National Colors

National Colors

Racial Classification and the State in Latin America

MARA LOVEMAN

OXFORD
UNIVERSITY PRESS

OXFORD
UNIVERSITY PRESS

Oxford University Press is a department of the
University of Oxford. It furthers the University's objective
of excellence in research, scholarship, and education
by publishing worldwide.

Oxford   New York
Auckland   Cape Town   Dar es Salaam   Hong Kong   Karachi
Kuala Lumpur   Madrid   Melbourne   Mexico City   Nairobi
New Delhi   Shanghai   Taipei   Toronto

With offices in
Argentina   Austria Brazil   Chile   Czech Republic   France   Greece
Guatemala   Hungary   Italy   Japan   Poland   Portugal   Singapore
South Korea   Switzerland   Thailand Turkey   Ukraine   Vietnam

Oxford is a registered trade mark of Oxford University Press
in the UK and certain other countries.

Published in the United States of America by
Oxford University Press
198 Madison Avenue, New York, NY 10016

© Mara Loveman 2014

All rights reserved. No part of this publication may be reproduced,
stored in a retrieval system, or transmitted, in any form or by any means,
without the prior permission in writing of Oxford University Press,
or as expressly permitted by law, by license, or under terms agreed with
the appropriate reproduction rights organization. Inquiries concerning
reproduction outside the scope of the above should be sent to
the Rights Department, Oxford University Press, at the address above.

You must not circulate this work in any other form
and you must impose this same condition on any acquirer.

Library of Congress Cataloging-in-Publication Data
Loveman, Mara, 1972–
National colors : racial classification and the state in Latin America / Mara Loveman.
pages   cm
Includes bibliographical references and index.
ISBN 978-0-19-933735-4 (hardback)—ISBN 978-0-19-933736-1 (paperback)
1. Ethnic groups—Latin America.   2. Ethnicity—Political aspects—Latin America.
3. Demographic surveys—Political aspects—Latin America.
4. Latin America—Census—History.   I. Title.
F1419.A1.L69   2014
305.80098—dc23   2014005732

1 3 5 7 9 8 6 4 2
Printed in the United States of America
on acid-free paper

CONTENTS

Tables vii
Figures ix
Preface xi
Acknowledgments xvii

CHAPTER 1. Introduction: Ethnoracial Classification and the State 3

CHAPTER 2. Classifying Colonial Subjects 43

CHAPTER 3. Enumerating Nations 79

CHAPTER 4. The Race to Progress 121

CHAPTER 5. Constructing Natural Orders 169

CHAPTER 6. From Race to Culture 207

CHAPTER 7. "We All Count" 250

CHAPTER 8. Conclusion: The International Politics of Ethnoracial Classification 301

Appendix: The Database on Diversity in Latin American Censuses 327
Bibliography 331
Index 363

TABLES

3.1 Timeline of the Creation of National Statistics Agencies in Latin America   103
3.2 Latin American Participation in the International Statistical Congress, 1853–1876   108
3.3 Race or Color Questions in Latin American Censuses, 1810s–1940s   113
3.4 Latin American Participation in the International Statistical Institute, 1887–1933   116
6.1 Race or Color Questions in Latin American Censuses, 1810s–1980s   208
6.2a Visibility of Indigenous Peoples in Latin American Censuses, 1810s–1980s   233
6.2b Approaches to Enumerating "Indians" in Latin American Censuses, 1810s–1980s   234
6.3 Visibility of Afrodescendants in Latin American Censuses, 1810s–1980s   241
7.1a Visibility of Afrodescendant and Indigenous Peoples in Latin American Censuses, 1980s–2010s   253
7.1b Approaches to Enumerating Afrodescendant and Indigenous Peoples in Latin American Censuses, 1980s–2010s   254
7.2 Questions about Ethnoracial Diversity in Latin American Censuses, 2000s–2010s   256
7.3 Latin American Signatories to ILO 169 (1989)   273

FIGURES

2.1　Constructing the Sociedad de Castas in Colonial Spanish America   64
2.2　A List of Castas from Colonial Mexico   65
2.3　A Series of Casta Paintings   67
4.1　Language Groups Reported in the Census of Mexico, 1921   136
4.2　Language Groups Reported in the Census of Guatemala, 1921   138
4.3　A Demonstration of the "Excellent" Effects of Ethnic Selection in the Census of Brazil, 1920   141
4.4　Nationality of Immigrants Who Entered Brazilian Ports between 1820 and 1907   150
4.5　Population Growth in Argentina and Other "Principal Nations," 1895   152
4.6　Guatemala's "Two Principal Groups" in the 1893 Census   159
4.7　A Comparison of Races in the Census of Panama, 1920   162
4.8　The Racial Composition of the Population of Panama, 1930   163
5.1　The Razas of Mexico, 1921   181
5.2　The Nationalities of Argentina, 1869   184
5.3　Changes in the Racial Composition of Peru, 1876 vs. 1940   185
5.4　The Pueblos in Argentine Territories, 1912   190
5.5a　The Racial Composition of the Argentine Population, 1895   194
5.5b　The Racial Composition of Argentina's Foreign-born Population, 1912   194

5.6a   The Bolivian Population Classified by Race, 1900   196
5.6b   The Bolivian Population Classified by Race, with Blacks Omitted, 1900   197
5.7   The Brazilian Population Postabolition, 1890   202
5.8   The Cohesive Argentine Nation, 1895   204
6.1a   Whites and Others in Cuba's Population, 1899–1953   230
6.1b   The Racial Composition of Cuba's Population, 1899, 1943, and 1953   231
6.2   The Shoe-Wearing Population of the Republic of Peru, 1961   238
8.1   Publicity for the Todos Contamos campaign in Mexico   315
8.2   Protesting the Belo Monte Dam Project in Brazil, 2012   323

PREFACE

What is your race? The answer that first comes to mind when you are confronted with this question—and, indeed, whether a specific category comes immediately to mind at all—has much to do with where you grew up. In the United States of America, where official racial classification has been historically ubiquitous, people generally have a ready answer. Americans are asked to identify their race in multiple institutional settings over the course of their lives. When they enroll for school, apply for a driver's license or a job, fill out health forms, or participate in the census, for example, they are asked to check a box to indicate their racial group membership. Through both implicit and explicit socialization, most Americans grow up knowing which box to check on official forms. They know, that is, how others in American society see them and which racial category is meant to include someone like them. Even the growing number of Americans who identify with multiple racial origins typically know which combination of boxes to check (when checking more than one box is permitted), or what to write in as an acceptable answer on the line provided for "Other."

For the majority of those who grew up in Latin America, in contrast, the experience of being asked to identify their race on official forms is not familiar at all. Most Latin Americans alive today have lived their entire lives—at least, until recently—without ever having to check a race box on an official form. As a result, if or when they are asked to state their race for official purposes, they may not have a ready answer. Without iterated rehearsals, they are not practiced in answering the question. Indeed, they may well respond with a category that most people who grew up in the United States would not recognize as a racial category at all: "My race? Well, I'm Brazilian...Mexican...Venezuelan...Argentine."

The invocation of a nationality category in response to a question about race may seem, to North American readers, to be a straightforward category mistake. In reality, however, such responses are true to the specific ways that race was historically constructed in the region. Generations of Latin American children grew up learning that race was constitutive of nationality. At school, on television, in print media, and in public celebrations of national holidays, children learned that race—or more specifically, race mixture—was what defined them as members of a distinctive people. In Mexico, for example, children were taught that the nation was created through the mixture of Spaniards and Indians; to be Mexican was to be *mestizo*. In Brazil, national myths championed the fusion of Africans, Indians, and Portuguese into a new human type; as Brazilians, children were told, they were racially mixed. In Cuba, the story went, "a nation for all" was forged through the absorption of differences; Cuban race and nationality were declared to be one and the same. Even in Chile and Argentina, where national ideologies celebrated the supposed racial and cultural homogeneity of the population, children learned origin myths that credited historic *mestizaje* for the creation of Chileans or Argentines as distinct national types. Latin American national myths long celebrated the idea that distinctive peoples were formed through the mixture of races and thus *dissolution* of racial differences.

As a corollary to these national myths, many Latin American states declared themselves officially colorblind, actively discouraged individual racial identification, and highlighted the supposed absence of racial divisions or discrimination within their nations. Their citizens knew better. Myths of racial democracy rooted in mestizaje did not keep Latin Americans from noticing physical and cultural differences among their friends and neighbors. Latin Americans use rich and varied lexicons to mark even subtle distinctions. From the wheat-colored *trigueño* in Nicaragua, to the light-but-not-quite-white *castizo* in Colombia, to the slightly-lighter-than-black *morena oscura* in Brazil, the everyday languages of distinction in Latin America make clear that the region's populations are not colorblind.

The fluidity of racial terminology in everyday language may give the illusion of a fluid social order. But Latin American societies are deeply stratified along socioeconomic and ethnoracial lines. An "Indian" child who sheds traditional clothing to attend school in Guatemala City may be socially redefined as *mestizo*. But a Guatemalan who is born "Indian" is much less likely to graduate from high school than a child who is born "ladino." A brown-skinned Brazilian who enters a prestigious occupation may be socially redefined as white. But on average, Brazilians with darker skin tone are much less likely to enter prestigious occupations, and those who do so will likely suffer a wage penalty for the color of their skin.

As in the United States, Latin American societies are thoroughly racialized: Ideas about essential and heritable differences among humans have profoundly shaped—and continue to shape—the structure and dynamics of social relations. But the racialization process did not unfold the same way throughout the Americas. Historically, racial ideas shaped social structures, relations, and identities differently in different parts of the region.

This book began as an inquiry into how, why, and with what consequences the meanings of race, national identity, and the relationship between them differ across the Americas. I first became intrigued by the fact that "race" means different things to different people in different parts of the Americas when I studied abroad as an undergraduate student in Rio de Janeiro. In a seminar on "The Anthropology of Brazil," a discussion of historian Thomas Skidmore's *Black into White,* segued into a heated debate over the critical question of whether or not the actress Halle Berry was black. ("Well, in the United States she's black," I insisted. "That's ridiculous!" came the Brazilian reply). Over the course of the semester, in the more measured and informed discussions that ensued, we explored how dividing lines that we grew up seeing as "givens"—such as the line between who is black and who is white—were in fact cultural impositions upon the natural fact of physical variation among human beings. Differences within populations obviously exist, but different societies perceive that variation differently, develop different rules for drawing distinctions, and attach different meanings and consequences to their classifications.

When I returned to UC Berkeley to finish my undergraduate degree, I took classes in Latin American history and literature and read poetry, novels, political treatises, and histories of social thought that revealed how the social meanings of race in the Americas were tied, inextricably, to narrative constructions of nationhood. The public articulations of national-racial identities in Latin America differed in their specifics, but they shared a common foundation in the trope of mestizaje, which undergirded mythologies of racially egalitarian nations.[1] Meanwhile, in classes on international political economy and the politics of development in what was then called "the Third World," I became aware of how trajectories of development in Latin American countries were indelibly marked by their

---

[1] As Radcliffe and Westwood (*Remaking the Nation*, 35) note, "Racial projects are to be found throughout Latin America that seek to privilege a 'fictive ethnicity' woven together within the discourses of racial democracy."

disadvantaged position in the world system of states and their uneven and unequal incorporation into a global capitalist economy.

It was not until my second year in graduate school at UCLA, in a seminar with Rogers Brubaker on theories of nationalism, that I began to recognize that what I had taken for two very separate sets of issues—the historical construction of narratives about race and nation on the one hand, and the international politics of development on the other—were in fact tightly bound. The historical agent that bound them together was the state. It became clear that to understand the micropolitics of racial classification and identification, inclusion and exclusion, required understanding the macropolitics of nineteenth- and twentieth-century nation making and state building.

National Colors shows how mundane administrative practices of classifying populations by race or ethnicity are tied historically to large-scale cultural and political projects of building modern states and defining national communities. Empirically, this is a book about the politics and practices of ethnoracial classification in censuses in Latin America from the colonial period until the first decades of the twenty-first century. More generally, it is a book that explains the centrality of racial thought to the construction of political and cultural communities in modern Latin America. The language of race figured only marginally in the popular-revolutionary nationalisms of France and the United States.[2] *National Colors* offers an explanation for why the idea of race, and especially the idea of race mixture, anchored official constructions of modern nationhood in Latin America.

Neither colonial legacies nor the brute facts of ethnic demography predetermined the racialist constructions of nationhood that crystallized in postcolonial Latin America. Rather, the majority of Latin American nations were defined ethnoracially due to international influences on nationalist aspirations. Latin American nation makers fastened on racialist constructions of nationhood as they reconciled domestic political projects with prescriptions for national progress set by international institutions and scientific epistemic communities. When international norms for how to be a modern nation and how to pursue national progress underwent revision around the mid-twentieth century, and again at the turn of the twenty-first, so did the ways that Latin American states deployed ethnoracial categories to describe their populations and prescribe their path to national development.

---

[2] Hobsbawm *Nations and Nationalism Since 1780*, 19–20.

In contrast to the United States, where official racial distinctions *excluded* segments of the population from membership in the political and cultural community of the nation, in many Latin American countries, racial language was used to draw boundaries around those to be *included* in the nation. Yet for most Latin American countries, for most of their histories, the discursive inclusion of ethnoracial minority (sometimes the numerical majority) populations was accompanied by de facto repression, marginalization, subordination, or paternalistic incorporation. Toward the end of the twentieth century, the enormous gap between national myths and socioeconomic and cultural realities set the stage for political struggles to renegotiate the relationship between Latin American states and their ethnoracially diverse citizens. The questions and categories used in national censuses to count minority populations have become a focal point of these still-unfolding battles. This book sheds new light on the stakes of census-reform politics by placing contemporary debates over official ethnoracial classification in Latin America in comparative and historical perspective.

This book also contributes to general sociological understanding of the role of states in the naturalization of ethnoracial divides. My analysis is grounded in what sociologist Michael Banton identified as a critical task of twenty-first-century scholarship on race: understanding "when, why, and how social differences are represented as natural differences."[3] Of course, the state—or more precisely, the myriad agencies and organizations staffed by human beings that together constitute the state—does not bear sole responsibility for making historically contingent group boundaries appear to reflect the natural order of things. But since at least the eighteenth century, the emergent nation-state has been the key protagonist in the demarcation, institutionalization, and politicization of ethnoracial divides. Comparative and historical analysis of how, when, and why states classify their populations in ethnoracial terms is essential to understand and explain the varied meanings and consequences of race in the Americas.

---

[3] Banton, "Finding, and Correcting, My Mistakes," 473.

ACKNOWLEDGMENTS

I am grateful to several teachers who paved the way for this book by impressing on a younger me the importance of understanding other times and places on their own terms: Ron and Fran Chilcote, Heloisa Corrêa, Julio Diniz, Tulio Halperín, José Sávio Leopoldi, Beatriz Manz, Ilmar R. de Mattos, José Luis Passos, Candace Slater, and the Suarez-Samper family.

The extraordinary intellectual community at UCLA in the late 1990s introduced me to sociology, filled my head with new questions, and equipped me with new tools to pursue the answers. I am grateful for the opportunity I had to learn from and with Rogers Brubaker, Michael Mann, Ivan Szelenyi, Roger Waldinger, David Lopez, Bill Roy, Edward Telles, Rebecca Emigh, Maurice Zeitlin, Jeffrey Alexander, Emmanuel Schegloff, Joel Andreas, Rachel Cohen, Dylan Riley, Jon E. Fox, Peter Stamatov, Catherine Lee, Stanley Bailey, David Fitzgerald, David Cook-Martín, and, at UCSD, Dain Borges and Richard Biernacki.

I wrote this book as a member of the sociology faculty at the University of Wisconsin, Madison. I could not have hoped for a more stimulating and supportive environment in which to work. I am grateful to the entire department—colleagues, students, and staff—who sustain the exceptional community that is UW-Madison Sociology. Though it is really impossible to convey the extent of my gratitude in this context, I especially want to thank Gay Seidman, for invaluable intellectual guidance and professional advice, and for her friendship; Erik Olin Wright, for being a steadfast source of intellectual and personal inspiration, and for teaching me through example the true meaning of community; and Pamela Oliver, for her no-nonsense mentorship and practical advice that helped me learn to balance commitments to research, teaching, service, and family.

Several colleagues generously made time to read and comment on earlier versions of the manuscript. I am especially grateful to Rogers Brubaker, Gay Seidman, David Fitzgerald, David Cook-Martín, Rebecca Emigh, Aliza Luft, Martina Kunović, Brian Loveman, and the anonymous reviewers for providing written comments on the entire manuscript. Though I surely failed to follow all of their sage advice, the final product is much the better for their respective interventions. I also want to thank colleagues who read and commented on portions of the manuscript at various stages, including Mark Burkholder, Bruce Castleman, Miguel Angel Centeno, Jim Cohen, Jonathan Eastwood, Mustafa Emirbayer, John French, Derek Hoff, Oriol Mirosa, Carmen Salazar-Soler, Tatiana Alfonso Sierra, and Eddie Telles. I am extremely grateful for outstanding research assistance from Matías Cociña, Rodolfo Elbert, Martina Kunović, and Oriol Mirosa.

Many ideas in this book crystallized through dialogue with colleagues and students at invited talks and conferences. While I cannot possibly name every individual who offered a question or criticism that sharpened my thinking, I am sincerely grateful to participants in the following venues for lively and generative conversations: the UC Berkeley Sociology Colloquium; the Watson Institute at Brown University; the UW-Madison William H. Sewell Memorial Lecture; the Latin American Studies lecture at Gettysburg College; the UW-Madison Seminar in Sociology of Economic Change and Development; the UW-Madison Institute for Research in the Humanities, and the 2012 ASA session on Nations and Nationalism. I had the privilege to share ideas and learn from some of my intellectual heroes at the conference on "Paper Leviathans: State and Nation-Building in Nineteenth-Century Latin America," organized by Miguel A. Centeno and Agustín Ferraro at Princeton in 2009; at the conference on "Racing the Republic: Ethnicity and Inequality in France in American and World Perspective," organized by Loïc Wacquant, Tyler Stovall, and Heddy Riss, at UC Berkeley in 2007; and at the conference "Des catégories et de leurs usages dans la construction sociale d'un groupe de référence: 'race', 'ethnie' et 'communauté' aux Amériques," organized by Véronique Boyer and Sara Le Menestrel at the Ecole des Hautes Etudes en Sciences Sociales in Paris in 2006.

Several colleagues provided critical insight and encouragement at different stages of this project. My thanks to Margo Anderson, George Reid Andrews, Robyn Autry, Peter Beattie, Katherine Curtis, Ivan Ermakoff, Myra Marx Ferree, Robert Freeland, Joan Fujimura, Susan Friedman,

Alice Goffman, Chad Goldberg, Jill Harrison, Alexandra Hunneus, Iván Jaksic, Heinz Klug, Peter Kolchin, Cathie Lee, Elizabeth Lira, Cameron MacDonald, James Mahoney, Florencia Mallon, James Montgomery, Jeffrey Needell, Rob Nixon, Teju Olaniyan, Joel Perlmann, Tania Salgado Pimenta, Anne Sætnan, Francisco Scarano, Paul Schor, Patrick Simon, Steve Stern, Loïc Wacquant, Andreas Wimmer, and Eviatar Zerubavel. Though I have never met him, the scholarship of Thomas Skidmore has been a cornerstone for my own.

The research for this book was undertaken with support from the Social Science Research Council, the Andrew W. Mellon Foundation, the Norwegian Research Council, the Wisconsin Alumni Research Foundation through the Graduate School at University of Wisconsin-Madison, and a UW-Madison Vilas Life Cycle Fellowship. A residential fellowship at the UW-Madison Institute for Research on the Humanities provided that elusive luxury of academic life—time to write—at a pivotal moment in the development of the manuscript. Thank you to Susan Friedman, my co-fellows at the Institute, and the participants in the interdisciplinary IRH colloquium for the stimulating intellectual community and for insightful and incisive comments on the project. At Oxford University Press, I am grateful to editor James Cook for welcoming the manuscript, and to Peter Worger, Gwen Colvin, and the production staff for efficiently ushering the final manuscript through to production.

My deepest gratitude is to my family, for their (respective takes on) love, humor, and support: Sharon and Brian Loveman; Taryn and Lynn Loveman; Carly and Jim Lutz; Ryan and Eveli Loveman; Ben Loveman and Camille Langlois; Ric and Amy Siem; Linda Metz; Kate, Max, Matai, Cecelia, Sean, and Colin (for keeping it real); and the memories of my grandparents, Bernard Loveman (aka Sherriff Bernie the Kid), and Martin and June Siem. With love and gratitude, this book is dedicated to Jay Sundu, my partner in life, and to Risa and Nico, *mis hijos queridos*, from whom I have learned so much.

National Colors

CHAPTER 1 | **Introduction**
Ethnoracial Classification and the State

MODERN STATES ROUTINELY CLASSIFY the populations they seek to govern. States classify populations by *sex* and by *age*, for example, to track population trends and to determine the distribution of rights and obligations, entitlements and responsibilities among their citizens. States classify populations by *citizenship* to regulate both physical and political access to the sovereign community in whose name they claim to legitimately govern. And in the day-to-day administration of social and political life, states routinely classify their populations by multiple other criteria such as civil status, place of residence, parenthood, veteran status, physical disability, and employment status, to name but a few. Categorical identification of segments of the population is central to modern bureaucratic administration, which is, according to Max Weber, the definitive and irreplaceable foundation of the modern state's exercise of legal-rational domination.[1] Through the bureaucratic lens and in the administrative practice of the myriad agencies that constitute modern states, populations are routinely divided into categorically distinct kinds.

This book is concerned with a particular subset of state classification practices: those that draw ethnoracial distinctions within human populations. While official classification by sex and age is ubiquitous in modern bureaucracies, official ethnoracial classification has been historically uneven. Some states have routinely classified their populations by ethnicity or race. Others have steadfastly refused to do so, regardless of the rationale. Most states have fallen somewhere in between, engaging in official ethnoracial

---

[1] Weber, M., *Economy and Society*, 217–26. In modern polities, the administration and ordering of everyday affairs necessarily privileges the categorical identification of individuals over and above their relational identification (Calhoun, *Nationalism*).

classification intermittently over the course of their histories or at particular moments for specific ends.

Why do some states classify their citizens by race or ethnicity while other states do not? What purposes does official ethnoracial classification serve, at whose cost, and to whose benefit? How are contemporary struggles over official ethnoracial classification created and constrained by the ways states classified their populations historically?

Much of what we know about these questions comes from research on the most historically egregious examples of racial classification by states. Apartheid South Africa, pre-civil rights United States, and Nazi Germany, to take the most well-known examples, all lay bare how official ethnoracial classification enables the social stigmatization, legal subjugation, economic exploitation, political repression, or outright physical annihilation of subject populations. In these contexts, official ethnoracial classification undergirded antidemocratic polities, segregated societies, and repressive, violent, even genocidal state projects. The state's classification of individuals by race provided the administrative foundation for the construction of explicitly exclusionary nations, grounded on principles and structures of racial inequality.[2]

States have also engaged in official ethnoracial classification of citizens in order to combat entrenched inequality, counteract pervasive discrimination, or protect vulnerable minority communities. In the contemporary United States, South Africa, or Brazil, for example, official ethnoracial classification enables states to administer affirmative action programs, monitor compliance with civil rights laws, and extend collective protections to indigenous communities.[3] Official ethnoracial classification has facilitated the implementation of policies that seek to advance goals such as substantive democratization, social integration, and the protection of civil and human rights. The state's classification of individuals by race creates the administrative foundation for efforts to reconstruct historically exclusionary nations as inclusive political and cultural communities.

Of course, these contradictory reasons for official ethnoracial classification—to target segments of the population for exclusion or for inclusion, for discrimination, or for redress—are not mutually exclusive. In most cases, in

---

[2] Bauman, *Modernity and the Holocaust*; Burleigh and Wippermann, *The Racial State*; Evans, *Bureaucracy and Race*; Fredrickson, *White Supremacy*; Gross, *What Blood Won't Tell*; Haney-Lopez, *White by Law*; Müller-Hill, *Murderous Science*; Pascoe, *What Comes Naturally*.

[3] Skrentny, *The Ironies of Affirmative Action*; Guiilebeau, "Affirmative Action in a Global Perspective"; Htun, "From 'Racial Democracy' to Affirmative Action."

fact, they are historically connected: Targeted constraints on the freedoms of one group may be coupled with targeted opportunities for others; targeted exclusion or repression in one period may generate resistance which culminates in organized demands for targeted benefits later on.

Whether the immediate motivation is to exclude or to include, states that formally link individual racial classification to the delivery of benefits or penalties *institutionalize* racial distinctions within populations. Official racial categories are enshrined in social policy and law, and racial classification becomes a routinized basis for distinguishing among citizens. States that legally institutionalize racial distinctions "make race" by making race matter, directly and explicitly, in the lives of individual persons.[4] To date, such states have been the primary focus of research that investigates the significance of official ethnoracial classification in modern societies.

Yet states that refrain from legal racial discrimination among citizens may also engage in the political construction of ethnoracial divides. In this book, I draw attention to states that make race *indirectly*, through strategies of governance that officially recognize ethnoracial distinctions within populations without formally linking individual-level classification to administrative allocation.[5] I analyze the politics and practice of official ethnoracial classification in nineteen Latin American states over more than two centuries.[6] In these contexts, as the chapters that follow reveal, states classified their citizens by race or ethnicity to construct formally *inclusionary* nations, but on deeply hierarchical grounds.

For readers not familiar with Latin American history, it may at first seem an odd choice to focus on this region to improve understanding of why states engage in official ethnoracial classification of their populations. When Latin American countries make an appearance in comparative race scholarship, it is often to note the *absence* of institutionalized racial discrimination in those contexts. This serves to highlight the momentous *presence* of legal racial domination in the history of the United States.[7] In contrast to the United States, none of the states in postcolonial Latin America constructed the administrative and legal architecture to institutionalize legal racial discrimination. In postcolonial Latin America, states

---

[4] Marx, *Making Race and Nation*.

[5] On administrative allocation, see Batley, "The Politics of Administrative Allocation."

[6] The nineteen countries are: Argentina, Bolivia, Brazil, Chile, Colombia, Costa Rica, Cuba, Dominican Republic, Ecuador, El Salvador, Guatemala, Honduras, Mexico, Nicaragua, Panama, Paraguay, Peru, Uruguay, and Venezuela.

[7] For example, Degler, *Neither Black nor White*; Marx, *Making Race and Nation*.

generally avoided the practice of formally linking rights or restrictions of citizenship to official ethnoracial classification of individual persons.[8]

Yet Latin American states did not abstain from official ethnoracial classification altogether. The evidence of official ethnoracial classification in postcolonial Latin America sits transparently in a wide array of archival sources used by historians to reconstruct various aspects of these societies' pasts. In addition to records pertaining to African slavery and Indian tribute—which remained legal for decades after independence in some countries—examples of official ethnic and racial classification can be found in birth and death records, testaments and wills, police reports, prison records, army recruitment forms, court documents, public school archives, public health statistics, and—most visibly, even to those who do not spend time in archives—population censuses. Thus, while we lack comprehensive studies of the history of official ethnoracial classification in individual Latin American countries, much less for the region as a whole, an array of historical research provides evidence of state officials making ethnoracial distinctions among citizens. Such distinctions were recorded in multiple bureaucratic domains, from the local to national level, across the region, and at various points in time.

The question, then, is not *whether* Latin American states engaged in official ethnoracial classification of their citizens, but *when* they did so, *toward what ends*, and *with what consequences*. If they had no interest—until recently—in the legal racial differentiation of citizens, why did they bother classifying their populations by race at all? This is the first book to systematically investigate these questions for all of Latin America. I chart the history of official ethnoracial classification across nineteen Latin American states from independence through 2012, focusing on a particularly significant institutional domain: state agencies charged with conducting national censuses and producing demographic portraits of Latin America's populations.

National statistics agencies and the censuses they conduct represent a strategic site to investigate ethnoracial classification and the state. From the mid-nineteenth century, national statistics agencies were positioned at

---

[8] There are significant exceptions to this generalization, which I discuss at greater length in later chapters. Most notably, the continuation of Indian tribute in Andean countries for several decades after independence meant that "*indio*" was retained as an administrative category. Latin American states also made ethnoracial categorical distinctions among potential immigrants. See Cook-Martín and Fitzgerald, "Liberalism and the Limits of Inclusion"; Fitzgerald and Cook-Martín, *Culling the Masses*; Lesser, *Negotiating National Identity*; Skidmore, "Racial Ideas and Social Policy in Brazil, 1870–1940."

the intersection of three driving projects of modernization: the political project of developing the administrative infrastructure and authority of a modern state, the cultural project of constructing the communal bonds (the imagined community) of a modern nation, and the scientific project of generating demographic information to inform the enlightened pursuit of national progress. The distinctive ways in which these three modernizing missions—state-building, nation-making, and the scientific promotion of national development—were intertwined in the work of central statistics agencies makes them privileged sites for an investigation of when, why, and how modernizing states engage in ethnoracial classification of citizens.

The historical analysis tackles three central questions. First, why did the avowedly color-blind liberal republics of postcolonial Latin America engage in ethnoracial classification of their citizens? Almost every postcolonial Latin American state included a direct question about race or color on an early national census. And those that did not often published ethnoracial statistics in census reports regardless.[9] The inclusion of race questions on Latin America's early national censuses is puzzling because the historical momentum after independence was decisively against official racial classification of citizens. The Latin American republics that emerged from the independence wars against Spain in the early nineteenth century were founded on promises to eradicate the odious "caste" distinctions that undergirded colonial rule. This stance is nicely captured by the oft-quoted words of the liberator José de San Martín: "In the future the aborigines shall not be called Indians or natives; they are children and citizens of Peru, and they shall be known as Peruvians."[10] After independence,

---

[9] Among Latin American states that conducted their first national census during the nineteenth century, only Argentina and Venezuela never included a query to capture race or color. Chile would also be included in this group were it not for the fact that its first attempt at a national census, in 1813, included a query on "origins" that classified individuals as "American Spanish," "European Spanish," "Asiatic, Canary and African Spanish," "Foreign European," "Indio," "Mestizo," "Mulatto" or "Black." The first four of these categories were grouped together as "Spanish and Foreign European" while the last four were grouped together under the denomination "castas." A second census planned for 1824 was set to use the same query, but the enumeration was cancelled. See Jaramillo, "Un Alto en el Camino," p.56; Chile. Instituto Nacional de Estatísticas. *Retratos de Nuestra Identidad*, appendix.

[10] Decree of August 27, 1821, cited in Lynch, *The Spanish American Revolutions*, 277. This quotation by San Martín is cited by Benedict Anderson to illustrate his argument about Latin American "creole pioneers" of modern nationalism (Anderson, B., *Imagined Communities*, 50). In Brazil, the continuity of official racial classification after independence is more easily understood, since political independence from Portugal predated the founding of the republic by more than six decades. A negotiated end to colonial rule in 1822 left the King of Portugal's son at the helm of an independent Brazilian monarchy. Not until the rebirth of Brazil as a republic in 1889 does the foundational contradiction between the liberal rhetoric of equality of all citizens before the law and the routine practice of official ethnoracial classification call out for explanation. See Barman, *Brazil*.

Latin American republics explicitly rejected the path charted by the United States of using official racial classification to legally enshrine inequality. So why not emulate France, and abstain from official ethnoracial classification altogether?

This initial historical puzzle is supplemented by two others. Tracing the questions and categories used in Latin American censuses over the course of the twentieth century reveals that around midcentury, nearly all states in the region dropped race questions from their censuses.[11] Why did "race" disappear from most Latin American censuses in the second half of the twentieth century? At the end of the twentieth century, the picture changed yet again. By 2010, questions about race and ethnicity had reappeared on national censuses throughout the region.[12] What explains this dramatic turnabout? Why did Latin American states reintroduce official ethnoracial classification on censuses at the dawn of the twenty-first century?

Not surprisingly, the answers to these historical questions differ in their specifics across countries and over time. In general terms, however, the answer to each question is the same: Official ethnoracial classification on Latin American censuses is driven by politics. More specifically, over the course of nearly two centuries, census taking in Latin America has been oriented to two basic political projects: (1) a descriptive project, to describe and thus define the nation through its statistical representation; and (2) a prescriptive project, to diagnose the population's strengths and weaknesses in order to chart the path to a better future. In the nineteenth and early twentieth centuries, this latter project was understood as the pursuit of "progress"; since the mid-twentieth century, it has usually been discussed under the rubric of "development."

Censuses are not mirrors of demographic realities; they do not merely reflect existing lines of distinction within a society at a given point in time. The analyses herein refute any such naïve demographic hypothesis. Nor do national censuses simply reproduce prenational or colonial practices of categorization.[13] Rather, censuses are both stakes and instruments of

---

[11] Only Cuba and Brazil (with the exception of 1970) continued to ask about race or "color" on national censuses throughout the second half of the twentieth century. These cases are discussed in chapter 6.

[12] With a single exception: Only the Dominican Republic had not added a question about racial or ethnic origins to the national census by 2010. This case is discussed in chapter 7.

[13] Hirschman, "The Meaning and Measurement of Ethnicity in Malaysia"; Dirks, "Castes of Mind." More generally, the significance and consequence of ethnoracial distinctions in postcolonial contexts did not simply reproduce colonial hierarchies; they were reinvented and reinscribed in the construction of independent nation-states. See Quijano, "Coloniality of Power and Eurocentrism in Latin America"; Mignolo, "Misunderstanding and Colonization."

politics. Census categories, in turn, are political products. The political nature of census categories has been documented in studies of censuses in numerous different contexts.[14] My analysis builds on the core insight that censuses are political, but my argument differs from prior work in this vein in a critical respect.

Most research on the politics of censuses focuses on politics *within* a given national context over time. In contrast, I find that the political struggles that take place within national arenas do not suffice to explain why and how Latin American states used censuses to count and classify their populations. The political field that shaped the development of modern census taking in Latin America was not confined by national borders. The ways that Latin American states classified their populations on censuses were shaped by *international* criteria for how to be a modern nation and how to promote national development, as these criteria reverberated through domestic scientific and political fields. When prevailing international understandings of what made a political and cultural community a "modern nation" changed, so too did the ways that Latin American states counted and classified their populations. The influence of *international* norms and actors on *national* census taking in Latin America started out diffuse and indirect, and became stronger and more direct over time.

Of course, the specific questions and categories included on national censuses varied considerably across countries and over time, reflecting different historical and demographic conditions as these were refracted through the perceptions and aspirations of national political elites. These perceptions and aspirations, in turn, bore heavy marks of influence by prevailing currents of thought in international scientific and organizational fields. In particular, the content of Latin American censuses over time reflected shifts in internationally accepted standards of what a modern demographic census should ask, and how the "progress" of a society should be measured and defined. As a result, notwithstanding country by country idiosyncrasies, there are notable "period effects" on the ways that Latin American census officials chose to describe ethnoracial diversity within their populations and to diagnose its implications for national development.

Official ethnoracial classification on censuses took different forms and served different purposes in the colonial period, the first century of

---

[14] A partial list of notable examples include: Ipsen, *Dictating Demography*; Lee, "Racial Classifications in the US Census"; Nobles, *Shades of Citizenship*; Patriarca, *Numbers and Nationhood*. For Latin America, Ferrández and Kradolfer, *Everlasting Countdowns*, is a recent volume of case studies focused on the political nature of ethnic and racial census categories.

nation-state building (1820s–1930s), the decades of nationalist integration and modernization (1940s–1980s), and the decades of struggle to radically redefine the cultural and legal meaning of national belonging (1990s-present). In this book, I explain how and why state officials used censuses to produce knowledge about ethnoracial distinctions within their populations in each of these historical periods. Taken together, the historical analyses also provide leverage to reflect on more general questions about the relationship between ethnoracial classification and the nation-state. Comparative and historical analysis of nineteen cases across centuries makes visible general regional and temporal trends that would be difficult if not impossible to discern through analysis of individual cases. These findings, in turn, challenge conventional approaches to thinking about the scale and sites of census politics, the power of state classification to shape individual and collective subjectivities, and the relationship between official ethnoracial classification and institutionalized social exclusion.

As noted, most existing research on the history and politics of census taking focuses on developments and struggles within nationally delimited political fields. As a result, the geographic and political boundaries which censuses themselves helped to naturalize as self-evident containers of "national" communities are taken to delimit the scope of analysis for understanding the politics of census categories. Simultaneous consideration of nineteen Latin American cases suggests that the tendency to treat each nation-state as an isolated case yields an incomplete understanding of census politics. Like scholars who have researched the history of census taking in individual countries, I find that in Latin America national censuses became symbolically potent vehicles for political and scientific elites to advance particular political projects to define the nation and to promote national progress.[15] My analysis also reveals, however, that census politics within national political fields were profoundly shaped by their embeddedness within international political and scientific fields—where Latin American elites were not the dominant players. In general terms, this suggests that the history of census taking—like the history of nation making more broadly—cannot be properly understood apart from

---

[15] There is now a large literature on the political nature of censuses. See especially: Nobles, *Shades of Citizenship*; Kertzer and Arel, *Census and Identity*; Alonso and Starr, *The Politics of Numbers*; Hirschman, "The Meaning and Measurement of Ethnicity in Malaysia"; Lee, "Racial Classifications in the US Census"; Andrews, *The Afro-Argentines of Buenos Aires, 1800–1900*, ch. 5; Loveman, M., "The Race to Progress"; Skerry, *Counting on the Census*; Anderson and Fienberg, *Who Counts?*; Peterson, "Politics and the Measurement of Ethnicity"; Senra and Camargo, *Estatísticas nas Américas*; Ferrández and Kradolfer, *Everlasting Countdowns*.

the coincident history of the emergence of a world system of (census-taking and nation-making) states.[16] Historically, the relative position of national political and scientific elites within international political and scientific fields influenced the contours and contents of national census politics.[17]

Comparative and historical analysis of nineteen Latin American cases also complicates the standard account of how official classification may shape the identities of the classified. Prior research on the political construction of race and ethnicity highlights the power of states to constitute individual and collective identities, and thus structure social boundaries, by linking official classification to systems of administrative allocation or legally enforced segregation.[18] The Jim Crow United States, apartheid South Africa, and post-civil rights United States stand out as notorious examples.[19] Bringing nineteen Latin American countries into the field of comparison makes it clear that legal institutionalization of ethnoracial categories is not a necessary condition for the political construction of racial or ethnic boundaries. Official classification of individuals does not have to be directly tied to administrative allocation of benefits or penalties, or to the enforcement of legal segregation, to become consequential in the construction of political and cultural divides. Official ethnoracial classification can make ethnoracial distinctions matter indirectly and diffusely, through a range of symbolic and political practices that fall short of legally institutionalized racial domination but nonetheless contribute to making ethnoracial boundaries a social reality, with attendant "socially real" consequences.[20]

At some points in my analysis, I underline how the state's symbolic power lends credence to its classifications; official categories make some ethnic and racial distinctions seem self-evidently "real" and socially salient,

---

[16] Poggi, "The State"; Meyer "The World Polity and the Authority of the Nation-State."

[17] The relative inattention to the international dimension of the history of national censuses is somewhat ironic given the internationalist motives behind the development of the national census as a fundamental state practice since the mid-nineteenth century (Ventresca, "When States Count"). Among scholars of the US Census, the tendency to neglect the international dimension may owe to the fact that US Census Bureau officials appear to have been willfully, if selectively, unconcerned with international census-taking standards and norms. In comparative perspective, the US appears to be an outlier in this respect. Though I do not investigate this question in this book, it may be that the ascending position of the US within international politics afforded US Census officials the luxury to engage selectively with international developments in the field.

[18] Jenkins, "Rethinking Ethnicity"; Cornell and Hartmann, *Ethnicity and Race*.

[19] Marx, *Making Race and Nation*; Nagel, "American Indian Ethnic Renewal"; Mora, *Making Hispanics*.

[20] For example, Stuchlik, "Chilean Native Policies and the Image of the Mapuche Indians."

while obscuring others from view. But my account also cautions against overstating the power of states to naturalize ethnic and racial divides. Whether the state ties classification to specific policies or not, official ethnic or racial categories are never imposed on a blank slate. An array of social institutions and ordinary citizens may draw different lines of ethnoracial distinction that the state actively ignores. In some contexts, the classified may rise up to contest the terms of their classification. I attend to both the potential and the limits of the state's capacity to impose its own vision of the relevant ethnoracial divisions within human populations.

Finally, analysis of nineteen Latin American cases challenges us to reconsider whether, or better, when, official ethnoracial classification serves as a technique of exclusion versus inclusion. Prior research on the political construction of race or ethnicity tends to fall on one or the other side of this question, depending on the case and time period under investigation. My analysis shows that states may classify citizens into ethnic or racial categories for both inclusionary and exclusionary purposes, even simultaneously. My analysis also shows that the *absence* of official racial classification can itself be a powerful means of exclusion. Drawing on insights gleaned from historical analysis of nineteen cases, I argue that the act of official ethnoracial classification per se is not intrinsically inclusionary or exclusionary. Nor is official ethnoracial classification inherently at odds with liberal ideals of equality and justice. The compatibility of official ethnoracial classification with liberal democratic principles hinges on what states *do* with the categorical distinctions they draw.

In the remainder of this introduction I set the theoretical stage for the analyses that follow. I elaborate on why official ethnoracial classification merits attention as a subject of sociological and historical research. I explain why national censuses represent a strategic site to anchor a comparative-historical sociology of official ethnoracial classification. And I describe the analytic approach and comparative scope of the research and provide a brief overview of the substantive chapters.

Official Ethnoracial Classification

Why study the politics of official ethnoracial classification? A comparative and historical sociology of state classification practices promises to advance theoretical understanding of the relationships among race, nation, and state in the modern world. In particular, this line of research illuminates how official classification contributes to the naturalization of racial and ethnic boundaries in modern societies; how theories of racial and ethnic difference informed the construction of nation-states; and how contemporary battles over the meaning and membership of national communities are shaped by the ways states drew ethnoracial distinctions among citizens in the past.

Naturalizing Social Divides

Comparative historical analysis of official ethnoracial classification promises to advance theoretical understanding of the state's role in creating and naturalizing categorical boundaries within populations.[21] Human beings exhibit a broad range of phenotypic traits and learned behaviors; absent the human imposition of categorical divides, variation in physical appearance and cultural practices tends to be continuous. Differences in human skin color, for example, are gradual; one tone shades into the next. The dividing line between "white" and "black" in any given time and place is not given in nature; it is socially determined. The act of racial classification imposes categorical divisions upon a continuous underlying reality in such a way that the resulting groupings appear to be naturally discrete subsets of the population.

The naturalization of social distinctions is a phenomenon that is central to the social construction of race. The common sociological refrain that "race is socially constructed" refers to the fact that racial categories are human constructs. Human variation obviously exists. But that variation is not, by nature, neatly partitioned into a finite set of mutually exclusive categories. The fact that someone who is socially defined as black in the United States may not be socially defined as black in the Dominican Republic or Brazil, or that Mexicans were considered white on the US Census in 1940 but not in 1930, or that the same American child may be classified as black by a teacher and white by a parent, are typical examples used to make the point that racial categorization schemes are cultural impositions on human diversity, not merely descriptive of that diversity.

Historically, states have played a prominent role in the imposition of particular categorical orders onto the varied dimensions of diversity among the populations within their borders. When states classify populations by race, they sort people into categories based on real or imagined markers of fundamental similarity among some humans, and difference from others. In some contexts, the substance of that similarity has been construed in

---

[21] Bourdieu, "Rethinking the State"; Goldberg, *Racist Culture*.

narrowly biological terms, a matter of shared ancestry or blood; in others, it has been viewed as cultural in origin, the result of long-term adaptations to diverse environmental and social milieu. Often, biological and cultural conceptions of racial difference are inextricably intertwined. However the distinguishing characteristics are conceived, official racial categories help to naturalize socially drawn divisions. Official categories inscribe a particular, simplified, order on the complicated mess of human diversity, even as they appear to merely describe already existing categorical divides within human populations.

States have employed an array of official vocabularies for categorizing what are identified as naturally distinct "kinds of humankind" within their borders.[22] Terminologies of race, caste, tribe, origins, nationality, linguistic group, and ethnicity have all made their appearance in official records of various sorts, artifacts of the modern state's particular concern with "difference."[23] Many social scientists draw sharp analytic distinctions between these terms, but they also recognize their family resemblance as ways of delineating collectivities that share ancestral or cultural roots. In the context of modern bureaucratic administration, these varied lexicons of difference can be seen as alternative ways to register the presence of distinct "ethnoracial" kinds of human beings within a population.[24]

When state bureaucracies classify people into discrete racial or ethnic categories, they make those particular categorical distinctions administratively relevant (and render others administratively irrelevant). Official ethnoracial classifications thus elevate the salience of some lines of distinction within a population and suppress the salience of others. The act of official classification is an act of *selective* recognition; the state takes a small subset of all socially recognized lines of difference and, in effect, "sanctions them, sanctifies them, consecrates them, making them worthy of existing, in conformity with the nature of things, and thus 'natural.' "[25] To the extent that individuals "recognize" that they belong to the categories named by the state, official classification shapes their subjective

---

[22] Hirschfeld, *Race in the Making*.

[23] Some of these do not always denote putative essential similarity; *religion*, for example, may be conceived in some contexts as a heritable and enduring trait and in others as a matter of personal choice. *Nationality* may refer explicitly to country of legal citizenship irrespective of membership in any other "natural human kinds"-type category. The specific meaning of any of these categories, and their meaning in relation to each other, is not stable across time and place and may have multiple uses in a single context. Considerable analytical caution is therefore required to avoid conflating terms with concepts. This is especially crucial for undertaking comparative research.

[24] Goldberg, *Racial Subjects*; Hirschfeld, *Race in the Making*, Introduction.

[25] Bourdieu, "Identity and Representation," 222.

understandings of the "kind" of person they are in relation to the other kinds that officially comprise a given society. In this way, official ethnoracial classification naturalizes racial and ethnic divides: social differences and social relationships come to be seen as natural differences and natural relationships.[26]

States do not construct race out of nothing. Rather, states "make race" by endowing particular axes of variation within a human population with symbolic weight and material consequence. Official classifications are especially likely to shape individual subjectivities when they have direct and systematic consequences for those classified. Ian Hacking has suggested that certain types of classifications have the peculiar capacity to "make up people," or constitute subjects as instances of a category precisely by labeling them as such.[27] Hacking considers how, for example, the behavior of those classified as schizophrenic has historically been "strongly interactive" with changing conceptions of schizophrenia. Awareness of being classified in a particular way "can change the ways in which individuals experience themselves—and may even lead them to alter their behavior."[28] The weight of scientific or legal authority vested in official

---

[26] Banton, "Finding, and Correcting, My Mistakes," 473; Hirschfeld, *Race in the Making*, 21; Goldberg, *Racist Culture*, 77.

[27] In this respect, Hacking's argument is in the same spirit as earlier interventions in symbolic-interactionism and labeling theory (cf. Goffman, *Stigma*; McIntosh, "The Homosexual Role"; Hacking, "Making Up People"). Hacking's more general argument is explicitly indebted to Foucault's work on the discursive (and disciplinary) constitution of subjects. Lawrence Hirschfeld has provocatively argued that ethnoracial human kinds are of a different sort than the human kinds analyzed by Hacking, products of "the conjunction of the enumerating state and the application of statistical reasoning to questions of human behavior" (Hirschfeld, *Race in the Making*, 20). Hirschfeld suggests that the historical constitution of ethnoracial human kinds does not hinge on official classification in the same way as Hacking's "interactive" human kinds. Rather, Hirschfeld argues, human beings may have a *universal* cognitive disposition that makes "race" easy to think, with historical *variations* in racial thinking "situated in—and guided by—the distinct ways in which humans organize knowledge of the social world." Even if this is correct, modern states have *also* engaged historically in classifying putatively natural "human kinds" (in Hirschfeld's sense of the term), and in some contexts such official classifications have significantly transformed "ethnoracial ways of being," creating ethnic or racial "human kinds" in Hacking's sense of the term. Thus, Hacking's notion of "interactive kinds" is well suited to the consideration of the historical constitution of particular ethnoracial kinds of human beings. Even if racial thinking is indeed, "situated in—and guided by— the distinct ways in which humans organize knowledge about the social world," as Hirschfeld contends, much more relevant for understanding historically specific instantiations of racialized ways of thinking and being are the distinct ways in which the social world—and especially the modern state—organizes knowledge about humans.

[28] Hacking, "Taking Bad Arguments Seriously," 15. Hacking's work focuses on those "kinds" of people that came into existence in tandem with the nineteenth-century development of the science of "moral statistics" (i.e., schizophrenic, vagrant, lunatic, suicidal). The creation of new scientifically classified types of deviance made possible new ways of being, in part, by sculpting out new "islands of meaning" (Zerubavel, *Social Mindscapes*), or new ways for people "to be."

classifications may at times be sufficient to influence the self-concept of those categorized.

In the case of official ethnoracial classification, the reflexive interaction between category and categorized—what Hacking refers to as the "looping effect"[29]—is likely to be greatest when official classifications are at the same time directly attached to individual bodies *and* deeply implicated in the structure and functioning of bureaucratic administration.[30] This was historically the case, to cite an obvious example, in apartheid South Africa, where "race" was officially registered at birth, stamped on official identity papers, and made pivotal for structuring differential access to political rights, economic opportunities, and social resources. It is not surprising under such circumstances that "race" became a defining basis of individual identification.[31] In another example, official classification of individual "nationality" in the former Soviet Union created a system of "obligatory ascribed status" that structured individual opportunities in domains such as higher education and employment; these legally imposed categories came to figure centrally in the configuration of post-Soviet nationalisms in the region.[32] In colonial Latin America, to cite an example directly germane to the present study, it was the colonizing state that invented "Indian" as a kind of person one could be. As historian Alan Knight notes, "The attribution of Indian identity began, of course, with the Conquest: 'it was the European who created the Indian.' No common Indian sentiment preceded the Conquest; it was only in the wake of the Conquest that the generic concept of 'Indian' could be formulated in negative contradistinction to the dominant Spaniard/European."[33]

Cases such as these suggest that where official ethnoracial classifications are mandatory, ascribed, pegged to the individual, and determinative for social experience, they will come to be recognized—if not always entirely shared—by those classified. Official categorical distinctions may not perfectly mirror

---

[29] Hacking, "The Looping Effect of Human Kinds"; Hacking, "Taking Bad Arguments Seriously."

[30] Caplan and Torpey, "Introduction"; Steinmetz, *The Devil's Handwriting*.

[31] Evans, *Bureaucracy and Race*; Marx, *Making Race and Nation*.

[32] Brubaker, *Nationalism Reframed*.

[33] Knight, "Racism, Revolution, and Indigenismo," 75; de la Peña, "Orden Social y Educación Indígena en México." Knight continues: "'Indian', as a term either of abuse or of praise, was conceived and applied by non-Indians.... It defined those who were not Spanish or mestizo and it lumped together a wide range of Indian groups, languages, and communities. The Indians themselves lacked any shared sentiment of Indian-ness (pan-Indianism is a very recent creation); they often lacked even the 'tribal' allegiances imputed to them, in that they gave their primary loyalty to the community—to the old Mesoamerican *atlepetl*, which the Spaniards had seen fit to conserve (or, with the *congregación*, to replicate) in the interests of social order and economic organization."

those used in informal interaction and subjective identification, but they will tend to approximate each other as the symbolic boundaries imposed by the state approach congruence with the social boundaries operative in daily life.[34] These cases also suggest that, under the right circumstances, officially ascribed classifications can become the unifying basis for mounting collective claims or sustained opposition against the classifying state.[35]

Official ethnoracial classification may contribute to "making up people" either directly and acutely, as when particular categories are attached to individual bodies and used to structure administrative allocation or other dimensions of lived experience, or indirectly and diffusely, as when such categories are employed to depict the national collectivity to which individuals "imagine" they belong.[36] Most modern states have lacked the infrastructural capacity or the political desire to construct and maintain an elaborate, discriminatory bureaucratic edifice on a foundation of official ethnoracial classification. Still, almost all modern states have classified their populations according to some ethnoracial criteria, either continuously, or in particular historical periods for specific pragmatic or symbolic ends. Where official ethnoracial classification is attached to individual bodies at particular moments (birth, marriage, death), but such classifications do not "stick" to individuals in their daily lives and are not used for purposes of administrative allocation, official classifications are less likely to become fundamental to individual self-understandings. Further, in such contexts, the symbolic boundaries imposed by official ethnoracial classification are likely to be more loosely coupled with the range of social categories and distinctions operative in daily interactions.

Where official ethnoracial classifications are not attached to individual persons at all, or not in socially consequential ways, they may nonetheless exert an indirect and diffuse influence on individual self-understandings. As Pierre Bourdieu argued, "The act of categorization, when it manages to achieve recognition or when it is exercised by a recognized authority, exercises by itself a certain power: 'ethnic' or 'regional' categories, like categories of kinship, institute a reality by using the power of *revelation* and *construction* exercised by *objectification in discourse*."[37]

---

[34] Lamont and Molnár, "The Study of Boundaries in the Social Sciences"; Wimmer, "The Making and Unmaking of Ethnic Boundaries."

[35] Marx, *Making Race and Nation*; Omi and Winant, *Racial Formation in the United States*.

[36] Hacking, "Making Up People"; Bourdieu, "Rethinking the State"; Anderson, B., *Imagined Communities*. On the "diffuse" power that stems from the self-evident nature of many state practices, see Mann, *The Sources of Social Power*, vol. 1, 8.

[37] Bourdieu, "Social Space and Symbolic Power," 223.

Thus, for example, when states use ethnoracial categories to *name* or to *describe* the constituent kinds of human beings that comprise the nation, notions of national identity may become inextricable from notions of ethnoracial identity. Individuals classified (and socialized) as part of the *national* community may come to understand themselves in *ethnoracial* terms not by virtue of their individual classification but through their subjective association with the ethnoracially depicted nation. For instance, while many Brazilians may be unsure of the "correct" response to a researcher who asks "what color/race are you?," most will readily acknowledge—in addition to (and often regardless of) however they opt to describe themselves as an individual—that *as a Brazilian*, they are "racially mixed."[38]

This does not mean states can call social groups into existence out of nowhere, simply by naming them. The state's classifications must be *recognized* by the classified in order to become reified in social practice.[39] Official classifications are more likely to become naturalized when they align with categorical distinctions that people already draw in daily interactions. The naturalizing power of official classification is bolstered when it corresponds with the unofficial categorical schemes deployed tacitly by individuals in everyday life.

Informal classification is inevitably implicated in formal bureaucratic processes, in part because individual discretion nearly always enters into administrative practice. The "spirit of formalistic impersonality" that characterizes modern, rational bureaucratic administration in its ideal-typical form is rarely fully realized in practice.[40] When public functionaries draw distinctions among citizens by relying on tacit cultural knowledge or discretionary preferences that diverge from official rules of classification, they may subvert the naturalization of the latter.[41] When informal classification processes align with official classification, on the other hand, the naturalizing repercussions of state-drawn distinctions are amplified.[42]

---

[38] Sheriff, *Dreaming Equality*. Common popular sayings such as "we all have one foot in the kitchen" (alluding to a space traditionally occupied by African-descended slave women) reproduce this idea in daily life.

[39] Jenkins makes the analytical distinction between *nominal* identity ("a name") and *virtual* identity ("a practical meaning or an experience"), noting that "it is an important contrast because one can change without the other doing so" (Jenkins, *Rethinking Ethnicity*, 56).

[40] Weber, *Economy and Society*, 225; Jenkins "Rethinking Ethnicity," 213.

[41] An example of this is the failed effort of the US Census Bureau to impose the US racial classification system in early twentieth-century Puerto Rico. See Loveman and Muniz, "How Puerto Rico Became White"; Loveman, M., "The U.S. Census and the Contested Rules of Racial Classification."

[42] This point is central to Charles Tilly's theoretical account of the role of categorization in the production of durable inequality. Tilly, *Durable Inequality*.

Official and informal classification are closely related phenomena, and in practice, they almost inevitably operate side by side.[43] In a sense, as sociologist Richard Jenkins argues, "the contrast between the formal and the informal is not a sharp distinction" but rather "a continuum of emphasis."[44] In key respects, the implications of ethnoracial classification for the lives of the classified hinges not on whether the classifications are formal or informal, but on the nature of the power relationship between the categoriz*ers* and the categoriz*ed*.[45]

Yet official, state-sanctioned ethnoracial distinctions do differ from informal classifications in a critical respect. Official classifications bear the weight of the accumulated symbolic authority of the modern state—an authority frequently backed by the threat of physical coercion.[46] Modern states hold (or at least claim to hold) unique and privileged positions of power with respect to the populations within their borders.[47] The classifications used by states to describe, regulate, and govern their populations have the power to shape individual existence in ways that informal classifications typically do not. Official ethnoracial classifications may seem to simply denote natural lines of distinction within populations, but the categories used by state bureaucracies can endow such distinctions with more "social reality" than they would otherwise have, effectively enabling, or even encouraging, the continuous *misrecognition* of social differences as natural differences.[48]

Making Nation-States

The study of official ethnoracial classification also clarifies the intimate connection between scientific theories about human difference and projects to construct nation-states, as both evolved over time. The perceived diversity of ethnoracial kinds within a given population was often seen as problematic for modern states in ways that it was not for earlier forms of

---

[43] As Richard Jenkins notes, "Formality and informality are specific kinds of social relation which have developed, historically, side by side: 'The formal is simultaneously an absence and a presence within the informal, and vice versa'. Each depends upon and takes part of its meaning from the other." (Harding and Jenkins, *The Myth of the Hidden Economy*, 137, cited in Jenkins, *Rethinking Ethnicity*, 64).

[44] Jenkins, *Rethinking Ethnicity*, 63–64.

[45] Jenkins, *Rethinking Ethnicity*.

[46] On the state and symbolic power, see Bourdieu, "The Social Space and the Genesis of Groups"; Bourdieu, "Rethinking the State"; Loveman, M., "The Modern State and the Primitive Accumulation of Symbolic Power"; Mitchell, "Everyday Metaphors of Power."

[47] Poggi, *The State*.

[48] Bourdieu, *Pascalian Meditations*, 177; Bourdieu and Wacquant, *An Invitation to Reflexive Sociology*, 167–8.

political organization. The diversity of subject populations was not a fundamental preoccupation, for example, for the rulers of expansionary patrimonial polities such as the Aztec or Ottoman empires, or the precolonial African polities of Azur, Azande, and Nupe, so long as it did not obstruct the extractive activities of the state.[49] The "quality" of the population *as a whole* was of little concern for states so long as these were not construed as the states *of* and *for* their citizens. Diversity within the governed population became an explicit cause for concern in modern states, because they were self-consciously organized as sovereign *nation*-states—states of and for a particular "people."[50]

Ethnoracial diversity of the population residing within the state's borders became a matter of concern once political legitimacy came to rest firmly on the radical notion of popular sovereignty. The idea that the legitimate political existence of any particular state ascended upward from "the people," rather than downward from the heavens, required some means of identifying who belonged to "the people" and of distinguishing one potentially sovereign "people" from others.[51] The move toward democratic forms of governance thus encouraged the identification of basic similarities within would-be sovereign populations and basic differences across them.

State builders deployed the idiom of nationhood to describe the traits that made a given population a distinctive "people." The claim to be a nation entailed assertions that "the people of a country constitute a socially integrated body, a meaningful whole."[52] The unity of "the people-as-nation" could be portrayed in relatively more "civic" or more "ethnic" terms. At one end of the continuum, the bonds of nationhood could be construed in terms of a voluntary adherence to a set of shared values and political principles, as in Ernest Renan's "daily plebiscite."[53] At the other end of the continuum, the bonds of nationhood could be construed in terms of primordial attachments of shared ancestry and communal life linked to common origins in some remote past.[54] Early waves of scholarship on nationalism

---

[49] Some degree of linguistic and cultural uniformity was achieved in the Aztec empire with the spread of Nahuatl, but after reviewing the evidence anthropologist R.D. Grillo concludes that in the Aztec empire, as in other cases of patrimonial, extractive states, "there was no policy of cultural homogenization affecting the population as a whole" (Grillo, *Pluralism and the Politics of Difference*, 73).

[50] Grillo, *Pluralism and the Politics of Difference*; Wimmer "Who Owns the State?"; Mann, *The Sources of Social Power, vol.2*; Giddens, *The Nation-State and Violence*.

[51] Bendix, *Kings or People*.

[52] Calhoun, *Nationalism*, 77.

[53] Renan, *Qu'est-ce qu'une nation?*

[54] Smith, A., *The Ethnic Origins of Nations*.

tended to characterize constructions of nationhood in a given country as either civic or ethnic. But as Rogers Brubaker has argued, the ethnic versus civic contrast is best construed as a difference of degree, not a difference in kind.[55] Further, in most countries, civic and ethnic conceptions of nationhood have coexisted, with their relative emphasis shifting at different points in time and in different contexts within the same nation-state.[56]

The particular challenge posed to modern states by various kinds of human diversity depended largely on the dominant conception of nationhood.[57] Where the nation was conceived first and foremost as a community rooted in primordial bonds, for example, non-coethnic residents were more apt to be seen as a threat to the integrity of the nation, and domestic nation-making projects were more likely to pivot on principles of exclusion or eradication of internal others. Where civic conceptions of the nation predominated, in contrast, internal heterogeneity was more likely to be construed as problematic only insofar as it obstructed integration into political culture (however "civically" or "ethnically" that political culture was, in actual practice, defined).[58] Differences within the population were seen as barriers to national progress, but not insurmountable ones. In such contexts, nation-making projects were more apt to turn on principles of assimilation and integration.[59]

Whether they espoused primarily civic or ethnic principles, nineteenth- and early twentieth-century nation-making projects in the Western Hemisphere shared a common font of inspiration: race science. The burgeoning field of science devoted to describing and explaining the variety of humankinds that populated the planet influenced nation-state building throughout the region.[60] Race science influenced how state builders construed the challenge of nation making and the pursuit of national progress.[61] The manifestations of this influence varied, in part depending on whether policymakers understood their nations in more civic or more ethnic terms.

---

[55] Brubaker, *Citizenship and Nationhood in France and Germany*, 2; Brubaker, "The Manichean Myth."

[56] Smith, R., *Stories of Peoplehood*.

[57] Brubaker, *Citizenship and Nationhood*.

[58] Wimmer, "Who Owns the State?"; Wimmer, *Nationalist Exclusion and Ethnic Conflict*; Smith, R., *Stories of Peoplehood*.

[59] Brubaker, *Citizenship and Nationhood*; Weber, E., *Peasants into Frenchmen*.

[60] Actually, saying nationalists drew inspiration from race science is probably an understatement, since many of the most influential contributors to nineteenth-century race science participated actively in nation-making projects within their own countries, and their scientific contributions bear marks of their nationalist interests. Banton, *Racial Theories*.

[61] Stepan, *The Hour of Eugenics*; Schwarcz, *O Espetáculo das raças*.

But in all cases, state-builders' views about putatively natural differences among categorically defined kinds of human kinds influenced policymaking in pursuit of national progress.

The influence of racial thought on the construction of nation-states is evident in the widespread use of official ethnoracial classification to restrict membership in national communities by regulating access to national territories. Even where nationhood is officially defined in "civic" terms, immigration policies often belie underlying ethnoracial understandings of legitimate belonging. Throughout the Americas, states have selectively excluded "undesirable" races, ethnicities, or nationalities from admission or the possibility of naturalization. Such policies defined rules of membership in the nation-state qua political community in ways that exposed the ethnoracial foundations of membership in the nation qua cultural community. The use of official ethnoracial classification in exclusionary immigration policies helped state builders define what the nation was by delimiting what it was not.[62]

Prevailing scientific theories about natural hierarchies of humankind also influenced how nation-state builders dealt with "differences" that already existed within their borders. Ethnoracial classification could be employed to monitor, segregate, exclude, or exterminate those living inside the state's borders but perceived as remaining outside the boundaries of the national community. States could also classify their populations along ethnoracial lines in order to target particular individuals, neighborhoods, or regions for projects that aimed to facilitate assimilation or integration. In addition, states could employ ethnoracial classification toward symbolic ends, to acknowledge or champion the presence of some types of people within the nation, while rendering others officially invisible.

It is not the case that only those states that championed "ethnic" conceptions of nationhood deployed official ethnoracial classification to differentiate among citizens. States that embraced "civic" national identities also routinely classified their populations into ethnoracial categories. The categorical distinctions imposed by states to deal with diversity beyond and within their borders played a fundamental role in defining the rules and terms of membership in the nation-state as both a political and ethnocultural

---

[62] This formulation is adapted from Zolberg, "Matters of State," 85. As Zolberg notes, "national identity always involves a negative aspect as well: we are who we are by virtue of who we are not." See also: Brubaker, *Citizenship and Nationhood*; Joppke, *Immigration and the Nation-State*; Zolberg, "International Migration Policies in a Changing World System"; Torpey, *The Invention of the Passport*; Fitzgerald, *The Face of the Nation*; Skidmore, *Black into White*; Lesser, *Negotiating National Identity*; Fitzgerald and Cook-Martín, *Culling the Masses*.

community. The use of official ethnoracial classification to exclude or include, to marginalize or to integrate, did not merely advance the interests of already existing nation-states, as policymakers might contend; it helped constitute nation-states as such. Historical analyses of states' use of ethnic and racial categories thus promises to expose the constitutive role of racialist social thought and racist scientific theory on the construction of modern polities and societies.

Defining and Redefining "the People"

Nation-states, once constructed, do not remain forever set in stone. Research into the politics and practice of official ethnoracial classification provides a window onto ongoing struggles over the power to define the symbolic and political boundaries of national communities. The official definitions of nationhood that prevail at pivotal moments weigh heavily in subsequent contests over rules and terms of national belonging. Hegemonic constructions of nationhood in a given period do not determine the outcome of later rounds of political struggle; but they do set constraints on the stakes and terms of contestation.

Domestic political battles to control states and define nations erupted regularly over the course of the nineteenth and twentieth centuries. A common stake in these struggles was the power to determine who could fully participate in the cultural and political life of the national community.[63] In the Americas, ethnoracial distinctions figured prominently in competing visions of political elites who fought for the power to direct the course of national development. In the late nineteenth and early twentieth centuries, nationalist elites selectively embraced race science as a pillar for their nation-making projects. As race science evolved into variants of eugenics, and then into different branches of anthropology, elites construed different facets of human diversity as scientifically and politically relevant to their projects for national development. Changes in the science of human difference over time reverberated in domestic political struggles, influencing how elites drew ethnoracial distinctions within their populations and how they framed the task of dealing with them in pursuit of their nation- and state-building goals.

As a template for the organization of political and cultural communities in the modern world, the nation-state prescribes congruence between the

---

[63] On the competing visions of national belonging in the history of the United States (restrictive versus expansive, and civic versus ethnic) see Smith, R., *Stories of Peoplehood*; Gerstle, *American Crucible*.

boundaries of political communities and the boundaries of cultural communities.[64] In the Americas, this template has proven to be ill-suited to social, cultural, and ethnodemographic realities. In the political struggles of the first decades of the twenty-first century, opponents continue to fight over alternative visions of nationhood. They also fight over alternatives to the nation-state model itself. The politics of official ethnoracial classification figures prominently in these unfolding debates. Historical analysis of state classification practices provides leverage to understand how official approaches to dealing with diversity in the past shape struggles to renegotiate relationships between individuals, communities, and states in the present day.

The National Census

National censuses are a strategic site for comparative and historical analysis of official ethnoracial classification and the state in the Americas. Historically, census taking played a significant role in the political and infrastructural development of states, in the symbolic construction of nations, and in the production of knowledge about national populations that served to inform (or justify) political projects in the name of national development. The importance of censuses to state building, nation making, and the politics of development make them an ideal institutional site to anchor an investigation of how ideas about race shaped nation-states, and how nation-states, in turn, shaped the generation of knowledge about race and its consequences for national development.[65]

The Modern Census and the Modern State

The production of official statistics, and census taking in particular, is among the most basic activities of modern states. Originally developed to facilitate tax collection and conscription for war, censuses played a pivotal role in the history of modern state formation in Western Europe and in European imperialist enterprises overseas.[66] The logistical demands of conducting even limited population counts contributed to the early development of

---

[64] Gellner, *Nations and Nationalism*, 1.

[65] On censuses as instruments of state formation, see Woolf, "Statistics and the Modern State." On censuses as instruments of nation making, see Anderson, B. *Imagined Communities*, ch.10. On censuses as instruments (and displays) of science, see Desrosières, *The Politics of Large Numbers*.

[66] Tilly, *Coercion, Capital, and European States*; Starr, "The Sociology of Official Statistics"; Woolf, "Statistics and the Modern State"; Porter, T., *The Rise of Statistical Thinking*; Giddens, *The Nation-State and Violence*.

"durable state structures" and bolstered the incipient infrastructural capacity of modernizing states.[67] State-builders conducted censuses to render the populations under their control "legible," translating heterogeneous agglomerations of people and places into orderly tables of numbers tied to particular geographic locales.[68] Organized lists of conscriptable men and taxable properties facilitated the extraction of resources toward their state-building ends.

In the mid-nineteenth century, a new model for taking a "modern" demographic census crystallized under the direction of leading European statisticians. The rationale and prescriptions for taking a modern census differed from various historical predecessors in several key respects.[69] First, in its idealized form, the modern national census differed from earlier data gathering activities with respect to its primary purpose. Reflecting the historical status of "population" as in the first instance a resource for its rulers, the primary purpose of historical population counts was to facilitate the extraction of fiscal and human resources. Historical censuses thus sought to collect information about specific, *concrete* individuals who might later be tapped to advance the state's interests. Modern censuses, in contrast, are supposed to be detached from the surveillance and taxation apparatus of the states that undertake them.[70] Reflecting the status of population in modern "governmental states" as "the ultimate end of government,"[71] modern censuses are supposedly conducted in the interests of enlightened public policy for the betterment of the society that is counted. As a consequence, in modern censuses it is only the *abstract* individual that is of interest, as in Adolphe Quetelet's nonexistent yet somehow powerfully real "Average Man."[72]

---

[67] On "durable state structures," see Tilly, *Coercion, Capital and European States*, 70; on infrastructural power of modern states, see Mann, *The Sources of Social Power*, vol. 2, 59–61.

[68] Scott, *Seeing Like a State*.

[69] The following discussion of the differences between colonial and modern censuses draws on Ventresca, "When States Count," which provides an insightful typological analysis of the differences between modern censuses, colonial censuses, and historical population counts.

[70] In modern states, the differentiation of the statistical apparatus and its associated personnel from other functions and functionaries of the state was an important step toward legitimizing the new purpose behind collecting information about the population. Not surprisingly, however, the historical association of population counts with extractive activities was a hard one to shake (and continues to create obstacles for modern census implementation in some contexts). Of course, in many contexts, the association between enumeration and extraction was not merely historical; the continued use of traditional forms of counting for specialized, extractive aims alongside the development of modern census taking in many places helped substantiate popular suspicions about the designs of census takers.

[71] Foucault, "Governmentality," 100.

[72] Desrosières, *The Politics of Large Numbers*, 73–7. Quetelet was a Belgian astronomer who is frequently referred to as the father of modern statistics (Desrosières calls him "the one-man band of nineteenth-century statistics.") In the 1830s and 1840s, Quetelet "disseminated the argument

The ideal modern census also differs from historical population counts with respect to its prescribed content. As techniques for assessing the general condition of "the people" for whom the state governs, modern censuses are explicitly intended to be comprehensive and inclusive, encompassing all individuals within the entire physical territory of the nation-state. Moreover, because modern censuses are meant to produce statistically useful information about general trends, the individuals enumerated respond to a standardized questionnaire that covers an array of potentially useful subjects. Ideally, modern censuses are taken at regular (five- or ten-year) intervals, permitting systematic evaluation of the population's characteristics and needs. In contrast to the modern census model, earlier population counts were irregular, targeted, and customized to respond to specific pragmatic ends. As mechanisms for rulers to extract resources from subjects, they rarely intended to cover an entire population of a delimited territory *irrespective* of particular characteristics; rather, censuses singled out individuals based on attributes such as sex and age (for military conscription), property ownership (for hearth censuses and tax registers), or race or caste (for labor tribute lists, tax liabilities, and allocation of privileges and immunities).

The organization and implementation of modern censuses also differ from their earlier relatives in ways that are indicative of the (theoretical) flattening of the hierarchical relationship that historically existed between ruler and ruled. Historically, the enumeration of *subjects* relied on the threat of physical or spiritual coercion exercised by an array of intermediary agents, all working in the name of their superiors in a hierarchical network of reciprocal relations that stopped only at the King. In modern states, in contrast, the enumeration of *citizens* typically relies on voluntary compliance with a specialized, professional staff of individuals who, as specially trained citizens themselves, are horizontally rather than hierarchically related to the individuals they set out to count.

Finally, reflecting a distinct conceptualization of the state-society relationship, the modern census model broke with earlier forms of enumeration

---

connecting the theory of probability and statistical observations. This construct held together both the random, unpredictable aspect of individual behavior and the contrasting regularity (and consequent predictability) of the statistical summation of these individual acts, through the notion of the *average man*" (Desrosières, *The Politics of Large Numbers*, 10, 78); cf. Igo, *The Averaged American*). As discussed in chapter 3, Quetelet was the driving force behind the creation of statistical bureaus in several European countries. He also organized the International Statistical Congress that met beginning in the 1850s to promote statistical science and develop international conventions for the production of comparable statistical data.

with respect to the intended dissemination of the results. Information collected in earlier counts was considered to belong to the state, and was often closely guarded as state secrets. In the immediate predecessors to modern European censuses, the secretive treatment of information about the population was inspired in part by mercantilist views, which deemed population statistics "too valuable to statesmen to be made public."[73] In modern censuses, in contrast, at least in democratic settings, it is assumed that individual privacy will be protected in the process of collecting and analyzing information, on the one hand, and on the other, that the general information produced through the aggregation of individual data will become public property.

Though the information provided by modern censuses may be of use to states, it does not *belong* to them; it is expected that the results will be made public and put to use in the interests of society. In these respects, as Paul Starr notes, modern censuses invert the earlier pattern: "In the pre-modern census, the state obtained information about persons and kept secret information about its population. The modern census is ideally expected to assure anonymity to persons and publicity to facts about population."[74] Moreover, the public that has a claim to modern census results is not limited by the boundaries of citizenship. Indeed, the development of the international statistics regime over the past two centuries was driven by the expectation that all countries should take general censuses and contribute to the general pool of comparable and standardized population data.[75] In stark contrast to the secret status of earlier population counts, modern census results are expected to produce knowledge that will become a part of world patrimony. It is precisely the international currency of the national population census that made it so amenable to state-builders' efforts to define and legitimize their nations.[76]

---

[73] Glass, *Numbering the People*, 13. As one example of this, Glass notes "the original results of the Austrian census of 1754 were assumed to have disappeared. Treated as confidential material, they lay buried in the archives until they were rediscovered in the present century." On mercantilist views of population in eighteenth-century Europe see also Torpey, *The Invention of the Passport*.

[74] Starr, "The Sociology of Official Statistics," 12. Of course, the protection of individual privacy, the autonomy of the census taking agency from coercive, extractive, or surveillance arms of the state, and the public nature of the results are all *ideally* characteristic of a modern census. The reality sometimes fell far short of the modern ideal. See Seltzer, "On the Use of Population Data Systems to Target Vulnerable Populations"; Seltzer and Anderson, "Census Confidentiality under the Second War Powers Act (1942–1947)."

[75] Ventresca, "When States Count."

[76] Of course, these characteristics of the "modern census" describe a normative and scientific model; the censuses that were actually conducted by states in the nineteenth and twentieth centuries varied tremendously in the degree to which they approximated the "modern census" ideal.

Census Taking and Nation Making

From the mid-nineteenth century, censuses became one of those things that modern nation-states do that demonstrates and documents their existence as such.[77] While the act of taking a national census itself became a symbolic claim to membership in the international system of states, the published reports of census results described the key attributes of the nation to both domestic and international audiences. Capturing a foundational irony of the nationalist worldview, census reports described the distinguishing features of populations using a standard template and measures; all nations could thus be equated with others, each with its own constitutive source of distinctiveness. Census reports thus served as national portraits. They helped to objectify and sharpen the symbolic boundaries of each nationally imagined community within an international gallery of others.

While concretizing the abstraction of "the nation" in order to render it internationally recognizable and comparable to others of like kind, national censuses also helped constitute and reify boundaries *within* the enumerated population. The categorical distinctions used on census questionnaires made it possible to generate a picture of the nation divided into those categorical types. Whether they were occupational, regional, linguistic, religious, or racial categories, the distinctions drawn on censuses helped to engender the very diversity of the population that the national survey intended to measure.

In part, census classification can help constitute the reality under investigation because the design of census forms and the analysis of results entail cognitive acts of "lumping and splitting."[78] To create the "classes of equivalence" necessary for statistical description and analysis requires grouping things of a certain "kind" together under a single heading, which in turn can contribute to making certain *kinds of things* into cognitive and social realities. By lumping together persons, places, and things that could just as easily (and in theory, indefinitely) be split apart, statistical categories necessarily impose a selective and simplified order on various dimensions of difference. By deliberately omitting certain categorical distinctions, they can also eclipse lines of difference from view.[79] Censuses promote particular images of the constitutive parts or substantive elements of a nation,

---

[77] Meyer, "The Changing Cultural Content of the Nation-State"; Ventresca, "When States Count."

[78] Zerubavel, "Lumping and Splitting."

[79] An example is the case of Argentina's historical omission of a census category to register the presence of Argentines of African descent. Andrews, *The Afro-Argentines of Buenos Aires, 1800–1900*.

even as they reinforce the view of the nation itself as a clearly delineated and unified whole.

Censuses may also influence the social facts they seek to measure through unintended feedback effects.[80] In early U.S. censuses, for example, the differential occupational classifications for men and women helped to solidify the (still prevalent) idea that household work constitutes "ungainful" employment.[81] The organization of nineteenth-century Italian statistics according to *compartimenti*, or regions, "effectively reinforced pre-existing divisions by reifying them into stable entities" even as the authors of Italian statistical works envisioned the gradual elimination of regional differences.[82] In colonial Southeast Asia, where the organization and administration of social life was guided by the "imagined map" of ethnoracial difference constructed by census classifications, the identity categories used by colonial administrators eventually took on a life of their own.[83] And in the post–civil-rights-movement United States, the direct use of census counts to track compliance with antidiscrimination laws has inadvertently contributed to the crystallization of ethnic group boundaries along the lines drawn by census categories.[84]

The creators of national statistics were often attuned to the potentially constitutive power of their enumerating endeavors. In postrevolutionary France, statistics were used to demonstrate and to help bring about the celebrated (if largely imagined) unity of the nation.[85] Italian statisticians produced "patriotic statistics" in the decade leading up to the unification of Italy with the explicit aim of demonstrating the viability and potential strength of a unified Italian nation.[86] Likewise, in nineteenth-century Latin America, census officials produced official reports that depicted politically fractured, ethnically divided populations as coherent and cohesive nations. The act of describing the nation in numbers advanced the idea that national integration was a foregone conclusion. This helped to constitute the nation

---

[80] Starr, "The Sociology of Official Statistics"; Kertzer and Arel, "Census, Identity Formation, and the Struggle for Political Power"; Hacking "Making Up People"; Patriarca, "Statistical Nation Building and the Consolidation of Regions in Italy."

[81] Anderson, M., "The History of Women and the History of Statistics"; Hutchinson, "La História Detrás de Las Cifras."

[82] Patriarca, *Numbers and Nationhood*; Patriarca, "Statistical Nation Building."

[83] Anderson, B., *Imagined Communities*, 169; Hirschman, "The Meaning and Measurement of Ethnicity in Malaysia"; Hirschman, "The Making of Race in Colonial Malaya."

[84] Skerry, *Counting on the Census?*, 72; Rodríguez, *Changing Race*; Skrentny, *The Ironies of Affirmative Action*; Mora, *Making Hispanics*.

[85] Bourguet, *Déchiffrer La France*; Weber, E., *Peasants into Frenchmen*.

[86] Patriarca, *Numbers and Nationhood*.

as a social fact. Against the reality of blurry, indeterminate, and sometimes stridently contested physical and cultural boundaries, printed volumes of national census results projected the nation as a clearly delineated set of individuals within a clearly bounded geographic space. Thus, national censuses provided an ideal forum for projecting nationalist desires on often uncooperative social and political realities.

The Census and the Science of Human Progress

Of course, censuses were not the only forum for the projection of nationalist aspirations on the international stage. But as depictions of modernizing nations, census reports enjoyed a particular legitimacy that derived from the combined authority of science and the state.[87] In the nineteenth and early twentieth centuries—and arguably still today for most countries— censuses were unrivaled in their credibility as a source of knowledge about the conditions and characteristics of national populations. Whatever the shortcomings of particular enumerations, censuses often figured as the source of first resort for demographic information about a given nation. Historically, the international recognition of census reports as *the* authoritative descriptions of national populations was directly tied to the scientific prestige of statistics as a revolutionary field of science. Following "the era of statistical enthusiasm" in the first half of the nineteenth century, statistics became the privileged media for describing, comparing, and diagnosing the defining attributes and developmental rankings of human populations.[88] The creation of central statistical bureaus beginning in the early nineteenth century institutionalized the merger of the science of probability and the practice of public administration, until then largely autonomous enterprises. Situated simultaneously within the field of science and technology and the field of government, the work of nascent statistical bureaus was somewhat ambiguously directed toward two distinguishable goals: objective, technical *description* and enlightened, policy-oriented *prescription*.[89] The particular manner in which public statistics was institutionalized and practiced in pursuit of these goals varied across countries, reflecting (and helping to reproduce) prevailing relationships between

---

[87] According to Desrosières, "Within the legitimacy enjoyed by state institutions, statistics occupied a particular place: that of *common reference*, doubly guaranteed by the state and by science and technology, the subtle combination of which constituted the originality and particular credibility of official statistics." (Desrosières, *The Politics of Large Numbers*, 148; italics in original).

[88] Westergaard, *Contributions to the History of Statistics*.

[89] Desrosières, *The Politics of Large Numbers*, 9.

state and society. But in all contexts, the ultimate utility of statistics for the state inhered in its ability to bridge knowledge and action, description and prescription, by "making things that hold."[90]

By identifying and objectifying consistencies in social relationships, containing them within standardized classifications, and crystallizing them in numerical form, statistics carved out cognitive "islands of meaning" and consecrated them as scientifically verifiable, enduring "things."[91] Thus, for example, "the average man," the "sex ratio," and the "mortality rate," presented as mere descriptions of things-that-are-true about a particular population, in fact helped to constitute these abstract conceptualizations as concrete, inter-nationally comparable "things." Thanks to national censuses, "populations" were equated with nations, and nations became directly comparable through the medium of statistics.

With the advent of regular and increasingly standardized national censuses, the door was open for the international ranking of nations according to statistical indicators of demographic well-being. Debates ensued among scientists in international venues over which rates or measures mattered most for ranking the prosperity of nations. In domestic arenas, meanwhile, political elites and census officials honed in on official statistics that aligned with their own theories and visions for national development. Official population statistics were used to assess the current state of the nation and to chart the path toward a brighter national future. Sanctioned by the combined authority of science and the state, national censuses became privileged platforms to document national progress—however it might be defined—for both domestic and international audiences.

In sum, the history of modern censuses is inextricable from histories of modern state building, nation making and the production of scientific knowledge about human diversity and its relevance for development. This makes national censuses a strategic site for comparative and historical analysis of the influence of racial thought on the construction of modern societies and polities. At the start of the twenty-first century, censuses remain central to political struggles over the definition of national identity and the meaning and future course of national development. Throughout contemporary Latin America, national censuses are symbolic stakes and pragmatic tools in the contentious politics of recognition, rights, and redress. In this book I provide a comparative and historical vantage point

---

[90] Desrosières, *The Politics of Large Numbers*.
[91] On cognitive islands of meaning, see Zerubavel, *The Fine Line*.

for understanding the contemporary politics of official ethnoracial classification and the state in Latin America.

Before turning to the historical analysis, I briefly introduce my distinctive analytic approach, note some advantages—and pitfalls—of this book's broad comparative scope, clarify my use of terminology, and provide an overview of the contents of remaining chapters.

Analytic Approach, Comparative Scope, and a Note on Terminology

Researching Race without Races

In making official ethnoracial classification my primary analytic focus, I depart from most social scientific scholarship on race. The sociology of race in the United States has concentrated historically on the analysis of racial groups and the relations between them. The group-focused paradigm encompasses an array of different theoretical traditions and it has generated some of the discipline's most influential and lasting contributions.[92] But this traditional paradigm is not well suited to the analysis of when, why, and how racial boundaries are drawn and socially instantiated, because it encourages researchers to take the group boundaries extant in a particular context as given. Even in research that is explicitly about the social construction of race, the observation that particular categorical divides are invented—that they are "a cultural imposition upon the brute fact of human phenotypic variation"—often appears in tandem with analyses that take both the boundaries and the boundedness of racial groups at face value.[93] As a result, the reality that any particular racial boundary is itself an artifact of historical struggles over the social meaning of physical and cultural differences slips out of view.

To some extent, reification of group boundaries may be inevitable in scholarship on race and ethnicity. The categories researchers use to parse the societies they study are partly products of those societies.[94] Even if crude forms of essentialism are avoided, the mere act of naming a collectivity has potentially reifying effects. Compounding this issue, many researchers of

---

[92] For an informative synthesis of this vast literature, see Daynes and Lee, *Desire for Race*; Emirbayer and Desmond, *The Racial Order*.

[93] This is the case even in otherwise exceptional works, such as Anthony Marx's *Making Race and Nation*. I elaborate on this point in Loveman, M., "Making 'Race' and Nation in the United States, South Africa and Brazil."

[94] Gellner, *Nations and Nationalism*, 34; Bourdieu, "Rethinking the State," 12–6.

racial dynamics rely on census data or other large-scale social surveys in which the racial or ethnic categories come predefined. In using such sources, it is all too easy to treat the official survey *categories* as synonymous with the social *groups* that exist in a given time and place. Historian Robert Jackson drew attention to this problem in reference to sources from colonial Latin America, noting that the official classification schemes "are seductive for modern researchers, because they carry with them the authority of written documents and are easily quantified."[95]

Official data sources, however, reflect a partial view; the politics of their production must be taken into account to understand the political and social meaning of the data they provide. The same note of caution is warranted for researchers who work with official demographic surveys to research race in the present. As political scientist Melissa Nobles showed in her comparative study of census politics in the United States and Brazil, the categories included on censuses are political artifacts.[96] The decisions of politicians, scientists, and bureaucrats who are positioned to influence the content of censuses can determine which ethnic or racial distinctions in society are statistically visible and thus seemingly self-evident and which are hidden from view. And as I show in the chapters that follow, the determinants of political choices about how to count and classify populations are varied, including both domestic and international sources of influence.

Adopting an analytic approach that makes boundary-making practices a primary focus does not immunize researchers against inadvertently contributing to the naturalization of social divides. But it can help minimize analytic reification by sharpening the distinction between *categories* and *groups*.[97] That is, rather than assuming congruence between official ethnoracial categories, on the one hand, and salient lines of ethnoracial distinction in everyday life, on the other, the degree of correspondence between official categories and experientially existing social groups is taken as an empirical question. Official census categories may map neatly onto salient social boundaries, in which case researchers can speak with relative confidence about the relations between groups in society based on analysis of population categories in official census data. But the congruence between official categories and social boundaries is one possibility

---

[95] Jackson, "Race/Caste and the Creation and Meaning of Identity in Colonial Spanish America," 2.
[96] Nobles, *Shades of Citizenship*.
[97] For more on the analytic distinction between categories and groups in the study of race and ethnicity, see Jenkins, "Rethinking Ethnicity"; Brubaker, "Ethnicity Without Groups"; Loveman, M., "Is 'Race' Essential?"; Brubaker et al., "Ethnicity as Cognition."

among others. Where census categories misalign with social boundaries or omit critical distinctions altogether, conclusions drawn from census data about prevailing intergroup relations may seriously miss the mark.[98]

Some scholars suggest that focusing the analytic lens on boundary-making processes instead of already constituted groups represents a detour away from fundamental concerns of sociological research on race.[99] But rejecting a group-focused analytic framework does not imply denial that ethnic and racial groups exist, much less an abandonment of the effort to improve understanding of historic and contemporary reasons for racial inequality and injustice. The politics and practices of demarcating categorical divides and naturalizing them as group boundaries are *endogenous* to the processes that generate racial inequality and injustice, not exogenous to them. An analytic approach focused on boundary-making processes does not rule out analysis of relations between groups, but it recognizes the boundedness of groups as variable and contingent, and it includes struggles to demarcate both the boundaries and boundedness of groups *within* the frame of analysis. Research that seeks to improve understanding of how, when, and why ethnic and racial distinctions get drawn and become instantiated in the organization of political and social life is critical to advance knowledge of how social distinctions become naturalized. Such research is critical, in other words, for the further development of sociological theories of racial domination, and its alternatives.[100]

Widening the Comparative Lens

With this book, I seek to expand the frame of comparative reference in scholarship that aims to theorize the links between race, nation, and states in the modern world. A broadened scope of comparison changes how we view the cases that have traditionally set the theoretical agenda for comparative race scholarship. For too long, scholars have treated the United States and South Africa as if they were classic cases of racial formation, instead of the historical outliers that they are.[101] This tendency is exemplified in books

---

[98] For more on this point with illustration from the contemporary Brazilian context, see Loveman, et al., "Brazil in Black and White?"

[99] For very different versions of this argument, see Bonilla-Silva, "The Essential Social Fact of Race"; Calhoun, "'Belonging' in the Cosmopolitan Imaginary"; Modood, *Multiculturalism*, ch5.

[100] See Wimmer, "The Making and Unmaking of Ethnic Boundaries"; Wacquant, "For an Analytic of Racial Domination"; Hollinger, "*Amalgamation and Hypodescent.*"

[101] For more on this issue, see Loveman, M. "Making 'Race' and Nation in the United States, South Africa and Brazil."

such as Anthony Marx's *Making Race and Nation*, which built a theory of how states "made race" that rests on the view of Brazil as historically "remarkable" for abstaining from institutionalized legal discrimination. "Including Brazil is pivotal," Marx explained, because it "remind[s] us that legal racial domination was not inevitable."[102] Yet when we expand the analytic lens, it becomes immediately evident that nation-state building projects anchored in legally institutionalized racial exclusion were the historical anomalies. To advance general understanding of how states make race we need to develop theories that fit more than one or two exceptional cases. We need more systematic investigations of how states construct race in the absence of legally institutionalized racial domination.

Widening the frame of comparative reference also promises to enrich our understanding of how states exercise power to shape the societies they govern. Accounts of states that engage in *de jure* racial discrimination tend to emphasize how states exercise administrative and coercive power to directly "racialize" populations. States assign individuals to racial categories and then subject them to targeted distribution of rewards or punishments based on their classification. Racial domination through bureaucratic administration is backed by the state's monopoly of "legitimate violence."[103]

Yet states also exercise symbolic power, which can contribute to the naturalization of racial boundaries indirectly and diffusely. Broadening the analytic scope beyond states that institutionalized legal racial domination draws attentions to how the political construction of ethnoracial divides relies not only on states' material and coercive power, but also on their symbolic power.[104] A broadened comparative scope promises to generate more nuanced and multifaceted understandings of how, exactly, various state practices may shape—or fail to shape—ordinary citizens' visions and divisions of the social world.[105] Including a wider range of cases in the analysis can ward against the allure of overly simplistic, determinist accounts of states' power to constitute social groups. State classification schemes may carry a distinctive kind of symbolic weight, but they exist alongside and sometimes in competition with classificatory schemes

---

[102] Marx, *Making Race and Nation*, 7.

[103] Weber, M., *Economy and Society* vol. 1, 54–56.

[104] Of course, the exercise of symbolic power is also important in contexts with institutionalized racial domination. But it tends to be theoretically neglected in accounts of such cases because it is overshadowed by the dominant story of legal institutionalization of racial divides backed by coercive force.

[105] Bourdieu, "The Social Space and the Genesis of Groups."

derived from other sources (such as the family, local community, religious order, etc.). Comparison of official ethnoracial classification and its consequences across a wide range of cases reveals the contingency of the state's capacity to create groups by naming them.

In addition to the analytic and theoretical advantages, a widened comparative lens expands our collective base of knowledge and enables the process of historical discovery. By researching ethnoracial classification practices in the national censuses of nineteen Latin American countries over the entire course of their existence as independent states, I discovered regional and period trends in how states classify their citizens that would be difficult to discern from research on a small number of cases. In particular, the broad comparative scope coupled with the long-term historical view exposed the critical influence of the international politics of nation making on national census taking in the region. Projects to build nation-states in Latin America were shaped from the beginning by the coterminous emergence and consolidation of an international system of nation-states. Nation-state building was thus inherently *relational*. The terms of incorporation into the international club of "civilized nations" influenced the cultural and political construction of modernizing nations.[106] The comparison of multiple cases over almost two centuries revealed regional trends that can only be explained by supranational political dynamics.[107] A wide analytic lens thus helps to correct for the teleological bias in many national(ist) histories of nation-state formation.

Finally, a broadened comparative perspective generates new knowledge about less frequently studied cases. This is important both as a means to better understand these societies on their own terms, and to disrupt the inclination in comparative race scholarship to treat Latin America as a single, unitary case.[108] A contemporary debate in the sociology of race in the United States, for example, centers on whether the US racial order is becoming "Latin Americanized"—as if Latin America were a single country characterized by a single type of racial order.[109] The variation in

---

[106] Much like the terms of incorporation into the global economy and world-system of states influenced the structure of national political economies. Cardoso and Faletto, *Dependency and Development in Latin America*; Bulmer-Thomas, *The Economic History of Latin America since Independence*; Coatsworth and Taylor, *Latin America and the World Economy since 1800*.

[107] These supranational dynamics include institutional connections and the flow of ideas across borders. See Cooper, "Race, Ideology and the Perils of Comparative History"; Morillo-Alicea, "'Aquel Laberinto de Oficinas'," 133.

[108] Of course, for many questions of concern to sociologists who study race, it is equally problematic to treat the United States as a unitary case. But that is a topic for another book.

[109] Bonilla-Silva, "We Are All Americans!"; Sue, "An Assessment of the Latin Americanization Thesis."

racial and ethnic dynamics throughout different parts of Latin America calls into question the underlying premise of this debate. Though there was, and is, significant shared history across the region—some of which is reported in this book—the range of racialized social dynamics found in Latin America defy a unitary, stylized generalization. Racial dynamics and politics work very differently in Argentina than they do in Brazil; indigenous-state relations in Mexico bear little resemblance to those in Chile and Uruguay. Within countries, as well, there are often striking variations by region, class, or generation in how racial or ethnic distinctions are understood and operate as a basis of social inclusion or exclusion in daily life. The adoption of a broad comparative scope brings dimensions of similarity and difference in racial dynamics across Latin America into clearer view.

The analytic, theoretical, and historical payoffs of adopting a wide comparative lens do not come without a cost. Most obviously, the panoramic breadth inevitably entails some sacrifice of historical, case-specific depth. One of the greatest challenges of writing a book that covers nineteen countries over two centuries has been the keen awareness that nearly every sentence that seeks to generalize about historical processes carries with it some caveat, partial exception, or countervailing case. (And the more research I did, the more the caveats seemed to multiply). I uncovered a number of country-specific idiosyncrasies and apparent anomalies that are not addressed in the existing secondary literature. I draw attention to these new historical puzzles at various points in the chapters that follow, but I do not resolve them all within the scope of this book. Thus, the answers to some of the questions raised herein await future research.

Clarifying Terminology

A final introductory note is necessary on terminology. As in everyday life, so in the world of scholarship, the communication of ideas about race often entails navigating tricky semantic terrain. I find it useful, for this purpose, to employ an analytical vocabulary that maintains some distance from the specific terminologies used in the times and places under study. In this book, I use the term *ethnoracial* as a generic, umbrella descriptor to refer to any categorical distinction that names or delimits sets of human beings who are construed to belong together naturally, as a collectivity or community, due to some source of heritable similarity. *Official ethnoracial classification*, in turn, refers to acts of ethnoracial classification carried out by agents of the state in their official capacities.

The term *ethnoracial* is admittedly a bit cumbersome; it does not flow as naturally off the tongue as either of the two descriptors that make it up. In some parts of the text, I rely on the simpler language of *racial* or *ethnic* classification in the interest of readability. But I use ethnoracial as the preferred descriptor where more theoretical precision is necessary. I also use it in some contexts to maintain a separation between the classificatory terms used by historical actors and my analysis of those classification practices, in order to avoid simply reproducing the naturalizing terminologies that are a primary object of my analysis.

Adoption of *ethnoracial* as a capacious analytic term also helps safeguard against the tendency to fall back on commonsense understandings derived from a particular time and place to decide which categories or groups are "racial" versus "ethnic."[110] Introductory sociology textbooks in the United States often insist on a neat distinction between "race" as a biological category and "ethnicity" as a cultural category. But the clarity of this distinction has never really held up to the variety of ways that human beings think, write, and talk about the diversity of other human beings. In practice, notions of biological and cultural difference are often inextricably intertwined. Indeed, as the chapters that follow show, racial lexicons in Latin America have often drawn on notions of heritable cultural differences, while the use of ethnic terminologies often elided underlying assumptions about essential and enduring biological traits. Thus, for example, instead of deciding a priori that indigenous groups should be described as "ethnic" and Afrodescendant groups as "racial," I analyze the politics and practices of classifying both within a common framework.[111]

Comparative and historical research on race requires a framework that recognizes a distinction between the *terms* people use and the *concepts* they invoke as they *do things* with categories.[112] The use of *ethnoracial* as an umbrella term provides leverage to analyze the often slippery usage of the languages of race and ethnicity in practice throughout Latin America, and to recognize how elite conceptions of indigenous, Afrodescendant, Asian, and even European populations have often trafficked precisely in

---

[110] On the implicit parochialism of most efforts to retain a sharp distinction between "race" and "ethnicity," see Wacquant "For an Analytic of Racial Domination"; Banton, "Analytical and Folk Concepts of Race and Ethnicity."

[111] On the need for unified frameworks for the analysis of the relationships between Latin American states and indigenous and Afrodescendant peoples, see Wade, *Race and Ethnicity in Latin America*, ch. 1.

[112] On "doing things" with categories, see Brubaker "Ethnicity without Groups," 169–70; Brubaker et al. *Nationalist Politics and Everyday Ethnicity in a Transylvanian Town*.

the *blurring* of distinctions between biological and cultural conceptions of human difference. In parts of Latin America, for example, Indians were described by elites in biological racial terms *and* they could become non-Indians when they migrated to urban areas, put on shoes, cast off indigenous clothing, joined unions, earned salaries, and thus became *mestizos*, *cholos*, *ladinos*, or members of other categories whose names could be used either descriptively or pejoratively.

Overview of Chapters

The chapters are organized chronologically, beginning with an analysis of ethnoracial classification in colonial Latin America in chapter 2. Chapters 3, 4, and 5 examine different facets of national census taking in Latin America in the first century after independence. I analyze post-World War II developments in chapter 6. In chapter 7, I examine the politics of census classification in the first decades of the twenty-first century. Each chapter addresses a separate historical puzzle or set of previously unanswered questions, while also helping to build or illustrate my overarching arguments.

Chapter 2 sets the historical stage for the analysis that follows through a critical examination of the ways Spanish and Portuguese imperial states counted and classified their colonial subjects in the Americas. In contrast to the postindependence view of population as a *nation* that justified the existence of the state, imperial states saw colonial populations first and foremost as a *resource* for advancing their extractive aims. Official ethnoracial classification in Spanish America dictated the distribution of debts and duties owed to the colonial state. The legal relationship between ruler and ruled hinged on each subject's official ethnoracial classification. The elaborate and consequential status distinctions institutionalized by imperial states in the Americas exemplify how the administrative use of ethnoracial categories can instantiate and naturalize social distinctions within populations.

After independence, the Spanish American polities stood poised to become color-blind republican nations. Glossing over the constitutive contradiction of accommodating African slavery and Indian tribute within the formal legal architecture of liberal republicanism, political elites declared the creation of modern liberal republics comprised of formally equal citizens. Yet over the next several decades, nearly all Latin American states engaged in official ethnoracial classification of citizens. Why did those charged with conducting early national censuses in the region break with the symbolic proclamations of universalist, color-blind republicanism, take up the colonial-tainted practice of state racial classification, and deliberately draw attention to racial differences in their populations? Chapters 3 and 4 provide an explanation for this unexpected regional trend.

Chapter 3 brings into focus how international developments in the emergent scientific field of statistics shaped both the form and content of Latin America's early national censuses. Independent Latin America's first census officials looked to authoritative European sources for instructions on how to conduct a modern census. The status of the national census as an internationally legitimate form and forum for documenting the progress of nations made it particularly appealing to Latin American state builders intent on joining the community of "civilized nations." But they also wrestled with how to adapt those models to Latin American realities. The modern census model did not simply disseminate across the region through emulation of the superficial attributes of an institutional form; Latin American census officials selectively adapted the international model to accomplish their own pragmatic and ideological ends.

In chapter 4, I document how early national censuses from across Latin America underscored the *racial* particularity of populations to bolster claims of *national* distinctiveness. I argue that state officials fastened on the idea of race—and in particular, of race mixture—to ground their claims of modern nationhood due to the temporal coincidence of Latin America's early phase of nation making with the international rise of race science. Prevailing theories denied Latin American states the possibility of future membership in the international club of "civilized nations," on racial grounds. Latin American statesmen used national censuses to craft an explicitly racialist response. In the "race to progress" in an age of scientific racism, Latin American census officials led the charge to document—in the internationally prestigious language of statistics—the inevitable "racial improvement" ("whitening") of their populations. The racial statistics collected in national censuses became the raw materials for crafting statistical portraits of racially regenerative nations-in-the-making.

Taken together, chapters 3 and 4 show how the production of racial statistics in late nineteenth- and early twentieth-century Latin America responded to scientific and organizational developments on the world stage. Prior research on the history of census taking in individual Latin American countries points to the direct involvement of census officials in domestic political projects, struggles, and debates. Domestic politics are pivotal for explaining the idiosyncrasies of censuses in each country, but they cannot account for the regional trends documented in this book.

The ways that Latin American states counted and classified their populations in early national censuses reflected the international embeddedness of nation-building projects. Census officials' orientation to international criteria for constructing modern nations shaped their statistical descriptions of ethnoracial diversity and their prescriptions for mitigating its toll on national development.

In chapter 5, I delve more deeply into the methods used to produce racial statistics in late nineteenth- and early twentieth-century Latin America. The chapter demonstrates that to understand the political and social meaning of official racial statistics requires close attention to the tacit cultural assumptions that inform their production. By scrutinizing the practices through which population statistics were collected, aggregated, and displayed, I show how racialist understandings of human differences informed the production of putatively objective knowledge about those differences. Census officials' tacit racial assumptions shaped how they organized and analyzed demographic data. Statistical tables conveyed officials' implicit views about natural hierarchies of human kind, helping to affirm their explicit arguments that equated national progress with "racial progress."

As the twentieth century wore on, national censuses came to play an increasingly prominent role in the politics of national development. In the wake of World War II, however, the explicit equation of national progress with racial progress came under critical scrutiny. Chapter 6 examines how Latin American census officials reconciled their commitments to the continued pursuit of national progress with the global discrediting of "race" as a scientific concept and "racial improvement" as a political project. The majority of Latin America countries abstained from direct race questions on censuses in this period, substituting questions about cultural characteristics such as maternal language or forms of dress. As a consequence, national censuses drew increasing attention to indigenous populations within the nation, while eclipsing those of African origins from view. While the terms for describing diversity within populations were recast, census officials still pointed to statistics showing the gradual disappearance of minority populations as evidence of national progress.

In chapter 7, I document and explain the resurgence of official ethnoracial classification in Latin American censuses since the 1990s. This resurgence coincides with an extraordinary moment of renegotiation in the relationships between states, ethnic minorities (who in some countries are numerical majorities), and broader publics in Latin America. By the early twenty-first century, the production of official ethnoracial statistics had become both a critical stake and a powerful tool in unfolding struggles over recognition, rights, and redress for historically marginalized populations in the region. Following a descriptive overview of changes to ethnoracial data collection in Latin American censuses between the 1980s and 2010s, I analyze the specific confluence of domestic and international interests that brought these changes about. In a few countries, census reforms resulted primarily from domestic activism, with ancillary support from international organizations. In most of the region, however, census reform happened in response to pressure from international organizations. I describe how the stated priorities and norms of the major international development organizations underwent a "multiculturalist" revision in this period, and I identify the specific mechanisms through which the revised priorities and norms of international organizations translated into a renaissance of official ethnoracial classification in Latin America.

In the conclusion, I place the contemporary politics and practice of official ethnoracial classification in Latin American censuses in historical perspective. In some respects, the new era of official ethnoracial classification is strongly reminiscent of the past. There is an underlying continuity across decades in Latin American states' use of ethnoracial population data to define their national identities and to chart the path to national progress. In other respects, however, the contemporary politics of official ethnoracial classification in Latin America break with historical precedent in the region. Of particular note, the field of census politics has opened up to include newly politicized historical actors. Those who would be counted demand more control over the instrument states use to count them. The legitimacy of the census increasingly hinges on prior negotiation with a broad range of interested actors, while the authority of the census as a neutral source of demographic information is challenged by the transparently political nature of such negotiations. In the final pages of the book, I comment on the implications of the new politics of official ethnoracial classification in Latin America for efforts to combat inequality, deepen democracy, and promote national development in the region as the twenty-first century unfolds.

CHAPTER 2 | Classifying Colonial Subjects

POPULATION WAS A KEY strategic resource of the Spanish and Portuguese empires in the Americas. The paramount objectives of the early phase of colonial rule—defense of territory against rival imperial powers, extraction of massive quantities of minerals from beneath Earth's surface, and development of agrarian production—demanded control over the colonial population. More precisely, the extractive aims of empire hinged on the domination and exploitation of specific, categorically defined segments of the colonial population.[1] As historian John Lombardi observes of the Spanish American context, "Without Indian labor all the wealth of Potosí and Mexico would have been wasted, locked in the ground awaiting the advent of a technology capable of extraction without a large number of human workers."[2] But "Indian labor" was itself a colonial invention. "Indian" did not exist as a *kind* of person prior to the categorical lumping of indigenous peoples by the colonizers, who gave life to the category through a combination of ritualized social interaction, law, and brute force.[3] Official racial classification in colonial Latin America was

---

[1] There is a large literature on colonial labor systems in Spanish America and Brazil. Illustrative sources include: Schwartz, "Colonial Brazil, c.1580–c.1750"; Schwartz, *Sugar Plantations in the Formation of Brazilian Society*; Sherman, *Forced Native Labor in Sixteenth-Century Central America*; Cole, *The Potosí Mita, 1573–1700*; Stern, S., *Peru's Indian Peoples and the Challenge of the Spanish Conquest*.

[2] Lombardi, "Population Reporting Systems," 13.

[3] As historian Alan Knight argues, the term "Indian" "defined those who were not Spanish or mestizo and it lumped together a wide range of Indian groups, languages, and communities. The Indians themselves lacked any shared sentiment of Indian-ness (pan-Indianism is a very recent creation); they often lacked even the "tribal" allegiances imputed to them, in that they gave their primary loyalty to the community—to the old Mesoamerican *atlepetl*, which the Spaniards had seen fit to conserve (or, with the *congregación*, to replicate) in the interests of social order and economic organization (Knight, "Racism, Revolution, and Indigenismo," 75; Bonfil Batalha, *Utopía y Revolución*, 19; Hacking, "Making Up People," 222–36).

integral to a system of imperial rule designed, in the first instance, to facilitate orderly extraction of agricultural, mineral, and fiscal resources from the colonial domains.

Population counts in colonial Latin America differed in significant ways from the population censuses that would be taken by post-independence Latin American states in the nineteenth century. Whereas national states in Latin America would (re)conceive population as *the people*—the set of citizens in whose name the state claimed to legitimately govern—the Spanish and Portuguese imperial states construed population first and foremost as a *resource* among others to which the Crowns laid claim. Distinct official visions of the natural order of societal bonds and the legitimate relationship between state and society would translate into different means and motivations for counting population in colonial versus national states in Latin America.

This chapter analyzes the practices used by Spanish and Portuguese imperial governments to count and classify the populations of their American colonies. Drawing on an array of examples from the colonial historiography, I provide a synthetic analysis of how imperial efforts to count and classify colonial subjects helped instantiate a particular ethnoracial social order in the colonies. Institutions that engaged in official racial classification were crucial sites of articulation between imperial visions of the colonial population and the pragmatic aims of imperial rule. Whether conducted by local priests, military officers, civil functionaries, or the courts, official racial classification helped to constitute categorically different kinds of colonial subjects.

Colonial Spanish and Portuguese America exemplify how the legal codification and administrative use of racial categories can instantiate and naturalize social divisions within human populations.[4] The population of the Americas from the 1500s to the 1800s encompassed tremendous variation in physical, linguistic, and other cultural traits. Operating within (and upon) this diverse human landscape, agents of Iberian imperial states imposed particular visions of the relevant divisions within colonial populations. From multiple dimensions of heterogeneity in the population, imperial law and administrative practice made some dimensions of difference

---

[4] Historians sometimes use the term *race/caste* to refer to the status of individuals in colonial Latin America, accentuating the point that individual position in the *sociedad de castas* was not strictly a matter of ancestry. The same is of course true of "racial" distinctions made in modern Latin America. In the interest of readability, and to underline the social determination of "racial" status in both colonial and postcolonial Latin America, I have opted to use the term *racial* rather than *race/caste* to describe the classification system in colonial Latin America.

socially consequential, while ignoring others. Like all schemes for racially classifying human populations, the particular lines of demarcation imposed and enforced by imperial administrators entailed cognitive acts of "lumping and splitting."[5] Through legal and administrative institutionalization of certain categorical divisions and not others, imperial governments in the Americas actively constituted social groupings within the colonized population that came to be perceived as natural groupings.

Official racial categories were the legal and administrative frame on which the bureaucratic infrastructures of the Spanish and Portuguese American imperial states were built. Legally enshrined racial categories bolstered Iberian empires in the Americas both materially and ideologically. Official racial categories structured imperial regulation of such fundamental aspects of colonial society as the division of labor, education, occupation, property ownership, and the distribution of individual privileges and obligations under the law. Likewise, racial distinctions constituted, to a large degree, the symbolic economy of honor and status prestige in the colonies. Official racial classifications also served to knit the material and symbolic economies of the colonies tightly together, as is especially evident in the ways racial categories informed laws governing marriage, legitimacy of children, and inheritance.[6]

In the colonial period (just like today), the term *raza* was not a stable signifier; it took on different meanings depending on the context of its use. In some contexts, *raza* was used to refer narrowly to family lineage or "purity of blood," while in others *raza* signified a broader complex of physical and cultural attributes. Categories that contemporary scholars (myself included) routinely refer to as "racial"—such as "white," "black," "indio," and "mulato"—appear in colonial population tables under diverse headings, including *raza*, *casta* (caste), *color, clase* (class), and *calidad* (quality). That the word *calidad* was often used interchangeably with *raza* or even *color*, suggests how the concept of race in colonial Latin America encompassed more than just lineage, on the one hand, or appearance, on the other. As historian Robert McCaa observes, "*Calidad*, typically expressed in racial terms (e.g., indio, mestizo, español), in many instances was an inclusive impression reflecting one's reputation as a whole. Color, occupation, and wealth might influence one's *calidad*, as

---
[5] Zerubavel, "Lumping and Splitting."
[6] For example, Lewin, *Surprise Heirs I*.

did purity of blood, honor, integrity, and even place of origin."[7] In addition to these characteristics, other factors that might have contributed to racial ascription included language, dress, hair type, stature, place of residence, and legitimacy of birth. An array of individual characteristics and socially defined traits thus combined to determine racial classification in colonial Latin America.

Analysis of colonial racial classification must attend to the historically embedded understandings of the sources and nature of putatively essential differences within human populations. At the same time, at least four dimensions of variation must be kept in mind as backdrop to any discussion of why and how Iberian imperial states counted and classified their colonial subjects in the Americas. First, the historiography of colonial Latin America warns against generalizing from the experience of any single locality in the imperial domains to the empire as a whole, much less from Spanish to Portuguese colonial contexts.[8] Second, the colonial historiography also cautions against generalizing from one moment in time to the entire "colonial period," as if social relations and modes of governance remained static across more than three centuries of imperial rule. Third, recent contributions to colonial Latin American history emphasize the heterogeneity of lived experiences and subjectivities forged under colonial rule; preferring to narrate colonial Latin American histor*ies* rather than histor*y*, recent scholarship reveals that colonial Latin America looks quite different when viewed through the lens of subaltern social actors rather than elites, and from the peripheries of an empire rather than its center.[9] Fourth, and finally, important recent contributions to the broader interdisciplinary field of colonial and postcolonial studies make plain the error of adopting simplistic analytical binaries, such as colonizer/colonized, to investigate colonial pasts. Just as "subaltern" experiences of colonial rule varied, so too did the intentions and understandings of the different kinds of social actors who made up "the imperial state." Missionaries and religious authorities, political elites, mid-level and local bureaucrats, military officers, absentee landowners, and the operators of plantations and mines no doubt envisioned the colonial population through only somewhat overlapping lenses.[10] Taken together,

---

[7] McCaa, "*Calidad, Clase,* and Marriage in Colonial Mexico," 477–8; McCaa et al., "Race and Class in Colonial Latin America."

[8] See, for example, Rappaport, "'Asi lo Paresçe por su Aspeto'," 606.

[9] Fisher and O'Hara, *Imperial Subjects*; Thurner and Guerrero, *After Spanish Rule*; and in the postcolonial context, Appelbaum, *Muddied Waters*.

[10] Stoler, "Rethinking Colonial Categories."

these dimensions of heterogeneity across time, geography, and categories of social actors render problematic any facile generalizations about "colonial Latin America."

Yet the recent historiography of colonial Latin America also provides leverage to investigate aspects of colonial administration that traversed different historical moments, contexts, and agents of empire. The wealth of rich case studies informed by advances in theories of empire and coloniality, subaltern studies, and the anthropology of the state, provide fresh insight into imperial modes and motives of rendering colonial Latin American populations "legible" to the state.[11] Even as different types of colonial agents attended to different lines of distinction within colonized populations, certain fundamental assumptions about the nature and purpose of colonial populations seem to have crosscut even the most varied circumstances. The underlying similarities in Iberian efforts to count and classify colonial populations across the vast temporal and geographic spaces of empire in the Americas bring the shared imperial vision of population as resource into sharp relief. Analysis of Iberian efforts to count and classify colonial populations also illuminates shared mechanics of naturalizing social differences through seemingly mundane, administrative acts of imperial governance. Finally, historical evidence of individual and collective efforts to contest or evade official racial classification highlights how imperial categories shaped and constrained—but never fully contained—the subjective self-understandings of colonial subjects.

Counting the Colonial Population: Motives and Methods

Prior to imperial conquest of the Americas, the Spanish and Portuguese crowns had already amassed considerable experience counting targeted segments of their respective populations. With some antecedents in the fourteenth century and even earlier,[12] the use of censuses, lists, and registers had become more common in Europe by the fifteenth century.

---

[11] Scott, *Seeing Like a State*.

[12] These include the Norman Domesday book (1086), the first Venetian census (circa 1268), and the Ottoman hearth registries (fourteenth century) (Alden, "The Population of Brazil in the Late Eighteenth Century," 174 fn9; Ventresca, "When States Count," 26). Other notable examples include the regular household censuses of Castile beginning in 1482, and the *descrizioni* of the Italian states beginning in the sixteenth century. On early population counts, see Emigh et al., *How Societies and States Count*, ch2; Wolfe, A.B., "Population Censuses Before 1790"; Willcox, "Census"; Knibbs, "The Evolution and Significance of the Census."

The ability to take stock of taxable resources and conscriptable men was crucial in a context where the survival of states depended on their ability to fend off predatory advances from their neighbors.[13]

The drive to mobilize armies for war stimulated the development of enumerating states in Western Europe.[14] The military impetus of most enumerative endeavors of early modern European states is clearly evident in their scope. On the Iberian Peninsula, fifteenth-century household counts (*cadastros*) were undertaken by individual kingdoms, or cities within kingdoms, to meet specific fiscal and military needs. For example, a census taken in the City of Gerona in 1462 sought to identify males old enough to be soldiers and who had not yet formed a family. Categories of men who were not considered conscriptable, such as priests and Jews, were not counted in the census.[15]

In part, the motives and methods of counting populations in colonial Latin America mirrored those deployed to count populations on the Iberian Peninsula both before and during more than three centuries of colonial rule in the Americas. But the Spanish and Portuguese crowns also adapted their approach to tracking colonial populations in ways that reflected their visions of the particular conditions and purpose of their colonial possessions.[16]

---

[13] Tilly, *The Formation of National States in Western Europe*; Tilly, "Epilogue"; Finer, "State- and Nation-Building in Europe"; Downing, *The Military Revolution and Political Change;* Porter, *War and the Rise of the State*; Ertman, *Birth of the Leviathan*; Centeno, *Blood and Debt*.

[14] The administrative apparatus for conducting military censuses and lists of taxable households was thus part of the "durable state structure" that emerged as an offshoot of the extractive and coercive activities of early modern European states. Tilly, *Coercion, Capital, and European States*; Woolf, "Statistics and the Modern State."

[15] Sobrequés i Vidal, "Censo y Profesión de los Habitantes de Gerona en 1462," 194–6.

[16] Historians have carefully documented a wide array of colonial Latin American census records, providing both general overviews of available sources and scrutinizing the details of specific censuses. The discussion that follows draws on the historiography to provide a synthetic account of the general practices and principles of population registers in colonial Latin America. Inevitably, this means that local- and regional-level discrepancies in how enumeration occurred, as well as idiosyncratic details of specific population lists, are glossed over in the interest of providing a general sense of how and why the Iberian powers went about counting their colonial populations. Useful general surveys of the types of colonial population records available to historians and their strengths and weaknesses for questions of concern to historical demographers include: Lombardi, *People and Places in Colonial Venezuela*; Lombardi, "Population Reporting Systems"; Cook and Borah, *Essays in Population History,* vols 1, 2; Cook and Borah, "The Historical Demography of Aboriginal and Colonial America: An Attempt at Perspective"; Alden, "The Population of Brazil"; Sánchez-Albornoz, "Population"; Sánchez-Albornoz, *The Population of Latin America*; CLASCO, *Fuentes Para la demografía histórica de América Latina*; Marcílio, "Levantamientos Censitarios da Fase Proto-Estatística do Brasil"; Marcílio, "Population"; Arretz et al., *Demografía Histórica en América Latina;* Consejo Latinoamericano de Ciencias Sociales. *Fuentes para la demografía histórica de América Latina;* de Souza e Silva, *Investigações Sobre os Recenseamentos*. Among numerous close

Through the mercantilist lens of the time, population size was considered a sign of strength—as with bullion, the more the better. If population was deemed crucial to national vitality at home, in the colonies its strategic importance was magnified. Bodies were needed to lay effective claim to colonial territory, while *brazos* (arms) were indispensable for the extraction of raw materials from the territories claimed. The enumerative practices of Iberian states in the Americas thus focused on counting population with two principal aims: the establishment and maintenance of colonial militias or armies and the management of large-scale systems of coerced labor.

In a context where the reigning principle of *uti possidetis* meant that claims to territory often hinged on sustained occupation, the Iberian powers had good reason to be concerned about the size and fixity of their colonial populations.[17] In Portuguese America, this concern was reflected in the continuous establishment and fortification of *colonias* in contested regions throughout the colonial period.[18] In Spanish America it was evident in the deliberate, urban-based method of colonization and administration. The imperial state prioritized the establishment of towns and monitored individuals through their connections to urban centers.[19] But settlement was not always sufficient to deter the ambitions of rival powers; the only real way to demonstrate occupation, when challenged, was to defend the claim militarily.

Censuses were used to gather information about the potential military force of the colonies and about the potential fiscal resources to support military endeavors. Royal concern with military strength was perennial, but it intensified in the latter part of the eighteenth century due to the

---

studies of specific population counts are Barickman, "Reading the 1835 Censuses from Bahia"; Bromley, "Parish Registers as a Source in Latin American Demographic and Historical Research"; Peachy, "The Revillagigedo Census of Mexico, 1790–1794"; Robinson, *Studies in Spanish American Population History*. In addition to these sources, journals of national historical institutes such as the *Revista do Instituto Histórico e Geográfico Brasileiro* are rich sources for descriptions of specific colonial censuses.

[17] The principle of *uti possidetis*, which recognized the sovereignty of whomever's subjects actually occupied the territory, was legitimized in the Treaty of Madrid in 1750. Before that, the division of the "New World" between Spain and Portugal was supposedly determined by an imaginary north-south line drawn 370 leagues west of the Cape Verde Islands, as established by the Treaty of Tordesillas in 1494.

[18] Among the most important of these for Brazil was the Colonia Sacramento, established on the borders of the Río de la Plata (located between present-day Argentina and Uruguay) to ward against Argentine expansion northward. Contests over the territory eventually led to war (1825 to 1828), and the establishment of Uruguay as a buffer state between Argentina and Brazil.

[19] Lombardi, "Population Reporting Systems," 15–17.

"increasingly bitter rivalry for hegemony in the New World."[20] Thus, in his discussion of available sources for the historical demography of colonial Venezuela, historian John Lombardi notes that there is "evidence of a considerable body of data collected in the 1770s in a government effort to assess the military strength of the empire."[21] The breakdown of the age brackets in the imperial censuses from this period reveal concern with enumerating the male population of fighting age.[22]

Population lists were also created to administer and enforce systems of coerced labor. Labor was the single most valuable resource in the Spanish and Portuguese American colonies; without it the riches of the soil and the mines would remain beyond the reach of the Spanish and Portuguese.[23] As Lombardi notes, "The problem in America in the early years when the basic elements of the reporting system were established was never a lack of natural resources to exploit but the availability of human resources to do it."[24] Surviving examples of colonial population counts reflect the centrality of labor extraction to the imperial enterprise in Latin America.

In the Spanish American colonies, an array of coercive labor practices served to fix indigenous peoples to the land and systematize their exploitation. Systems of labor extraction varied in their details across local contexts, but each had its accompanying practices of counting and classifying targeted sectors of the population. Tributary and head-tax systems such as the *encomienda*, and later, the *repartimiento* (*mita* in the Andes), depended on detailed registers of *indios útiles* (literally, "useful Indians").[25] Over time, the repartimiento developed separately as an apportionment of Indian labor to selected colonial enterprises, apart from the encomienda tribute system, making the Spanish colonial state the "dispenser" of Indian labor to favored clients.[26]

Tellingly, lists of tributary populations make up the bulk of sixteenth-century colonial population data that have been uncovered by historians.[27] Tribu-

---

[20] Alden, "The Population of Brazil," 176.

[21] Lombardi, *People and Places in Colonial Venezuela*, 32.

[22] Alden, "The Population of Brazil."

[23] The aversion of Iberian colonizers to manual labor is an oft-repeated theme in colonial Latin American historiography. See, for example, Burkholder and Johnson, *Colonial Latin America*, 197.

[24] Lombardi, "Population Reporting Systems," 12–13.

[25] For a detailed discussion of the tributary system with attention to the changing Spanish classification of tributaries from the fifteenth to the eighteenth centuries in one local context, see Villaramín and Villaramín, "Colonial Censuses and Tributary Lists of the Sabana de Bogotá Chibcha," 45–92. For the pitfalls in using tributary lists see, by the same authors, "Native Colombia."

[26] See, for example, Kramer, *Encomienda Politics in Early Colonial Guatemala, 1524–1544*.

[27] Cook and Borah, *Essays in Population History*, vol. 2, 182; Keith, *Conquest and Agrarian Change*; Simpson, *The Encomienda in New Spain*.

tary lists did not directly track demographic trends within indigenous populations, however. In practice, the lists came to reflect the outcomes of political and legal battles between local colonial officials and the leaders of indigenous communities. As historian Steve Stern showed for the case of Huamanga communities in early colonial Peru, Indian leaders learned to exploit schisms within the colonial elite, claim rights promised to them in colonial law, and petition for recounts (*revisitas*) of their populations to lower tributary demands.[28] Though not all petitions were successful, by the early seventeenth century, Huamanga communities had managed to significantly reduce their tributary obligations. Given the entrenched resistance of local colonial authorities to Indians' revisita petitions, this feat "represented a considerable native achievement against formidable odds rather than an inescapable consequence of objective demographic trends."[29]

Nothing like the encomienda system developed in colonial Brazil, where the Portuguese encountered a much smaller and more geographically dispersed indigenous population. Yet in Brazil, too, colonizers subjected indigenous peoples to coerced labor. In the first decades of colonization, this took the form of direct enslavement: Captured Indians labored in the first northeastern sugar mills. Indian slavery was legally abolished in 1570, but it continued thereafter thanks to legal exceptions for Indian slaves taken in "just war."[30] The owners of sugar mills kept books that listed captive Indian laborers alongside African slaves. The former comprised the majority of their workforce into the 1570s. By the 1590s, however, African slaves had displaced Indians from most jobs in the mills, owing to the growing supply and legality of African slaves, their perceived superiority as laborers, and the decimation of Indian populations due to exposure to disease.[31]

Information about Indian populations in colonial Brazil also comes from records kept by Jesuit missionaries, who competed with sugar mill owners for control of Indian labor. Jesuits sought to convert Indians to Catholicism and transform them, in the process, into reliable and dependent agricultural workers. In Bahía, the Jesuits established villages (*aldeias*) of (supposed) converts and kept counts of "their" Indians, while calling out the illegal and immoral enslavement of Indians on neighboring

---

[28] Stern, S., *Peru's Indian Peoples*, ch. 5.
[29] Stern, S., *Peru's Indian Peoples*, 127.
[30] Schwartz, *Sugar Plantations in the Formation of Brazilian Society*, 36.
[31] Schwartz, *Sugar Plantations in the Formation of Brazilian Society*, 68–72.

plantations. Jesuit missionaries reported the number of converted Indians in their charge to colonial authorities until the order was expelled from Brazil as part of Pombal's reforms in 1759.[32]

From the 1600s onward, the Portuguese government in Brazil relied primarily on imported African slaves to fill the labor needs of the colony. Like Indians in Spanish colonial America, slaves were carefully counted by Portuguese authorities. And just as Spanish efforts to track Indians were susceptible to corruption by local officials and subterfuge by Indians themselves, official slave counts in colonial Brazil did not always faithfully track demographic reality. Since African slaves were most often tracked as property, however, the population estimates derived from archival sources, such as records of port activity and property deeds, are probably more accurate than the tributary lists of Indians in the Spanish colonies.

In addition to targeted methods for tracking the supply of Indian and African labor, Spanish and Portuguese authorities collected population data through household censuses of urban areas and surrounding regions. The Spanish household censuses, or *matrículas*, provided information on the size of the population within particular administrative jurisdictions in addition to detailed information about the size, composition, and physical location of individual families within the town's sociogeographic space.[33] Household censuses were also attempted in colonial Brazil, both to track young men for obligatory military service and to assess property taxes, the latter in part to finance public works such as the construction of roads and bridges.[34]

In both Spanish and Portuguese America, royal attempts to gather demographic information depended entirely on the cooperation of local officials. Such cooperation was not always forthcoming. This is hardly surprising given the presumed and actual ends of household-by-household counts: to

---

[32] Maclachlan, "The Indian Labor Structure in the Portuguese Amazon, 1700–1800," 221, notes the fragmentary nature of statistics on "Indians" in the Portuguese Amazon in the eighteenth century. The Jesuit order was expelled from the Spanish colonies in 1767.

[33] Lombardi, "Population Reporting Systems," 14–17.

[34] Milliet, "Recenseamentos Antigos," 145–6. A survey of colonial census-taking efforts in Brazil, listed by province and by date, can be found in de Souza e Silva, *Investigações Sobre os Recenseamentos*; see also Botelho, "População e Nação no Brasil do Século XIX." An assortment of original examples of the forms and tables constructed by local authorities to count the colonial population is compiled on microfilm, available at the National Archive in Rio de Janeiro (Códice 808, 4 volumes). There is also a collection of original manuscripts of colonial population tables at the National Library in Rio de Janeiro, Manuscript Section.

facilitate the crown's extraction of local resources.[35] In colonial Brazil, it was not unusual for local officials to "passively oppose" orders to count the population under their jurisdiction: "Alleging the impossibility of collecting the information...they falsified the exact number of inhabitants, increasing it to obtain certain privileges or to reduce individual quotas."[36]

Household censuses were also complicated by the overlapping jurisdictions of secular and ecclesiastical authorities.[37] Adapting a practice long established in Europe, Spanish and Portuguese colonial authorities often called on the Church to collaborate in their efforts to track sectors of the population in their American colonies. In colonial Latin America, the monopoly over the power of salvation often proved more effective than the monopoly over the means of physical coercion as a foundation upon which to build a durable administrative apparatus that directly penetrated the lives of individual colonial subjects.[38] In contrast to the Iberian context, the papal concession of the *Patronato Real* to the Spanish monarchs in the colonies meant that the Church hierarchy was formally subordinated to the power of the Crown. The papal grant of December 13, 1486 gave the Spanish Crown "the right of patronage and presentation to all the major ecclesiastical benefices" in the newly conquered territories.[39] Thus, colonial authorities were apt to treat the administrative capacity of the Church bureaucracy as part and parcel of their own (though not without friction). From the perspective of the Spanish and Portuguese colonial authorities, parish priests in the Americas were essentially specialized agents of the Crown.[40] The Iberian states

---

[35] Indian flight and migration also complicated enumeration. See Powers, *Andean Journeys*; Wightman, *Indigenous Migration and Social Change*.

[36] Milliet, "Recenseamentos Antigos," 146.

[37] Alden, "The Population of Brazil," 180–3.

[38] Of course, colonial Latin America was not unique in this respect. See, for example, Gorski, *The Disciplinary Revolution*.

[39] Elliott, *Imperial Spain, 1469–1716*, 101.

[40] Most European states that survived into the modern era would struggle to reduce their reliance on the Church in this regard, either by usurping the information gathering infrastructure of religious authorities, or introducing new forms of obligatory civil registration alongside religious registration procedures. The movement to establish civil registration, either as a substitute for or alongside parochial registers, corresponded with the transformation in the conceptualization of state-society relations as constituted by the contractual relationship of *citizenship*. Thus, the implementation of civil registration was one of the first items on the agenda in post-Revolutionary France (Noiriel, "The Identification of the Citizen"). Somewhat surprisingly, such efforts did not meet with significant opposition from either the clergy or the populace in France. A similar initiative in mid-nineteenth century Brazil spurred a violent revolt in the rural northeastern backlands (Loveman, M., "Blinded Like a State"). See also Glass, *Numbering the People*, on controversies over civil registration and the first census in England.

often depended upon the cooperation of these royal agents to furnish basic information about the colonial population.[41]

In the "New World," as in the "Old," the Church and its agents had their own reasons for maintaining population registers of various kinds; information collected for purposes of the Church, however, was often put to use in the interests of the State. As in the Iberian Peninsula, parish priests in the colonies maintained registries of baptisms, marriages, and deaths, in addition to communion lists (of individuals over seven years old), which were supposed to be aggregated and forwarded up the Church hierarchy on a regular basis. Additionally, the Church sometimes conducted its own censuses of households, which could be used in combination with birth and death registers to reconfigure parish boundaries, track the collection of tithes at the local level, or keep track of the activities of local clergy.[42]

For the local clergy, in turn, the keeping of registers could be a significant source of social power. In addition to providing a steady source of supplementary income through the various prescribed and/or customary fees attached to the acts of registration, the classificatory choices of parish priests could potentially affect the social status, and thus legal rights and proscriptions of their parishioners. Control of birth, marriage, and death records thus put parish priests in a privileged position to give and receive favors.

Because parochial registers were compiled for ecclesiastical ends, the data they provided to secular authorities were apt to exclude anyone whose existence fell outside the local clergy's domain of responsibility or awareness, such as unconverted natives, itinerants, members of remote rural households, and unbaptised children.[43] Still, much of the information collected by priests could be adapted to serve the interests of imperial authorities.[44] Thus, for example, parish priests could be called upon

---

[41] In nineteenth-century colonial contexts, missionaries often supported the imperialist projects of European states, acting as an "informal extension of the state domain" (Young, "Ethnicity and the Colonial and Postcolonial State in Africa," 78). Ralph Grillo suggests that in some respects missions in colonial contexts were Althusserian "Ideological State Apparatuses," though he notes that this view tends to make the "'colonial state' seem a more widely ramifying, planned, coherent, totalitarian entity than it was." (Grillo, *Pluralism and the Politics of Difference*, 99). See also Stoler, "Rethinking Colonial Categories."

[42] Arcaya Urrutia, *Censo de Venezuela en 1807*.

[43] The systematic omission of nonparishioners from Church population records was perceived as a problem for the developing states of England and France as well, bolstering arguments for the development of secular population registration systems. Glass, *Numbering the People*, 15; Noiriel, "The Identification of the Citizen."

[44] Eighteenth-century parish house lists in Spanish America typically noted the physical location of the household in the town and the names of household members (generally ranked by status in the household). John Lombardi notes that sex and marital status can be derived from names and their

to compile household-level tables summarizing the population of their parishes, working from their existing lists as a base.[45] Illustratively, the governor of Bahia in 1708, Luiz Cesar de Menezes, asked the vicars to use their confessional rolls (*roles de desobriga*) to supply him with lists of heads of households and the number of male children and their ages.[46]

The Spanish and Portuguese imperial states also garnered information about the population from general descriptive surveys submitted by colonial authorities. These were essentially catalogs of natural and human resources to be found in a given administratively demarcated zone, sometimes produced on private initiative, but most often in response to questionnaires sent down from higher level royal authorities. The Spanish sixteenth- and seventeenth-century *relaciones geográficas* included "descriptions of principal geographic features, economic conditions, agricultural conditions, military advantages, and population resources of a given locality."[47] Portuguese colonial authorities submitted very similar reports in response to royal orders. A surviving example compiled from the reports of local officials of the Island of Santa Catharina in 1796 includes detailed nominal lists of the varieties of birds, trees, fruit, fish, monkeys, snakes, and tigers to be found in the area, in addition to tables reporting the "population belonging to the Government."[48]

As part of a generalized intensification of efforts to extract revenues and centralize administrative control in the last quarter of the eighteenth century (the Bourbon reforms), the imperial government stepped up efforts to collect information about the population of their colonies.[49] In part, late eighteenth-century enumerative activities resembled earlier colonial counts, with extraction of human and material resources as their ultimate aim. But they also reflected the increasing importance placed by European states on information per se as a foundation of state power. As anthropologist Arjun Appadurai notes, "By the end of the eighteenth century...the idea had become firmly implanted that a powerful state could not survive without making enumeration a central technique of social control."[50]

---

order, suggesting they were not explicitly recorded. "Racial designations" were recorded irregularly (Lombardi, "Population Reporting Systems," 33–6).

[45] Alden, "The Population of Brazil"; Lombardi, "Population Reporting Systems."

[46] de Azevedo, *As Ciências no Brazil*, 32.

[47] Lombardi, *People and Places in Colonial Venezuela*, 31; Hidalgo Pérez, "El Contenido de las *Relaciones Geográficas* Mexicanas y Venezolanas."

[48] Biblioteca Nacional do Brasil, Rio de Janeiro, Seção Manuscritos, II-35,30,3.

[49] Lynch, Spanish Colonial Administration, 1782–1810.

[50] Appadurai, "Number in the Colonial Imagination," 117.

In the second half of the eighteenth century, England, Portugal, and Spain all issued orders for general counts of the populations of their American colonies. The English in 1761 ordered North America's governors to provide "frequent & very full Information on the State and Condition of the Province under Your government," specifying that reports should include the number of "whites," "blacks," and "Indians."[51] Spain and Portugal followed suit in 1776, calling for population counts of their colonial domains in the Americas as well.[52] Spain ordered governors of the Indies to submit regular tables (*padrones*) listing the colonial population "with proper distinction of classes, [marital] status, and castes of all persons of both sexes, without omitting the infants."[53] Portugal, meanwhile, issued a call for the enumeration of all inhabitants of Brazil, by sex and age group, with the exception of regular troops, officials of the church, and "uncivilized indians."[54]

In their aspiration to cover (almost) the entire population of the colonial territories, including both sexes and all ages, these censuses differed significantly from the long tradition of generating targeted population lists for conscription or labor-tribute purposes. The late eighteenth-century censuses approximated the modern census ideal of full coverage of a territorially defined population. Yet they also retained the vestiges of earlier counting procedures. The information collected was often kept secret (which is why it often remained "undiscovered" for years in historical archives).[55] The data were explicitly intended to serve the interests of the state, rather than the interests of society. And the job of composing the lists fell to local clergy or municipal officials, rather than specialized staff or trained citizens.

Surviving household records from late colonial enumerations reveal that local officials exercised discretion in deciding what information to collect from which houses. It appears that colonial officials tasked with taking these censuses collected the information they deemed relevant, and

---

[51] Circular of April 28, 1761 in Benton, Jr. (1905: 27–30), as cited in Alden, "The Population of Brazil," 177. For a detailed account of the eighteenth-century population controversy in England, including the debates over proposals for a general census, see Glass, *Numbering the People*.

[52] Prior to the call for a general imperial census in 1776, smaller scale enumerations were conducted of delimited geographic units within the empire. For a bibliographic index of Latin American censuses taken during the colonial period, see Platt, *Latin American Census Records*.

[53] Text of the Spanish *cedula* of November, 1776, as cited in Alden, "The Population of Brazil," 177.

[54] Alden, "The Population of Brazil," 179.

[55] Charney, *Indian Society in the Valley of Lima, Peru, 1524–1824*, ch. 1.

did not bother with the rest. The Spanish imperial census of 1776 is a case in point. Even though the official instructions circulated by the Spanish authorities specified that officials should report the "race" of each individual in the household, in practice, racial classifications were reported only erratically.[56] The disjuncture between royal directive and local practice may owe to the fact that local officials saw no immediate purpose for racial ascriptions in the context of a census divorced from immediate pragmatic ends. Notably, the inverse situation was the case for the Portuguese imperial census of the same year. Even though the official instructions did not ask local authorities to report the "color" or the "condition" (slave/free status) of the enumerated population, "nevertheless, some of the governors, notably those who had reason to be concerned about the large number of unfree Negroes confined to their jurisdictions, directed their subordinates to include such information in their reports."[57] Tasked with taking a general count of the population without a specific, predetermined purpose, local colonial officials adapted the census procedures issued by the imperial state to make the resulting information useful for their own immediate ends.

Perhaps it is just as well that local officials adapted the general census to their pragmatic needs, as there is no indication that the general census results were effectively used by the Spanish or Portuguese imperial governments for other purposes. The most likely reason is that the imperial states lacked the administrative capacity to handle the enormous volume of information they amassed. As Lombardi explains for the Spanish case, Spain was "unable to develop a management system equal to the size and complexity of the empire" it was creating.[58] The failure of the Spanish and Portuguese imperial states to fully assimilate and use the information garnered from general population counts may also have been conceptual. The fact that imperial governments amassed large quantities of facts about their colonial populations does not mean that they were "thinking statistically." As sociologist Paul Starr notes:

> It is one thing to record and number people and things, but another matter entirely to create bodies of manipulable data. The records and results from early forms of data gathering, such as census taking, were not used to think statistically. Although the seventeenth-century Spanish empire may have

---

[56] Lombardi, *People and Places in Colonial Venezuela*.
[57] Alden, *The Population of Brazil*, 196.
[58] Lombardi, "Population Reporting Systems," 20.

kept more comprehensive accounts than did the English or its colonies, the English led in statistical analysis. They gathered less numerical data, but they produced more statistical information.[59]

It should come as no surprise that Spain failed to use the data it amassed from its enumerating activities in the Americas to produce useful statistical information; by the time the foundational concepts of statistical thinking were invented and disseminated among European statesmen, Spain had lost nearly all its American colonies. It was only in the first decades of the nineteenth century, and especially from the 1820s—around the time of independence for most of Latin America—that the field and form of knowledge called "statistics" had crystallized as a "moral science" concerned with the regularities of human daily life, including suffering and deviance. During the height of the Spanish and Portuguese American empires, "chance" had not yet been "tamed."[60]

Even without the capacity to incorporate statistical thinking into the practice of governance, the straightforward numerical description of the colonial population was a mode of exerting symbolic power that facilitated social control. Appadurai has argued that Britain's production of official statistics detailing every aspect of its Indian colony helped to "create the sense of a controllable indigenous reality."[61] The same was no doubt true of the Spanish and Portuguese empires, though without the analytical tools available to the British in the nineteenth century, especially the ability to conceptualize aspects of human existence in terms of lawlike numerical regularities, the collection of numerical data by the Iberian states probably did less, relatively speaking, to "tame" the colonial milieu. Still, the stepped-up efforts to enumerate the colonial population from the mid-eighteenth century may have contributed to maintaining the *illusion* of bureaucratic control, even as that control was slipping further away as the century drew to a close.[62]

---

[59] Starr, "Social Categories and Claims in the Liberal State," 17. Not even the English were transforming aggregate data into useful statistical information prior to the first few decades of the nineteenth century. It was only in the nineteenth century that the idea that numerical laws governed everything from cycles of births and deaths to criminal activity, idiocy, and sickness took hold in the minds of bureaucrats (Hacking, "Biopower and the Avalanche of Printed Numbers").

[60] Hacking. *The Taming of Chance*.

[61] Appadurai, "Number in the Colonial Imagination," 117.

[62] Historian Javier Morillo-Alicea argues that the creation of the illusion of bureaucratic control was key to actual Spanish control in those colonies it retained in the second half of the nineteenth century (Morillo-Alicea, "Aquel Laberinto de Oficinas."). In this regard, see also Scarano, "Censuses in the Transition to Modern Colonialism."

Contributing to the erosion of royal authority in the colonies was the waning ideological legitimacy of the fundamental hierarchical principles upon which that authority rested, and according to which colonial society had been constructed. From the initial colonization of the "New World" by the Iberian powers, the creation and maintenance of bureaucratic control over the colonial population entailed the imposition of a legally inscribed ethnoracial status hierarchy. As in other colonial contexts, at its core the bureaucratic order of colonial Latin America was an order founded on the presumed superiority of the colonizers and inferiority of the colonized. The hierarchical structure of imperial domination was ordered along what the Iberian rulers considered to be natural ethnoracial lines. In the first years of the colonial endeavor, the boundaries between European colonizers, indigenous peoples, and African slaves appeared self-evident and sharply drawn. Within a few generations after the conquest, however, the once clear boundaries had significantly blurred. From then on, it was the bureaucratic imposition of categorical distinctions that transformed a population characterized by a continuous distribution of phenotypical and social traits into the naturalized social hierarchy that was the *sociedad de castas*.

Counting Heads, Constituting Difference

Far from straightforward exercises in counting and accounting, colonial enumerative practices helped to constitute the kinds of people they purported simply to count. The racial categories used in colonial administration both reflected and inscribed imperial visions of the relevant divisions of colonial populations.[63] Official racial classifications made some categorical distinctions socially and legally consequential, while rendering others irrelevant.

Historians and social scientists often note the situational instability of racial classification and identity in the Americas, pointing to the movement of individuals across categories. But the arbitrariness of the overarching racial categorical schemes per se often goes uncommented. Official data sources impose culture-laden classificatory and organizational schemes on the people, places, and things they portend to simply describe. In the colonial context, the official categories used to count populations were plainly

---

[63] This phrasing borrows from Bourdieu, "Social Space and Symbolic Power."

"artifacts of [colonial] policy"; they did not aim to capture lines of social distinction most salient to the classified.[64]

Official population counts are partial and imperfect sources when the aim is to describe the full range of salient ethnoracial distinctions within colonial populations.[65] But such counts are invaluable for analyzing how imperial administrative practices worked to *inscribe* a particular subset of social distinctions in the guise of merely describing natural distinctions. At one level, the surviving records of colonial Latin American population counts can be usefully analyzed as cultural artifacts, revealing the "cognitive commitments" of those who produced them.[66] As Lombardi suggests, Spanish American colonial census materials "can be made to reveal much about the Spanish colonial self-image, about imperial priorities, about local understanding of social structure, and a host of other non-numerical topics."[67] Read as "texts," colonial population tables may reveal more about the counters than the counted.

Yet colonial population counts were not simply "texts." They were pragmatic instruments of administrative rule over subject populations. Thus, they not only reflected imperial ways of seeing subject populations; they also stamped imperial schemas onto the colonial social order. Population reporting practices were a means through which the cognitive schemes and material interests of imperial rulers were transposed onto the bodies of colonized subjects and into the social structures of colonial society. Through the act of official racial classification, colonial officials actively constituted particular kinds of colonial subjects.

The categorical distinctions codified in law and deployed in administrative practice did not merely reflect preexisting groupings of colonial subjects. Official racial classification served to *demarcate* legal and social divides within the colonial population, to group together sets of human

---

[64] Jackson, "Race/Caste and the Creation and Meaning of Identity," 172–3. Recent work has illuminated the imperfect fit between imperial categories and lived identities, while drawing attention to dynamics of negotiation and contestation over official racial classifications. See, for example, Althouse, "Contested Mestizos, Alleged Mulattos."

[65] This does not mean such data cannot or should not be used by analysts to better understand systems of racial stratification, past or present. In many cases, official data are the best or only information available. Attention to the conditions of production of racial demographic data can help ward against analytic reification, in part by exposing the myth that such data are merely descriptive. On the need to rely on such data despite limitations, see Andrews, *Afro-Latin America*, epilogue.

[66] On analysis of population statistics as cultural artifacts, see Hirschman, "The Meaning and Measurement of Ethnicity in Malaysia"; Anderson, M. "The History of Women and the History of Statistics"; Hutchinson, "La História Detrás de las Cifras"; Starr, "The Sociology of Official Statistics"; Barickman, "Reading the 1835 Censuses of Bahia."

[67] Lombardi, "Population Reporting Systems," 11.

beings according to a particular principle of classification, to accord them different sets of rights, responsibilities, and restraints in both law and practice, and thus to *constitute* colonial subjects of particular *kinds*. Examining the use of racial classifications in colonial population records thus provides insight into the cognitive commitments of imperial rulers *and*—albeit with varying degrees of coherence and comprehensiveness—into a foundational means of instantiating imperial priorities and power through the governing structures of colonial society.

Ruling with Racial Categories

A legal hodgepodge of corporate privileges and proscriptions, duties and exemptions, reigned in Castile on the eve of colonial expansion to the Americas. This system of status-based *fueros* was transplanted to the colonial context, and adapted to encompass new categories of people—Indians, Africans, and castas. The casta system was not only an elaborate system of social stratification; it was also, as anthropologist Claudio Lomnitz-Adler notes, the basis for creating different *kinds* of colonial subjects, through differential modes of subjugation. For example, while "Indians" were most often incorporated as members of collective units (*repúblicas de indios*), Africans and their descendants were denied collective recognition and excluded from most potential avenues of upward mobility.[68]

The constitutive power of official classification in the colonies hinged on the fact that individuals' racial designations set the terms of their relationship to the state and to other colonial subjects within the hierarchical social order. Legal codes specified different individual rights and restrictions on the basis of numerous categorical distinctions, including "race, sex, age, family lineage, religion, marital status, place of birth, occupation, wealth, and personal attributes."[69] Like the legal system on the Iberian Peninsula, the legal order in the American colonies was pluralistic: there were multiple sources of law with overlapping jurisdictions, and the legal codes applicable to a given situation depended on the categorically defined status of those involved.[70]

The official rules of the game in colonial Latin America were thus different for different categories of colonial subjects. Discriminatory legal

---

[68] Lomnitz-Adler, *Exits from the Labyrinth*, 269. Official restrictions on paths to mobility did not always succeed in the face of determined resistance. See Andrews, *Afro-Latin America*, ch. 1.

[69] Mirow, *Latin American Law*, 54.

[70] Mirow, *Latin American Law*; Benton, *Law and Colonial Cultures*.

codes governing all aspects of life in the colonies bolstered the interconnected imperial designs of control over population and resource extraction.[71] Crosscutting most other categorical distinctions, racial or caste distinctions were foundational. Racial classification had implications for marriage, guild membership, military service, municipal posts, residence, tax or tribute obligations, bearing of arms, school admissions, criminal punishment, property ownership, inheritance, and even style of dress. In Portuguese America, as well, colonial subjects faced different legal constraints and obligations depending on their officially designated "quality" or "condition."[72]

The underlying impetus to the particular regimes of ethnoracial domination implanted in the American colonies has been traced to the perennial Iberian obsession with *limpieza de sangre*, literally, "cleanness of blood." Official discrimination based on limpieza de sangre appeared in a series of fifteenth-century edicts that sought to protect Iberian Catholics from threat of contamination by non-Catholics, including Jews and converted Jews, Moors, and heretics.[73] Transposed to the American colonies, the legal tradition of preserving full rights and privileges exclusively for those with "clean blood" became a foundational organizing principle of colonial society.

Belief in the natural superiority imbued by limpieza de sangre provided ideological justification for the maintenance of a privileged caste of colonial rulers.[74] At the same time, limpieza ideology, as translated to the colonial context, supported the differential subjugation of different kinds of colonial subjects. There was some disagreement among colonial officials over the particular nature of the "defect" introduced to lineage by mixture with Indians or Africans. But generally, they viewed the "stain" of African origins as indelible, while the stigma of Indian mixture could be overcome over generations. Supposedly, the logic of racial inheritance worked to cleanse the blood when the mixture involved Indians, but not when it involved Africans. The tortured logic of this belief system is evident in the following excerpt from a report on New Spain, published for an Iberian audience:

---

[71] Mirow, *Latin American Law*, 54. Chance, *Race and Class in Colonial Oaxaca*; Chance and Taylor, "Estate and Class in a Colonial City."

[72] Boxer, *Race Relations in the Portuguese Colonial Empire, 1415–1825*; Boxer, "The Colour Question in the Portuguese Empire, 1415–1825."

[73] Twinam, "Purchasing Whiteness," 145.

[74] See Martínez, *Genealogical Fictions*; Villella, "Pure and Noble Indians."

It is known that neither Indian nor Negro contends in dignity and esteem with the Spaniard; nor do any of the others envy the lot of the Negro, who is the "most dispirited and despised".... If the mixed-blood is the offspring of a Spaniard and an Indian, the stigma disappears at the third step in descent because it is held as systematic that a Spaniard and an Indian produce a *mestizo*; a *mestizo* and a Spaniard, a *castizo*; and a *castizo* and a Spaniard, a Spaniard.... Because it is agreed that from a Spaniard and a Negro a *mulato* is born; from a *mulato* and a Spaniard, a *morisco*; from a *morisco* and a Spaniard, a *torna atrás* [return-backward]; and from a *torna atrás* and a Spaniard, a *tente en el aire* [hold-yourself-in-mid-air], which is the same as *mulato*, it is said, and with reason, that a *mulato* can never leave his condition of mixed blood, but rather it is the Spanish element that is lost and absorbed into the condition of a Negro.... The same thing happens from the union of a Negro and Indian, the descent begins as follows: Negro and Indian produce a *lobo* [wolf]; *lobo* and Indian, a *chino*; and *chino* and Indian, an *albarazado* [white spotted]; all of which incline towards the *mulato*.[75]

The elaborate and peculiar progenerative arithmetic that underlay the abstract conceptualization of the Spanish society of castes gave rise to a rich vocabulary of racial classifications. In theory, each new combination demanded a new category to describe the progeny (with the exception of "Spanish"/"castiza" unions, as noted above). The extent of preoccupation with tracking lineage is exemplified in surviving examples of taxonomic lists of the variety of castes in the colonies. As seen in figures 2.1 and 2.2, some such lists included upward of fifteen categories, while others included more than fifty ordered combinations. Of course, even the most elaborate of such attempts to impose order were destined to fail, undermined by their own classificatory logic. Since the number of hypothetical combinations increased exponentially with each successive generation, the reality of human reproduction would always be a few steps—and innumerable would-be racial classifications—ahead of even the most detailed taxonomic scheme.

---

[75] O'Crouley, *A Description of the Kingdom of New Spain*, 20; cited in Katzew, "Casta Painting," 11–12. According to Katzew, this text appears to have been written at the author's own initiative, but the same idea appears in manuscripts that seem to respond directly to questionnaires issued by the Spanish Crown. One such manuscript, titled *Origen, costumbres, y estado presente de mexicanos y philipinos* (1793), describes the various castas of Mexico, noting that "These are, among the vast types of peoples of New Spain, the main castas or generations that it contains, originated from the introduction of Blacks.... If this Kingdom had freed itself from the mixture with that nation, it would by now be purely Spanish without any corruption. Since Indians belong to a pure nation, upon mixing with Spaniards they become perfectly Spanish on the third step" Bafarás, *Origen, costumbres, y estado presente de mexicanos y philipinos*, vol. 2, B50, cited in Katzew, "Casta Painting," 11.

CLASSIFYING COLONIAL SUBJECTS | 63

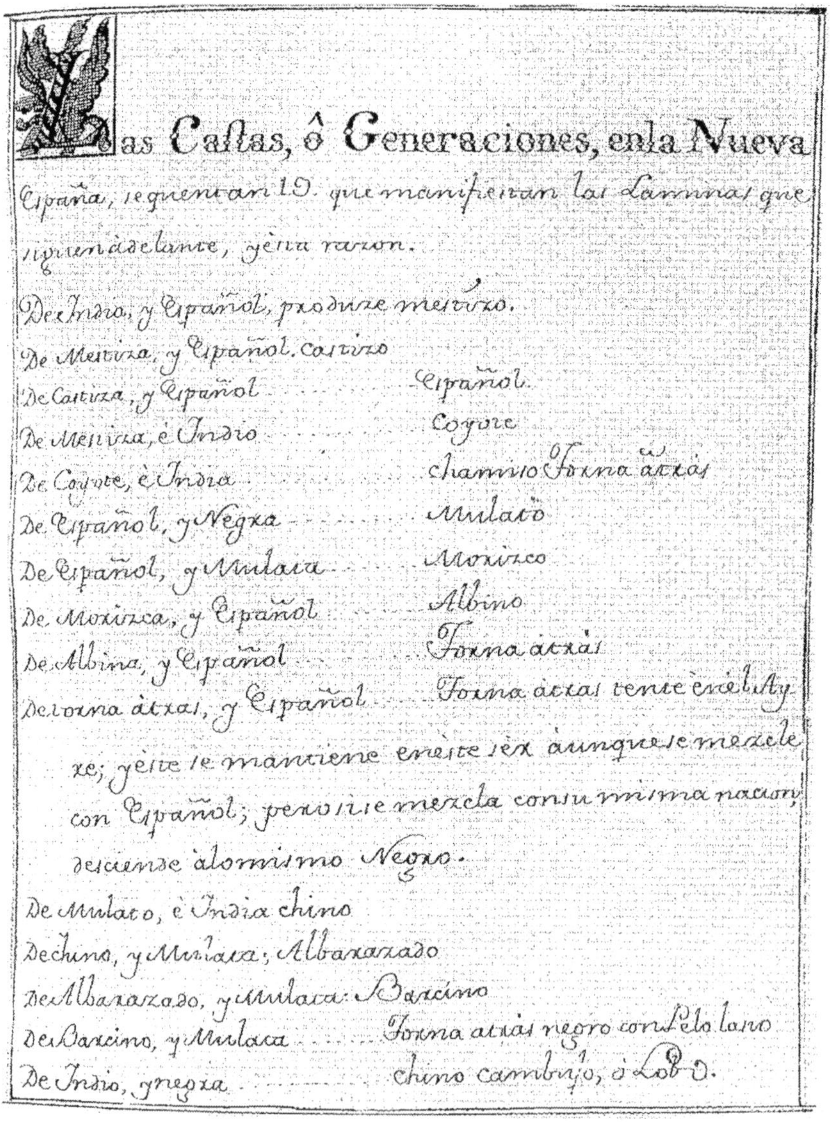
Las Castas, ô Generaciones, enla Nueva España, se quentan 19. que manifiestan las Laminas que siguen adelante, y en su razon.

De Indio, y Español, produze mestizo.
De Mestiza, y Español, castizo
De Castiza, y Español ..... Español.
De Mestiza, è Indio ..... Coyote
De Coyote, è India ..... chamiso Torna atràs
De Español, y Negra ..... Mulato
De Español, y Mulata ..... Morisco
De Morisca, y Español ..... Albino
De Albina, y Español ..... Torna atràs
De torna àtras, y Español ..... Torna àtras tente en el Ayre; y este se mantiene en este ser aunque se mezcle con Español; pero si se mezcla con su mismo nacion, desciende alo mismo Negro.
De Mulato, è India chino
De chino, y Mulata; Albarazado
De Albarazado, y Mulata: Barcino
De Barcino, y Mulata ..... Torna atràs negro con Pelo laso
De Indio, y negra ..... chino cambujo, ò Lobo.

FIGURE 2.1 Constructing the Sociedad de Castas in Colonial Spanish America.

SOURCE: Basarás, Joachin Antonio de, *Origen, costumbres, y estado presente de mexicanos y philipinos*. New York: Hispanic Society of America, 1763. Courtesy of The Hispanic Society of America, New York.

The famous casta paintings from this period are symptomatic of Spanish attempts to maintain the illusion of colonial society as a neatly ordered ethnoracial hierarchy despite the increasing messiness of social reality.[76]

[76] In their attempt to impose order on the "exotic" and unknown, the Spanish casta paintings are in a sense analogous to the British imposition of caste classifications on the population in colonial censuses of India. In both cases, formal classification helped to "tame" colonial "others" in the interests

LAS CASTAS

Casta	Cruce de:
1. Ahí o hay te estás (sic)	No te entiendo con india
2. Albarasado	Tente en el aire con mulata
3. Albino	Español con morisca
4. Barzino	Albarasado con india
5. Cambujo	Chino con india
6. Campa mulato o calpamulato	Barzino con india
7. Castizo	Mestizo con blanca
8. Castizo cuatralvo	Blanco con mestiza
9. Coyote	Indio con mestiza
10. Coyote mestizo	Chamizo con mestiza
11. Cuarterón	Blanco con tercerona
12. Cuarterón de chino	Blanco con china
13. Cuarterón de mestizo o español	Blanco con mestiza
14. Cuarterón de mulata	Mulata con blanco
15. Chamizo	Coyota con indio
16. Chino	Lobo con negra
17. Cholo	Mestizo con india
18. Español o españolo	Castiza con blanco
19. Genízaro	Barzino con sambaiga
20. Galfarro	Negro con mulata
21. Gente blanca	Blanco con requinterona de mulato
22. Gíbaro	Lobo con china
23. Grifo o tente en el aire	Indio con loba
24. Harnizo	Blanco con coyote
25. Jarocho	Negro con india
26. Limpios	Blanco con gente blanca
27. Lobo	Indio con negra
28. Lunajero	(?)
29. Mequimixtos	(?)
30. Mestindio	Indio con mestiza
31. Mestizo	Blanco con india
32. Morisco	Blanco con mulata
33. Mulato	Blanco con negra
34. Mulato obscuro	Indio con mulata
35. No te entiendo	Tente en el aire con mulata
36. Octavón u ochavón	Blanco con cuatralva
37. Puchuela	Blanco con octavón indio
38. Puchuela de negro	Blanco con octavón negro
39. Quinterón	Blanco con tercerón negro
40. Quinterón de mestizo	Blanco con cuarterona de mestizo
41. Quinterón de mulato	Blanco con cuarterón de mulato
42. Requinterón de mestizo o español	Quinterón de mestizo con requinterona de mestizo
43. Requinterón de mulata	Quinterón de mulato con requinterona de mulato
44. Rayados	(?)
45. Sambayo o sambahigo o sambaigo	Cambujo con india
46. Saltatrás	Blanco con albina
47. Saltatrás cuarterón	Negro con tercerona
48. Saltatrás quinterón	Negro con cuarterona
49. Tente en el aire	Cambujo con india
50. Tercerón o cuarterón cuatralvo	Blanco con mulata
51. Tresalvo	Indio con mestiza
52. Zambo	Indio con negra
53. Zambo prieto	Negro con zamba

FIGURE 2.2 A List of Castas from Colonial Mexico.

SOURCE: León, Nicolás. *Las Castas del México Colonial o Nueva España*. Mexico: Talleres Gráficos del Museo Nacional de Arqueología, Historia y Etnografía, 1924. Reproduced in Castelló Yturbide, "La indumentaria de las castas del mestizaje," 79.

The paintings, most dating from the mid-eighteenth century, depicted the human kinds that resulted from the mixture of Spanish, Indian, and African in the Spanish American colonies.[77] Casta paintings, such as the exemplar reproduced in figure 2.3, provided naturalistic portrayals of the colonial social-racial hierarchy; depictions of a man, woman, and resulting child, each bearing both the physical and social marks of their caste, naturalized the social hierarchy and rendered unproblematic the thorny issue of inheritance of social status.[78]

The elaborate racial taxonomies portrayed in casta paintings were not put to use, as such, in the enumeration and administration of the colonial population.[79] The business of running the colonies was different from the business of producing naturalistic depictions of the varieties of humankind to be found there. The taxonomic impulse on display in the casta paintings may have informed the tacit reasoning and varied terminology used by colonial officials in the course of their official work. For the most part, however, colonial officials did not need to make such fine-grained distinctions to carry out the tasks of imperial governance.

To apply the relevant law, assess the appropriate tax, or impose the requisite punishment, cruder categorical distinctions usually sufficed. Indeed, for most purposes, colonial officials concentrated on the demarcation and enforcement of three foundational categorical divides: Indians versus non-Indians; free persons versus slaves; and "whites" (the putatively untainted descendents of "pure" Spanish or Portuguese lineage) versus everyone else. These three axes of distinction intersected with each other and with other legally foundational categorical distinctions—such as sex, religion, and legitimacy of birth—to demarcate the principal faultlines, social positions, and legally differentiated types of colonial subjects.

---

of imperial rule. Cooper and Stoler, "Introduction. Tensions of Empire," 611; Appadurai, "Number in the Colonial Imagination."

[77] The audience for such works was mostly Spanish government officials in Spain and in the Americas. Paintings were also commissioned for display in public spaces such as the Natural History Museum in Madrid. The works appear to have been quite popular, although there were also some critics. More than one hundred separate series of casta paintings have been identified to date. On the audiences for casta paintings, see Deans-Smith, "Creating the Colonial Subject," 189–92.

[78] Katzew, "Casta Painting," 13.

[79] For example, Castleman ("Workers, Work, and Community in Bourbon Mexico") notes that in a late-eighteenth-century colonial census of Orizaba, children of "indian" mothers and "mestizo" fathers were labeled "mestizos," not "coyotes," the proper term according to the taxonomic rules depicted in casta paintings. The terminological variety used in everyday life no doubt exceeded the subset of categories used by colonial authorities for official business. But the complexity of colloquial terminology no doubt also fell short of the elaborate taxonomic treatises to the Iberian obsession with genealogy represented in the casta paintings.

FIGURE 2.3 A Series of Casta Paintings Katzew, Ilona. *Casta Painting: Images of Race In Eighteenth-Century Mexico*, 100.

In the Spanish American empire, the official distinction between Indians and *gente de razón* (literally, "people of reason") was paramount.[80] Reflecting the belief that Indians, like women and children, could not be held to full responsibility under European law, a separate corpus of legal codes applied to those classified as "Indian."[81] These laws institutionalized the perverse combination of paternalistic protection and coercive exploitation of indigenous peoples.[82] Most important, as noted above, classification as "Indian" subjected individuals and communities to systems of forced labor. At the same time, being "Indian" meant exemption from certain taxes and from obligations of military service.

Of course, the generic classification of indigenous peoples as "Indian" overwrote tremendous diversity of the indigenous population. Communal

---

[80] According to Cook and Borah, in colonial Yucatán and central Mexico, "gente de razón" included "Spaniards and other Europeans; *mestizos*...; Negroes, whether slave or free; and all mixtures with some proportion of Negro genetic stock" (*Essays in Population History*, 75).

[81] Cook and Borah, *Essays in Population History*, 188.

[82] See Jackson, *Race, Caste, and Status*.

distinctions were fundamental to the administration of both the Aztec and Incan empires, and significant lines of intra-Indian differentiation remained (and remain) socially salient—to those able or willing to discern them—long after the conquest.[83] Local colonial authorities attended to salient distinctions between and within indigenous communities pragmatically, to accomplish specific aims. For example, they often collaborated with recognized Indian leaders to extract tribute labor from diverse indigenous communities. For most purposes, however, application of the crude category "indio" served colonial administrative needs.

The legal distinction between free and slave was also foundational to the construction and maintenance of the colonial hierarchy. Slaves were at the very bottom of the colonial hierarchy, deprived of that most fundamental right upon which most other rights in the colonies were predicated: freedom.[84] The primacy of the divide between slaves and free persons was reflected in colonial population tables: separate columns for slave and free superseded the subclassification of population by sex, age, color, or "race." In colonial Brazil, the "slave" totals were sometimes subdivided into "blacks" and "mulatos" or "pardos." More often, however, it was only within the free population that distinctions by "color" or "race" were deemed relevant.[85] In colonial Venezuela, the category "black" was reserved for recently freed slaves. Thus, individuals with the same skin color could have been assigned to separate categories based on their proximity to slave status, and an individual classified as "negro" could have been lighter than an individual classified as "pardo."[86]

Within the subset of the colonial population that was both free and non-Indian, the most consequential legal and social divide was the distinction between those with limpieza de sangre, on the one hand, and would-be risers and other castas afflicted with the "stain" of impurity, on the other.

---

[83] Cahill, "Colour by Numbers"; Grillo, *Pluralism and the Politics of Difference*.

[84] There is an expansive literature on slavery in colonial Latin America. Recent contributions emphasize variation in slave experiences across place and time. Useful overviews include Klein and Vinson, "African Slavery in Latin America and the Caribbean"; Kraay, "Transatlantic Ties"; Mörner, "Slavery and Race in the Evolution of Latin American Societies."

[85] These observations are drawn from a review of colonial population tables held at the Biblioteca Nacional in Rio de Janeiro, Brazil (BN-Seção Manuscritos, II-30,35,5; I-32,10,6; I-31,19,7; I-31,19,5; I-32,10,5; I-31,19,16; II-35,30,3; 3,1,38; 8,3,30; 11,4,2; 9,4,2;11,3,17.) The category set used to describe the free population in colonial Brazil typically included "white," "indian," "pardo" or "mulato," and "black." In some reports additional categories were also included, such as "*cabra*," "*mameluco*," "*caboclo*," or simply "*de côr*" (literally, "of color"). For a discussion of racial categories in colonial São Paulo, see Nazzari, "Vanishing Indians."

[86] Lombardi, *People and Places in Colonial Venezuela*, 43.

Official recognition of "clean blood" opened access to the highest ranking positions within the colonial state and society. Designated in official documents as "Spanish" or "white," this privileged category could include *peninsulares* (those born in Spain), *criollos* (Spaniards born in America), and mestizos (when recognized by their Spanish fathers, or when able to pass due to wealth or social status).

At times, official population counts distinguished creoles and mestizos from Spanish-born Spaniards. This distinction was apparently more salient in some parts of the colonies than others. In parts of late eighteenth-century colonial Mexico, for example, the distinction between mestizo and castizo appeared regularly in census lists; in censuses taken in Venezuela around the same time, the distinction was absent.[87] Censuses taken in the present-day city of Oaxaca in 1777 and 1791 suggest that identification of Spanish-born Spaniards became relevant toward the onset of the wars for independence. The 1777 census lumped Spaniards together while the 1791 census tellingly distinguished European-born Spaniards (denoted as "*europeo*" or "*español europeo*") from others.[88]

While distinctions between American-born "whites" and their Iberian-born counterparts became highly salient in some moments, maintaining the categorical divide between whites and everyone else was more fundamental for the administration of the colonies. Free blacks and castas were subject to a broad range of legal restrictions that blocked paths to mobility and imposed stigma of inferiority. Legal exclusion from most respectable trades, for example, helped to ensure that the colonial socioeconomic hierarchy mapped reasonably well onto the ethnoracial hierarchy. Detailed legal restrictions also proscribed forms of behavior and dress deemed unfitting for those without "clean" blood. Men of casta status could not own or carry guns, while women of African descent "were forbidden to wear silk garments, pearls, or gold."[89]

For some purposes, colonial officials distinguished among castas according to the source of impurity. Though the distinctions they drew were generally much cruder than those portrayed in casta paintings, they reflected the same ideological inconsistency in the treatment of those with "Indian" versus "African" ancestry. As one example, responding to an appeal by colonial administrators in Mexico, the Spanish government

---

[87] Castleman, "Social Climbers in a Colonial Mexican City"; Castleman, *Building the King's Highway*; Lombardi, *People and Places in Colonial Venezuela*.
[88] Castleman, "Workers, Work, and Community," 152.
[89] Stern, P., "Gente de Color Quebrado," 189.

clarified that under a 1778 law regulating intermarriage mestizos and castizos (the progeny of Indians and Spaniards) should be distinguished from other castas, and considered to be of the same condition as Spaniards. In the matter of military service, as well, mestizos would sometimes be conscripted together with Spaniards; those with African ancestry, in contrast, could serve only in segregated pardo or black militias.[90] In colonial Mexico, the maintenance of segregated militias was facilitated by the segregated collection of population data. The Revillagigedo military census of Mexico (1789–1793) was organized "in solid blocks according to race. Thus there might be a complete census which included all the españoles and mestizos living in a certain town, a second embracing only mulattos and Negroes, and so on. The totals immediately segregate the numerical values for the groups."[91] The separate blocks represented the separate population pools from which recruits could be drawn. (Reflecting their legal exemption from military service, "Indians" were excluded from the census altogether).[92]

Given the elaborate legal and administrative apparatus created to protect the boundary of whiteness in the colonies, it is fascinating to discover that the state also created a legal avenue to cross over the caste divide and become officially recognized as "white." In the latter part of the eighteenth century, colonial subjects could legally petition the crown for a *cédula de gracias al sacar*. Literally a "certificate of thanks for letting out" (of status restrictions), the cédulas were a legal means of removing barriers imposed on individuals due to sources of impurity in their ancestry.[93] The cédula could be "acquired in recompense for distinguished service or substantial financial contribution," and would open up access to a university education and certain "honorable" professions, such as surgery or law.[94] The fact that a "white" classification could be purchased or earned illustrates how official racial categories could be divorced, at a bureaucratic whim, from the tyrannical hereditary logic on which they were supposedly based. At the same time, the fact that the petitions were very few and rarely granted

---

[90] Voelz, *Slave and Soldier*, 118–22; Vinson, *Bearing Arms for His Majesty.*

[91] Cook and Borah, *Essays in Population History*, 186; Peachy, "The Revillagigedo Census of Mexico, 1790–1794."

[92] Souto Mantecón, "Composición familiar e estructura ocupacional de la Población de Origen Español en Jalapa de la Feria (1791)."

[93] On the institution of gracias al sacar see Twinam, "Purchasing Whiteness"; Twinam, *Public Lives, Private Secrets.*

[94] Lombardi, *People and Places in Colonial Venezuela*, 42; Burkholder and Johnson, *Colonial Latin America*, 206.

underscores that colonial officials remained determined to enforce the tight link, both conceptual and legal, between genealogical "purity" and privileged social status in the Spanish American colonies.[95]

The petitions to obtain legal certification of "whiteness" also draw attention to another crucial observation about the colonial social order: Colonial subjects did not always acquiesce to their official racial classification. Those who filed gracias al sacar petitions to be legally recognized as white sought to use colonial institutions to carve out a narrow path to upward mobility within the hierarchical system. They were not alone in this objective. Colonial subjects found a range of ways to evade, resist, or directly challenge the imposition of particular racial classifications and the legal burdens or social stigma these entailed.

Resisting Racial Categories

Precisely because official racial classification was usually purposeful—that is, the ascription of a racial label was done in relation to specific administrative ends—colonial officials exercised direct power over those they classified. Colonial subjects, however, did not always concede to their classification. Given the stakes, it is hardly surprising that the classifiers and the classified did not always see eye-to-eye. At times the stakes were material, such as tribute obligations or ability to inherit property. In others, the stakes were primarily symbolic, involving diffuse or acute preoccupations over status, honor, and family reputation. The interests of each party could also change depending on the context: "Whereas the Indian might wish to pass for a *mestizo* in order to escape paying tribute, the *mestizo* might find it convenient, in certain cases, to present himself as an Indian to escape the jurisdiction of the Inquisition."[96]

There was not always room for maneuvering when colonial subjects came into contact with classifying agents of the state. But in a range of different contexts, colonial subjects found ways to evade, resist, or directly challenge the terms of their official classification. Against the portrait of colonial society as a static and rigid caste system, recent research draws attention to liminal spaces within the empire, such as places where the administrative apparatus of the imperial state did not reach, where lowly functionaries

---

[95] Twinam documented 26 official requests for royal certification of whiteness in the last decades of colonial rule. Petitions for gracias al sacar were more commonly made to request legal erasure of other forms of institutionalized stigma, such as illegitimacy of birth, which routinely obstructed upward mobility in the colonies. Twinam, "Purchasing Whiteness."

[96] Mörner, *Race Mixture in the History of Latin America*, 69–70.

exercised classificatory discretion, or where colonial subjects learned to use colonial institutions to directly contest their categorization.[97]

Efforts to evade the classifying state were facilitated by the imperial states' limited capacity. While the law on the books described colonial Latin America as a rigidly hierarchical society with different legal rights, responsibilities, and exclusions tied to official racial designations, in practice, there were substantial gulfs between legislation and social reality.[98] Pointing to new laws prohibiting castas from bearing arms in 1547, 1574, 1583, 1589, and 1595, for example, historian Peter Stern argues that "The repeated promulgation of royal laws intended to control mestizos and mulattos is testimony to their failure as instruments of social control."[99] The challenge of making laws "stick" was exacerbated by the geographic dispersion of colonial populations. Large swaths of the colonial population lived remote from the centers of administrative control. Indeed, "the centers, not the peripheries, were the exceptions"[100] in terms of colonial subjects' "exposure" to the regulative apparatus of the Spanish or Portuguese imperial states.

For at least some colonial subjects, the limited infrastructural reach of the colonial state made flight a viable means of escaping the burdens of stigmatized classifications. For Indians, migration could be an effective strategy for wrestling free of undesired tributary obligations.[101] For slaves, flight could be a path to freedom.[102] Of course, many obstacles impeded the free movement of individuals across the vast expanses of the American empires—not least of which was the inhospitable nature of nature itself. For those who could manage it, however, migration to areas effectively beyond state control could be a means to evade strictures of official racial classification.

Where populations remained under the nominal purview of colonial authorities, some classificatory mobility was still possible thanks to the discretionary power of local officials. Not surprisingly, low-level bureaucrats

---

[97] See Fisher and O'Hara, *Imperial Subjects*.

[98] Mörner, *Race Mixture in the History of Latin America*, 70.

[99] Stern, P., "Gente de Color Quebrado," 204.

[100] Cutter, *The Legal Culture of Northern New Spain, 1700–1810*, 6; cited in Mirow, *Latin American Law*, 31.

[101] Cahill, "Colour by Numbers," 336. David Robinson found high rates of Indian migration in the Yucatán in the late eighteenth century, and suggested the primary motivation may have been the desire "to avoid the burdens of tribute" (Robinson, "Indian Migration in Eighteenth-Century Yucatán," 168).

[102] On runaway slave communities in the Americas, see Price, *Maroon Societies*; Thompson, *Flight to Freedom*.

and parish priests varied in their zeal for compliance with directives from above. Some authorities charged with counting and classifying colonial subjects did so methodically, while others were content to supply rough, incomplete, and occasional estimates, or to ignore instructions for maintaining population records altogether.

In both Spanish and Portuguese America, local authorities exercised considerable autonomy in determining when and how to classify colonial subjects. This was clearly the case for parish priests in colonial Mexico, whose surviving registries of baptisms, marriages, and burials reveal tremendous inconsistencies in racial classification practices: "Some recorders examined carefully the origin of each person; some lumped great masses of people together under a single designation; some cited the racial group within which the head of a family fell and ignored the wife and children."[103] While the standard practice was for authorities to decide the racial classification as they saw fit, there is evidence that in some contexts self-identification was allowed. For example, the parish priest of Santiago de Querétaro, Mexico, in 1777 noted that he accepted his parishioners' self-declarations of calidad when reporting the membership of his parish, without checking the declarations against baptismal, marriage, or tribute lists.[104]

The idiosyncratic classification practices evident in surviving colonial parish records points to an important source of discretionary power enjoyed by local authorities. Parish priests could classify individuals according to their own predilections, usually without oversight or accountability. While this discretionary power was probably exercised most often in the interests of local landowners,[105] it could also provide openings for colonial subjects to "earn," or buy, a more desirable classification for themselves or their children. Historian George Reid Andrews notes the "easy corruption of the parish priests who maintained the church's birth, marriage, and death registries" in this regard.[106] In general, local officials could use their clas-

---

[103] Cook and Borah, *Essays in Population History,* 190. Cook and Borah also note that "In certain parishes and jurisdictions, no racial information whatever is given, or it is so meager as to be useless" (191).

[104] Archivo Histórico del Arzobispado de México, Fondo Episcopal, Secretaría Arzobispal. Ramo Padrones, caja 9 CL/libro 6. Cited in Sánchez Santiró, "El Nuevo Orden Parroquial de la Ciudad de México" 64, n. 4.

[105] For example, historian Robert Jackson argues that the apparent decline in the number of "indios" in a subregion of Cochabamba, Bolivia, from the colonial period into the nineteenth century reflects reclassification in response to *hacienda* labor demands and government policies, not underlying demographic trends. Jackson, "Race/Caste and the Creation and Meaning of Identity," 5.

[106] Andrews, *Afro-Latin America,* 48.

sificatory authority to show deference, return a favor, or offer a reward, as they saw fit. On the flip side, of course, local authorities could also deploy their classificatory power to show scorn, extract a favor, or deliver punishment.

Interacting with colonial officials' instrumental motivations for classification, the tacit rules of racial ascription prevailing in particular regions of the colonies also created some limited opportunities for mobility within the caste system. Close scrutiny of classification patterns within and across colonial population records reveals that the racial classifications of individuals in colonial registers were often not independent from other attributes recorded, such as place of residence, the color of a spouse, occupation, or legitimacy of birth.[107] For example, historian Bruce Castleman documented a pattern of upward "racial drift" among individuals enumerated in both the 1777 and 1791 censuses of Orizaba (known today as Oaxaca). Of 1012 individuals he was able to positively link between censuses, 333 had "drifted" from one racial classification to another.[108] The majority of these had moved into higher status classifications, often matching the classification of their spouse.[109] Castleman also found evidence of intergenerational racial drift. The children of indio/mestizo unions were often classified as mestizo, and the children of mestizo/castizo unions were often classified as castizo. The children of pardos and creoles or pardos and indios, on the other hand, were classified as pardos. Thus, in this context, upward racial mobility was foreclosed for children with a parent of African ancestry.[110]

One important consequence of the local-level sources of flexibility in the official classificatory regime was that this arbitrariness, however delimited, could suddenly become visible to the classified. When the discretionary aspect of official racial ascription became transparent, colonial subjects sometimes leveraged the opportunity to openly contest their racial classification. Occasionally, colonial subjects mobilized collectively to contest their racial designation, as when mestizos in Cochabamba revolted against attempts by authorities to reclassify them as indios in an early

---

[107] Cf. Jackson, "Race/Caste and the Creation and Meaning of Identity"; Castleman, "Workers, Work and Community"; McCaa, "*Calidad, Clase,* and Marriage."

[108] Castleman, "Workers, Work and Community," 168.

[109] Such upward drift was not the universal pattern in colonial Mexico. McCaa ("*Calidad, Clase,* and Marriage") linked parish records with a census document from the same period considered by Castleman and found an overall tendency to drift downward.

[110] In other contexts, avenues of upward racial mobility were sometimes open to those of African descent as well. See Andrews, *Afro-Latin America,* ch. 1.

eighteenth-century census.[111] More often, direct challenges to official racial classification were brought by individuals who sought to remove barriers to their mobility within the colonial hierarchy.

Direct challenges to official racial designations became more common in the final decades before independence, as colonial subjects became increasingly adept at using colonial institutions toward their own ends. The petitions for certificates of whiteness, referenced above, provide one clear example of this. But the phenomenon of using colonial institutions to contest racial classifications or their consequences was more widespread than the few dozen attempts to acquire legal recognition of whiteness would suggest. For instance, colonial subjects exploited small openings created in the context of judicial proceedings about other issues to claim mestizo rather than mulato status.[112] Indigenous leaders filed repeated requests for reinspections to try to reduce tributary counts in their communities.[113] Men of African descent petitioned for exemption from the law forbidding blacks from bearing arms.[114] Even runaway slaves and free persons sometimes used the courts to fight for legal recognition of their freedom.[115]

Efforts to legally challenge official classifications should not be confused with "passing." The surreptitious crossing of racial boundaries to assume a more privileged racial status was a different form of agency within the constraints of the colonial hierarchy. The fact that passing was viewed as threatening is evident in the many social conventions and legal codes that aimed to prevent it. Because passing obscured individuals' "true origins," it was seen as a particular threat to reputable families (and the integrity of their estates). Unlike legal challenges, however, passing did not usually expose or call into question the arbitrary power of colonial authorities to assign individuals to their positions in the status hierarchy in the first place.

On a case-by-case basis, neither passing nor legal strategies for individual mobility posed much of a threat to the status order as a whole. Those who exploited opportunities for racial mobility in colonial Latin America evinced "constrained creativity"[116] in challenging their own

---

[111] Pearce, "The Peruvian Population Census of 1725–1740," 84–7.

[112] Althouse, "Contested Mestizos, Alleged Mulattos."

[113] Stern, S., *Peru's Indian Peoples*, ch. 5.

[114] Schwaller, "'For Honor and Defence.'" In this case, the goal was to obtain a right reserved to those of higher status *without* changing racial classification, by asserting that exemplary behavior or service to the crown should override the relevance of ancestry before the law.

[115] Chalhoub, *Visões da liberdade*.

[116] Fisher and O'Hara, *Imperial Subjects*, introduction.

racial subjugation. Yet individual mobility strategies also tended to recognize and thus reinforce the basic hierarchical principles of the colonial social order. As a result, they could be seen to inadvertently legitimize the naturalized hierarchy that simultaneously organized and justified colonial rule in the Americas.

Yet when considered altogether, the cumulative effect of myriad small acts of resistance to the colonial classificatory regime contributed to the erosion of its legitimacy. The society of castes depended in principle on assigning individuals the "proper" racial classification, as if this were a matter of mere description, not active and instrumental attribution. In practice, however, especially toward the end of the colonial period, the *régimen de castas* was undermined by increasing visibility of arbitrariness in official classificatory practices, on the one hand, and increasing distrust of individuals to reveal (or know) their "true" calidad, on the other. (An illustration of how colonial officials charged with enumeration admitted to their uncertainty are the following entries from a tax list from New Spain: "Manuel Hilario López, Spaniard as he says, but of very suspect color"; "Juan Antonio Mendoza, Castizo of obscure skin.")[117]

Given the hierarchical distribution of rights, obligations, and status according to racial classification, such explicit suspicion of the poor fit between the official classification and the reality it claimed to name was an unlikely foundation for the smooth operation of the colonial administration of the régimen de castas. The legal and administrative architecture was constructed on the premise that each individual's racial classification could be easily identified and would remain fixed. If the precise order of the racial status hierarchy in Spanish colonial law never exactly matched the operative hierarchy of prestige and disdain in everyday social interaction,[118] the administration of the former became increasingly difficult as the ambiguities and flexibility of the latter grew. By the end of the colonial period, the legal apparatus of racial differentiation, segregation, and discrimination thus became less and less connected to the complex workings of colonial social reality.[119] The disjuncture helped expose the fact that the colonial social hierarchy was not, in fact, merely an institutionalized expression of a natural hierarchy. The society of castes was a human invention, and as such, it could be undone.

---

[117] From Aguirre Beltrán, *La Población Negra de México*, 273-4, cited in Mörner, *Race Mixture in the History of Latin America*, 69.

[118] Mörner, *Race Mixture in the History of Latin America*, 60.

[119] Mörner, *Race Mixture in the History of Latin America*, 68–70.

Race and Republic

During the independence wars in Spanish America from 1810 to 1826, the *sistema de castas* came under direct attack. Slaves, former slaves, Indian peoples, mestizos, and other castas fought on both sides of the wars for independence, as both sides held out promises of emancipation and equality. The promises of independence leaders and royalists alike would turn out to be mostly illusory. The political revolutions that brought an end to Spanish imperial rule in the Americas did not suddenly upend entrenched ethnoracial hierarchies in the region. The end of empire did, however, bring with it explicit repudiation of the ideological rationale and legal architecture upon which the hierarchical society of castes had been created. Across the region, newly penned republican constitutions declared the practice of official ethnoracial classification to be historically obsolete.

Yet the practice of official ethnoracial classification did not disappear with the birth of Latin American republics. The liberal promises of independence-era leaders notwithstanding, postcolonial bureaucrats continued to draw ethnoracial distinctions among colonial subjects- turned-citizens in an array of different contexts. In many cases, the continued use of ethnoracial classification by local authorities in the years after independence can probably be attributed to bureaucratic inertia; everyday administrative practices at various levels of government across the expanse of the former colonial territories were not instantly revamped by the promulgation of liberal republican constitutions by political elites in the capital cities. But not all instances of official ethnoracial classification in postcolonial Latin America can be easily dismissed as colonial holdovers. In some contexts, official racial classification was effectively reincarnated by nation-building elites to accomplish new and distinctively nationalist political and symbolic ends.

This was the case, as I show in the chapters that follow, for the use of official ethnoracial classification in the context of national censuses. Given the efforts by Latin America's early nationalist leaders to discursively relegate the practice of official ethnoracial classification to the colonial past, it is rather surprising to discover that the majority of early national censuses in the region classified populations by race. Even though independence-era leaders had vowed to end state-imposed racial distinctions, census takers throughout much of Latin America in the nineteenth and early twentieth centuries were tasked with racial classification of their fellow citizens. While the contradiction between liberal promises and state practices was hardly unprecedented, the national census was a highly visible and thus particularly surprising site for such a blatant violation of liberal ideals. In the next chapter, I explain why the fact of pervasive ethnoracial classification in Latin America's early national censuses calls out for explanation, pointing to both domestic and international pressures that might have lead things to be otherwise.

CHAPTER 3 | Enumerating Nations

AFTER WINNING INDEPENDENCE, THE spokesmen of newly created Latin American republics uniformly pronounced their intentions to destroy colonial racial hierarchies and create formally equal, *national* citizenries.[1] The founding documents of these new polities, the first republican constitutions in Latin America, emphasized rupture with the colonial past by defining the new nations in civic terms and explicitly proscribing official racial distinctions among citizens.[2] As the "liberator" and supreme director of newly independent Chile, Bernardo O'Higgins decreed in 1818, "After the glorious proclamation of our independence, sustained with the blood of her defenders, it would be shameful to permit the use of formulas invented by the colonial system, among them the denomination as Spanish of those who in their *calidad* are not mixed with other races."[3] In the new Chile, the decree proclaimed, it would be illegal to distinguish officially between Spaniards and Indians; they were both to be called Chileans. Likewise, in a decree abolishing the practice of labor tribute, the liberator José de San Martín declared that "in the future the aborigines shall not be called Indians or natives; they are children and citizens of Peru, and they shall be known as Peruvians."[4] In Argentina, the 1819 Constitution proclaimed

---

[1] Nearly all of the new polities of Latin America emerged from the independence wars as constitutional republics. The key exceptions were the Empire of Brazil, which became independent in 1822 but remained a monarchy until 1889, and the brief monarchical interlude from 1821 to 1823 in Mexico.

[2] In theory, the Spanish Constitution of Cadiz (1812) anticipated this shift by starting to erase legal distinction between freeborn colonials and Spaniards. See Mirow, *Latin American Law*, 145.

[3] Decree of June 2, 1818. Archivo Nacional de Chile. Oficio N.8 (12).

[4] Decree of August 27, 1821, cited in Lynch, *The Spanish American Revolutions*, 277. This quotation by San Martín is cited by Benedict Anderson to illustrate his argument that Latin Americans were "creole pioneers" of modern nationalism (Anderson, B., *Imagined Communities*, 50).

Indians "equal in dignity and rights to other citizens."[5] In Venezuela, the 1811 Constitution revoked the special status of indigenous people before the law, and also included an article that "revoked and annulled, in every sense, the ancient laws which imposed a civil degradation on that part of the free population of Venezuela, hitherto known under the denomination of *pardos*; these shall all remain in the possession of their natural and civil rank and be restored to the imprescriptible rights belonging to them, in like manner as the rest of the citizens."[6] In Mexico, in turn, independence leader and Catholic priest José María Morelos proclaimed in the 1814 constitution, "Slavery is forever prohibited, as well as distinctions based on race (*castas*), leaving everyone equal, and only vice and virtue will distinguish one American from another."[7] In Latin America's new republics, the official ethnoracial distinctions that had undergirded and rationalized the colonial hierarchy were declared obsolete.

Of course the words of Creole nationalists were, for the most part, just that. In reality, these declarations were blatantly contradicted by everyday administrative practices that continued to rely on colonial-era ethnoracial distinctions. Whatever the new constitutions promised, local authorities did not generally abstain, one day to the next, from official ethnoracial classification. This was particularly true for the use of categorical distinctions that were integral to the continued administration of coercive-extractive labor regimes. To cite just the most obvious examples, official identification of tributary "Indians" remained an important revenue source in Andean countries until the 1850s at least, and in some localities this practice endured much longer than that.[8] The legal distinction between "slave" and "free" also endured, for decades after independence in some cases.[9] The existence and continual growth of free populations of color meant the slave/free distinction was never perfectly coterminous with racial categorical divides. But the legality of slavery in much of early republican Latin America inescapably reinscribed the colonial-era stigma of African origins. In short, Independence did not miraculously erase

---

[5] Levene, *Manual de historia del derecho argentino*, 462, cited in Mirow, *Latin American Law*, 146.

[6] Federal Constitution for the States of Venezuela (1811). Articles 201 and 203. Translation from: http://scholarship.rice.edu/jsp/xml/1911/9253/1/aa00032.tei.html#index-div1-N107F5; Brewer-Carías, *Las Constituciones de Venezuela*.

[7] Tena Ramírez, *Leyes Fundamentales de México*, 22, cited in Mirow, *Latin American Law*, 145.

[8] Indian tribute was abolished in Peru in 1854; in the same year Peru abolished slavery. See Basadre, *Chile, Peru y Bolivia Independientes*, 271–2. Indian tribute was around 20 percent of government income in that year.

[9] See Andrews, *Afro-Latin America*, for dates of final abolition of African slavery in Latin America.

three centuries of combined de jure and de facto ethnoracial classification and subjugation. Declarative speeches and constitutional promises aside, everyday practices of drawing ethnoracial distinctions continued unabated throughout Latin America, together with entrenched ethnoracial hierarchies.[10]

While at the level of local administrative governance colonial-era classification practices continued after independence in many parts of Latin America, at the level of national political discourse would-be leaders championed the advent of governments that eschewed the outdated practice of differentiating racially among citizens. Political leaders pronounced their adherence to liberal principles; they decried the backwardness of the colonial caste system and they extolled the virtues of modern, liberal, color-blind governance. In high-profile public settings, nineteenth-century political elites sought to paint a proper liberal face on their nationalist aspirations. To underscore the symbolic and political breaks with the colonial past, variants of the idea that racial distinctions did not matter for membership in the nation became central to official discourses of nationhood throughout post-colonial Latin America.

It is curious, therefore, that when it came time to take stock of the human beings that made up their new nations by taking general censuses of the population, modernizing elites in most Latin American countries did not balk at the idea of asking census takers to mark down the race of their fellow citizens. Indeed, almost every Latin American country included a question about race or color in at least one of their early national censuses. Against the backdrop of liberal declarations that official racial distinctions were obsolete, the focus on race in the highly visible forum of the national census is striking. The attention to racial distinctions within national populations seemed to fly in the face of official, independence-era promises to reconstruct the former colonies of Spain as color-blind republican nations. Why engage in official ethnoracial classification in the politically and symbolically potent context of a national census?

The mystery is deepened, as revealed in this chapter, by the fact that domestic political momentum against the tainted practice of official ethnoracial classification was in stride with modern census-taking standards that developed independently in the international arena in this period. From the mid-nineteenth century, a group of Western European scientists formed the International Statistical Congress (ISC) and began to

---

[10] For example, see Guerrero, "The Administration of Dominated Populations," 293–5. Examples of color segregation in Argentina are noted in Andrews, *Afro-Latin America*, ch. 3.

hammer out a set of standardized guidelines for how modern states should conduct censuses of their populations. Thereafter, taking a national census that followed ISC guidelines became a way to demonstrate and document modern nation-statehood. By designing national censuses with reference to ISC recommendations, Latin American census officials sought to position their nations as plausible future members in the club of "civilized nations." Neither the ISC's guidelines nor those of its institutional successors recommended including questions about race on national censuses. The international statistics regime thus provided an authoritative source of external validation for conducting color-blind census-counts in postcolonial Latin America. Nonetheless, Latin American census officials often chose to draw attention to racial distinctions in their national censuses.

Official Ethnoracial Classification in Officially Color-Blind States

What explains census officials' decisions to produce racial statistics in early national censuses, despite domestic pressures and international "permission" to abstain from doing so? At first glance, racial classification in Latin America's early national censuses might seem like a straightforward case of bureaucratic inertia. As historians of the postindependence decades have shown, the advent of constitutional guarantees of equality did not suddenly erase hierarchical ideologies and social structures constructed over the course of centuries. While at the level of official discourse and law, the break from the colonial practices of racial differentiation and subjugation was sudden and sharp, on the ground and in practice, the shift away from administrative use of racial categories in postcolonial Latin America was gradual and uneven. The unthinking carryover of colonial bureaucratic practices was especially likely in administrative domains that were geographically or politically removed from the nation-making spotlight in the first decades after independence.[11] Changing ingrained bureaucratic habits proved an ongoing challenge, constitutional promises notwithstanding.

National censuses, however, were not just any administrative endeavor. They were highly visible—indeed, deliberately conspicuous—sites of postcolonial nation making. As such, national censuses were unlikely venues for the blatant contradiction between official rhetoric and government

---

[11] Guerrero, "The Administration of Dominated Populations."

practice with regard to racial classification of citizens. Indeed, postcolonial officials made concerted efforts to avoid overt racial classification of citizens in other politically conspicuous contexts. Explicit rejection of state-imposed racial distinctions among citizens was an important legitimizing move for postindependence political elites.[12] Their perceived need to denounce the practice of official racial classification may have stemmed in part from what historian Thomas Abercrombie characterizes as their "redoubled postcolonial predicament." In common with postcolonial elites in other contexts, Latin America's Creole elite faced the standard postcolonial predicament of wanting to simultaneously "distance themselves from their former imperial metropole, and to emulate it, depending on an imperially educated minority to build progress-oriented institutions for a new kind of nation-state." But for the Latin American Creole elite, this predicament was compounded: "In the first-wave nation-states of the Americas ... nation-building elites were not only schooled in Spanish traditions, but had been privileged above the native masses by *being* Spaniards, if suspect Creole ones, tainted by their tropical environs and by the milk of their Indian or African wet nurses."[13]

To resolve their postcolonial predicament without threatening their own privileged status, Latin America's republican elites eschewed the "colonial racial formula" of explicit racial discrimination in favor of nominally color-blind exclusionary policies. Through heavy reliance on property and literacy requirements for political participation, for example, Latin American elites maintained the de jure exclusion of the majority of the population from the benefits of citizenship without resorting to the discredited colonial mechanism of official racial exclusion.[14] In some contexts, political elites sought to lessen the evident contradiction between their promises of equality before the law and their continued support of ethnoracially targeted regimes of labor exploitation by "privatizing" the practice of ethnoracial ascription. Historian Andrés Guerrero argues from the Ecuadorian experience that postcolonial elites managed to reconcile their liberal promises with the continued differentiation of "Indians" from

---

[12] Larson, *Trials of Nation Making*.

[13] Abercrombie, "Mothers and Mistresses of the Urban Bolivian Public Sphere," 179–80.

[14] The theme of liberal exclusion of indigenous and Afrodescendant populations from Latin American republics has received extensive treatment in the Latin American historiography. Important recent contributions include Lasso, *Myths of Harmony*; Larson, *Trials of Nation Making*; de la Fuente, *A Nation for All*; Andrews, *Afro-Latin America*; Mallon, *Peasant and Nation*; Grandin, *The Blood of Guatemala*; Thurner and Guerrero, *After Spanish Rule*; de Carvalho, *Os Bestializados*; Appelbaum et al., *Race and Nation in Modern Latin America*.

regular "citizens" by devolving the power to inscribe and enforce "Indianness" to the owners of large haciendas.[15] Such strategies are symptomatic of the fact that conspicuous reliance on official ethnoracial classification for purposes of administrative governance became a political liability in postcolonial Latin America.

Given the intended public visibility of early national censuses, it is thus implausible that official racial classification in that context resulted from the unthinking reproduction of colonial approaches to enumerating populations. In contrast to low-level officials who conducted local government business for mostly local purposes, the directors of national censuses anticipated the glare of a national—and ideally international—political spotlight. High-level census officials typically earned their appointments thanks to their political or scientific prominence and their corresponding connections to other political elites. Census directors in this period did not feign disinterested objectivity; they engaged directly in the politics of nation-state building.[16]

This points, in turn, to another possible explanation for the practice of racial classification in early national censuses: the direct involvement of high-level census officials in national politics.

As prior research has shown, nineteenth- and early twentieth-century census officials used their positions to intervene in scientific debates, partisan conflicts, and regional disputes.[17] The political vision of high-level census officials and their position within domestic political fields helps to explain shifts over time in the specific content of national censuses in individual countries. This was especially true during the early years of the formation of national statistical fields, when individual census directors often enjoyed the leeway to shape the content of the census to advance their own scientific agendas or political projects.[18] Case studies of the production of racial statistics in nineteenth-century censuses in Brazil and Argentina, and in twentieth-century Ecuador and Peru, for example, suggest that the

---

[15] Guerrero, "The Administration of Dominated Populations." Of course, given the close relations between large landowners and local officials in many parts of Latin America in this period, it would have mattered precious little, to those classified, whether the person doing the classifying was technically an agent of the state. The fact of their legally enforceable and materially consequential classification remained.

[16] On Argentina, see Otero, *Estadística y Nación*; on Chile, see Jaramillo, "'Un Alto en el Camino para Saber Cuántos Somos'"; on Brazil, see Senra, *História das Estatísticas Brasileiras*; Loveman, M., "The Race to Progress."

[17] Cf. Nobles, *Shades of Citizenship*; Patriarca, *Numbers and Nationhood*; Lee, "Racial Classifications in the US Census"; Cole, J. H., *The Power of Large Numbers*. Otero, *Estadística y Nación*.

[18] Camargo, "Classificações Raciais e Formação do Campo Estatístico no Brasil (1872–1940)."

particular political aims and scientific ambitions of top-level census officials played a role in shaping official classification practices on censuses in this period.[19]

Yet the political projects of particular census officials in individual Latin American countries do not alone suffice to explain the region-wide tendency to bracket liberal promises of color-blind governance and deliberately draw attention to racial distinctions in national censuses. The politics of nation-state building in each individual Latin American country did not take place in isolation; they were embedded within and shaped by the coterminous development of an international system of nation-states. Attention to the international embeddedness of Latin America's nineteenth- and early twentieth-century nation-state building projects brings into focus the profound influence of developments in the international scientific and political fields on the national censuses in the region. First, as shown in this chapter, Latin American census officials crafted statistical portraits of their nations in reference to an emergent "global model" for how modern states should take modern censuses. And second, as described in chapter 4, census officials used national censuses to engage in international scientific debates about measures of modern nationhood and demographic predictors of national progress. It is the orientation of Latin America's nineteenth and early twentieth-century nation builders to both domestic and international political and scientific fields that explains why the region's early national censuses classified citizens by race.

The domestic politics of census-taking and nation-making in nineteenth- and early twentieth-century Latin America were shaped by the *international* politics of nation-state building. Even as they leveraged their positions within domestic political fields to influence debates at home, Latin American census officials engaged in international scientific debates with broader professional, scientific and general literate communities about the inherited quality and future prospects of their national populations. Engagement in these only-partly overlapping scientific and political fields exerted countervailing pressures on census officials. Attention to these countervailing concerns is necessary to understand why, despite considerable historical momentum to the contrary, several of Latin America's early national censuses distinguished citizens by race.

---

[19] Otero, *Estadística y Nación*; Loveman, M., "The Race to Progress"; Clark, "Race, 'Culture,' and Mestizaje"; López, R., "Demographic Knowledge and Nation-Building."

The Nation-State as Cultural Form

By the early nineteenth century, the nation-state had crystallized as the normative form for legitimate political units in the modern world. The nation-state was envisioned as a sovereign, autonomous, and differentiated political organization wielding a monopoly of coercive power over a delimited territory in the name of a national community. Ideally, the nation in whose name the state exercised authority would be internally homogenous, whether in civic values, ethnic ancestry, or both, and fully contained within the territorial limits of the state.[20] As a political form, the nation-state was never fully realized in practice; nominal nation-states varied tremendously in their degree of actual nation-stateness. But as a *cultural template* for how modern polities should *appear* to be organized, the nation-state was wildly successful.

Institutionalized at the level of the world polity, and bolstered by its modularity and adaptability, the nation-state as political and cultural form diffused across the globe over the course of the nineteenth and twentieth centuries.[21] As a consequence, despite extraordinary diversity of people, history, geography, polity, and economy, political units in the modern world exhibit a remarkable degree of "institutional isomorphism."[22] Striking similarities in formal political architecture, organizational appearance, symbolic accoutrements, and official "claims to purpose" overlay vast differences in substantive social realities across countries.

The cultural model of the nation-state helps to define what modern nation-states *are* by prescribing what modern nation-states *do*. Outward signs of compliance with the global model of nation-statehood are particularly evident across the array of polities that gained independence from first- and second-wave European empires. By working within the hegemonic cultural template for legitimate political organization, former colonies bolstered their claims to rightful membership in the modern international community. Indeed, a relatively straightforward way for former colonies to gain recognition as nation-states was to begin doing, and be seen doing, the things that modern nation-states are supposed to do.[23]

---

[20] Poggi, *The State*.

[21] Meyer, "The World Polity and the Authority of the Nation-State."

[22] DiMaggio and Powell, "The Iron Cage Revisited."

[23] For critical perspectives on this phenomenon, see Chatterjee, *Nationalist Thought and the Colonial World*; Badie, *The Imported State*.

Yet would-be modernizers of former colonial polities found that emulation of the international (Western European) template for modern nation-statehood was not always a straightforward task. In part, difficulties arose due to vast disparities in resources, administrative infrastructure, and prior regimes of political authority. But difficulties in realizing the ideal of modern nation-statehood also derived from the fact that in key respects the "global" model of the nation-state was in fact a Western European cultural and political construct that had been built upon a series of implied or explicit *oppositions* to the very former colonies that now sought to realize the "universal" nation-state ideal. Thus, nineteenth- and turn-of-the-twentieth-century modernization projects in Latin America evidence the intrinsic tensions in efforts to emulate a model of modern polity and society that was constructed, in key respects, in idealized *contrast* to the political, social, and demographic realities prevailing in their own countries.

International Origins of the National Census

Census taking, in its modern form, is one of those things that nation-states do to demonstrate and document their nation-statehood. Of course states do not take censuses merely as a nationalist performance. Censuses are designed to serve a range of political, economic, scientific, and administrative ends. But in addition to the many pragmatic motivations for taking national censuses, periodic censuses of the national population serve a legitimizing function in a world of nation-states.

Censuses provide official portraits of the "the state of the nation." Such portraits reify the nation as a bounded collectivity with specific, measurable characteristics that make it comparable to other nations. Depicted in the language of official statistics, the nation becomes legible as such, identical to other nations in *kind,* and thus comparable to other nations in quantifiable indicators of *substance*. Claims of national distinctiveness, ubiquitous in census publications, testify to the aspiration to be recognized as one nation among others.

National portraits embodied in the published results of national censuses display remarkable uniformity in style and form, even as they self-consciously describe the distinctive characteristics of each nation. This international uniformity in the form of modern censuses across states is not a historical coincidence. At mid-nineteenth century, there were a number of alternative conceptions and practices of "statistics" in use. By the end of the nineteenth century, a single model would emerge as the normative template for the production of official population statistics worldwide.

The convergence of statistical methods and census-taking practices across states was propelled by the establishment of an international epistemic community devoted to that outcome.[24] Following on nearly two decades of informal and private efforts to encourage the use and dissemination of statistical methods and knowledge in several European countries, the first International Statistics Congress (ISC) convened in 1853.[25] Under the leadership of the Belgian statistician Adolphe Quetelet, a group of European statisticians met at the Great Exhibition in London in 1850 to discuss the formation of an international statistical society. There they planned the first ISC, to be held in Brussels in 1853. Subsequent Congresses were held in Paris (1855), Vienna (1857), London (1860), Berlin (1863), Florence (1867), the Hague (1869), St. Petersburg (1872), and Budapest (1876).[26]

By the time of the first ISC, the utility of statistics for modernizing states was widely assumed. The previous decades saw what Ian Hacking refers to as "the avalanche of printed numbers." From the 1820s to the 1840s, there was an exponential increase in the printing of numbers of all sorts, tied to "the taming of chance" through conceptual innovations such as Quetelet's notion of "the average man" and the law of normal distribution.[27] The concept of the average man, which brought together descriptive statistical data and the theory of probability, made it possible to "transform subjective averages into objective ones."[28] In consequence, a myriad of previously unpredictable aspects of human life were suddenly rendered amenable to scientific quantification and, in theory, management.[29] These innovations constituted a revolutionary episode in the development of a biopolitics of the population "that gave rise to comprehensive measures, statistical assessments, and interventions aimed at the entire social body

---

[24] Haas, "Introduction: Epistemic Communities and International Policy Coordination."

[25] Sociologist Marc Ventresca identifies the founding moments of international statistics activity in the "series of novel and fragile international congresses that commence in 1853 and continue through the late 1870s" (Ventresca, "When States Count," 68).

[26] At the 1872 meeting, a permanent commission was created which met four times: in Vienna (1873), Stockholm (1874), Budapest (1876), and Paris (1878). On the history of the ISC, and its successor, the International Statistical Institute, see Westergaard, *Contributions to the History of Statistics*; Nixon, *A History of the International Statistical Institute, 1885–1960*; Porter, T., *The Rise of Statistical Thinking*.

[27] Hacking, "Biopower and the Avalanche of Printed Numbers."

[28] Desrosières, *The Politics of Large Numbers*, 238.

[29] Hacking, "Biopower and the Avalanche of Printed Numbers."

or at groups taken as a whole."[30] By the mid-nineteenth century, official statistics described an increasingly vast array of social conditions, from mortality and public health to the living conditions of the working class. Statistics were seen to provide invaluable information for states intent on promoting social improvement and material progress.[31]

As the avalanche of printed numbers threatened to continue unabated, and with key advances in statistical concepts and methods made by Quetelet and others, the incomparability across states of the massive collections of numbers being produced came to be seen as an obstacle to scientific—and thus human—progress. Prior to the 1850s, the specific methods, units, and nomenclatures used to generate official statistics varied widely across contexts. Distinctive traditions of statistics had developed in countries like France, England, and Prussia, reflecting specific historical dynamics of state formation.[32] The German field of *Staatenkunde* (from which the term "statistics" is derived), for example, developed in the seventeenth and eighteenth centuries and entailed the compilation of facts about a state, characteristically recorded in descriptive lists and organized into tables. In contrast to the descriptive methods of *Staatenkunde*, the seventeenth-century English tradition of political arithmetic advocated a more quantitative approach to the collection and presentation of facts.[33] These different approaches to producing official statistics made it difficult if not impossible to directly compare the characteristics and progress of nations.

The ISC was Quetelet's envisioned solution to this problem. The ISC was at the forefront of a broader movement by leading European scientists to standardize, across established and newly consolidating national borders, the methods and notations of specific fields of scientific inquiry.

---

[30] Foucault, *History of Sexuality*, vol. 1, 146.

[31] For example, the Scottish Poor Law Commission Statistics of 1844 reported on poor relief, parishes, food, prices, rents and wages, occupations, housing, rural facilities, language, and emigration.

[32] The literature on this theme is voluminous. Important contributions include: Desrosières, *The Politics of Large Numbers*; Woolf, "Statistics and the Modern State"; Hacking, "Biopower and the Avalanche of Printed Numbers"; Krüger et al., *The Probabilistic Revolution*; Porter, T., *The Rise of Statistical Thinking*; Westergaard, *Contributions to the History of Statistics*. The "endogenous" historical conditions that promoted the growth of state-sponsored statistics in specific countries did so in part because of the geopolitical pressures that drove modern state formation in Europe (Tilly, *Coercion, Capital and European States*; Poggi, *The State*; Downing, *The Military Revolution and Political Change*; Ertman, *Birth of the Leviathan*; Finer, "State- and Nation-Building in Europe"; Centeno, *Blood and Debt*). The more general point here is that modern state formation cannot be understood apart from the coincident emergence of a world system of nation-states (Poggi, *The State*, 23).

[33] The diverse historical traditions of social accounting by Western European states are summarized in Patriarca, *Numbers and Nationhood*, 12–21; see also Starr, "The Sociology of Official Statistics."

The second half of the nineteenth century witnessed an explosion in the founding of new international scientific organizations, whose congresses helped crystallize the boundaries of specialized disciplines.[34] The ISC was a trailblazer in the movement to construct such a transnational scientific field, predating the first international congress in the natural or physical sciences by seven years.[35]

Fueled by Quetelet's universalizing scientific vision, the main goal of the congresses was to establish a set of statistical "best practices" for adoption by all modern, or modernizing, states. Coordination of statistical methods and classificatory nomenclature across states would ensure international comparability of official numbers. Comparability of statistics, in turn, would enable the advancement of knowledge through assessment of the conditional factors governing various laws of population. This knowledge could then be put to use by governments in the form of enlightened public policies.

From the outset, Quetelet's universalizing vision had to compete with the nationalist predilections and political interests of many delegates. Attendees no doubt appreciated the benefits of international standardization of data and measurement in theory, but they tended to privilege their established administrative traditions and emergent nation-state building agendas in practice.[36] The ISC lacked any formal authority vis-à-vis states, and thus relied entirely on voluntary compliance to effect the diffusion of its recommendations. It adopted a pragmatic approach to this dilemma, promoting the progress of statistical science in general through the advancement of statistical science in individual states.

Implementation of congress recommendations was left to the discretion of each state. For the duration of the congresses, countries like England, Prussia, and France adopted ISC recommendations selectively at best, while aspiring European nation-states like Greece and Hungary adopted them more eagerly and with deliberate visibility.[37] Thus, somewhat ironically, when judged from their immediate impact on the statistical activities of the European states represented by the most influential delegates, the statistics congresses fell far short of their initial aspirations. But when judged by their influence on the statistical practices of less prominent

---

[34] Crawford, *Nationalism and Internationalism in Science, 1880–1939*.

[35] Crawford (*Nationalism and Internationalism in Science*, 39) lists the following partial list of first international scientific congresses: chemistry (1860), botany and horticulture (1864), geodesy (1864), pharmaceutical science (1865), meteorology (1873), geology (1878).

[36] Randeraad, "The International Statistical Congress (1853–1876)."

[37] Randeraad, "The International Statistical Congress," 60–1.

states, the success of the congresses—certain barriers to diffusion notwithstanding—becomes more evident.

The ISC institutionalized an authoritative, prescriptive template for how modern states should count and classify their populations. In so doing, it influenced the development of census taking in numerous countries in the nineteenth century. It also laid an influential foundation for future initiatives to coordinate statistical activities of states, which continued into the twentieth century.

How to Count Human Beings: Constructing a Global Model

Among the resolutions of the first ISC in Brussels was a call for states to take periodic demographic censuses with standardized content, following standardized procedures. At the congresses that followed, the rules of census taking were debated and revised. In the course of a few decades, the resolutions from these international congresses coalesced into a global model of how, when, and why states should count their populations.

Armed with the newest statistical discoveries about the lawlike regularities of human societies, the nascent science of "moral statistics" sought to improve the human condition through knowledge about its characteristic weaknesses, taken as a whole.[38] An unintended consequence of the enumerative mania that began with a bang in the first half of the nineteenth century was the proliferation of ways of classifying human beings, and thus, the proliferation of ways for human beings "to be."[39] To discern the laws governing abstract, average individuals required the grouping of concrete, subjective individuals into classes of equivalence: "enumeration demands *kinds* of things or people to count."[40]

The universal significance of the enumerative enterprise—and the centrality of scientific classification to that enterprise—was not lost on the select group of scientists invited to attend the ISC. The delegates convened with the aim of developing a standardized set of classifications and procedures for the production of official demographic data that would be

---

[38] Hacking ("Biopower and the Avalanche of Printed Numbers") suggests that such enlightened overt aims of the moral sciences did not generally bear fruit; much more consequential in the long run were its "subversive" ramifications.

[39] It also occasioned the proliferation of ways for human beings to *cease* being, such that today "It is illegal to die...of any cause except those prescribed in a long list drawn up by the World Health Organization" (Hacking, "Biopower and the Avalanche of Printed Numbers," 280).

[40] Hacking, "Biopower and the Avalanche of Printed Numbers," 280; Desrosières, *The Politics of Large Numbers*.

comparable across nations. Of course, representing the world in numbers in itself facilitates comparison by forcing what is numbered into standard, countable units. Numbers are an excellent way to obscure qualitative diversity. As historian Silvana Patriarca notes to illustrate this point, the replacement of topographical descriptions of regions with their numerical representation in terms of "square feet" literally "flattens" geographical diversity, homogenizing landscapes and transforming them into "things" that can be directly compared.[41]

But the mere reduction of reality to numbers was not sufficient to support the advancement of the science of statistics at mid-nineteenth century. Distinct national traditions of recording and reporting numbers got in the way of essential comparisons. The reduction of reality to numbers needed to proceed *in the same way* across contexts. The ISC developed recommendations with this pressing need in mind. By adopting standardized classification schemes, the universe of ostensibly equivalent cases in one country could be directly compared to the universe of cases of precisely the same *kind* in other countries across the globe.

Attention to statistical methodology in the meetings of the ISC was paired with a consideration of the *purpose* of moral statistics as a policy instrument for enlightened states. The particular "classes of equivalence" (or "human kinds") whose investigation would be recommended hinged on the *political* concerns of modernizing states. Thus, for example, the classification and production of statistical knowledge about the poor and sickly population received sustained attention from the very first meeting of the ISC, just as mortality and public health statistics had been of concern in major European states since the 1820s.[42]

Transformed from an "art" into a "science," governance demanded that human beings be counted—and thus classified—in a plethora of new ways.[43] As the taxonomies of human kinds grew more extensive and detailed, the methods used to count the brute number of human bodies took on a new urgency. For the knowledge gleaned about any particular class of individuals within the national population to be objectively (statistically) meaningful, it had to be placed in relation to the whole of which it was a part. The production of average rates of incidence of any given type of "human

---

[41] Patriarca, *Numbers and Nationhood*. On the concept and politics of commensurability, see also Espeland and Stevens, "Commensuration as a Social Process."

[42] Schweber, *Disciplining Statistics*; Starr, "The Sociology of Official Statistics"; Hacking, *The Taming of Chance*.

[43] Hacking, "Biopower and the Avalanche of Printed Numbers"; Foucault, "Governmentality."

kind"—whether idiots, assassins, the blind, or perpetrators of suicide—required placing particularly classified kinds in relation to a more generic class of kinds, and ultimately, in relation to the national population as a whole.

The delegates to the first and subsequent meetings of the ISC thus agreed on the vital importance of general censuses for the progressive aspirations of individual states and for the advancement of statistical knowledge construed in universal terms. Both the interests of statistical science and the interests of modern (European) states figured in the deliberations that led to the crystallization and dissemination of ISC recommendations for the standardized content of national census questionnaires.

Resolutions of the first Congress that convened in Brussels in 1853 included the following prescriptions for how states should identify and classify human beings in the context of a national demographic census:

1. family name and given name
2. age
3. place of birth
4. language spoken
5. religion
6. civil status
7. occupation (profession or condition)
8. permanent or habitual place of residence, whether temporary or in transit
9. obvious sickness or infirmities (blind, deaf-mute, confinement in public or private institutions, and mental retardation)[44]

These were recommendations for minimum content, covering the categories of human kinds singled out by the ISC as vital to the interests of all modern states. The ISC also noted that states could supplement these queries with others to meet their particular needs and circumstances. The inclusion of queries on language and religion on the ISC's original list of recommended census queries is noteworthy. With the 1848 revolutions in recent memory, these queries were likely included as proxies for "nationality," understood not in its civic sense as country of citizenship, but in its ethnoracial sense, as an essential attribute of individuals. Language,

---

[44] Additionally, the recommendations called for reporting of children who receive public or private education, distribution of housing by floor and number of rooms that serve as habitation for each family, and grounds contiguous to each home (Articles 5a and 5b).

especially, was considered in many European countries to be a useful indicator of ancestral ties or communal affiliations.[45]

At the 1860 congress in London, the criteria recommended for counting individuals at the first meeting were reiterated, with a notable modification. The 1860 congress attendees divided inquiries of population censuses into two categories, those "indispensable in all States" and those "properly included" in the censuses of all countries for which it may be "convenient and possible." The inquiries considered "indispensable" included:

1. family and given name
2. sex
3. age[46]
4. degree of relation by type to the family head
5. civil or conjugal status
6. occupation (profession or condition)
7. place of birth (specifying non-naturalized foreigners and their country of origin)
8. blind or deaf mute[47]

Both "language spoken" and "faith" were demoted to inquiries that should be made "where expedient and practicable."[48] Such questions could be impractical in contexts where language and religion were highly politicized indicators of ethnonational group membership.[49] National censuses were supposed to contribute to stability and human progress through rational governance, not unleash "primordial" hatreds that could fuel mass violence.

---

[45] Given the lack of linguistic unification within most Western European states in the 1850s, it is also possible that information on language was of interest in its own right, as a measure of the extent of intranational linguistic unification. The 1857 meeting of the ISC in Vienna explicitly discussed the counting of ethnolinguistic minorities in censuses.

[46] Revealing the connection between the implementation of civil registration and taking of national censuses, the recommendation to inquire about age included mention of the "desirability of corroborating by an authentic extract of birth certificate." See Ventresca, "When States Count," 182–6.

[47] The persistent concern with tracking physical impairments of the population is clearly linked to the idea that censuses should track the health and vigor of the nation (or lack thereof). Detailed inquiries of physical defects are common in nineteenth- and early twentieth-century Latin American censuses, and their usage is of particular interest in relation to medicalized imageries of the nation in literature and public discourse (Borges, "'Puffy, Ugly, Slothful and Inert'").

[48] Other characteristics to be recorded, where practical, included residence (whether habitual or temporary), domicile, number of children attending primary school (or receiving their instruction at home), and persons touched with grave illnesses or afflicted with permanent infirmities. All ISC resolutions from 1853 to 1876 pertaining to the "conduct and content" of population censuses can be found in Ventresca, "When States Count," 182–6.

[49] See Kertzer and Arel, *Census and Identity*.

The inner circle of invited delegates to the congresses displayed unquestioning confidence in the import of their work; they saw themselves as the vanguard in an effort to disseminate the illuminating glare of statistical inquiry across the globe. In the words of a participant at the 1860 meeting: "Thus from the mouths of the representatives of the principal civilized nations of the world, the Congress learnt, and we learn also, the general progress of statistical inquiry, and the estimation in which this branch of knowledge is held. Countries far behind others in many respects, not only appreciate its value, but desire to be directed by its light; and abundant evidence is afforded that the seeds sown by the Congress have already yielded a goodly harvest."[50]

With the publication of the ISC recommendations, the particular template for conducting a modern census (preferably decennial and in years ending in zero or five) gradually gained hegemony in Europe and the Americas over the next several decades. Representing "the first moments in the structuration of an international statistical field,"[51] the ISC established the basic formula for taking a *modern* census that would be recognized as such. Subsequent international conventions for how to take national censuses built from the recommendations put forth by the ISC. The institutional developments that followed helped disseminate the model and promote "adherence to the synthetic 'global' standards for national statistical purpose and practice."[52]

Adoption of the global census-taking model set by the ISC and its successors was never absolute, not even in the home countries of the delegates to the Congress. In most countries, adoption of certain aspects of the international model was coupled with deliberate adaptations of others. The delegates of the ISC themselves recognized that individual states might wish to supplement the minimal recommended inquiries, adding additional queries that might help states address their particular needs and interests. Indeed, the Congress's explicit acknowledgment that a national census, first and foremost, should produce statistics of use to the state that conducts it, helped ensure the legitimacy and broad acceptance of its recommendations.[53] For those states that would adopt the ISC's recommendations,

---

[50] Hammack, "Report to the Statistical Society on the Proceedings of the Fourth Session of the International Statistical Congress, held in London, July 1860," 14.

[51] Ventresca, "When States Count," 97.

[52] Ventresca, "When States Count," 97.

[53] This directive continues to legitimize the UN's imposition of international standards on census-taking practices throughout the world today (United Nations, *Principles and Recommendations for National Population Censuses*); it has also appeared in the form of specially tailored "regional" recommendations (United Nations, *Asian Recommendations for the 1970 Population Censuses*;

then, there was some room for legitimate maneuver in the adaptation of the model in order to take account of national idiosyncrasies. Efforts to meet international norms for minimum content were coupled with considerable variability in supplementary methods of counting, and hence classifying, human beings.

The ISC came to an abrupt end after the 1876 meeting, due in part to the decision by Bismarck to prohibit further participation in the congresses by Prussian statisticians.[54] A few years later, the International Statistical Institute (ISI) stepped into its place, taking up the same agenda with a slightly modified political posture. To appease the Prussian representatives, the activist stance of the ISC—which had gradually sought to increase its influence over the statistical activities of individual governments—was replaced by a more advisory and noninterventionist relationship to states.

With the outbreak of World War I, the work of the ISI was disrupted. There were no ISI meetings between 1913 and 1919, and no new recommendations for census taking emanated from Europe during this time: "The war of 1914–1918 dealt a severe blow to the Institute as to many other international organizations, but thanks to the creation of the Permanent Office in 1913, the Institute continued to function as such at its seat in the Hague. No biennial sessions or elections of members of officers were possible.... The number of members fell from 204 in 1913 to about 150 in 1919 and of these nearly 90 percent were Europeans."[55] The ISI continued to exist after the war, but it was gradually demoted (not without some resistance from members) from its position as organizational protagonist in the movement to standardize the production of statistical information worldwide.[56] It became

---

United Nations, *African Recommendations for the 1970 Population Censuses*). For example, the preface to the *Asian Recommendations for the 1970 Population Censuses* states: "The regional recommendations have been developed parallel with the world recommendations but the emphasis in the region has been placed on the development of topics and tabulations, particularly those which would take into account the characteristics as well as the statistical needs of the countries in the ECAFE [Economic Commission on Asia and the Far East] region" (United Nations, *Asian Recommendations for the 1970 Population Censuses*).

[54] Nixon, *A History of the International Statistical Institute*.

[55] Nixon, *A History of the International Statistical Institute*, 27–8.

[56] In the words of Robert Charles Geary, acting President of the ISI in 1957: "After the war it was inevitable that the statistical (or economic) divisions of the League of Nations and the International Labour Office should take over some of the functions previously exercised by the Institute, a tendency receiving added force from the ever-increasing tempo of development of official statistics. The new international organisations had political prestige and recognition, they disposed of the necessary funds and they had centralised statistical staffs, whereas the Institute had to rely largely on the dedicated spare-time labours of a few members often widely dispersed throughout the world. The Institute loyally co-operated with the new bodies in the spirit that it was enough that the essential work should be efficiently done somewhere." Geary, "Specific Comments," 6, cited in Ventresa, "Global

instead a willful collaborator to the interstate coordination activities directed by the League of Nations.

After World War I, the League of Nations took over the international coordination and standardization efforts of the ISI.[57] Under its purview, what had been the agenda of an international professional society only loosely connected to individual governments and without any institutional mechanisms to encourage compliance became a formally institutionalized international statistics regime. This international statistics regime gained additional momentum and resources after World War II, when the work of supporting and coordinating the development of statistics-gathering infrastructure across countries was transferred to the United Nations.[58]

International Models and Latin American Nationhood

During the time that the ISC was working to institutionalize regular demographic censuses as a normative activity for modern nation-states, the Latin American republics were emerging from decades of postindependence wars (or post-*Regresso* regional revolts in the case of monarchist Brazil), and gearing up to tackle the difficult challenges of state and nation building. In the decades following political independence in Latin America, *caudillos*, factions, and nascent political parties struggled, often violently, for control of the new states. In civil wars, regional conflicts, and local rebellions, they clashed over whether the new states would be centralist or federalist. They clashed over territorial and political boundaries. And they clashed over the power to direct the process of national development.[59] They did not, however, clash over the fundamental type of political unit they would build. The former colonies of Latin America were all conceived as variants of a single kind of political unit: the territorial nation-state.

While early-modern European states took form through long periods of violent competition among contending types of political organizations

---

Policy Fields." On organizational competition in this period, see also Nixon, *A History of the International Statistical Institute*, 34.

[57] The ISI continued to exist, but it morphed into a more traditional disciplinary-professional organization, shifting its attention toward creation of knowledge in the field and intradisciplinary pedagogy.

[58] Ventresca, "When States Counts." The post-WWII international statistics regime profoundly influenced the development of contemporary census-taking practices in "the global South," including Latin America, a point to which I return in chapters 6 and 7.

[59] Brading, "Nationalism and State-Building."

(kingdoms, fiefdoms, empires, city-states, etc.), in Latin America modern state formation occurred in the absence of contending forms of legitimate political organization.[60] By the first decades of the nineteenth century, when struggles for independence were waged throughout Latin America, the once varied field of potentially viable forms of political organization had already been narrowed down to a single realistic possibility: the nation-state.[61]

There was therefore no question, after independence was achieved and consolidated, that Latin American states would take on the formal properties of established nation-states. The new Latin American states borrowed constitutional models and legal codes from the United States and Europe. Like France, England, and the United States, Latin American states would have national flags, anthems, libraries, museums, monuments, currencies, legal regimes, armies, and ministries of education and health (with or without actually functioning education and health systems). Also like other modern states, Latin American states would conduct periodic national censuses of their populations.

Foremost on political agendas throughout Latin America from the mid-nineteenth century into the twentieth was the modernization of polities and societies. In the final decades of the nineteenth century and leading up to World War I, Latin American elites often envisioned their societies developing into extensions of Western European civilization. From Argentina to Mexico, political leaders and intellectual elites dreamed of turning their respective *patrias* into card-holding members in the international community of "civilized nations." To increase their chances of acceptance as members of the club, Latin American state-builders took pains to make their states *look like* already recognized members. They sought to build states that did—and were seen doing—the things that modern states were expected to do. Thus, many early efforts at modernization in Latin America

---

[60] In his introduction to a foundational collection of essays on the subject, sociologist Charles Tilly explicitly noted the historical peculiarity of Western European state formation in this respect. Though frequently taken to posit broad theoretical generalizations about the formation of national states, most of the theoretical literature on state formation explicitly speaks to the geographically and historically delimited context of fifteenth- to nineteenth-century Western Europe. (Tilly, *The Formation of National States in Western Europe*). For a discussion of the limitations of theories of Western European state formation for understanding state formation in Latin America, see Centeno, *Blood and Debt*; Centeno and López-Alves, *The Other Mirror*.

[61] As in Europe, the architects of newly independent Latin American states grappled with the questions of *where* sovereignty would reside (with individual states/provinces or with the national/federal government) and, in the Brazilian case of constitutional monarchy, *whether* and *how* it might be shared between hereditary monarchs and elected representatives. But the rejection of dynastic and colonial rule in favor of independent, territorial nation-states was unanimous.

entailed the emulation and adaptation of what were seen as the legitimate institutional forms and practices of modern nation-states.

In this context, Western European countries and the United States served as models for everything from the design of official buildings, to criminal codes, to the organization (and uniforms) of armed forces.[62] Census taking was one among several state practices whose development in Latin America was strongly influenced by external models of the modern. Along with so many other imported prescriptions for nation building, Latin American elites accepted the recently crystallized international norm calling on modern states to take modern demographic censuses.

Adopting the Modern Census in Latin America

The idea of conducting censuses of the population was obviously not itself a foreign import to Latin America. The Spanish and Portuguese imperial states conducted targeted counts of colonial subjects from the onset of colonization in the Americas, and their enumerative efforts became more expansive and encompassing over time. By the late eighteenth century, colonial censuses in the Americas aimed for full coverage of territorially delimited populations, approximating key features of what would become the modern census model.[63] Such grandiose enumerative ambitions mostly receded with the wars of independence in Spanish Latin America. But once the dust had settled, projects to count population emerged again, initially at the city or provincial level.

Census taking took on new significance in the context of independent Latin America. Though early national censuses drew on the practical experience of enumerative endeavors from years of colonial rule, in several key respects they were a different kind of enterprise than most colonial enumerations. From special-purpose, instrumental mechanisms for identifying and extracting resources from specific racially defined subjects, censuses became general-purpose efforts to take stock of *national* conditions and to assess the characteristics of anonymous individuals to get a picture of the population as a whole. Accompanying this shift in purpose, the content and coverage of censuses also changed, from tailored counts of particular segments of the population to generic information gathering

---

[62] Needell, *A Tropical Belle Epoque*; Loveman, B., *For la Patria*; Nunn, *Yesterday's Soldiers*; Centeno, *Blood and Debt*.

[63] Tovar Pinzón et al., *Convocatoria al poder del número*, 53–55; Scarano, "Censuses in the Transition to Modern Colonialism."

about the entire population. The methods of data collection also shifted, at least in theory, from involuntary extraction of individual information by religious and secular authorities to its voluntary provision to specially trained citizen-equals. And the final results of the census, in turn, were reconceived as public patrimony rather than state secret.[64]

The first postindependence census-taking initiatives were prompted by the political and resource needs of new governments. Early efforts to take population censuses were often tied to new electoral laws. Population counts were needed to determine the number of representatives to be elected to provincial legislatures or congresses. Toward this end, Chile attempted a census as early as 1813—before independence was consolidated, and with limited success.[65] Gran Colombia (which at the time included Ecuador, Venezuela, and modern-day Panama) took a census in 1825 that aimed to establish baseline counts for political representation. Officials also sought to determine the size and depth of their tax base, with an eye to undertaking infrastructure development projects and supporting incipient bureaucratic growth.[66]

The task of enumerating newly national citizenries presented enormous challenges for independent Latin American states. They lacked the requisite "stateness," both material and symbolic, to accomplish such a logistical feat.[67] The independence wars wrought havoc and destruction throughout much of the region, severely undermining already limited state capacities. The bureaucratic infrastructure of most of the new republican states did not reach far beyond capital and secondary cities. In imperial Brazil, officials based in the capital city of Rio de Janeiro referred to the entire rest of the enormous country as "the interior." Vast territories of the continent were nominally part of new nation-states, but in practice they were effectively stateless. Reliable means of transportation, communication, and coordinated administration across and between population centers were almost completely lacking—and with them, the capacity to even envision undertaking a simultaneous population count on a nationwide scale.[68]

---

[64] Ventresca, "When States Count."

[65] Jaramillo, "Un Alto en el Camino."

[66] Tovar Pinzón et al., *Convocatoria al poder del número*.

[67] On "stateness" as a matter of degree, see Nettl, "The State as Conceptual Variable"; Ozlak, "The Historical Formation of the State in Latin America."

[68] On infrastructural power and state-building, see von Hau and Soifer, "Unpacking the 'Strength' of the State." For a concrete sense of just how much and what kinds of infrastructural capacity states needed to conduct a comprehensive and simultaneous population count in the early nineteenth-century,

These logistical obstacles were compounded by the reticence of populations to cooperate with efforts to count them. The colonial experience made Latin America's new citizens wary of census-takers' aims, a fact that is lamented in official government reports from the period. For example, a Colombian official reporting on the 1825 census explained that residents "tried to avoid being enumerated, because many of them believed that the purpose of the census was to demand contributions [taxes] and conscript recruits."[69]

During the first part of the nineteenth century, census-taking capacity at the local or provincial level often outpaced central states' capacity to orchestrate a census. This was certainly the case in federalist Brazil, where provincial governments in São Paulo, Rio de Janeiro, and Minas Gerais took the lead in developing local census-taking capacities, long before the central government had either the vision or resources to attempt to do so on a national scale.[70] Population censuses in the first decades of the nineteenth century were mostly partial counts taken in particular towns or regions without national-level coordination of timing or content.

From the mid-nineteenth century, however, when Quetelet organized the first meeting of the ISC and a single legitimate model crystallized for taking a modern national census, piecemeal population counts conducted any old way simply would no longer do. As modernizing nation-states, the Spanish American republics and Brazil would take modern national censuses. During the second half of the nineteenth century, Latin American state-builders became aware of and increasingly oriented to international standards for how modern census taking should be done.

There is ample evidence that the central message promulgated first by the ISC and subsequently by the ISI—that statistics was the science of progress, which no modernizing state could do without—resonated with Latin America's state builders in this period.[71] One indicator of this resonance is the proliferation of state agencies dedicated to taking national censuses in the name of national progress. At midcentury, several Latin American countries had

---

see the detailed methodological description of Britain's 1851 census in Chesire, *The Results of the Census of Great Britain in 1851*.

[69] Archivo General de la Nación (Bogotá) *Secretaría de Guerra y Marina* 142, f.47r., cited in Tovar Pinzón et al., *Convocatoria al poder del número*, 54. On popular resistance to census taking in nineteenth-century Latin America, see Chace, "Protest in Post-Emancipation Dominica"; Loveman, M., "Blinded like a State."

[70] Botelho, "População e Nação"; Senra, *História das Estatísticas Brasileiras*. Alves, *O Desenvolvimento do Sistema Estatístico Nacional*.

[71] Senra and Camargo, *Estatísticas nas Américas*.

statistical offices in key provinces and some had ad hoc national statistical committees. At its first meeting in 1853, the ISC recommended that every state establish a central statistics agency charged with the regularized production of official demographic statistics.[72] In the wake of this recommendation, the diverse organizational arrangements for collecting official statistics across Latin American countries gradually converged around a single institutional form: a national statistics agency under control of the central state. The one clear exception to this pattern proves the rule: Chile's precocious establishment of a national statistics office in 1847 owed to a recommendation made by a French scientist hired by the government to create a scientific description of the country in the 1840s.[73] The recommendation made to Chile's government by the French scientist anticipated the recommendation made more broadly a few years later by the group of European scientists who comprised the ISC. Table 3.1 presents the dates that national statistics agencies were established in the nineteen Latin American countries under analysis.

Evidence that Latin American state builders embraced the idea that statistics was the science of universal progress and that censuses were necessary and noble activities of modern states also abounds in the public rhetoric of the nascent statistical agencies and their supporters. Illustratively, in the wake of a violent uprising in 1851 that forstalled the first general census of Brazil for two decades, an editorial clamored: "All the civilized countries proceed in this manner, the government of Brazil could not help but do the same!!!!"[74] The editorial insisted that census taking was a prerequisite for inclusion in the club of civilized nations, a view that came to be widely shared by Latin American political elites by the second half of the nineteenth century. As the introduction to the 1869 Argentine census proclaimed, the most advanced of the ancient pueblos, "upon arriving at a certain level of civilization" relied on censuses as a crucial resource of government.[75] Clearly, explained the

---

[72] United States, "Report of the Delegates to the International Statistical Congress," 4.

[73] Estefane, "Imperial Uncertainties and Republican Conflicts," 201. On Chile's precocious institutional development more generally, see Loveman, B. and Lira, E., *Las Suaves Cenizas del Olvido*; Loveman, B., *Chile*.

[74] *Diario de Pernambuco*, January 5, 1852, 2. The revolt became known as "the war of the wasps." See Loveman, M., "Blinded Like a State"; Palacios, "A 'Guerra dos Maribondos'"; Melo, "Guerra dos Maribondos"; Mattos, "Identidade Camponesa, Racialização e Cidadania no Brasil Monárquico"; de Oliveira, "Sobreviver à Pressão Escapando ao Controle."

[75] The Argentine census mentioned the registration of inhabitants by the Persians three thousand years earlier, the censuses of ancient Egypt and Asia Minor, the detailed registries of the ancient Chinese, the voter lists of ancient Greece, and the use of censuses in the formation and administration of the Roman Empire. Ancient American civilizations were also included among the litany of great civilizations that made use of statistics to solidify power over their domains. According to the Argentine census, Incan and Mayan rulers "had notions of statistics centuries ago—perhaps even

TABLE 3.1 Timeline of the Creation of National Statistics Agencies in Latin America

YEAR OF DECREE	COUNTRY	NAME OF THE CENTRAL STATISTICS AGENCY
1847	Chile	Oficina de Estadística
1853	Uruguay	Dirección General de Estadística y Censos
1861	Costa Rica	Oficina Central de Estadística
1864	Argentina	Oficina de Estadística Nacional
1871	Brazil	Diretoria Geral de Estatística
1871	Venezuela	Dirección General de Estadística y Censos Nacionales
1873	Peru	Dirección de Estadística
1879	Guatemala	Oficina Central de Estadística
circa 1880	Honduras	Dirección General de Estadística y Censos
1881	El Salvador	Oficina de Estadísticas
1882	Mexico	Dirección General de Estadística
1885	Paraguay	Dirección General de Estadística, Encuestas y Censos
1899	Cuba	Oficina del Censo
1900	Bolivia	Oficina Nacional de Inmigración, Estadística y Propaganda Geográfica
1903	Panama	Oficina Central de Estadística
1905	Dominican Republic	Oficina de Estadística
1905	Nicaragua	Dirección General de Estadísticas
1918	Colombia	Dirección General de Estadística
1944	Ecuador	Dirección General de Estadística y Censos

introduction to Uruguay's 1896 census, census taking was an activity "whose transcendence and importance everyone knows."[76]

The directors of Latin American statistical bureaus saw themselves as major players in the modernizing project. They also saw themselves as part of a world movement of similarly enlightened scientists who lent their services to their states for the progress of national societies and of humankind.

---

better than the [statistical notions] of the new *pueblos* that replaced them." Argentina, Superintendente del Censo, *Primer Censo de la República Argentina*, xi. Goyer and Domschke (*The Handbook of National Population Censuses*, 239) suggest that governors of the Mexican colony made use of archeological discoveries of population counts conducted by Indian tribes.

[76] The quotation comes from a letter by Señor Nicolás Granada to Señor doctor don Samuel Blixén, published in *La Razón*, afternoon edition, April 17, 1896, and reproduced in the 1896 census of Uruguay (Uruguay. Dirección General del Censo, *Censo General*, 258–62).

Exemplifying this view, the director of Brazil's 1872 census declared that the "glorious mission" of the population census is "so noble that the census agents should be considered apostles of civilization, of justice and of the happiness of peoples."[77]

Censuses not only promoted progress, they signified it; they were seen as markers of modern nationhood. Revealing of the symbolic significance of early national censuses, the presentation of census results evinced a clear orientation toward an international audience. The reports, typically published in decorative leather tomes, devoted many pages to presentation and analysis of comparative statistics that ranked countries of Europe and the Americas according to internationally recognized indicators of progress and civilization. The second national census of Argentina (1895), for instance, included tables and graphics that reported that Argentina was the fastest-growing nation in Europe or the Americas.[78] Brazil's first national census, to take another example, reported the number of schools and the number of students per capita (counting only the free population) in comparison to nine European countries and the United States. Brazil's poor showing in this ranking bolstered an appeal for government investment in public education.[79] The publication of carefully selected comparative statistics was a common practice in censuses throughout the region. While highlighting particular strengths of a given nation, such comparative tables simultaneously affirmed that Latin American nations were directly comparable to those of Europe, transforming them into objective, abstract things—modern, civilized nation-states—of the same basic "kind."

By successfully conducting a modern national census and publishing the results, Latin American census agencies positioned their respective nations as directly comparable to—and thus categorically equivalent to—the "civilized nations" of Western Europe. Viewed in hindsight, it appears that this symbolic function of Latin America's early censuses was often as

---

[77] Brazil, Directoria Geral de Estatística [DGE], "Recenseamento da População do Imperio...1872," 1–2).

[78] The proportional rate of growth was calculated based on the population figures from the last two censuses of each country. The previous Argentine census was nearly twenty-six years earlier, while the interval between the censuses of most other countries compared was ten years. The text accompanying the comparative table noted that if longer time periods were considered for other countries, their proportional growth might appear higher, but still the rate of growth of other countries "would always remain inferior to that of Argentina" (Argentina. Comisión Directiva del Censo, *Segundo Censo de la República Argentina*). Of course, the census commission could have used census results from earlier censuses in other countries to make the data more comparable, or adjusted the data to reflect the discrepancy in time elapsed.

[79] Brazil. Directoria Geral de Estatística, *Relatorio. Trabalhos Estatísticos*...1873, 27. For a discussion of the push by Brazil's DGE director for investment in education in the 1870s, see Loveman, M., "The Race to Progress."

important as their intended pragmatic functions at the time. Indeed, as the nineteenth century wore on, the ability of Latin American states to collect basic data from their entire populations and make the results usable for policy purposes remained very uneven.[80] When states did manage to overcome logistic hurdles and gather significant numbers of census returns, the modest staff of central statistics agencies often lacked the resources or capacity to do much with the piles and piles of census forms returned by enumerators. The absence of basic technologies that would later mechanize the processing of census returns meant that generating even the most basic summary statistics was an extraordinarily time- and labor-intensive endeavor. Directors of early national censuses frequently disavowed the thoroughness or reliability of the final results, complaining of inadequate resources or lack of cooperation from the populace, even as they trumpeted the census as a great accomplishment and reported results as if they were not political fictions. Notwithstanding these practical limitations, however, census officials touted their faith that statistical knowledge would contribute to the development and consolidation of modern nation-states, as European proponents of the new statistical science promised it would.

Implementing the International Model

In addition to recognizing central statistics agencies and modern censuses as indispensable instruments and indicators of the progress of nations, Latin American census officials signaled their acceptance of specific ISC resolutions regarding census procedures and content. In case there might be any doubt that the censuses conducted in Latin America were the same sort of enterprise as those conducted by civilized European states, official census reports often made explicit reference to the authoritative recommendations of the ISC.

To cite just a few examples of this practice, in his introduction to the published results of the 1865 census, the director of the Chilean Central Statistical Office included an extract of the recommendations made by "the distinguished Belgian statistician, Mr. Quetelet" at the 1853 meeting of the ISC. The Chilean director noted that Quetelet's program, which was "intended to standardize the official statistics of the European nations, has such close relations to our [census], that it could almost be said to have been formed

---

[80] For example, see Soifer, "Elite Preferences, Administrative Institutions, and Educational Development during Peru's Aristocratic Republic (1895–1919)."

according to its indications, without any differences other than those born of the special conditions of our nationality."[81] The preface to the 1864 census of Costa Rica explained that the substance of the census followed the recommendations of the 1860 ISC meeting in London.[82] The first Venezuelan census, in 1873, "solicited the information that constituted the minimum for a census of the time according to the recommendations of the International Statistical Congresses."[83] And the second, third, and fourth Venezuelan censuses followed the ISC's recommendations closely to ensure "the comparison of its data with that of other countries." Indeed, in Venezuela, the importance of following international census-taking conventions was explicitly signaled in legislation pertaining to the 1910 census. According to a 1910 law, "The Census will take place on December 31, 1910 and all its operations will refer to the 12m. of this day. Venezuela thus respects the recommendations made since 1874 by the International Statistical Congresses and Institutes and helps facilitate the comparison of its study with those of other countries."[84] In Argentina's 1914 census, to cite a final example, the inclusion of questions pertaining to fertility of married women was explained by the fact that "This topic was prioritized in all the civilized countries that take censuses, due to the initiatives on this subject recently adopted by the International Statistics Institute—the most respectable association that exists in the world, dedicated to promoting demographic and anthropologic studies—in its frequent biannual meetings."[85]

How did Latin American census officials learn of ISC recommendations? Very few Latin American countries ever participated directly in the international statistical congresses. The congresses were conceived as European affairs and explicitly organized as such. Representatives from a few non-European countries were invited to the first congress in 1853 (including the United States, Japan, and Sublime Porte [Ottoman Empire]), and invitations were extended to other countries for some of the subsequent meetings. Only four Latin American countries ever had a delegate invited to participate in the ISC (Costa Rica, Peru, Argentina, Brazil), and it appears that in most of these cases the invitations were either opportunistic or matters of diplomatic etiquette. Such was the case for an Argentine-Italian

---

[81] Chile. Oficina Central de Estadística. *Censo General de la República de Chile... 1865,* VIII.

[82] Costa Rica. Dirección General de Estadística y Censos (*Censo General de la República de Costa Rica,* section IX).

[83] This was reported in the introduction to the 1950 Venezuelan census. Venezuela. Dirección General de Estadística y Censos Nacionales, *Octavo Censo General de Población,* v.

[84] Regulamento de 7 de abril de 1910 (related to Decreto de 19 March, 1919), article 6. Cited in Venezuela. Dirección General de Estadística y Censos, *Octavo Censo General de Población,* v.

[85] Argentina. Comisión Directiva del Censo. *Tercer Censo Nacional de la República,* 40.

businessman who happened to be in Italy at the time of the 1867 meeting, for example, or the Brazilian minister in London in 1860. With the possible exception of the Brazilian Baron von Varnhagen's invitation to attend the 1872 ISC in St. Petersburg, the scientific credentials of Latin American invitees seemed inconsequential to their inclusion in the ISC program, suggesting their participation was more a symbolic gesture than a recognition of possible substantive contribution to the discussion. Published proceedings from the congresses suggest little Latin American influence on the substantive discussions. Table 3.2 provides an overview of official Latin American participation in the ISC.[86]

The reports sent by Latin American delegates back to their home governments were one conduit for transmitting ISC recommendations to Latin American census officials. Thus, for example, Varnhagen sent a report on the 1872 meeting to the director of Brazil's Directora Geral de Estatística (DGE) that summarized the highlights of the congress.[87] Brazilian consuls in Europe also helped the DGE get up to date, offering to secure important publications in the field of statistics on the DGE's behalf. Responding to inquiries sent from the Brazilian consuls in Prussia and Rotterdam about the topics that would be most useful to the DGE, the director of Brazil's statistics agency replied, "for this General Directorate [DGE] it would be useful to have knowledge of any and all statistical works of official origin published in all the states of Europe; but above all regarding legislation relative to the census and any statistical works about population. It would also be useful to have the reports of the statistical congresses, however for both these and [the other publications], it would be very difficult to make use of them if they are written in Dutch or even in German."[88]

In addition to the direct transfer of ISC resolutions via official channels, the latest statistical advances and recommendations reported in the congresses traveled to Latin America via established networks of scientists and political elites. Latin America's educated elite frequently studied abroad in Western Europe, and became conduits for the (selective) transfer of

---

[86] Table 3.2, which covers the full span of the ISC's existence, is based on information found in the following sources: Ventresca, "When States Count"; Nixon, *A History of the International Statistical Institute*; Westergaard, *Contributions to the History of Statistics*; United States. *Report of the Delegates to the International Statistical Congress*.

[87] See the report by the Baron of Porto Seguro (Francisco Adolfo de Varnhagen), Brazilian delegate to the St. Petersburg meeting, appended to the 1872 report of the Ministerio dos Negocios do Império. de Varnhagen, "Relatorio Acérca dos Trabalhos do Congresso Estatística."

[88] The letters were forwarded to the DGE director through the Minister of Foreign Affairs, in a letter dated July 1, 1871. Arquivo Nacional, Rio de Janeiro GIFI 5C264 (Ministerio do Imperio. 2a seção. 1868–74. cod.01. AA seção SDE).

TABLE 3.2 Latin American Participation in the International Statistical Congress, 1853–1876

YEAR OF CONGRESS	LOCATION	NUMBER OF COUNTRIES WITH OFFICIAL DELEGATES	DELEGATES FROM LATIN AMERICAN COUNTRIES	TOTAL NUMBER OF OFFICIAL PARTICIPANTS	NUMBER OF LATIN AMERICAN COUNTRIES WITH DELEGATES
1853	Brussels	26		153	0
1855	Paris	29	Costa Rica (Escalante, counselor at law; Lafond, Gabriel, insurance agent; Marie, Undersecretary of State). Peru (de Riveiro, Minister)	311	2
1857	Vienna	27		542	0
1860	London	24	Brazil (the Commander de Carvalho Moreira, the Brazilian Minister in London)	586	1
1863	Berlin	16 (grouping German delegates)		477	0
1867	Florence	23	Argentina (Prof. Mantegazza)	751	1
1869	The Hague	24		488	0
1872	St. Petersburg	25	Brazil (Baron F.A. de Varnhagen)	485	1
1876	Budapest	24	Brazil (official delegate)	442	1

scientific theories to their home countries. Influenced by positivists such as Comte and Spencer, for example, Mexico's "científicos" under the Porfiriato (1876–1910) recognized "the importance of statistics as an internationally approved gauge of progress" and thus "began organizing central statistical institutions that would compile and publish reports, annuals, and bulletins on a regular basis."[89] As the nineteenth century wore on, official reports and bulletins published by central statistics agencies facilitated the dissemination of statistical knowledge within Latin America. The directors of Latin America's nineteenth-century statistical agencies attempted to stay abreast of each other's work and at times would even cross-reference one another in the introductory essays to the published volumes of census results.

Taken together, the census volumes produced by Latin America's statistics agencies from the mid-nineteenth century make clear that their creators were aware of the international prestige of statistics as the state-builders' science. The creation of central statistics agencies charged with taking modern, national censuses in nineteenth- and early twentieth-century Latin America was itself fueled by state builders' orientation to the international cultural norm of census taking as necessary state practice, a norm consolidated through the work of the ISC. Latin American state builders accepted the ISC's claim that modern states should take modern censuses, and they accepted the ISC's authority to decide what made a census modern. They looked to ISC recommendations, then to the ISI (after 1885), for guidance on how states should count human beings within their borders. And they explicitly called attention to their knowledge of ISC norms in publications of census results.

Adapting the International Model

Latin American statistics agencies attempted to bring their census-taking practices into line with international conventions, and to advertise this compliance in print. When they deviated from the international recommendations, this fact was often explicitly noted, lest it appear that the discrepancy was due to oversight or ignorance. Adaptations to the international model were usually justified with observations that national census taking faced distinct challenges in diverse national settings, and that in the particular country concerned, census takers confronted certain nationally specific obstacles to the implementation of ISC recommendations.

---

[89] Contreras and Reich, "Numbers and the State," 1254–5.

Well into the twentieth century, the narrative introductions to published volumes of Latin American census results are riddled with explanations for the various shortcomings of the census efforts when compared with international standards for modern census taking. For example, in prefatory comments to the report on Costa Rica's 1864 census, the director noted that delays in printing the forms combined with the fact that it "absorbs from three to five days" to reach areas along the Pacific coast had made a simultaneous enumeration impossible. He explained that while "this inconvenience would have been of the utmost significance in other circumstances, because it destroys the simultaneity of the operation" in Costa Rica it was not really a problem since the population "is composed...almost entirely of landowners who, with their families, remain stationary in one location. There is no notable immigration or emigration, nor temporal absences...; the only real local population movement is of births and deaths...."[90] In other contexts, census directors explained that instead of conducting the enumeration in December, as the ISC recommended, they had conducted the census in June or July. The ISC had settled on December as the best month for taking a national census at its first meeting; it was decided that midwinter was a time when people were most likely to be home. But in the southern hemisphere, of course, December was midsummer. In a rare instance of "bottom-up" feedback influencing the ISC agenda, the Brazilian delegate to the 1872 congress in St. Petersburg placed this issue on the table for discussion. The ISC's recommendation was relaxed when it was pointed out that December was midsummer in the Southern Hemisphere, and thus not always ideal for finding people at home.[91] In contrast to their general lack of influence in setting the ISC agenda, noted above, on the matter of when states should count their populations Latin American delegates prompted an amendment of ISC recommendations. At the 1872 meeting, the ISC dropped the call for universal December censuses and recommended instead that states choose the date of their census in accordance with local seasonal conditions and migratory patterns.

On rare occasions, the authority of the ISC to act as ultimate arbiter of a proper modern census was rejected out of hand. Though not common, such a stance was one way that Latin America's census directors could preemptively defend themselves when a count taken under their supervision was widely recognized to be shoddy or incomplete. An Uruguayan census official, for example, called on the words of Chilean and Argentine

---

[90] Costa Rica. Dirección General de Estadística y Censos, *Censo General de la República de Costa Rica*, XIV–XV.

[91] de Varnhagen "Relatorio Acérca dos Trabalhos do Congresso Estatistica".

colleagues to emphasize the importance of avoiding complete dependence on "foreign theory," and relying on "native [national] means" to accomplish the census—"a work required for the progressive march of our aggrandizement."[92] To substantiate his point, he quoted the president of the Argentine National Census Commission, who reputedly insisted that only "the agents of our excellent personnel know the means we invented to be able to enumerate inaccessible zones of the Republic in one day and at the same time." According to this source, the methods invented by the Argentines to accomplish this feat were *sui generis,* so it was "only in principle" that the Argentine census was like those of other nations.[93]

Given that nearly all of Latin America's early census agencies lacked the capacity to take a census that complied with the ISC rules, it might seem surprising that rhetorical repudiation of the authority of the ISC was not more widespread. However, beyond the cultural and scientific legitimacy it held as the mouthpiece of "the representatives of the principal civilized nations of the world," the ISC facilitated acceptance of its authority by creating space for adaptation to local conditions *within* its prescribed census model. Built into the ISC's recommendations was the recognition that states needed some flexibility to mold the standardized census model to the specific conditions and concerns of national governments. Thus, states could adapt the model while still working within it, signaling that adaptations were not rejections by including explicit comments to this effect in explanatory notes. In this spirit, Latin American census texts frequently noted when specific prescriptions of the ISC were deliberately adapted to national contexts. Deviations from the ISC's authoritative recommendations were explicitly registered as such, with the specific rationale for the adaptation laid out in the methodological essays or prefatory comments that accompanied the publication of census results.

A Silent Adaptation of the International Model: The Question of Race

One widespread adaptation to the international census model for which no explicit justification was offered in census reports was the inclusion of race queries on census questionnaires. Given the general tendency to

---

[92] Uruguay. *Censo General (1895–1896),* 259, 262.
[93] As reported in Uruguay. *Censo General (1895–1896),* 262.

explicitly justify deviations and adaptations to the ISC model, the uncommented inclusion of race queries in Latin America's early census forms is striking. Not all Latin American states classified their populations by race in their early censuses. But the majority of Latin American countries included race questions in at least one and usually more of their nineteenth- and early twentieth-century censuses. Of the eighteen countries that attempted a modern national census prior to 1940, only Argentina and Venezuela never included an explicit query about an individual's "race" or "color" on a national census schedule.[94] Table 3.3 shows national censuses conducted in Latin American from the 1810s to the 1940s that did and did not include direct questions about race (raza) or color.[95] Usually, these questions took the form of a one-word prompt to enumerators (e.g., "Race:") followed by a set of categories from which to choose (e.g., "White, Mulatto, Black, or Indian"). In cases where the original questionnaire could not be located, a census is coded as including a direct race query if the official reported results refer explicitly to such a question or the data that it generated.

In the first few decades of the nineteenth century, only a few countries even pretended to have the capacity to count the population within their borders. These early efforts are not recognized by contemporary national statistics agencies as actual national censuses. They are seen as part of the protohistory of the development of statistical capacities of the state. Though the surviving records are thin, available archival evidence suggests that many of these early efforts to count (or estimate) populations recorded distinctions by race. By the 1880s and 1890s, most countries had attempted at least one national census, and among these, about half included direct questions about race. Between 1900 and 1940, thirteen of the nineteen countries analyzed included such a question on at least one

---

[94] Chile included a question on ethnoracial "origins" on the 1813 census, but then dropped the query in all subsequent censuses. Argentina excluded a query on race from national censuses, but took separate censuses of its territories that included queries about membership in indigenous groups. Argentina also compiled racial statistics from data on individual nationality, an issue I discuss in chapter 5.

[95] Note that Cuban censuses from the 1840s to the 1880s were colonial censuses, not national censuses. Information compiled in table 3.3 is drawn from a combination of secondary sources including Goyer and Domschke, *The Handbook of National Population Censuses*; Travis, *A Guide to Latin American and Caribbean Census Material*; Library of Congress, *General Censuses and Vital Statistics in the Americas*; Vandiver, "Racial Classifications in Latin American Censuses," and a wide array of historical monographs, articles, and primary materials on specific censuses in individual countries. See Appendix for more information on sources and methods used to construct table 3.3 and subsequent tables in this book that report census contents for all nineteen countries across multiple decades.

TABLE 3.3 Race or Color Questions in Latin American Censuses, 1810s–1940s

	1810s	1820s	1830s	1840s	1850s	1860s	1870s	1880s	1890s	1900s	1910s	1920s	1930s	1940s
Argentina														
Bolivia			?	R	R			?		R				
Brazil							R		R					R
Chile	R													
Colombia											R			
Costa Rica												R		
Cuba				R		R	R	R	R	R	R		R	R
Dominican Rep.												R	R	
Ecuador														
El Salvador							?	?	?	R			R	
Guatemala							R	R				R		R
Honduras							R		R	R			R	R
Mexico											R			
Nicaragua				R		R		R		?		R		?
Panama											R	R	R	R
Paraguay				R					?				?	
Peru		R					R							R
Uruguay					R									
Venezuela														

■ = Census taken   R = Race or color question   ? = Census taken but no data on questions

national census. Among the exceptions are Ecuador (no national census prior to 1940), Paraguay (available documentation does not suffice to determine the content of questionnaires), and Argentina, Chile, Uruguay, and Venezuela (to which I return in later chapters).

Table 3.3 provides an informative yet partial view of the attention devoted to race in Latin America's early national censuses. In several cases where no race data were collected, census reports nonetheless included extensive discussion of racial demographic trends. In the absence of contemporary data, census officials invoked historical statistics or rough estimates based on other types of government sources. (This practice is discussed in more detail in chapter 4). While illuminating, it is thus important to underscore that table 3.3 does not fully capture the extent to which Latin American census officials focused on racial distinctions in censuses in this period.[96]

The topic of racial classification in national censuses was never explicitly addressed in the international statistics congresses. This is not particularly surprising, since the Europeans did not generally use the language of race to describe the distinct "peoples" contained within their states'

---

[96] A clear understanding of the substantive significance of the information reported in Table 3.3 only emerges through close textual analyses of census reports in combination with historical analysis of the political and scientific contexts of their production, as undertaken in subsequent chapters. On this methodological issue more generally, see Biernacki, *Reinventing Evidence in Social Inquiry*.

continental borders. When ISC delegates discussed whether and how censuses should attend to "primordial" communal distinctions within their populations, they talked about *nationalities* or *language groups*—not races. The terminology of "race" was more likely to be used in reference to colonized populations. Yet even on the few occasions that the ISC directly addressed census taking in the colonies, the matter of racial classification on censuses did not arise.[97]

The ISC's inattention to the question of whether states should regularly collect racial data on censuses was only partly a matter of semantics. ISC delegates recognized the potential political volatility of producing official counts of various "minorities" within state borders. It was decided early on that states' domestic political considerations should weigh over any "universal" good that might come from collection of data on such axes of difference. Thus, when a delegate to the 1857 Congress in Vienna presented a map depicting the geographic distribution of ethnolinguistic groups in Prussia, the cartographic accomplishment was complimented by ISC delegates; but the idea that other states should strive, as a matter of course, to create analogous ethnic maps of their own populations was quickly subdued. From its third meeting in 1860, as noted above, the ISC removed language and religion from the list of items that all states should include on national censuses.

The ISC's abstention from opining on the matter of racial classification in national censuses carried over to its successor institutions through to the mid-twentieth century. The ISI, founded in 1885 to take up where the ISC left off, continued to promote the international uniformity of statistics by issuing recommended procedures for state census agencies.[98] Operating as a scientific association of disinterested professionals, a nongovernmental successor to the ISC, the ISI met biannually in European cities, amending and elaborating the ISC's model for how to count human beings in a census. A review of ISI congress proceedings up to the outbreak of World War I in 1914 revealed that the topic of racial classification in censuses was not addressed.

---

[97] For the most part, the ISC showed very little concern with colonial enumerative endeavors. Papers reporting on colonial censuses in some contexts were occasionally presented at a meeting, but there is no evidence that they generated any sustained or systematic attention to the matter by the ISC.

[98] The ISI was created at a conference convened in London to celebrate the jubilee anniversary of the London Statistical Society, where participants met "to consider what has been achieved by the International Statistical Congresses or by other means in the direction of uniformity of statistics and by what measures that object may be further promoted, and to consider the possibility of establishing an International Statistical Association." Statistical Society Jubilee Volume, pp. VIII and IX, cited in Nixon, *A History of the International Statistical Institute*, 11.

Given its European origins and predominant membership, it is perhaps not surprising that the ISI did not take up the issue of racial classification on national censuses during its years as an advocacy organization vis-à-vis national states. Relatively few non-European members were chosen to join the ISI, and none from colonial contexts.[99] Among Latin American countries, only Argentina, Brazil, Mexico, Bolivia, and Uruguay were represented before 1933. Any substantive contributions of Latin American participants to the ISI through the mid-twentieth century are not detectable from the official records of conference proceedings.[100] Table 3.4 lists Latin American countries invited to participate in the meetings of the ISI.

When World War I ended, the League of Nations stepped into the ISI's role of coordinating statistical activities across states. In August 1919, the League of Nations convened a conference in London on "International Coordination in Statistics." The aim of the meeting was to hammer out "the relations of the League with other international institutions, and also, in general, the way in which the League could profitably assist the development of international cooperation in statistics."[101] At this conference and another the following year in Paris, the recommended census content was reviewed and reiterated. The proceedings from these conferences leave no record of discussion of the matter of racial statistics. In later years, the League would consider issues related to demographic statistics of national minorities in some European contexts, but not as a matter of general concern for the mandating of topics to be included in the paradigm national census of modern states.

More surprisingly, perhaps, than the silence around racial statistics in the work of the ISC, the ISI, and the League of Nations is the fact that intraregional scientific congresses in Latin America also neglected this issue in the first half of the twentieth century. This neglect was evident even in venues explicitly devoted to discussing the standardization of demographic statistics in the region. The program for the first Pan-American Scientific Congress, which took place in Santiago, Chile, in

---

[99] Zahn, *50 Années de l'Institut International de Statistique*.

[100] It was not until the 1950s that a Latin American member of the ISI held an official post in the organization (Jorge Kingston, a professor from Rio de Janeiro, was appointed interim vice president of the ISI between 1956 and 1957). By this time, the ISI had long since undergone a major organizational transformation, moving definitively away from its historical role as an advisory body to state statistics agencies to become an academic-professional association, focused on advancement of statistics as an academic field of knowledge with practical applications. Nixon, *A History of the International Statistical Institute*, 159.

[101] Nixon, *A History of the International Statistical Institute*, 28.

TABLE 3.4 Latin American Participation in the International Statistical Institute, 1887–1933

YEAR OF CONFERENCE	LOCATION	COUNTRIES WITH DELEGATES	LATIN AMERICAN COUNTRIES	NUMBER OF OFFICIAL PARTICIPANTS	LATIN AMERICAN PARTICIPANTS
1887	Rome	21	Argentina, Brazil	156	3
1889	Paris	19	Argentina	167	2
1891	Vienna	22	Argentina	173	2
1893	Chicago	20	Argentina	171	2
1895	Berne	20	Argentina	170	2
1897	St. Petersburg	20	Argentina	168	1
1899	Christiania	21	Argentina	173	2
1901	Budapest	22	Argentina, Mexico	171	3
1903	Berlin	22	Argentina, Mexico	193	3
1905	London	22	Argentina, Mexico	210	3
1907	Copenhagen	23	Argentina, Mexico, Uruguay	220	4
1909	Paris	23	Argentina, Mexico, Uruguay	212	4
1911	The Hague	25	Argentina, Mexico, Uruguay	206	4
1913	Vienna	26	Argentina, Mexico, Uruguay	204	3
1923	Brussels	27	Argentina, Bolivia, Uruguay	155	3
1925	Rome	30	Argentina, Bolivia, Brazil, Uruguay	172	4
1927	Cairo	29	Bolivia, Brazil	175	2
1929	Warsaw	33	Bolivia, Brazil, Mexico	193	3
1931	Tokyo	32	Brazil, Mexico	185	2
1933	Mexico	37	Brazil, Mexico	198	2

1908–09, included a paper by an American representative, S. N. D. North, on the topic of "Uniformity and Cooperation in the Census Methods of the Republics of the American Continent." The paper extolled the virtues of harmonizing census methods across states in the Americas. Those in attendance seemed to agree with this agenda, in principle. Among the resolutions issued by the Congress was a decision to recommend to their respective Governments: "1. That a common date be chosen for taking the census in all the countries of the American Continent. 2. That, as far as possible, uniform subjects of inquiry be chosen which will facilitate comparison of the returns of the census in all the American Republics, and at the same time increase and perfect the materials required for sociologic, economic, and political studies."[102] The Congress did not attempt to specify, however, what those "uniform subjects of inquiry" should be.

The topic of regional standardization of census methods emerged again at the Fourth International Conference of American States, held in Buenos Aires in 1910. At that conference, a resolution with twenty signatories reiterated the existing international convention of holding a decennial census of the population "taking into account the advance of science and technical procedure."[103] The resolution further recommended "that steps be taken to effect a population census in all of the American States in the year 1920, if possible, in the same month, to be recommended beforehand by the Pan-American Union at Washington."[104] Again, there was no mention of what content the simultaneous 1920 censuses should include.

The call for coordinating census efforts throughout the Americas was reiterated at the second Pan-American Scientific Congress, held in Washington, DC, in 1915–16.[105] In a repeat appearance, S.N.D. North drew attention to his earlier (ineffective) call for census cooperation and emphasized the heightened significance of hemispheric integration in light of the disruption of transatlantic ties due to war in Europe. Along with an appeal to Latin American countries to abandon their national currencies in favor of a US-based gold standard, and a reciprocating call on the United

---

[102] International Union of American Republics, Bulletin of the International Bureau of the American Republics, "First Pan-American Scientific Congress," 590.

[103] Carnegie Endowment for International Peace, *The International Conferences of American States*, 200.

[104] Fourth International Conference of American States, Buenos Aires, July 12–August 30, 1910. The resolution also recommended taking industrial and other censuses "as science and practice counsel" on the same date. The resolution was signed by delegates for Argentina, Brazil, Chile, Colombia, Costa Rica, Cuba, Dominican Republic, Ecuador, Guatemala, Haiti, Honduras, Mexico, Nicaragua, Panama, Paraguay, Peru, El Salvador, United States, Uruguay, Venezuela (Carnegie Endowment for International Peace, *The International Conferences of American States*).

[105] North, "The Standardization of Census and Commercial Statistics."

States to give up its "prehistoric system of weights and measures" in favor of the metric system,[106] North underscored the importance of generating standardized, internationally comparable demographic and commercial statistics: "I dwell upon these things because it is becoming more and more evident, as the science of government develops, and particularly the government of democracies under the representative system, that statistics are, or ought to be, and eventually must be, the foundation upon which it rests, both in legislation and in administration."[107] The delegates were evidently on board with North's recommendations, at least with respect to census coordination. The Final Acts of the Congress included the following resolution: "The Second Pan American Scientific Congress deems it advisable that: The American Republics agree upon a uniform date for the taking of the census, and that uniform methods be adopted in the collection, arrangement, and presentation of commercial and demographic statistics."[108] But again, there was no record of any specific recommendations on the matter of census content, nor were there any mechanisms to translate the recommendation into action by the region's governments.

Finally, at the Fifth International Conference of American States, held in Santiago, Chile, in 1923, minimum content for population censuses in the Americas was specified: "The census shall contain data regarding the actual population, and if possible, also regarding those domiciled but absent from their place of domicile, of the entire country, as well as of each of its territorial units and populated areas, classifying the inhabitants at least according to sex, age, civil status, nationality, education, and means of livelihood or profession."[109] "Race" was not named among the attributes that should be queried in a national census. Uniformity of demographic statistics remained a topic of discussion at the Seventh International Conference of American States, which took place in Montevideo,

---

[106] On the subject of the metric system, North added: "There is a suggestion of Anglo-Saxon stubbornness and individualism in the refusal of Great Britain and the United States to take full advantage of the modern methods of metrology. One country with the world's greatest commerce, the other her near rival in that commerce, they tolerate this handicap chiefly through the power of inertia and iron rule of tradition" (North, "The Standardization of Census and Commercial Statistics," 623).

[107] North, "The Standardization of Census and Commercial Statistics," 619.

[108] Proceedings of the Second Pan American Scientific Congress, vol. 12. Final Act. Article 43, 39.

[109] Resolution adopted at the Twelfth Session (May 1, 1923) of the Fifth International Conference of American States (March 25–May 3, 1923) (Carnegie Endowment for International Peace, *The International Conferences of American States*). The resolution also reiterated the recommendation to American governments that they take a decennial census (now with the day and month fixed by countries in accordance with particular conditions, with preference for the season when a majority of residents are home).

Uruguay in 1933, as part of a proposal by the Mexican Delegation to establish an Inter-American Bureau of Labor. Again, the possibility of including "race" as part of the standard content for censuses in the hemisphere was not discussed.[110]

Thus, prior to World War II, neither international nor regional standards for conducting a modern census advocated inclusion of race queries on national censuses. Nonetheless, as the following chapter details, Latin American census officials opted to use the forum of the national census to draw attention to racial distinctions within their populations. In doing so, they underlined a fundamental difference between their nations and the European exemplars of modernity that they sought to emulate. They also suggested a fundamental similarity to the United States—where citizens were also routinely racially classified on censuses—in a domain in which they otherwise sought to claim the higher ground: postcolonial race relations.

Official decisions to draw attention to racial distinctions in national censuses did not owe to ignorance or indifference toward prevailing international standards for how a legitimate modern state should take a legitimate modern census. As we have seen, Latin American census officials announced their familiarity with international standards of modern census taking and sought to demonstrate adherence to those standards in other respects. Nor can official racial classification in postcolonial censuses be dismissed as a colonial administrative hangover. As noted at the outset of this chapter, significant ideological, political, and legal momentum weighed *against* introducing the colonial-tainted practice of official racial classification into the highly visible and politically charged context of a national census. What then explains the penchant for producing racial statistics in so many of Latin America's nineteenth- and early-twentieth century censuses?

An adequate answer this question requires a sustained look at the types of racial statistics that Latin America's nascent central statistics agencies actually produced. What information did they collect, how did they collect it, and to what purposes was it put? As the next two chapters reveal, nineteenth- and early twentieth-century Latin American censuses strayed far from neutral description of the ethnodemographic composition of populations. Though the pressure on census officials to conform to the international recommendations for census content was strong, it was dwarfed

---

[110] Hull, "Report of the Delegates of the United States of America to the Seventh International Conference of American States."

by countervailing pressure to craft an assertive response to the prevailing international scientific wisdom that condemned non-white nations to backwardness. Confronted with authoritative predictions by leading scientists that their nations were doomed to degeneracy, Latin American statesmen countered with racial statistics documenting the "regenerative" potential of Latin American populations.

CHAPTER 4 | The Race to Progress

A MAJOR ACCOMPLISHMENT OF early national censuses was to establish and help naturalize the commensurability of nations. With standardized methods for counting and classifying kinds of humankind, national censuses could render the most disparate and diverse populations directly comparable to each other on an array of indicators of national development. As the Colombians wrote in the introduction to their 1912 census, "This is the first time a work of this genre is published in this country...[it will] contribute to giving a clear idea, in both the interior and the exterior, of the true situation of Colombia, with respect to its population and resources, in the face of all other countries, and particularly those of the Hispano-American continent."[1] In the pages of leather-bound volumes of published census results, Latin American populations materialized as neatly delineated and self-evident nations that could be directly compared to others. Elite aspirations of nationhood appeared as a settled reality.

For Colombia, as for most other Latin American countries in this period, census results tended to reveal that their population lagged behind those of Western Europe and the United States on the road to national progress. When ranked by such measure as population density or schools per capita, for example, most Latin American countries fell on the bottom half of the list. Regardless, the fact that their progress was measured on the same scale as the most advanced nations of the time ratified Latin American nations as things of the same basic kind.[2] Further, the ordinal ranking of nations according to various indicators of development created the conceptual possibility of a shift in relative standing; Latin American nations

---

[1] Colombia. Ministerio del Gobierno, *Censo General de la República de Colombia... 1912*, 3.
[2] On the politics and power entailed in making things commensurable, see Espeland and Stevens, "Commensuration as a Social Process."

might eventually approximate or even surpass other nations in the race to progress. Thus, the ability to establish a fundamental, definitional symmetry between the emergent independent polities of Latin America and the core nations of Europe and the United States was an alluring feature of the national census in the eyes of Latin America's modernizing elites.

National censuses became strategic instruments of nation-making in nineteenth- and early twentieth-century Latin America. In addition to establishing that the Latin American polities were categorically similar to the nations of Europe and the United States, national censuses provided an ideal platform for describing the particular attributes of individual nations. Drawing attention to particularity might seem to be in tension with the goal of establishing categorical similarity. Yet espousing some kind of intrinsic and irreducible source of particularity was (and is) a key ingredient in the cultural formula for constructing a modern nation. Indeed, it is a defining, if oxymoronic, feature of modern nationhood that to be recognized as a nation among others requires making a credible claim to be fundamentally unique. Thus, even as ranked lists of countries implied the categorical equivalence of units labeled "Peru," "Argentina," "France," and "Belgium," early national census reports also included narrative sections that drew attention to attributes that made each individual nation historically one of a kind.

While all nations are alike in their claims to be built on some essential "something" that sets them apart,[3] they differ in the particular attributes selected by nationalizing elites to mark their distinction. In France and the United States, for example, nationalists touted their radically democratic civic bonds as the defining source of nationhood.[4] In Germany, they extolled the bonds created by shared ancestry of a homogenous *volk* (people). In Latin America, meanwhile, national elites tended toward a hybrid approach. In a nod to civic definitions of nationhood, they championed their allegiance to liberal ideals; in line with ethnic conceptions of nationhood, they pointed to *racial particularity* as the originating source of *national particularity*. In contrast to European variants of "ethnic nationalism" which aspired to make membership in the nation contingent on membership in a single ethnoracial group, Latin America's nationalisms

---

[3] Calhoun, *Nationalism*, 7.

[4] Brubaker, *Citizenship and Nationhood*; Smith, R., *Stories of Peoplehood*. Of course, underlying the claims to "civic" nationhood lay prior assumptions about the ethnoracial group that legitimately "owned the state" (Wimmer, "Who Owns the State?"). These assumptions erupted regularly in the form of xenophobic and exclusionary nationalist politics across the histories of these countries (Gerstle, *American Crucible*).

celebrated the forging of nations through processes that blended different races together. Latin America's founding fictions emphasized how new nations had been born and continued to develop through *race mixture*.[5]

It was not inevitable that Latin American nations would come to be defined in explicitly racial terms. Prominent "civic" models of nationhood were available to Latin America's postindependence leaders, and adopting them would have maximized the symbolic break with their colonial past. Yet Latin America's nation-state builders eschewed strictly civic definitions of nationhood and instead honed in on racial particularity, and especially on race mixture, as the constitutive foundation of their nations.

Why did Latin America's modernizing elites choose to underline racial particularity as the fundamental source of national particularity? The answer can be traced to the fact that intensification of state modernization projects in Latin America in the latter half of the nineteenth century and beginning of the twentieth (of which modern census taking initiatives were a part) coincided with the emergence and proliferation of racial determinist theories of societal development. By the 1870s and into the first decades of the twentieth century, Latin American intellectual and political elites were profoundly influenced by theories that linked putatively innate differences among human groups to prospects for national development.[6] According to the science of the times, populations composed of non-European "racial stock" were destined to lag perpetually behind in the race to progress; where there was extensive racial mixing, they might even move backward on the evolutionary trail.

Confronted with such ideas, and given Latin American elites' own perceptions of demographic realities in their respective nations, leading thinkers in the region embraced their demographic inheritance and set out to prove that it could in fact be a progressive demographic force. In this context, national censuses became privileged sites to confront the "civilized world's" predictions of a stagnant or regressive Latin American future. While taking a modern census in itself served as a formal signal of civilized nation status, published census reports served as ideal platforms

---

[5] Sommer, *Foundational Fictions*.

[6] The influence of European and North American racial theories on various aspects of Latin American political and intellectual development is the subject of a rich and still growing literature. See especially Stepan, *The Hour of Eugenics*; Graham, *The Idea of Race in Latin America*; Skidmore, *Black into White*; Helg, "Race in Argentina and Cuba, 1880–1930"; Hale, "Political and Social Ideas in Latin America"; Maio and Santos, *Raça, Ciência e Sociedade*, Lesser, *Welcoming the Undesireables*; Lesser, *Negotiating National Identity*; Schwarcz, *O Espetáculo das raças*; McCann, "The Formative Period of Twentieth-Century Brazilian Army Thought, 1900–1922"; Holloway, *Immigrants on the Land*; Bronfman, *Measures of Equality*.

for elaborating national statistical portraits that defied the grave predictions of racial determinist theories by presenting evidence of racially *re*generative Latin American populations.

In this chapter I analyze how Latin American officials used early national censuses to tell "stories of peoplehood,"[7] in the guise of neutral demographic description. More specifically, I examine how census officials produced and deployed racial statistics to craft narratives, build arguments, support claims, and draw conclusions about the essential nature and future prospects of Latin American nations. The analysis is based on a systematic review of all available national census reports produced by Latin American statistics agencies from independence through the 1940s, together with supplementary government documents, newspaper reports, and secondary sources.

The production of facts about racial demography in Latin America's early national censuses contributed to broad-based efforts by modernizing political and intellectual elites to reconcile the region's colonial inheritance—especially its demographic inheritance—with the idealized image of a modern nation-state. Supplementing international recommendations for modern census content, and eliding independence-era commitments to administrative color blindness, nearly all Latin American states distinguished citizens by "race" on at least one of their early national censuses. Even when race data were not collected in the census itself, census officials often drew on other sources to make observations about the racial makeup and trajectory of their populations in the context of census reports. Close reading of the statements made with racial statistics—and the silences imposed by their selective omission—reveals how the production of racial statistics served two principal and related nation-making aims: (1) to ground claims of national distinctiveness, and (2) to provide demographic evidence of national progress—defined in racial terms.

Against predictions that Latin America's racial demography blocked any real hope of development, census officials charted, in the internationally reputable language of statistics, the demographic pathways to recovery—and eventual prosperity—of Latin American nations. While the specific narratives told with statistics varied across the region and over time, the analysis reveals a common underlying plotline: Latin America's early national censuses showed populations undergoing progressive demographic movement toward a "whiter," or at least "lighter," future. Before turning to analysis of racial statistics in Latin America's early

---

[7] The phrase is borrowed from Smith, R., *Stories of Peoplehood*.

national censuses, I provide a brief overview of the ideological and political climate in which these statistical portraits of racially regenerative populations were produced.

Latin America through the Lens of Race Science

Viewed through the lens of the most influential nineteenth-century scientific theories of societal development, the future for most of Latin America looked rather grim.[8] The combination of racial determinism, social Darwinism, and Comptean positivism that suffused scientific thinking from around 1870 to the first part of the twentieth century all but condemned peoples of African or indigenous ancestry to perpetual backwardness. Racial determinist theories of human progress placed a dark cloud over the developmental aspirations of modernizing elites in much of Latin America.

Prevailing scientific theories predicted a less-than-glorious future for the emergent nations of Latin America. Even worse, leading intellectuals of the time explicitly invoked Latin American countries as *evidence* for their arguments concerning the perils of racial heterogeneity and intermixture for a nation's developmental prospects. Several prominent European and North American contributors to race science looked to Latin America to build and defend their theories that racial heterogeneity and intermixture lead to civilizational decline. Though there were some dissenting views, the dominant perspective described race mixture as detrimental to the vitality of a population as a whole, serving to decelerate or even reverse the progress of a nation. To take a notorious example, Arthur de Gobineau, the aristocratic French author of the *Essay on the Inequality of the Races* who is often cited as the founding father of the science of racial demography, pointed to Brazil's population as *prima facie* evidence of his theory that race mixture bred degeneracy. Drawing from his first-hand experience in Brazil during the 1870s as a diplomat for the French government, de Gobineau explained that "not a single Brazilian has pure blood because the pattern of marriages among whites, Indians, and Negroes is so widespread that the nuances of color are infinite, causing a degeneration of the most depressing type among the lower as well as the upper classes."[9]

---

[8] The following paragraphs provide a very brief overview of key themes in the well-developed literature on Latin American engagement with race science in the late nineteenth and early twentieth centuries. For more extended treatments of this issue, see works cited in note 6.

[9] de Gobineau, *Essai Sur L'Inégalité des Races Humaines*, cited in Skidmore, *Black into White*, 30.

The claim that miscegenation resulted in inferior offspring rested on the supposition that the traits of lesser races overcame those of superior ones upon extended contact. This contradictory proposition was argued explicitly by de Gobineau's student, Vacher de Lapouge, a lawyer-turned-anthropologist who spread the gospel of Francis Galton's theories of eugenics through his teaching and his influential book, *The Aryan and his Social Role* (1899). According to Lapouge, "[W]hen classes and races conflict, the inferior drives out the other.... Among well-known examples are the Antilles, where the white element has almost disappeared, and Haiti, where even the mulattoes have succumbed, giving way to African barbarism."[10] Lapouge saw in Latin America confirmation of the theory that race mixture yielded degeneracy. In another context, he pronounced that the Latin American republics had "arrived on the world scene too late, with a race which is too inferior. The only two nations of numerical importance are Mexico, where the Indian element has taken over, and Brazil, an immense Negro state returning to barbarism."[11]

One of the most prominent naturalists and zoologists of the nineteenth century, Louis Agassiz, also pointed to Latin America in support of his theories of innate racial inequality and the dire consequences of race mixture. Agassiz was born in Switzerland and studied and researched in Germany and France before moving to Harvard in the latter part of his career. In the United States, he became a vocal proponent of polygenecism (the theory of multiple Creations), by then a minority viewpoint among reputable scientists. Agassiz was most famous for his contributions to the natural sciences, but he leveraged his scientific authority to weigh in on the heated debates over race and social policy in the United States, arguing that desegregation and miscegenation were against the laws of nature (as designed by God). In a book coauthored with his wife and published in 1868 under the title *A Journey in Brazil*, Agassiz admonished, "Let any one who doubts the evil of this mixture of races, and is inclined, from a mistaken philanthropy, to break down all barriers between them, come to Brazil. He cannot deny the deterioration consequent upon an amalgamation of races, more wide-spread here than in any other country in the world, and which is rapidly effacing the best qualities of the white man, the Negro, and the Indian, leaving a mongrel nondescript type, deficient in physical and mental energy."[12]

---

[10] de Lapouge, *Les Sélections Sociales*, 66–7, cited in Skidmore, *Black into White*, 53, n39.

[11] de Lapouge, *L'Aryen*, 500, cited in Skidmore, *Black into White*, 53, n39.

[12] Agassiz and Agassiz, *A Journey in Brazil*, cited in Skidmore, *Black into White*, 31.

The dire predictions of race science concerning the implications of race mixture, along with the weight of evolutionary social thought more generally, bore heavily on the formation of Latin America's intellectual and political elite in this period. The ideas of Herbert Spencer, Arthur de Gobineau, and Gustav le Bon were particularly influential in Latin America.[13] Theories of racial difference combined with different measures of environmental, biological, or sociocultural determinism shaped the development of national scientific traditions and institutions in several Latin American countries.[14] The influence of evolutionary social thought also informed the design and implementation of an array of eugenicist-inspired state projects throughout the region that aimed to "civilize" Latin American populations, whether through educational reform, public health initiatives, military training, or other domesticating social institutions.[15]

If scientific treatises on the inequality of human races exerted a profound influence on leading thinkers and state actors in Latin America, this no doubt owed largely to the fact that they generally accepted the idea of natural inequality between races. Scientific racial theories found fertile ground in a region where centuries of colonial rule had presumed a natural hierarchy of humankinds and inscribed that hierarchy into law.[16] The idea of natural and inherent inequality between different types of humankind were not themselves novel imports to nineteenth-century Latin America. The elaboration and repackaging of these ideas as scientific knowledge, however, heightened the salience of racial social thought among Latin America's elite.[17] Scientific theories that asserted a direct link between a nation's racial composition and its prospects for development shifted the significance and raised the stakes of Latin America's colonial racial legacies.

Endowed with substantial—in some cases majority—populations of non-European descent, and with the weight of environmental and racial determinism conspiring against them, how could Latin American modernizers chart a viable path toward national progress? Just like foreign observers, Latin American leaders believed that large segments of their populations

---

[13] Stepan, *The Hour of Eugenics*. Charles Darwin was also influential, though his imprint on racialist and racist social thought in Latin America was more indirect and metaphorical than Spencer's or de Gobineau's, as his work on natural selection focused on plants and animals, not on "human kinds" (Guillaumin, "The Idea of Race and Its Elevation to Autonomous Scientific and Legal Status," 65, n3).

[14] Schwarcz, *O Espetáculo das raças*.

[15] See, for example, Holloway, *Immigrants on the Land*; Needell, *A Tropical Belle Epoque*; McCann, "The Formative Period of Twentieth-Century Brazilian Army Thought."

[16] da Costa, "The Myth of Racial Democracy."

[17] Schwarcz, *O Espetáculo das raças*.

were racially "impure," a product of miscegenation going back generations. In the words of nineteenth-century Brazilian liberal reformer Sílvio Romero, for example, "The Aryan race, combining here with two totally different races, has contributed to the creation of a mestiço and creole sub-race distinct from the European.... It helps little to discuss whether this is good or bad. It's a fact and that's enough."[18] It would seem, then, that the dominance of racial determinist theories of national development left Latin America's aspiring modernizers with little room for maneuver. Yet maneuver they did, crafting a range of scientific, literary, political, and practical responses to the challenge of making modern nations out of racially heterogeneous populations.

Crafting a Response

Many Latin American intellectual and political elites countered racial determinist theories with alternative theories of their own. As historian Thomas Skidmore demonstrated for the case of Brazil, leading thinkers refused to accept that "modern progress was meant only for white men in temperate zones."[19] In response to claims that their nations were tarnished by the presence of backward and inferior races, Latin American intellectuals crafted treatises, scientific papers, essays, literature, and art to champion the virtues of their *sui generis* national types, each forged through the mixture of distinct racial types.

Though they rarely rejected the foundational premise of a natural hierarchy of races, many Latin American writers broke from commonly held scientific views regarding the biological and social consequences of race mixture. Specifically, they sought to challenge the prevailing claim that race mixture necessarily led to deficient, inferior offspring and thus to the degeneration of national populations. A prominent critic of this view was João Batista de Lacerda, the director of Brazil's National Museum and author of an influential paper ("The Métis, or Half-Breeds of Brazil") presented at the First Universal Races Congress in London (1911). According to Lacerda, "Contrary to the opinion of many writers, the crossing of the black and the white does not generally produce offspring of an inferior intellectual quality."[20]

---

[18] The quotation is from 1888, as cited in Skidmore, *Black into White*, 35. Of course, and as discussed below, elites in different parts of Latin America differed in their assessments of whether and how much mestizaje would affect national development.

[19] Skidmore, *Black into White*, xxiii.

[20] Lacerda, "The Métis, or Half-Breeds of Brazil," cited in Skidmore, *Black into White*, 65.

In Brazil, he argued, "the children of métis have been found, in the third generation, to present all physical characters of the white race."[21] Back in Brazil, Lacerda's claim that the population would be whitened within the century sparked a heated debate—not so much over the substance of the prediction, but on the question of how long the whitening process would take.[22] In different contexts, intellectual and political elites drew on different strains of evolutionary science and pointed to different kinds of evidence to challenge theories of racial determinism.[23] Disagreements on finer points of fact and interpretation notwithstanding, many of Latin America's positivist-inspired modernizers converged in challenging the validity of the claim that miscegenation bred degeneracy.

Of course, there were significant exceptions. Some Latin American thinkers accepted the racial determinist argument that race mixture yielded degenerate human types. They lamented its consequences for their nations and advanced policies to mitigate its presumed-deleterious consequences. In Brazil, the doctor and scientist Nina Rodrigues, who worked to establish the fields of ethnology and legal medicine as a faculty member of the medical school in Bahia, invoked Agassiz's position on mixed-race degeneracy (cited above) and claimed that the presence of Africans in Brazil's population would "forever constitute one of the causes of our inferiority as a people."[24] In Bolivia, meanwhile, the intellectual Alcides Arguedas argued that the predominance of Indians—whom he compared with vicious disdain to domesticated animals—had condemned Bolivia to lag behind in its development:

> If Indian blood had not predominated, from the beginning the country would have had a conscious orientation to its life, adopting every means of material and moral perfection, and today it would be on the same level as many pueblos that were favored by immigrant streams from the old continent.[25]

---

[21] Lacerda, "The Métis, or Half-Breeds of Brazil," cited in Skidmore, *Black into White*, 66.

[22] Skidmore, *Black into White*, 65–9.

[23] See essays in Graham, *The Idea of Race in Latin America*; Bronfman, *Measures of Equality*. Historian Lilia M. Schwarcz (*O Espetáculo das raças*) showed how Brazilian scientists' perspectives on race and its implications for development were tied to their institutional connections to different sites and modes of knowledge production (ethnology, historical institutes, law schools, or medical schools). The nuances of their various arguments, elided here, mattered intently to these "men of science" at the time; they argued passionately over their different views.

[24] Rodrigues, *Os Africanos no Brasil*, 28, cited in Skidmore, *Black into White*, 60.

[25] Arguedas, *Pueblo Enfermo*, 32, cited in Zúñiga, "Las Metáforas del racismo," 41. Zúñiga notes that Arguedas' racist rationalizations for exclusion of indigenous peoples from national life remain influential in Bolivia to this day. In 2004, the conservative Bolivian president Carlos Mesa hailed the contemporary relevance of Arguedas' "sociological vision," calling for the re-publication of his complete works.

A contemporary of Arguedas, René Morelos, concluded in turn that Bolivia's progress required the exclusion if not elimination of highland Indians. Specifically, Morelos' modernization plan called for "the extinction of [the Indian] beneath the weight of European immigration, racial purification [*depuración*] to achieve unification of the national race, and mixture with [lighter-skinned, lowland] *camba* indians, but never with the [darker-skinned, highland] *aymara* and *quechua*."[26] In Argentina, to cite a final example, the scientist and author Carlos Octavio Bunge decried mestizaje as the fundamental problem with the region's populations. Bunge published cruel eugenicist tracts that applauded alcoholism, smallpox, and tuberculosis for their role in decimating Africans and Indians in the province of Buenos Aires.[27] In sum, a vocal subset of Latin America's modernizing elite dissented from the idea that race mixture was regenerative, and they contested the presumption that incorporation of Indians and blacks into the nation was inevitable, much less beneficial, for the pursuit of progress.

Overtly racial determinist arguments exerted some influence on nation-state building projects in this period, but they ultimately lost out to the influence of more "optimistic" views. The arguments of racial determinists probably received their most open reception in the context of debates over selective immigration bans; even strident defenders of the view that race mixture could be regenerative tended to agree with the determinists that it would be better not to add additional "inferior races" to the mix.[28] Racial determinist arguments also influenced domestic policies that actively marginalized or even sought to eliminate African or Indian populations in some contexts.[29] More broadly, however, those who steered national development projects in the late nineteenth and early twentieth century tended to discount pessimistic claims that miscegenation had put the evolutionary brake on development. Instead, they favored perspectives that embraced mestizaje as both an originating national trait and a key to national progress.

Among modernizing elites who believed that Latin America's populations could and would undergo processes of racial improvement, the men charged with conducting Latin America's early national censuses occupied

---

[26] Cited by Zúñiga, "Las Metáforas del racismo," 42.

[27] Terán, *Vida Intelectual en el Buenos Aires fin-de-Siglo*, 159, citing Bunge, *Nuestra América*.

[28] Fitzgerald and Cook-Martin, *Culling the Masses*; Skidmore, "Racial Ideas and Social Policy in Brazil"; Lesser, *Negotiating National Identity*.

[29] For example, "liberal" positivists who held racial determinist views championed campaigns to exterminate Indians in Argentina's "conquest of the desert" in the 1880s. Rodriguez, J., *Civilizing Argentina*.

a privileged place. The international legitimacy of the census as a means of collecting information about human populations, and the international legibility and authority of statistics as a medium for transforming that information into scientific knowledge, made official census reports ideal platforms for refuting the prognosis of populations in decline. Indeed, given the centrality of statistics to the original development and continued elaboration of racial determinist thought, there was no better medium through which to respond to its harsh condemnations of Latin America's populations.[30]

Contra the pessimistic pronunciations of international observers and their domestic adherents, Latin American census officials produced authoritative descriptions of populations moving steadily forward, not backward, in the race to progress. Published census reports combined textual narrative, graphic displays of data, and pages and pages of neatly ordered columns and rows of categorized numbers. The heavy tomes of presumed-to-be-factual information were presented to their audiences—principally political and scientific elites, domestic and international—as comprehensive, scientific portraits of modernizing nations. Using statistics—the same internationally legible and authoritative language that lent credence to racial determinist tracts—Latin American census officials presented evidence that mixture, in conjunction with other "progressive" demographic dynamics, generated racially "improved," (which nearly always meant "whiter") populations.

Of course, official accounts of the demographic progress of Latin American nations were far from uniform across the continent. In different parts of Latin America, distinct demographic realities set different "natural" constraints on the ways census officials could plausibly depict the racial status and projected transformation of national populations. In countries like Argentina and Chile, where by the latter part of the nineteenth century there were only small populations of African descent, surviving Indians were geographically and politically marginalized, and European immigration was on the rise, census officials could produce reports that projected a rapid and inevitable ascent into the ranks of homogenous, "white" nations. In contrast, in countries with significant indigenous populations, such as Mexico, Guatemala, Peru, and Bolivia, census officials tended to portray the demography of racial improvement in much more gradual terms. They trained their focus on the binary divide between those who were Indian

---

[30] The father of early eugenicist science, Francis Galton, was also a prolific contributor to the development of statistical methods.

and those who were not, and measured "progress" in evidence of movement across this divide—whether through mestizaje or because Indians stopped being "Indians" in the eyes of census officials when they moved to a city, stopped chewing coca leaves, and began to wear shoes. Meanwhile, in countries where the demographic legacy of centuries of African slavery was most profound, such as Colombia, Venezuela, the Dominican Republic, and, especially, Cuba and Brazil, census officials also presented the formation of national types as very much a work in progress. In these contexts, "progress" was often equated with evidence that blacks were being assimilated or absorbed, or were otherwise disappearing as a distinctive race within the nation.

In sum, in the late nineteenth and early twentieth centuries, the legacies of African slavery, the enduring presence of more or less loosely bounded indigenous populations, and immigration exerted varying degrees of influence on the political, economic, and ideological projects of modernizing Latin American nation-states. As a consequence, the plausible range of methodological and presentational strategies for elaborating statistical portraits of national populations varied as well. Census officials could exercise considerable creative license in their use of statistics to document regenerative demographic processes, as several examples presented in the sections that follow reveal. But to retain their credibility, official statistical portraits of the nation could not be completely divorced from prevailing perceptions of the objective demographic conditions they claimed to merely describe.

Documenting Racial Difference

As they conducted national censuses amid unfolding scientific debates about the limits of racial determinism, Latin American census officials in the late-nineteenth and early twentieth centuries marshaled racial statistics toward two distinct and somewhat contravening aims. On the one hand, the presentation of racial demographic data served to document the existence of originating racial heterogeneity, which was often parsed as the original font of national distinctiveness. On the other, racial statistics documented the gradual dissolution of that very heterogeneity; demographic processes were shown to be shifting populations toward a more homogenous and whiter future. The tension between these two uses of racial statistics was resolved in official census reports via discursive strategies that displaced diversity to the past or a transitory present, while heralding the disappearance of ethnoracial difference in the proximate or eventual future.

The presentation of demographic evidence that purported to document the decline of African or indigenous influence on the contemporary national population created space to acknowledge the distinguishing mark of non-European peoples on the nation's conception. In some census reports, this moment of conception was located far in the colonial past. In others, it was more ambiguously situated in or near the present. Either way, the constitutive racial elements of the nation were often described in great detail, underscoring not only the mixture of races at the founding of Latin American nations, but differentiating the particular kinds of each race that went into the mix as a way to distinguish each nation from all others.

In countries where census results showed large indigenous populations, for example, official reports often devoted sustained attention to cataloguing the internal diversity of the "Indian" category. Illustratively, the first national census of Bolivia included extended discussion of the diverse indigenous populations within its borders. A report on the 1846 Bolivian census titled "A Statistical Sketch of Bolivia" included an essay, "On the Races and their Relations," by the preeminent Bolivian social scientist Jorge Delance.[31] The essay described the component races of Bolivia, beginning with a brief mention of that "well-known race," the Spaniards, who are "endowed with physical qualities of a superior order, and with a natural intelligence" that put them among "the most favored *pueblos* of Europe." The majority of the essay, however, focused on the qualities of Bolivian "aborigines," defending their worth against likely inferences to the contrary, and asserting their close relation to the "Caucasian race." In the words of Delance:

> The Indians of our sierras...are not inept at the arts or sciences, nor inadequate at maritime trades, nor disquiet, nor fond of war, nor vindictive, any more than other men. In the vast cemeteries of Carangas, I've seen over one thousand [Indian] mummies; and I did not detect in their skulls anything but the same accidental diversity that is observed in the skulls of the Caucasian race, that is, that some are bigger than others, some more spherical and some less so, etc., and nothing that would otherwise distinguish them.

---

[31] According to historian Herbert Klein, Delance's "statistical work on national society clearly earns for him the title of the father of the social sciences in Bolivia. His efforts at the systematic reconstruction of the social and economic structure of the nation in the 1840s were unique, and the intelligence and sophistication of his work mark him as a social analyst conversant with the latest European developments" (Klein, *A Concise History of Bolivia*, 149–50).

> The intellectual force of our Indians cannot be placed in doubt, without infamy; indeed, it is notorious that despite the indifference with which they have always and continue to look at their [formal] education and instruction, to the extreme that many of them have never even seen their own parish priests, there cannot be found among them men as stupid as the miners of Cornwall and lower Brittany; it is also the case that of the small number of Indians that fate has driven to the profession of letters, many of them have distinguished themselves; the most eloquent and profound lawyer there has ever been in Charcas and who is an honor to Bolivians, was an Indian.[32]

Delance claimed that certain Bolivian Indians "demonstrate the same aptitudes as Europeans" and that this was no coincidence because the Bolivian aborigines of the sierras are related [*son parientes*] to whites, "another variety of the same [Caucasian] race." For this reason, the author argued, "these men of nature are indistinguishable from the Caucasian race, except in minor details...." The author continued: "Which is why I judge that just like the Hindustani [*Indostana*] family is reputed to be a variety of the Caucasian race, despite their color and wide heads, oval faces, smooth and dark hair, and small thin bodies, so our Quichua and Aimarae Indians are another variety of the same [Caucasian] race, despite their oval-shaped [*orvicular*] eyes and small feet." The Mojos and Chiquitos, in turn, "equal men of the European race in equal circumstances," while the Guarayos and Sirionós "are clearly descendants of the groups of Spanish explorers that got lost in the forests."[33]

The differentiation of indigenous tribes by name, the affirmation of their distinctive merits, and the assertion of their proximity to Spaniards on the family tree of a common humanity, all served to valorize the non-European elements that went into making the modern Bolivian nation. Delance's essay thus heralded the unique combination of ingredients that comprised Bolivians as a distinctive people. At the same time, the essay pitched a preemptive defense against those who would read the raw numbers of Boliva's racial composition at mid-nineteenth century through a racially determinist lens. The majority "Indian" population of Bolivia should not be misread as foreshadowing a less than prosperous future for the nation-in-formation.

Five decades later, in 1900, Bolivia's census showed a population that was still majority indigenous (50.91 percent). Again, the official census

---

[32] Delance, *Bosquejo Estadístico de Bolivia*, 199.
[33] Delance, *Bosquejo Estadístico de Bolivia*, 200.

report devoted several pages to describing the virtuous characteristics of the various pueblos, branches [*ramas*], and "nations" of Bolivia's indigenous peoples—only 9 percent of whom, it was reported, still lived "in a state of barbarism."[34] After proclaiming that the diverse indigenous races of Bolivia were destined to disappear, the author of the census report affirmed that each of them had "contributed to stamping the peculiar character of the nationality that has formed within the limits that today constitute the Republic of Bolivia."[35]

The distinguishing "stamp" of indigenous origins was also highlighted in the censuses of Guatemala and Mexico. In these cases, census reports often focused attention on the diversity of indigenous peoples who comprised the "Indian" segment of national populations by emphasizing the array of native languages spoken within the state's territory.[36] Linguistic diversity received extensive treatment in Mexican censuses. A language query was included on Mexican census questionnaires beginning in 1895, and published reports presented detailed tables of Mexico's indigenous population according to language spoken. The 1895 Mexican census report presented tables titled "population according to habitually-spoken language [*idioma habitual*]," with numbers of speakers of various indigenous languages broken down by state and municipality. The list was extensive, including twenty different indigenous languages.[37]

Mexico's 1900 census included a separate query on "Mexican languages." The varied responses were presented in tables grouped under the subheadings "Indigenous Languages," "Castellano," and "Foreign Languages." In the report on the 1920 Mexican census, in turn, indigenous and foreign languages were implicitly marked as the tongues of outsiders, juxtaposed to the "national language" in official tables. As seen in figure 4.1, the total population of Mexico was divided into speakers of three major language

---

[34] Bolivia. Oficina Nacional de Inmigración, Estadística y Propaganda Geográfica. *Censo General de la Población*, 28.

[35] Bolivia. Oficina Nacional de Inmigración, Estadística y Propaganda Geográfica. *Censo General de la Población*, 25.

[36] The attention to distinctive indigenous cultures within the nation coincided with the rise of *indigenismo* as a literary and political movement in the early twentieth century. For an introduction to the large literature on indigenismo, see Prieto, "The Literature of Indigenism." On Mexico, see also Stabb, "Indigenism and Racism in Mexican Thought," and Powell, "Mexican Intellectuals and the Indian Question, 1876–1911"; on Peru, Chevalier, "Official *Indigenismo* in Peru"; on Ecuador, Radcliffe and Westwood, *Remaking the Nation*.

[37] The languages listed in the 1895 Mexican census report included: cahita, ópata, pápago, pima, seri, zapoteca, otomí, chiapaneco, chol, chontal, maya, mexicano, tarasco, popoloco, tzendal, zoque, cora, huichol, huaxteco, chinateco.

ESTADOS UNIDOS MEXICANOS

CUADRO 8

IDIOMA NATIVO

IDIOMAS Y DIALECTOS	CENSO DE 1910			CENSO DE 1921		
	Hombres	Mujeres	TOTAL	Hombres	Mujeres	TOTAL
Nacionales						
Idioma Oficial: Español.........	6 505 809	6 637 563	13 143 372	5 118 804	5 463 802	10 582 606
Indígenas						
Amusgo..............................	4 688	4 536	9 224	2 400	2 407	4 807
Cochimí.............................	44	52	96	5	2	7
Cocopa o Cucapá..................	......	......	......	12	8	20
Cora.................................	3 950	3 518	7 468	173	168	341
Cuicateco...........................	2 140	2 577	4 717	4 661	4 926	9 587
Chañabal...........................	2 770	2 751	5 521	1	2	3
Chatinteco.........................	5 799	5 882	11 681	1	2	3
Chiapaneco........................	1	3	4	226	240	466
Chinanteco........................	10 415	11 330	21 745	9 925	10 564	20 489
Chocho.............................	......	......	......	719	833	1 552
Chol................................	6 278	6 059	12 337	5 296	5 039	10 335
Chontal............................	12 464	12 979	25 443	11 240	12 618	23 858
Huasteco...........................	26 340	25 723	52 063	14 947	14 746	29 693
Huave o Juave....................	2 193	2 183	4 376	1 575	1 656	3 231
Huichol............................	2 215	2 212	4 427	191	173	364
Kikapóo............................	146	116	262	164	155	319
Mame...............................	688	667	1 355	3 181	2 979	6 160
Matlatzinca o Pirinda...........	1 449	1 536	2 985	152	246	398
Maya...............................	112 426	115 457	227 883	119 020	115 655	234 675
Mayo...............................	8 588	8 197	16 785	6 219	5 969	12 188
Mazahua...........................	30 697	35 231	65 928	33 341	34 711	68 052
Mazateco..........................	17 245	18 931	36 176	19 396	20 205	39 601
Mexicano o Náhuatl.............	252 687	264 469	517 156	231 722	240 968	472 690
Mixe...............................	16 405	17 143	33 548	12 571	13 484	26 055
Mixteco............................	80 959	85 198	166 157	76 707	79 761	156 468
Opata..............................	23	20	43	18	26	44
Otomí..............................	98 706	110 934	209 640	103 820	108 391	212 211
Pame...............................	865	808	1 673	37	34	71
Pápago.............................	162	159	321	98	75	173
Popoloca...........................	5 554	6 411	11 965	7 236	8 069	15 305
Seri.................................	......	......	......	2	1	3
Tarahumar.........................	11 353	10 185	21 538	12 507	11 091	23 598
Tarasco............................	18 167	19 006	37 173	16 727	17 621	34 348
Tepecano..........................	......	......	......	14	2	16
Tepehua...........................	......	......	......	810	808	1 618
Tepehuano........................	4 353	4 088	8 441	986	848	1 834
Totonaco..........................	33 827	33 913	67 740	31 798	32 411	64 209
Triqui..............................	1 344	1 460	2 804	2 106	2 002	4 108
Tzendal o Sental.................	22 824	24 136	46 960	12 854	13 023	25 877
Tzőlzil.............................	22 183	22 598	44 781	10 819	10 537	21 356
Yaqui..............................	2 664	2 511	5 175	1 516	1 167	2 683
Zapoteco..........................	108 411	116 452	224 863	103 363	111 223	214 586
Zoque..............................	3 999	4 471	8 470	7 188	7 753	14 941
Otras lenguas indígenas, además de las enumeradas.......	5 345	5 528	10 873	30 830	31 671	62 501
Se ignora el idioma y dialecto que hablan.......................	15 838	14 671	30 509	......	......	......
SUMAS...............	956 205	1 004 101	1 960 306	896 674	924 270	1 820 944
Extranjeros						
Alemán............................	2 960	1 172	4 132	2 672	1 100	3 772
Arabe..............................	2 428	1 117	3 545	3 467	1 953	5 420
Catalán............................	......	......	......	207	59	266
Chino..............................	12 819	153	12 972	14 323	191	14 514

FIGURE 4.1 Language Groups Reported in the Census of Mexico, 1921.
SOURCE: Mexico. *Resumen del censo general de habitantes de 30 de noviembre de 1921*, 69.

groups (with various subclassifications): "National Languages" (with only one option, *Idioma Oficial: Español*), "Indigenous" (including forty-three categories plus an additional category for other indigenous languages beyond those enumerated), and "Foreign" (including twenty-two nationality categories—among them, "Hebreo"—and separate categories for "other" and "unknown." Only the first four nationality categories are shown in Figure 4.1).

The display of linguistic diversity in this format revealed the richness of Mexico's indigenous (and immigrant) heritage while suggesting the nationalist ideal of gradual linguistic assimilation. Becoming part of the *national* community was equated, via the categorical headings in the official tables, with acquisition of Spanish as the dominant language of daily life.[38]

In a similar vein, Guatemalan census reports showed how multiple indigenous languages coexisted alongside Spanish as the dominant linguistic force. The Guatemalan censuses of 1921 and 1940 included a question on "mother tongue" and the published results reported the numbers who spoke various indigenous languages. The resulting tables, such as the example reproduced in figure 4.2, highlighted the existence of a distinctive combination of indigenous elements within the nation, while leaving no doubt of the overwhelming and inevitable numerical dominance of the nation's Spanish-speaking, European face.

The tendency to underscore not only the racial heterogeneity of the nation's origins but the particular strains of each race that went into the mix was most common in countries with proportionately large indigenous populations. In some cases, this discursive approach was also deployed in countries with large and visible population of African descent. In the narrative prelude to Brazil's 1920 census results, for example, Brazilian author Oliveira Vianna penned a defense of the Brazilian racial type that relied, in part, on careful description of the particular varieties of Europeans, Africans, and Indians that had gone into the colonial mix.[39] Vianna argued, for example, that the "Nordic-European type"—pinnacle of de Lapouge's much-touted racial taxonomic hierarchy—played a more significant role in

---

[38] The net decline in Mexico's total population between 1910 and 1920, evident in Figure 4.1, owes primarily to massive loss of human life in the Mexican Revolution. See McCaa, "Missing Millions."

[39] The introduction to the 1920 Brazilian census was written by Oliveiro Vianna at the invitation of the Director of the *Directoria Geral de Estatística*, Bulhões Carvalho. The essay was subsequently published under Vianna's name with the title *Evolução do Povo Brasileiro*. But in the 1920 Census report it appeared anonymously, thus taking on the guise of institutional authority and neutrality as an integral part of the central statistics agency's preeminent official publication. On Oliveira Vianna's writings, see sources cited in Needell, "History, Race and the State in the Thought of Oliveira Vianna," 1, n1.

POBLACION NACIONAL

LENGUA MATERNA	Habitantes	Tanto %
Castellana	104,667	90.28
Quiché	1,219	1.05
Cakchiquel	4,483	3.87
Sutohil	254	0.22
Quekchi	246	0.21
Pocomchi	55	0.05
Mam	279	0.24
Pipil	97	0.08
Suma	111,300	96.00
Población de extranjeros	4,628	4.00
Total	115,938	100.00

FIGURE 4.2 Language Groups Reported in the Census of Guatemala, 1921.
SOURCE: Guatemala. Ministerio de Fomento. Dirección General de Estadística. *Censo de la población de la república levantado el 28 de agosto de 1921.* Guatemala: Talleres Gutenberg, 1924.

the early colonization of Brazil than the less-remarkable Portuguese. The white element in Brazil's conception was thus of premier racial quality.[40] The particular African and indigenous races that went into the Brazilian mix were also specified, with comments to the effect that the majority of Africans brought to Brazil as slaves were not of the "most inferior types," and some of them even approximated "European standards of beauty."

The discursive emphasis on the specific racial kinds implicated in the conception of distinct national types was a common trope in Latin American census reports in the late nineteenth and early twentieth centuries. Heterogeneous racial origins were explicitly acknowledged as a constitutive fact of national demographic history. Originating racial heterogeneity imbued each Latin American nation with its ineffably unique essence, making it a distinctive nation among others. Even as the influence of non-European races in the original constitution of modern Latin American nations was openly acknowledged, however, it was simultaneously dislocated to a mythic founding moment or a transitory present.

Looking to the future, the authors of census reports affirmed that traces of African and Indian influence would be submerged and dissipated by unfolding demographic processes. The foundational kernel of distinction born of race mixture would remain, but the outward manifestation of "the people," the nation, would trend in a progressively more homogenous—and whiter—direction.

---

[40] This claim, which degraded the role of the Portuguese in the development of Brazilian civilization, was the primary focus of the essay's contemporary critics (Vianna, *Evolução do Povo Brasileiro*, foreword to second and third editions).

Charting Racial Progress

The presentation of selected facts of racial demographic history served to establish the distinctive origins of Latin American nations, but this was not the overriding purpose to which racial statistics in census reports were put. More often, and more emphatically, racial statistics were presented and parsed as critical indicators of the nation's future prospects.[41] Emblematic of this perspective, the introduction to the 1930 Honduran census proclaimed:

> No statistics are more important than those that refer to Demography, because [demographic statistics] reveal with the eloquence of numbers the vital power of the race, and it is according to demographic statistics that state elites [*estadistas*] are to form their hopes for the future.[42]

From an array of numerical indicators that spoke to the level of development of Latin American nations, the authors of census reports tended to underscore demographic statistics— especially racial statistics—as uniquely critical and revealing. Latin American state and nation builders came to read facts of racial demography as pivotal measures of national progress.

In Latin America's early national censuses, national progress was frequently defined in racial terms. This did not always or necessarily mean that progress was understood to inhere strictly in biological evolutionary processes. Like other scientists and intellectuals who wrote about race in this period, those who authored the official reports on census results often trafficked in the haziness of the boundary between biology and culture; cultural phenomena were often naturalized, while physiological attributes were often attributed to cultural practices.[43] Census officials drew on strains of racial thought that acknowledged natural racial hierarchy while also admitting some degree of mutability of inherited traits at the individual or collective level, either within or across generations. Census officials described race as given (by nature or God), yet they also asserted that races could change. Indeed, while they sometimes wavered in their predictions of its pace and ultimate destination, they never questioned the *possibility* of racial change as a means of national improvement.

---

[41] Part of this section is drawn from Loveman, M., "Whiteness in Latin America."

[42] Honduras. Dirección General de Estadística, *Resumen del Censo General,* 12.

[43] On the concepts of culture and biology in Latin American social thought, see the work of anthropologist Peter Wade, especially, *Race, Nature and Culture*. On the way racial ideologies in general traffic in the multivalent meanings of the race concept, see Wacquant, "For an Analytic of Racial Domination."

Latin American census takers confronted varied demographic and social realities as they endeavored to chart the racial progress of their nations. Real differences in social and demographic conditions were refracted through the sometimes idiosyncratic analytical lenses of particular thinkers who were charged with authoring the first census reports in the region. Yet running through the varied narrative threads contained in the census reports of different countries, and the shifts in narrative emphasis in the census reports of the same country at different points in time, there is a striking similarity in the basic underlying story: populations steadily undergoing racial-demographic change in a "progressive" direction.

Latin American census reports from this period drew attention to three principal demographic processes fueling the racial improvement of populations: natural and social selection, immigration, and race mixture (*mestizaje*). With varying weight in different contexts, these demographic processes were parsed in census reports as both engines and indicators of national progress. The authors of census reports used official statistics—including, at times, their selective omission—to document and demonstrate how these fundamental demographic dynamics moved Latin American populations in a progressively whiter direction.

Natural and Social Selection

Late nineteenth- and early twentieth-century census reports often showcased statistics that purportedly showed selective processes gradually yielding whiter populations. Side-by-side comparison of fertility and mortality rates by race revealed higher rates of reproduction among whites and lower rates of reproduction by Indians and blacks. For the most part, those who penned census reports showed little interest in sorting out the underlying reasons for these racial disparities. They simply reported the numbers matter-of-factly, perhaps adding subtle or not-so-subtle comments welcoming the evidence that whites were gradually overtaking other racial elements in the national population. When the causes of racial disparities in fertility or mortality were broached at all, they were apt to be glossed as evidence of natural inferiority of blacks or Indians. That the disparities might be socially generated rather than biological in origin did not usually warrant comment in official census reports.[44]

---

[44] In broader fields of scientific and policy debates within individual countries, the sources of such disparities were a focus of debate. Social reformers in many countries highlighted environmental and cultural obstacles to demographic vitality, arguing for improvement in access to basic sanitation, nutrition, and education as crucial for national progress.

Higher rates of natural increase for whites were reported in census publications of several Latin American countries in this period. For instance, the author of the report on the 1848 Bolivian census concluded his discussion of "the Races and their Relations" with the presentation of comparative data on the rates of reproduction of whites and indios. Notwithstanding the paragraphs of text devoted to establishing the near-whiteness of Bolivia's indigenous peoples, the author finished his report by presenting numbers that showed a higher birth rate for whites than for Indians. Sizing up these numbers, he concluded with an air of relief, "the white is multiplying more than the other."[45]

Arranged in misleadingly clear comparative tables, official statistics seemed to provide irrefutable evidence of populations trending naturally in a whiter direction. Most of the time, such tables were presented without too much in the way of editorial comment. But sometimes the accompanying commentary was decidedly triumphant. Such was the case in Vianna's introduction to the 1920 Brazilian census. Presenting a table comparing the racial composition of the population in 1872 and 1890, Vianna wrote: "The delicate and complex mechanism of ethnic selection has been explained in the previous paragraphs; however, the demonstration of the excellence of its effects is this statistical table" (See figure 4.3).

ANNOS	Brancos %	Negros %	Indios %	Mestiços %
1872	38.1	19.7	3.9	38.3
1890	44.0	14.6	9.0	32.4

FIGURE 4.3 A Demonstration of the "Excellent" Effects of Ethnic Selection in the Census of Brazil, 1920.
SOURCE: Directoria Geral de Estatística. *Recenseamento do Brazil... 1920*, v.1, 343.

Analyzing the numbers, Vianna celebrated the increase in the white share of the population at the expense of blacks and *mestiços*, while glossing over the substantial increase in the Indian share of the population:

> As can be seen, the coefficient of *Homo afer* in our population declined, in less than twenty years, from 19.7 to 14.6....Although there was a certain increase in the contingent of *Homo americanus*, the two most impressive facts of this table, which shows the ethnic balance of our people [povo] in

---
[45] Delance, *Bosquejo Estadístico de Bolivia*, 205.

less than twenty years of evolution, are those that refer to the Aryan contingent and the numerous mass of *mestiços*. The latter, which make up 38.3% of our population in 1872, are reduced, in less than twenty years, to 32.4%. A large number of these *mestiços* were eliminated by death while others, lightened [*clarificados*] through the subtle work of sexual selection, passed over to the white column. The whites, who represent 38% of the population in 1872 are already 44% in 1890: that is, as the blacks declined by 5.1% and the mestiços by 5.9%, the volume of the white population increased by nearly 5.9%."[46]

Vianna was even more excited about the demographic trend in the southern region of the country. Presenting a second table with data only from Rio Grande do Sul, he noted that "the reduction of the coefficient of the inferior races is even faster" in "certain zones of intense aryan immigration." The table showed the white share of the population increasing from 59.4 percent to 70.2 percent between 1872 and 1890, while the black and Indian shares declined from 18.3 percent to 8.7 percent and from 5.9 percent to 5.4 percent, respectively. He chose to omit the mestiço category, perhaps because the results for that column were less "impressive" in the south (assuming the total across categories summed to 100 percent, the mestiço column would have shown a 0.7 percent increase across censuses). Summing up the statistical trend, Vianna enthused, "See how fast the destruction of the black population is in the extreme south.... In contrast to the descendent evolution of the two inferior types [we can see] the magnificent ascendant movement of the aryan type."[47]

The presentation of descriptive statistics showing change in racial composition between two censuses appeared to vividly document a dramatically shrinking black share of Brazil's population and a gradual but inevitable dominance of the white share over the others. Meanwhile, however, fundamental changes in the composition of the category set used for enumeration between 1872 and 1890 went uncommented. Moreover, there was no discussion of the significant—and by then openly recognized—deficiencies in the execution of the 1890 census that rendered the results dubious at best.[48] The official statistics were reported as transparent facts; the numbers could not be refuted. Further, the differential growth rates were invoked to slam the predictions of race scientists as

---

[46] Brazil. Directoría Geral de Estatística, *Recenseamento do Brazil*, 343.
[47] Brazil. Directoría Geral de Estatística, *Recenseamento do Brazil*, 344.
[48] See M. Loveman, "The Race to Progress"; Senra, *História das Estatísticas Brasileiras*.

demonstrably incorrect. In the text beneath a statistical table that reported birth and death rates by race, Vianna noted:

> Processes of natural and social selection accelerate extraordinarily among us the rapidity of the process of reduction of the ethnically inferior elements.... Even if the initial numbers of each group were equal, the ultimate preponderance of the white group would be inevitable.... Neither Lapouge nor Le Bon foresaw this surprising outcome of the operation of ethnic selection in the tropics.... When those great scholars, with their high authority as anthropologist and sociologist prophesize that 'Within a century Brazil will become an immense Negro state, so long as it does not return to barbarism, which is quite probable,' we have, without doubt and without the slightest irreverence, the right to smile.[49]

While such direct confrontation with specific race theorists was unusual in census reports, it was a common tactic to report statistics that contradicted predictions of overall population decline by showing more rapid increase of white segments of the population.

A triumphal tenor also reverberated in the presentation of results from Cuba's 1899 census.[50] Taken immediately after gaining independence from Spain, while the country was still under US military occupation, the published census report (which appeared in English) was composed by officers of the US War Department and was clearly oriented to a North American audience. Perhaps for this reason, the description of statistics that showed a decline in the "colored" population revealed a particularly blatant social-Darwinist spin. For instance, following a table that reported the changing percentage of the Cuban population that was "white" and "colored" from 1775 to 1899, the report's author explained:

> The reason for the great increase in the number and proportion of the colored up to 1841 is doubtless the continued importation of blacks from Africa, which persisted, in the form of smuggling, long after its official

---

[49] Brazil. Directoría Geral de Estatística, *Recenseamento do Brazil*, 340.

[50] In some respects, the Cuban census was a different sort of document than the other censuses mentioned so far because it was conducted and published under the auspices of the US War Department, following the US victory in the Spanish—(Cuban)—American war. The census was taken while Cuba was under direct US military control, with the express purpose of discovering the number and type of eligible voters under newly promulgated election laws. The enumeration was thus restricted to males over 21 years of age. In contrast to the other published censuses considered, then, this census was not a self-portrait of a modernizing nation. Rather, it was a snapshot taken by an imperialist state with clearly defined pragmatic ends.

prohibition. Their diminution relative to the whites, during the last half century, is doubtless but another illustration of the inability of an inferior race to hold its own in competition with a superior one, a truth which is being demonstrated on a much larger scale in the United States.[51]

Unlike the other censuses considered, the presentation and analysis of racial statistics in this Cuban census reflected the imperialist and racist gaze of the US War Department. It is thus interesting to note that the "survival of the fittest" imagery in the Cuban census, which suggests explicit and fatal competition between the races, contrasts with the image of more inadvertent and pacific selective processes highlighted in the censuses of other Latin American countries. Still, the Cuban census report was like others in pointing to the more rapid increase of the white share of the population and attributing this advantage, at least in part, to naturally unfolding "selective" processes.

In addition to noting the more rapid increase of whites, the authors of census reports also drew explicit attention to statistics that suggested the slow growth or even rapid decline of African or indigenous shares of the population. For example, the Bolivian census of 1900 relied on comparative estimates from 1846 to observe that "the black race in Bolivia is rapidly diminishing."[52] Similarly, the introduction to the El Salvadoran census of 1929 noted that "in our judgment the percentage of *negros* and *amarillos* [members of 'yellow races']—races that for reasons of eugenics can be considered *non gratas*—is shrinking."[53] Remarkably, this judgment was offered despite the acknowledged "absence of earlier censuses for comparison," which made it impossible "to affirm if the percentages are increasing or diminishing."[54]

The absence of actual data on fertility and mortality by race rarely stopped the authors of census reports from noting that populations of indigenous and African descent were naturally declining as a share of total populations. Emblematic of this, Argentina's census reports included detailed accounts of the factors that contributed to the disappearance of Africans and Indians from the nation. Among the mechanisms reported to be at work, disparities in life expectancy featured prominently. The report

---

[51] United States. War Department, *Census of Cuba 1899*, 97.

[52] Bolivia. Oficina Nacional, *Censo General de la Población*, 30.

[53] El Salvador. Dirección General del Censo, *Censo de Población*, 52. This was a census of the Municipality of San Salvador, taken in preparation for the national census of 1930.

[54] El Salvador. Dirección General del Censo, *Censo de Población*, 52.

on Argentina's second national census, in 1895—which did not include a race query—cited as fact that "the African race, just like the Indian race, is less fertile than the Caucasian; in addition, more of their children succumb during infancy; pulmonary disease wreaks havoc among blacks and mulattos, and their fertile period is shorter than that of white women."[55] Africans' putatively higher mortality was noted repeatedly in Argentine census reports from the late nineteenth century through the mid-twentieth. Such claims supported the broader assertion that Afro-Argentines had disappeared from Argentina's population, while helping to justifying the lack of race queries in censuses that might have generated demographic data to the contrary.[56]

In Argentina as elsewhere, differential rates of "natural" increase were said to be gradually shifting populations in a more homogenous and whiter direction. Parsed as the unfolding of selective processes, racial disparities in fertility and mortality were seen as steady and sure engines of demographic change. But as engines of desired demographic change, selective processes were also seen to be lamentably slow. Perhaps for this reason, census directors and their staffs rarely pinned their assessments of racial progress exclusively on differential rates of growth among existing segments of their populations. In addition, they looked optimistically to statistics that measured the influx of new bodies into the nation.

Immigration

The authors of Latin America's early national census reports greeted evidence of the arrival of immigrants with great enthusiasm. More specifically, they celebrated the arrival of Europeans. Best estimates indicate that some 13 million European immigrants arrived in Latin America from 1870 to 1930 (not taking into account return migration). Most went to Argentina, Brazil, and Cuba, with more moderate flows to Venezuela, Chile, Mexico, and elsewhere.[57] Immigration to Latin America grew steadily in

---

[55] Argentina. Comisión Directiva del Censo, *Segundo Censo de la República Argentina*, II: XLVII, cited in Otero, *Estadística y Nación*, 363, n53. According to Otero, some other state agencies collected race data in this period. It is possible that studies based on data from those agencies informed comments in census reports (though there is no citation to other data in the census report).

[56] On this point, see Otero, *Estadística y Nación*, 361–2; Andrews, *The Afro-Argentines of Buenos Aires*.

[57] See Mckeown, "Global Migration, 1846–1940"; Thistlethwaite, "Migration from Europe Overseas in the Nineteenth and Twentieth Centuries"; de Lapouge, *Les Sélections Sociales*; Sánchez-Alonso, "Algunas Reflexiones Sobre las Políticas de Inmigración en América Latina"; Hatton and Williamson, *The Age of Mass Migration*.

the final decades of the nineteenth century, reached a peak in the 1910s, and declined by the 1930s.[58] Whether census results revealed a flood of European immigrants or a scant trickle, the influx was construed as a much-welcomed booster shot for the demography of racial "improvement." Statistics that showed growing numbers of European immigrants were frequently heralded as both a sign and an assurance of national advancement.

Census officials did not necessarily see all kinds of European immigrants as equally desirable. During the last decades of the nineteenth century and the first of the twentieth, Latin American statesmen and scientists debated the relative merits of different kinds of European immigrants. These debates echoed, rather faintly, the often vicious debates over the variable quality of different European nationalities pouring into the United States in these decades.[59] It is important to recall in this context that during this period, different nationalities were often seen as racially distinct. Scientists wrote of the racial differences between Germans, French, and Italians—and even subsets of these—even as governments in the Americas classified all of them as "white."[60] In the realm of immigration policy, these debates translated into incentive programs for some types of European immigrants (such as promotional campaigns in countries of origin, direct subsidies for travel and settlement, easy naturalization regimes) and obstacles to immigration for others (such as targeted restrictions against non-Catholics or "anarchists").[61] In the context of national census reports, however, concerns about the relative merits of different European races were not usually belabored. Statistical tables broke down numbers of arrivals by country of origin, but the analyses typically lumped Europeans together in generalized assessments of the beneficial influence of "whites."

Statistics that pointed to the immigration of Africans or Asians, in contrast, were typically downplayed or outright ignored. Nearly all countries in the Americas imposed legal restrictions to bar or slow the entrance of "undesired" immigrants at some point during this period.[62] In some contexts, these restrictions took the form of explicit racial bans—against,

---

[58] For a regional overview of immigration laws and flows to the Americas in this period, see Cook-Martin and Fitzgerald, "Liberalism and the Limits of Inclusion."

[59] See Guglielmo, *White on Arrival*; Roediger, *Wages of Whiteness*; Ignatiev, *How the Irish Became White*; Kolchin, "Whiteness Studies."

[60] Guglielmo, *White on Arrival*; Kolchin, "Whiteness Studies."

[61] Fitzgerald and Cook-Martín, *Culling the Masses*; Lesser, *Welcoming the Undesirables*.

[62] See Fitzgerald and Cook-Martín, *Culling the Masses*.

for example, members of "yellow races," regardless of country of provenance.[63] Proponents of restrictive immigration laws often levied explicitly racist arguments to justify selective exclusion of immigrants. In Brazil, for example, legislators opposed a proposal by planters to import Chinese workers in the 1870s on the grounds that the "degenerate" Chinese would "pervert and corrupt our race even further."[64] On occasion, muted versions of this type of concern appeared in the pages of national census reports. For the most part, however, census officials simply elided discussion of statistics that tracked the arrival of non-European immigrants, focusing on the inflow of "whites" instead.

Statistics that documented the arrival and permanence of European immigrants filled pages of Latin American census reports in this period. How *many* pages devoted to analysis of immigration statistics varied greatly by country; the authors of Argentine census reports had a lot more material to work with than their counterparts in Guatemala, El Salvador, or Bolivia. Yet even countries that witnessed very little European immigration in these decades often took space in their official census reports to flag the importance of European immigration to the future prospects of the nation.

A prime example of such an unlikely suspect heralding the significance of European immigration for national progress is Guatemala. The director of Guatemala's 1893 census noted in the introduction to his official report, "immigration has been encouraged for many years, but we have not been able to devote resources to promoting it due to the current requirements for organizing public services within the country in accordance with the demands of our epoch. But despite this, foreign immigrants constantly arrive in the country and the conditions are expeditious for [immigrants] to prosper."[65] It was suggested that the "shadow" cast over Guatemalan development and progress by the "indifference" and "passive attitudes" of the indigenous numerical majority could be counteracted [*neutralizado*], in part, "by European and North American immigrants, who are energetic and hardworking, if not as numerous as would be ideal." In addition to their cultural and economic contributions to the vitality of the nation, the author of the report noted, immigrants would help to improve the "quality"

---

[63] In other contexts, selective sourcing of immigrants was managed through religious or ideological proscriptions (barring entrance to "anarchists," for example). For discussion of categories used to selectively ban or limit immigration to Latin American countries in this period, see Cook-Martín and Fitzgerald, "Liberalism and the Limits of Inclusion."

[64] Skidmore, *Black into White*, 26, citing abolitionist Joaquim Nabuco.

[65] Guatemala. Dirección General de Estadística, *Censo General de la República de Guatemala... 1893*, 15.

["calidad"] of the national population through their "contribution to national robustness."[66]

In part, the benefits of European immigration for Latin American populations were construed in sociocultural terms. European immigrants were welcomed for their desired labor skills, mental discipline, and industrious habits. But such claims often spilled over seamlessly into arguments that alluded to the self-evident benefits of European immigrants by virtue of their *being* European, and thus superior, "white," specimens of humankind.[67] Exemplified by the Guatemalan report, the notion that European immigrants contributed to the overall quality of the population due to their "vitality" or "robustness" invoked racialist notions of intrinsic, embodied traits characteristic of all members of the category. From the perspective of political and scientific elites who ran Latin American census agencies in this period, the natural superiority of Europeans could be transfused into Latin American populations via the addition and incorporation of immigrants into the national mass.

In some countries, this racialist understanding of the demographic benefits of European immigration was taken to an extreme. The influx of European immigrants was identified in census reports as indispensable to counteract the presence of large numbers of African-origin individuals in the national population. In Cuba, for example, results from the 1899 census showing that blacks and mulattos comprised one third of the population elicited public calls for white immigration as the only viable antidote to this looming racial-demographic danger for the nation. As historian Alejandro de la Fuente notes, the census results "ratified the worst fears of the white elite, who had repeatedly stated throughout the nineteenth century that population—that is, the ethnic factors that constitute it—was the country's greatest problem."[68]

The call for European immigration as a means to "improve the race" of the national population was similarly explicit in Brazil. Oliveiro Vianna's introductory essay to the 1920 Brazilian census unabashedly championed the influx of Europeans as a mechanism for accelerating the whitening of the population.[69] For instance, the introductory essay included a table

---

[66] Guatemala. Dirección General de Estadística, *Censo General de la República de Guatemala... 1893*, 14–15.

[67] On the lack of a neat distinction between cultural and biological understandings of race in Latin America in this period, see Wade, *Race and Ethnicity in Latin America*.

[68] de la Fuente, *A Nation for All*, 47–8, citing an editorial in *Diario de la Marina* ("El Censo" April 22, 1900). The terms *etnico* and *racial* were used interchangeably in this context.

[69] The Brazilian government encouraged European immigration by providing travel subsidies and access to land in the decades after abolition of slavery (1888). On the politics of this policy, see Holloway, *Immigrants on the Land*.

reporting the absolute numbers of Portuguese, Spanish, Italian, Russian, German, Austrian, French, English, and Dutch immigrants who entered into various Brazilian ports between 1908 and 1920. Assessing the statistics, Vianna noted that in these years Brazil witnessed an annual influx of 100,000 immigrants of "the best European races, who distribute themselves among the mass of our population, influencing powerfully the reduction of the index of blackness (*nigrescência*) of our people."[70] Lauding this process as "admirable," Vianna observed that immigration from Europe "not only contributes to the rapid augmentation of the coefficient of the pure Aryan mass in our country; additionally, by crossing and re-crossing with the mestiça population, it contributes with equal rapidity to raising the Aryan element of our blood."[71]

The introduction to Brazil's 1920 census was particularly blatant in the use of racist pseudoscientific discourse to document and champion whitening as synonymous with national progress. But the argument for European immigration as a means of demographic progress built on a theme that had been present in Brazilian census reports, in less explicitly racist form, since the first national census in 1872.[72] In an official report on the 1872 census, the director of Brazil's national statistics agency lamented the negligible success of efforts to attract European immigrants to settler colonies in the country's interior. Yet he concluded on an optimistic note by expressing the hope that soon "a robust, hard-working, moralized population will flow into our country, bringing with them new germs of life."[73] Concern with tracking the arrival and incorporation of immigrants as a measure of the population's overall vitality heightened after the abolition of slavery in 1888 and the creation of the republic in 1889. The 1890 census included additional queries to track the incorporation of foreign-born in Brazilian society, and official reports produced by the census agency in the first decades of the twentieth centuries underscored time and again how European immigration propelled Brazil's population forward on its progressive, evolutionary path.

By the early 1900s, Brazil's immigration picture had brightened. While it still lagged far behind the United States and Argentina, Brazil had become a major destination for European immigrants to the Americas. Brazil's national statistics agency touted the presence of Europeans in the population in

---

[70] Brazil. Directoria Geral de Estatística, *Recenseamento do Brazil*, 336.

[71] Brazil. Directoria Geral de Estatística, *Recenseamento do Brazil*, 337.

[72] For a historical analysis of the increasing attention to immigration statistics in the work of Brazil's Directoria Geral de Estatística from 1872–1920, see Loveman, M., "The Race to Progress."

[73] Brazil. Directoria Geral de Estatística, *Relatorio, Trabalhos Estatísticos 1873*, 37.

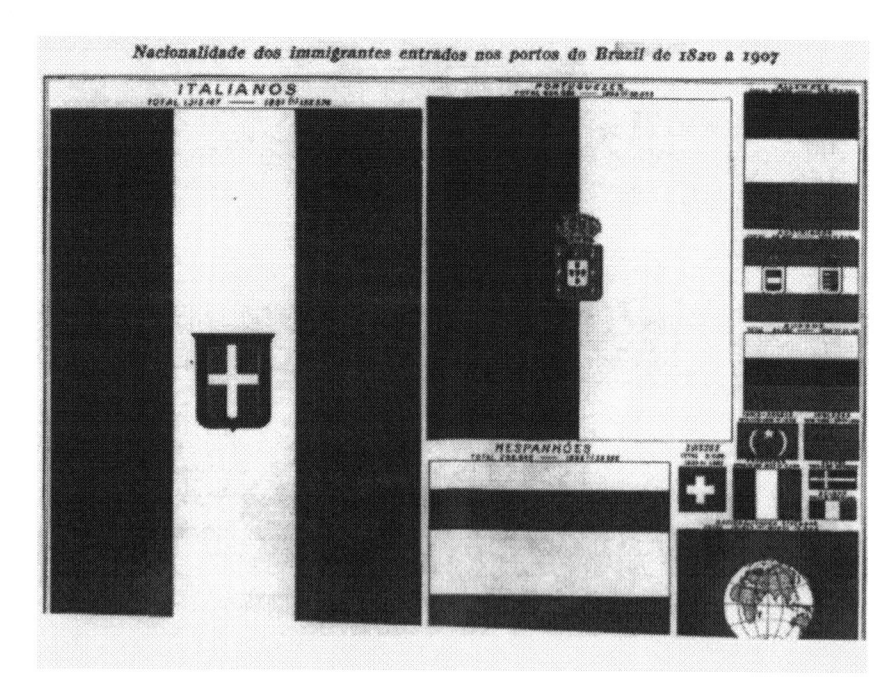

FIGURE 4.4 Nationality of Immigrants Who Entered Brazilian Ports between 1820 and 1907.
SOURCE: Brazil. Directoria Geral de Estatística. *Boletim Commemorativo da Exposição Nacional de 1908*, 84.

publications that aimed to boost immigration even more. For instance, in 1908, the agency produced a high quality commemorative volume for the centennial celebration of Brazil's independence that was geared toward international audiences. Among the glossy pages filled with photographs of Brazil's modern buildings and neoclassical statues, the volume included immigration statistics, by nationality, for all immigrants who had arrived in Brazilian ports between 1820 and 1907. The numbers were conveyed visually with an image of brightly colored national flags, roughly scaled according to the relative weight of each nationality to the total inflow. Notably, with the exception of a small flag for "Turkish-Arabic" immigrants; all other non-European immigrants were lumped together under the category "diverse nationalities," represented with a flag that showed an image of the globe in the bottom right hand corner of the page.[74] (See figure 4.4).

More than any other country in Latin America, Argentina made immigration a primary focus of analysis in reports on national censuses in this period. Census officials bragged that Argentina's population was growing proportionately faster than any other in the Americas, thanks to the flood

---

[74] Brazil. Directoria Geral de Estatística. *Boletim Commemorativo da Exposição Nacional de 1908*.

150 | National Colors

of European immigrants. A bar graph published in the 1895 census, for example, suggested that Argentina's "proportionate population growth" was in a league of its own (See figure 4.5).[75]

Argentina's census reports left no doubt that the rapid growth of the population owed to immigration, that nearly all arriving immigrants were European, and that the influx therefore contributed to the racial improvement of the Argentine nation. Pointing to statistics on the nationality of immigrants to Argentina, the author of the 1895 census report claimed: "It is enough just to read these statistics to understand how large the ethnic influence of the foreign element is in the Argentine Republic, and that a new race has formed and continues to form, intelligent and vigorous, since in accordance with the laws of natural selection the products of the recombination [*la refundición*] are superior to each of the beings that gave them life."[76] With the addition of European immigrants to the mix, the "Argentine race" was recast.

According to Argentina's 1895 census report, the regenerative influence of European immigration owed not only to the magnitude of the inflow, but also to the preponderance of men. The unbalanced sex ratio of immigrants was cheered for accelerating the reconstitution of the Argentine population, in the desired direction. For example, a table that described "The Argentine population by race"—based on statistics derived from reported nationality—was summarized with the following observation:

> Thus, the Latin race makes up the immense majority of the population, with 975 out of every 1000 persons; but the Germanic, Anglo-Saxon and Scandinavian [races], with the remaining 25, contribute to the improvement [of the majority race], giving origin to a new race through the fusion of the diverse elements. It must also be taken into account that the predominance of the masculine sex among foreigners, constituting two thirds of the total, contributes to their union with native-born women, making the transformation of the races even more active.[77]

By the time Argentina conducted its third national census, in 1914, immigrants were construed as more than a beneficial supplement to the native-born

---

[75] The legend explained: "The annual growth of the population is represented by red vertical columns, 4 mm high for every one [percent growth] per one thousand. Within each column is the name of the country, the date of [the last] census, and the proportional growth per 1000 per year."

[76] Argentina. Comisión Directiva del Censo. *Segundo Censo de la República Argentina*, II: XLIII, cited in Otero, *Estadística y Nación*, 355.

[77] Argentina. Comisión Directiva del Censo. *Segundo Censo de la República Argentina*, II: XLV. This table is discussed in chapter 5, figure 5.5a.

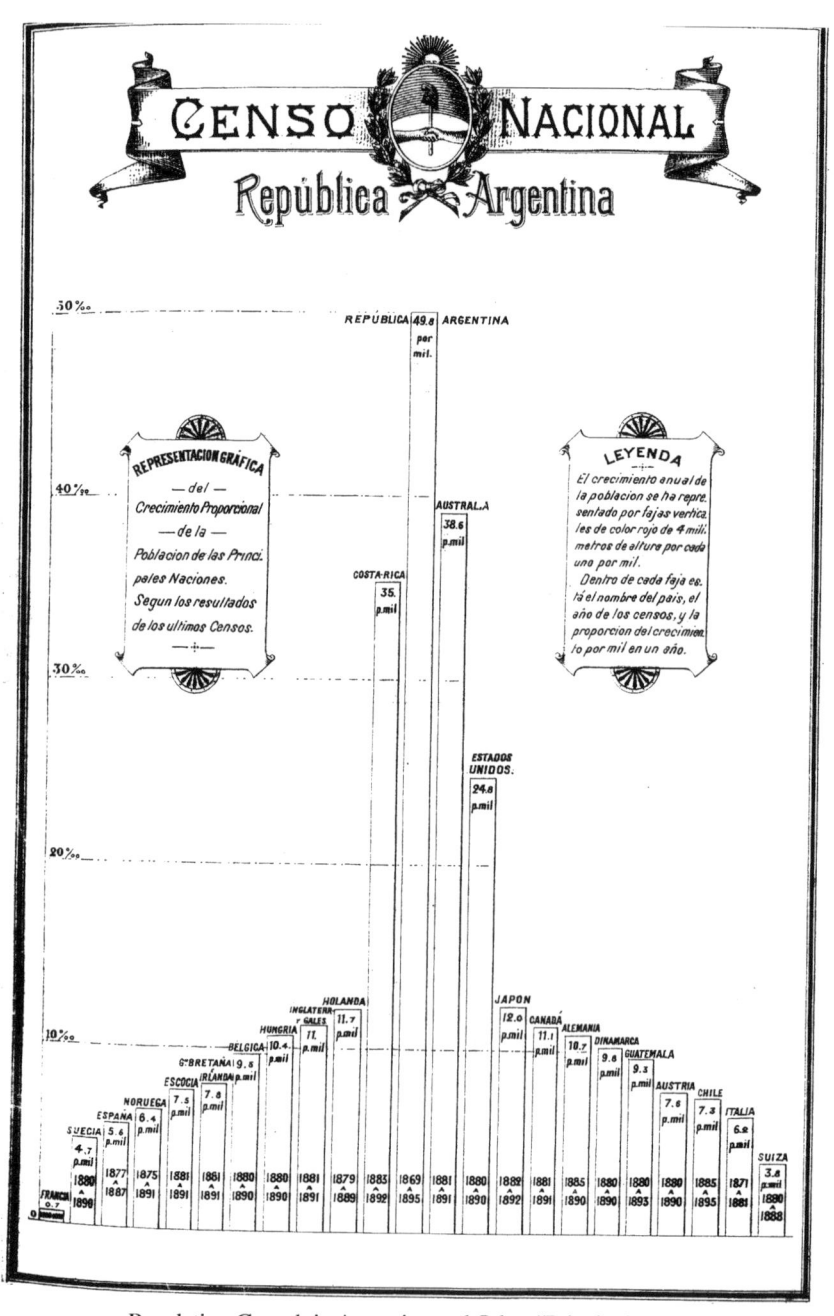

FIGURE 4.5 Population Growth in Argentina and Other "Principal Nations," 1895.
SOURCE: Argentina. Comisión Directiva del Censo. *Segundo Censo de la República Argentina, Mayo 10 de 1895.*

population. In the view of Alberto Martínez, president of the commission in charge of the third national census, European immigrants and their descendants comprised the backbone and the core essence of the nation: "The foreign population... has constituted and constitutes still the Republic's principal force (*la principal fuerza*) and its primary element of progress and labor."[78] The overall picture projected by Argentine censuses in this period was of a nation forged through the fusion of different European nationalities—construed as distinct races, all of them "white"—on Argentine soil. These newcomers integrated rapidly into the native-born population, itself composed almost entirely of the progeny of prior immigrant arrivals, to form a new white race: the Argentine race.

While Argentine censuses stand apart from others in the region in the privileged place allotted to immigrants in the statistical representation of the nation, the foundational notion that European immigrants were a means for demographic progress and prosperity was broadly shared. Across the region, those who penned census reports extolled the virtues of European immigration for contributing to the advancement of national populations. European immigration was construed as an inherently progressive demographic force, capable of improving the overall quality of the people who made up the nation.

Latin American census officials saw the demographic benefits of European immigrants accruing through two principal mechanisms: the raw increase of whites in the population, and the intergenerational elevation of the native population through immigrants' "integration." The net inflow of white bodies into the national territory increased the total number of whites relative to blacks and Indians, diluting the influence of less-desired components of the population. At the same time, by blending biologically and socially with native-born populations, European immigrants contributed to the racial-cultural uplift of the next generation of nationals from within. The discursive emphasis placed on the integration of European immigrants in many Latin American census reports from this period directs attention to a third demographic dynamic frequently underlined as an engine of progressive transformation of Latin American populations: mestizaje.

Race Mixture

Nearly all Latin American censuses from this period advanced the view that race mixture—mestizaje—gradually and steadily improved the quality of populations. In making this claim, census officials rejected the prevailing

---

[78] Argentina. *Tercer Censo Nacional*, I: 201, cited in Otero, *Estadística y Nación*, 368.

assumption among most leading scientists that race mixture bred intergenerational degeneracy, retarding or completely halting a nation's progress. Instead, they used a combination of discursive arguments and official statistics to assert that race mixture fueled the progressive evolution of their populations. The projected end point of this evolutionary process varied by country and over time, as did the specific explanations for how and why mestizaje had demographically beneficial effects. But in a broad sense, the authors of Latin American census reports converged in identifying race mixture as an unstoppable demographic dynamic that worked to transform populations in a desirable direction.

The pros and cons of mestizaje were actively debated by Latin American intellectual, scientific, and political elites in this period. Debates about the nature of race and race mixture and their consequences for national development fueled contentious public exchanges and political battles over the shape of public policies. There was never consensus among leading domestic thinkers on questions of race. For some, racial diversity and intermixture would be their nation's undoing; for others, mestizaje held the key to their nation's redemption. Operating within this cacophonous ideological field, the men charged with producing official demographic portraits of Latin America's modernizing nations nearly always came down on the side of racial redemption. National census reports projected the gradual improvement of populations. And the demography of mestizaje featured centrally in these "optimistic" projections.

Mestizaje could be construed as an agent of progressive demographic change because it was understood to act differentially on the component races in the mix. As a demographic phenomenon, mestizaje purportedly favored the "superior" races at the expense of the "inferior" ones. Collectively, mestizaje was presumed to reduce the relative influence of Indianness or Africanness on the nation, while enhancing the influence of Europeanness or native "whiteness"—never the reverse.[79] In some countries, the demographic end-product of successive generations of mixture was projected to be a homogenously white national type. In others, the face of the nation was predicted to stabilize as a uniform *mestizo* type, but one that was construed as *almost* white, if not quite.[80]

---

[79] The view that race mixture could be equally effective for the racial redemption of blacks as it was for Indians differed from the colonial-era treatment of "black blood" as a stigma that could never be fully erased (see chapter 2).

[80] On this latter point, see especially Martínez-Echazábal, "*Mestizaje* and the Discourse of National/Cultural Identity in Latin America, 1845–1959"; Rahier, "The Study of Latin American 'Racial Formations.'"

The censuses of different Latin American countries offered different accounts of the sociodemographic mechanisms through which mestizaje moved national populations in a whiter direction. One explanation for the putative whitening effect of mestizaje was that the superior races, being superior, naturally dominated over the inferior in the process of intergenerational inheritance. This reasoning was laid out explicitly in the introduction to Brazil's 1920 census: "It is known that in the crossing of animals, the qualities of the superior race can be grafted little by little to an inferior race, in order to form, through successive selections, a new ethnic type, that while of spurious origin, possesses the most excellent attributes of the superior race."[81] While the comparison to animal breeding might have been read as advocacy for a eugenic policy agenda, the more immediate aim of the analogy in the introduction to Brazil's 1920 census was to establish an empirical foundation for the claim that race mixture in the human population entailed selective transmission of superior human traits to the next generation.

A nearly identical claim appeared in the early national censuses of Argentina, which invoked the animal-breeding comparison to explain how the distinctive and superior Argentine race had emerged out of a history of racial mixture:

> The confirmed finding that the offspring of superior animal species improve by crossing races has been reproduced with application to the human species wherever it has been possible to make observations. These theories have had splendid confirmation in the Argentine Republic, where it can be observed that new generations resulting from the mating [*entroncamiento*] of European men and American women, and vice versa, are stronger and more beautiful than the individuals that preceded them.[82]

Notably, the only parties to the mixture according to this excerpt from Argentina's second national census, taken in 1895, were Europeans and "Americans"—the latter an ambiguous term that admitted the possibility of prior mixture with Indians and Africans without naming either. In another context, it was clarified that the "Argentine" ["American"] type had emerged through the original fusion of Europeans with Indians and Africans, followed by the subsequent subordination of the latter via selective dynamics:

---

[81] Brazil. Directoria Geral de Estatística. *Recenseamento do Brazil,* Introduction.
[82] Argentina. Comisión Directiva del Censo. *Segundo Censo de la República Argentina,* II: XLIII, cited in Otero, *Estadística y Nación,* 355.

> Three races came together... in the physical and moral genesis of early Argentine society [*la sociabilidad del Plata* ...]; the European or Caucasian as the active part, the Indian [*indígena*] or American as auxiliary, and the Ethiopian [*etiópica*] as complement. From their fusion resulted this original type, in which European blood has prevailed due to its superiority, regenerating itself constantly via immigration, and at whose side that other race of mixed black and white has continued to improve, and has assimilated the physical and moral qualities of the superior race.[83]

This quotation from Argentina's third national census, taken in 1912, is particularly interesting given the overriding tendency toward erasure of the African contribution to the nation's demographic, social, or political history over the course of the twentieth century. In this context, the Argentine census official acknowledged not only a "complementary" African presence in the original conception of the Argentine national type, but also the continued coexistence and improvement of an Argentine "mulatto" population alongside the dominant "race" that is "regenerated constantly" by European immigration.

The idea that the children of mixed unions more closely resembled the "superior" parent was common in census officials' accounts of mestizaje as a demographic process. Sometimes this was noted in census texts as a simple point of fact. For example, Delance's essay on the 1846 Census of Bolivia concluded with the observation that "the offspring of white men and Indian women are in every respect identical to their fathers; although, they sometimes tend to be a bit wheat-colored [*trigueños*] and show a few subtle characteristic traces of their mothers." The combination of white males and Indian females thus generated the "almost-white" progeny—to whom, Delance noted, "Bolivia owes its political independence."[84]

Discussions of mestizaje in national census reports often underscored that each of the contributing races left a mark on the national type, a discursive tactic that enabled claims of national distinctiveness, as discussed earlier. But in many census texts, even greater emphasis was placed on the power of mestizaje to erase racial diversity in the present and future. The authors of national census reports described mestizaje as a demographic

---

[83] Argentina. Comisión Directiva del Censo. *Tercer Censo de la República Argentina*, 198–9. This was written by Alberto Martínez, president of the Third National Census Commission, quoting Bartolomé Mitre's work in *Historia de Belgrano*. Cited in Otero, *Estadística y Nación*, 357.

[84] Delance, *Bosquejo Estadístico de Bolivia*, 206. The original reads: "*Los hijos de blanco y india son en todo idénticos a su padre; sin embargo, suelen ser a veces un poco trigueños y mostrar algunos rasgos ligeros característicos de su madre. A estos debe Bolivia su independencia política.*"

process that homogenized national populations; almost inevitably, this transformation was envisioned to take place at the primary expense of Indian or African-descent populations.

Mestizaje of the national population was confirmed, not surprisingly, in the published results of the Mexican census of 1921—the only modern Mexican census to include an explicit race question and the first census after the 1910 Revolution. Matter-of-factly, the census reported that the majority of the Mexican population corresponded to the *raza mezclada* (literally, the mixed or "blended" race), followed by the *raza indígena*, and then the *raza blanca*. The blunt reporting of absolute numbers of each race was followed by a lengthy discussion of the various indigenous languages and archaeological treasures to be found in different parts of Mexico. The statistical description of a predominantly mestizo present (and implicitly, future) population was thus followed by the narrative evocation of the glorified indigenous past upon which modern Mexican *mestizo* national identity was constructed.[85]

Census reports in countries with small or geographically isolated indigenous populations often included assertions that "uncivilized" Indians were declining in number, a trend attributed in part to their intermixture with the "civilized" population. In most cases, such pronouncements lacked empirical foundation, since "uncivilized" Indians were, by definition, those who lived beyond the reach of census enumerators. Wars of conquest and disease were also recognized to play a part, but mestizaje, census reports explained, fueled the disappearance of "savage tribes" from the territory. For example, Argentina's census reports routinely announced that Indians were disappearing into the national mass. The 1914 Argentine census put the estimated total of remaining Indians at 58,979. This precise-looking estimate was immediately followed with the assurance that although the numbers were not diminishing "with the rapidity that was expected," the indígenas "become mixed (*se mestizan*), become civilized, and become diluted in the general mass of the population."[86] Similarly, the introduction to Venezuela's 1936 census report noted "The indigenous population, which once comprised important population clusters, had been blending with the civilized population."[87] With concern, the Venezuelan report

---

[85] Mexico. Departamento de la Estadística Nacional, *Resumen del censo general de habitantes, de 30 noviembre de 1921*, 51–3. On the role of archeology in the construction of national identities, see Kohl, "Nationalism and Archaeology"; Hobsbawm and Ranger, *The Invention of Tradition*; Anderson, B., *Imagined Communities*.

[86] Argentina. Dirección General de Territorios Nacionales, *Censo de Población de los Territorios Nacionales*, 34.

[87] Venezuela. Dirección General de Estadística. *Resumen General del Sexto Censo de Población*, 5.

noted the possible slowing of this trend, as some tribes were retreating from contact with the "civilized" population to escape from exploitative authorities, the aggressions of other tribes, and the devastation of epidemic diseases. The opening page of Venezuela's 1936 census report called for government action to ensure the continued absorption of Indians into the nation: "It is necessary to attract them to the modern life using all possible means, as an imperative of patriotism and of humanity."[88]

On the other end of the spectrum, Latin American countries whose census results showed large indigenous majorities also hailed mestizaje as a gradual means to shift the demographic balance of their nations in the direction of "civilization." Civilization, needless to say, was construed as European and white. Thus, the introduction to the 1893 Guatemalan census conceded that two-thirds of the national population was indígena, but then went on to note that "in some districts, and especially near the centers of the white population, the indígena race has suffered declines as a consequence of mixing (*cruzamiento*) in various degrees."[89]

The notion that *mestizaje* worked to shift the population away from Indianness was made plain by the categories used to organize statistical tables of census results (see, for example, figure 4.6).

The tables showed Guatemala's population divided into "the two principal groups": Indians and Ladinos. Notably, the ladino category encompassed both "whites" and "the mixture of the European with the indígena." The propriety of this categorical lumping was justified with the observation that in Guatemala "the mixture of the European with the indigenous race has produced neither facultative decrease nor intellectual or moral debilitation."[90] Mestizaje was construed as a demographic process whose momentum moved Guatemala's population toward whiteness, never the reverse.

While Guatemalan census officials deemed the boundary between white and *mestizo* inconsequential, they described the divide between ladinos and indígenas as sharply demarcated and fundamental. Guatemala was portrayed as a dual society, composed of two races—ladinos and indígenas— that did not "move to the same compass."[91] The "aptitude for the arts and industry" and "urbanity, education and good sense" of the former was

---

[88] Venezuela. Dirección General de Estadística, *Resumen General del Sexto Censo de Población*, 5.

[89] Guatemala. Dirección General de Estadística, *Censo General de la República de Guatemala... 1893*, 15.

[90] Guatemala. Dirección General de Estadística, *Censo General de la República de Guatemala... 1893*, 14.

[91] Guatemala. Dirección General de Estadística, *Censo General de la República de Guatemala... 1893*, 15.

RESUMEN DEL CENSO DE LA REPÚBLICA DE GUATEMALA.

Cuadro Número 1.

RAZA Y SEXO.

DEPARTAMENTOS	LADINOS H.	LADINOS M.	INDIOS H.	INDIOS M.	TOTAL H.	TOTAL M.	TOTAL DE POBLACIÓN
Guatemala	46,241	52,995	25,011	23,593	71,252	76,588	147,840
Sacatepéquez	6,463	9,398	13,878	12,974	20,341	22,372	42,713
Chimaltenango	6,980	7,347	21,794	21,056	28,774	28,403	57,177
Amatitlán	11,447	11,694	5,976	6,270	17,423	17,964	35,387
Escuintla	12,045	10,595	5,058	4,303	17,103	14,898	32,001
Santa Rosa	18,753	18,473	5,118	4,949	23,871	23,422	47,293
Sololá	4,251	4,087	31,610	30,091	35,861	34,178	70,039
Totonicapam	1,498	1,366	41,900	44,574	43,398	45,940	89,338
Quezaltenango	16,232	17,028	37,029	40,849	53,261	57,877	111,138
Suchitepéquez	6,014	5,889	13,285	12,608	19,299	18,497	37,796
Retalhuleu	6,228	4,909	8,950	7,690	15,178	12,599	27,777
San Marcos	12,881	13,810	31,005	31,626	43,886	45,436	89,322
Huehuetenango	9,493	11,393	47,244	48,997	56,737	60,390	117,127
Quiché	8,116	7,236	38,880	38,521	46,996	45,757	92,753
Baja Verapaz	8,420	10,305	17,941	18,150	26,361	28,455	54,816
Alta Verapaz	2,703	2,922	48,603	46,531	51,306	49,453	100,759
Petén	2,351	2,170	1,132	1,099	3,483	3,269	6,752
Izabal	2,842	2,330	1,145	1,084	3,987	3,414	7,401
Zacapa	14,869	13,193	9,214	10,086	24,083	23,279	47,362
Chiquimula	10,588	10,999	21,441	20,718	32,029	31,717	63,746
Jalapa	7,843	8,283	8,600	8,559	16,443	16,842	33,285
Jutiapa	19,723	19,542	6,677	6,914	26,400	26,456	52,856
Sumas	235,981	245,964	441,491	441,242	677,472	687,206	1.364,678

FIGURE 4.6 Guatemala's "Two Principal Groups" in the 1893 Census.
SOURCE: Guatemala. Dirección General de Estadística and Victor Sanchez Ocaña. *Censo general de la república de Guatemala... 1893.*

contrasted to the "systematic passivity and invincible suspicions" of the latter. These differences were not, however, "organic": "the Indians who enter into any type of immediate relations with the families or services of the active society, quickly develop an amount of energy disproportionate to what you would presume from a glance at the race as a whole, and this phenomenon is especially noticeable among the Indian women." Through both sexual and social contact, the boundary between Indians and ladinos could be easily crossed. But it could only be crossed in one direction. The development and "progress" of the Guatemalan nation hinged, according to the census, on the gradual absorption of Indians into the ladino population.[92]

"Indians" also comprised the majority of Bolivia's early twentieth-century population, and as in Guatemala, the census predicted that their numerical dominance would eventually decline as a consequence of mestizaje. The author of the 1900 Bolivian census report underscored that the "raza mestiza" was the next largest group after Indians. Mestizos, the report explained, were the product of the initial contacts between Spanish men and "women of the conquered race," over which "the foreign [European] element continued to operate" thereafter. The mestizo may have been "inferior to the Spanish race, but was very much superior to the indígena race." According to the report's author, once mestizos were better educated and cured of their inclination to vice—especially pernicious "ever since their participation in politics had been legalized"—they would form the mass of the nation, becoming "useful to the country, as citizens, as industrial laborers and as soldiers."[93] In striking contrast to the 1893 Guatemalan census, the 1900 Bolivian census portrayed the boundary between Indians and mestizos as porous (again, in one direction only), while maintaining a clear symbolic divide between mestizos and whites. Whites were construed as descendants of Spaniards, with different culture and character than the mestizo mass who were projected to make up the manual workforce of the future. Quoting "a foreign writer, P. Liminana," the census report's author explained, "the white race, descendant of the Spanish, whose most illustrious names are found here in profusion, is the smallest in number but has retained over all the others the supremacy

---

[92] Guatemala. Dirección General de Estadística, *Censo General de la República de Guatemala... 1893*, 14–15. In the meantime, the Guatemalan census presented a tolerant, even mildly appreciative, stance toward the indígena population (a stance which unfortunately never took hold among the political and military elite of the country): "Ladinos and Indians are in reality two distinct societies in the same country: the first marches with hope and hard work along the paths that progress advises and imposes; the other is immobilized, outside the intellectual and political atmosphere, sustaining its ancient customs and habits with obstinateness. The Indians do not contribute to [the development of] civilization, but they don't obstruct it either with any resistance other than passivity. In any case, despite their indolence, they contribute the majority of the labor that makes the earth produce and creates the wealth of the nation." Needless to say, the author of the report did not seem aware of the obvious contradiction between the claim that "the Indians do not contribute" to the development of civilization and the observation that "despite their indolence" the Indians "contribute the majority of the labor" that feeds the population and "creates the wealth of the nation."

[93] Bolivia. Oficina Nacional de Inmigración, Estadística y Propaganda Geográfica. *Censo General de la Población*, 30.

[the white race] obtains in all places." Positions of national leadership, then, would remain with Bolivia's "white" minority.[94] While this Bolivian census report was unusual in drawing a solid boundary between whites and mestizos, it nonetheless shared in the broader, regional conception of mestizaje as a process that shifted populations collectively in a "better" direction.

Of course, not every census official construed mestizaje in this way. One notable exception was the author of Panama's 1920 census report, who insisted that the original traits of distinct races persisted across multiple generations, despite mestizaje. In a somewhat confusing prelude to several pages of statistical tables that reported various population traits (sex, legitimacy, religion, etc.) cross-tabulated by race, the author explained how the "principal races" of Panama endured:

> the effect of mixture upon the principal races is subject to certain restrictions, such that the characteristics of the more numerous race always prevail over four or five generations. If a *mestizo* crosses with a white, the white race will predominate...This is the only way that the attributes of a people can persist in the majority of inhabitants and over many years, despite the influence that climate, race mixture, and the progress of civilization may have over them. From this, comes the deduction that in Panama many of the physiological traits of the principal races are maintained.[95]

In this census official's view, when a white crosses with a mestizo, the "white race" predominates not because whites are superior, but because the white component of the mix is numerically larger. (In the crude math of racial biology: 1 white + 1 mestizo [½ white + ½ Indian] = ¾ white and

---

[94] If mestizos would make up the mass of the nation as soldiers, workers, and citizens, leadership would remain firmly in the control of "the white race," which included both foreigners and Bolivians. According to the introduction to the Bolivian census of 1900, foreigners could be further subdivided into two branches: European ("the most important of the two branches") and American (the most numerous of the two branches). These branches, in turn, could be broken down by national origins (for example, the "easily assimilable Italians," the Spanish—"conquerors and señores for three centuries," the Germans—"who bring with them good work habits and ability to assimilate," and the French—whose character is "the most like that of the Bolivians.") Meanwhile, Bolivians—"the genuine inhabitants [*pobladores*] of the national territory"—"are composed of *more or less pure* descendants of Spaniards, first of all, and secondly of other Europeans who immigrated during the nineteenth century" [my emphasis]. Bolivia. Oficina Nacional de Inmigración, Estadística y Propaganda Geográfica. *Censo General de la Población*, 30.

[95] Panama. Dirección General del Censo. *Boletin N°. 1*, 18. The explanation continued: "Among the whites, the type who are of Spanish color predominate, while among the blacks, the type like slaves from 1549 are most evident. The *indios* also retain their racial traits (*carácteres*)."

¼ Indian). With subsequent crossings over generations, whiteness wins out. Immediately following this explanation came several tables that reported the racial composition of the population in different ways, including a breakdown of the "Predominant Race" (by district), a "Comparison of Races, 1920–1911" which showed a growth of 2.6 percent and 5.73 percent in the share of "whites" and "blacks," respectively, and a 9.9 percent decline in the share of "mestizos," and a "Comparison between the White, Black and *Mestiza* Races" (see figure 4.7).

The 1920 census of Panama thus showed the population reverting to the "principal races," with blacks predominating due to their numerical advantage over whites. Trying to make sense of these statistics, the report's

SECCION IV

COMPARACIÓN ENTRE LAS RAZAS BLANCA, NEGRA Y MESTIZA

COMPARACION

RAZA			DIFERENCIA	
Blanca	14,645	14,10%	N 23,898	23,00%
Negra	38,543	37,10%	M 7,257	7,00%
Mestiza	45,800	44,10		

SECCION V

COMPARACIÓN DE RAZAS 1920—1911

Las razas principales, exceptuando la raza amarilla han aumentado de su número desde 1911. La raza mestiza, ha disminuido.

AÑO	BLANCA	%	DIFERENCIA	%
1920	14,645	14,10	6791	2,6
1911	7,854	11,5		

AÑO	NEGRA	%	DIFERENCIA	%
1920	38,543	37,10	17276	5,73
1911	21,267	31,37		

AÑO	AMARILLA	%	DIFERENCIA	%
1920	1586	1,53	332	
1911	1254	1.84		0.31

AÑO	MESTIZA	%	DIFERENCIA	%
1920	45,800	44,11	9166	
1911	36,634	54,07		9,96

FIGURE 4.7 A Comparison of Races in the Census of Panama, 1920.

SOURCE: Panama. Dirección General del Censo. *Boletin N°. 1. Censo demográfico de la Provincia de Panamá, 1920*, 21.

República de Panamá									Cuadro No. 9

Cuadro de población por razas y sexo

República	Hombres	Mujeres	Total	H	M	T
Blancos............	38,862	39,951	78,813	8.42	8.44	18.14
Negros.............	36,738	32,845	69,583	7.95	7.02	14.67
Mestizos............	125,055	124,528	249,583	26.85	26.54	52.36
Mulatos............	11,764	10,681	22,445	2.53	2.20	4.80
Amarillos	3,350	788	4,138	0.71	0.17	0.87
Indios	23,730	19,167	42,897	5.07	4.10	9.16
Total..........	239,499	227,960	467,459	51.53	48.47	100.00

FIGURE 4.8 The Racial Composition of the Population of Panama, 1930.
SOURCE: Panama. Dirección General del Censo. *1930 Censo Demográfico*.

author concluded that this outcome "could only be explained" by the tendency for race mixture to yield to the proportionately dominant component of the mix.

Ten years later, however, Panama's divergent demographic trajectory was put back on course. As can be seen in figure 4.8, the 1930 census results showed a dramatic shift in the racial composition of the population, with a large majority mestizo population, followed by whites, and then blacks. Evidently, the social definition of "mestizo" became more capacious between censuses; enumerators classified many Panamanians as "mestizo" in 1930 whom they had classified as "black" ten years before.[96] From 1930, Panama's population dynamics looked more like those of other Latin American countries in this period, on course for a gradual but inevitably whiter future.

Thus, with few exceptions, Latin American census reports from this period depicted the demographic momentum of *mestizaje* pulling

---

[96] I was not able to locate copies of the original enumerator instructions for these two censuses, so it is not clear whether the shift in racial composition owes to changes in the official rules of classification or changes in the tacit, informal rules of classification. Other demographic and political processes may have also played a role, including perhaps the early influence of the United States in Panama followed by Panama's increased integration into hemispheric politics. In another context, I demonstrate how possible explanations for such dramatic short-term changes in racial composition according to official census results can be teased apart and empirically assessed (Loveman and Muniz, "How Puerto Rico Became White"). On the history of ethnic and racial classification in Panama's censuses, see Mauri, "The Social and Political Construction of Race and Ethnic Categories in National Censuses of Panama, 1911–2010."

populations away from their indigenous and African-descendant roots and toward more European-looking and -acting populations. Some census reports projected that race mixture would dilute the traits of "inferior" races to the point of social erasure, yielding new kinds of "white" humankind. Others implied that race mixture moved populations in the direction of whiteness without positing that the nation would ever be fully "white" in the end. But in general, *mestizaje* was identified as a prevalent phenomenon in Latin American populations, and one that fueled demographic change in a "progressive" direction.

The authors of Latin American census reports in this period pointed to mestizaje –their evolutionary Achilles heel in the view of determinist racial theories of the time—and inverted its causal significance, transforming it into a demographic means of racial evolutionary salvation. Census reports described a variety of mechanisms through which mestizaje was supposed to be generating beneficial demographic effects. Sometimes mestizaje played a starring role as an efficient agent of selective evolutionary processes or collective biological regeneration. Other times, mestizaje was said to promote racial progress by diluting or absorbing the "inferior" races in the mix. In some census reports, claims that mestizaje improved the racial quality of the population were explicit and overtly celebratory. In others, the desirability of mestizaje's "uplifting" effects was merely implied. In one critical respect, however, depictions of mestizaje in official census reports converged. Crosscutting the particularities of different national contexts and the idiosyncrasies of the reports' authors, mestizaje was construed as a mechanism of demographic improvement. According to census reports, the effects of race mixture on Latin American populations were neither detrimental nor demographically neutral; mestizaje advanced populations forward on the march to national progress.

The Race to Progress: Projecting a Brighter (Whiter) Future

Latin America's nineteenth- and early twentieth-century censuses charted the gradual but inevitable demographic "improvement" of national populations. The authors of census reports deployed racial statistics to depict the observable diversity of their populations as a transitory demographic state. The combined momentum of demographic trends, including natural selection, immigration, and mestizaje, was projected to fuel the transformation of the region's populations, in a progressive direction. In most cases, demographic progress was construed as movement away from racial diversity toward homogeneity, via the erosion of distinguishable indigenous and African-descendant populations and the bolstering of European or "white" elements in the mix.

In some tension with these projections, census reports from this period often documented the continued existence of distinct racial groups within Latin American populations. Analytic narratives related tales of nations birthed through the fusion of distinct combinations of European, African, and Indian races. The categorical divisions used to organize tables of census results—which I analyze more closely in the following chapter—presented pictures of populations composed of clearly divided racial groups. And even where race data were not collected in censuses, census reports often included lengthy discussions of the racial or ethnically differentiated minorities found within the territorial boundaries of the nation.

Census officials reconciled descriptions of actually existing ethnoracial diversity with projections of a more homogenous and whiter future by imposing a linear, evolutionary narrative structure on the demographic trajectories of Latin American populations. Racial heterogeneity anchored the past. Accounts of originating race mixture grounded claims of national particularity, and thus legitimized Latin American nations as nations among others. Most census reports also acknowledged that racial diversity still weighed heavily in the present. This may not have been ideal, but nor was it cause for serious concern; the demographic present was depicted as merely a snapshot of a trajectory still very much in motion. From the transitory present, active demographic forces were propelling Latin American nations along their determined path to progress—toward a whiter and more homogenous steady state in the future. Against the predictions of racial determinist theories, Latin American censuses showed that racial heterogeneity and intermixture did not block the evolutionary path to progress.

Thus, Latin America's nineteenth- and early twentieth-century census officials collected and used racial statistics to document the distinctive origins of their nations and to craft demographic portraits of racially improving (i.e., whitening) populations. The question that still demands a fuller answer is *why?* What motivated the men in charge of Latin America's early census-taking endeavors to collect and scrutinize racial statistics, and to dwell on discussions of racial demography even when race data were not collected?

Here it becomes useful to consider the audience that census officials likely had in mind as they wove racial narratives through carefully crafted statistical portraits of their nations. At one level, the authors of national census reports clearly directed their commentaries and analyses to their domestic peers and colleagues, state officials, political elites, intellectuals, and especially other "men of science." Census reports were taken as opportunities to intervene with authority in domestic scientific disputes, or to shape the contours of ongoing political debates. To take just one example, Vianna's introduction to the 1920 Brazilian census leveraged racial statistics to challenge a rival theory of the racial formation of "the Brazilian type." A contemporary journal of military medicine had published statistical studies which concluded that Brazil's population would ultimately coalesce around two regionally distinct racial types. Vianna used the forum of the national census to reject the evidentiary base for this claim, and to reaffirm his thesis of the inevitable convergence of Brazilians into a single, quasi-white racial type.[97] In other contexts, too, historical analyses of particular censuses reveal how officials used census reports to intervene in proximate scientific disputes and political debates over the racial character and future prospects of their respective nations.[98]

At the same time, and perhaps even more centrally in many cases, the authors of census reports in this period also directed their observations about racial demographic change to an international audience. As described in chapter 3, one central motivation for undertaking the onerous task of a national census in this period was to be recognized by the international community of "civilized nations" as a member of the club. Taking a modern census was a way to demonstrate modern *statehood*. Producing racial statistics as part of the census, in turn, was a way for Latin America's former colonial polities to demonstrate modern *nationhood*. The censuses of each Latin American country depicted the enumerated population as a historically unique *nationality*, a *sui generis* community forged through a distinctive combination of originating racial parts. Demographic reports of originating racial difference within populations thus grounded claims to national difference—a minimum requirement for international recognition as a modern nation. Demographic reports of gradual racial improvement, meanwhile, confronted and refuted international scientific theories that proclaimed Latin America's racial heterogeneity an obstacle to national development. By producing and analyzing racial statistics, Latin American census officials inserted themselves into international

---

[97] For more on this debate, see Loveman, M., "The Race to Progress."

[98] For example, see Otero, *Estadística y Nación*, on the way political context shaped statistical production in Argentina from 1869–1914, and the ways census officials, in turn, participated in national politics.

scientific debates about the necessary ingredients for a nation's social and economic progress.

In addition to the international field of scientists, politicians, and intellectuals who followed learned debates on questions of race and prospects for human development, Latin American census officials also sought at times to engage a very different international audience: potential European immigrants and sources of foreign capital. Indeed, even as they crafted census reports to accomplish rather abstract tasks of symbolic, political, and scientific legitimation of their nations, census officials often had more immediate and pragmatic objectives in mind. They sought to use census reports to promote national development—not merely describe it. In practice, this often meant crafting and disseminating optimistic pictures of economic, social, and demographic conditions. In addition to sending census reports to their official counterparts in statistical offices abroad, Latin American statistics agencies produced an array of complementary statistical bulletins, pamphlets, journals, and reports for dissemination to national and international readerships. In some countries, statistics agencies also helped produce materials for marketing a "civilized" and whitening image of their country to prospective immigrants, targeting attendees of national expositions, World Fairs, or residents of particular European cities.[99] Efforts to package official statistics to attract "desirable" immigrants were more evident in some countries than others. But rarely was some note of boosterism aimed at potential immigrants entirely absent from census reports in this period.

The production of racial statistics in Latin America's early national censuses thus served a variety of ends. Racial statistics provided the empirical grounding for nationalist "foundational fictions";[100] they anchored the (partial) repudiation of international race science; they intervened in domestic political debates; and at times, they bolstered efforts to market Latin American societies as outposts of European civilization, ripe with opportunities for industrious European immigrants. Of course, there was much variation across countries and time in the specific audiences targeted by the authors of particular census reports. Yet running through these historical specificities was a common trend in the use of racial statistics. Facts of racial demography were presented to convey a custom-fitted variant of

---

[99] On the deliberate marketing of a "European" national image by Brazilians and Argentines in their competition for potential European immigrants in the late nineteenth and early twentieth centuries, see Skidmore, *Black into White*, 124–44.
[100] Sommer, "Irresistible Romance."

the same basic argument: neither originating racial diversity nor race mixture thereafter would derail the promise of a prosperous national future.

In order for Latin American census reports from this period to make this case, facts of racial demography had to be presented and analyzed with considerable care. Chapter 5 provides a close look at how the racial statistics contained in Latin America's early national censuses were collected, coded, and often creatively displayed. Scrutiny of the methods used to assemble and report racial statistics in this period reveals that the production of racial demographic facts was truly an act of *production*, although it masqueraded as an act of mere description. Latin American census takers capitalized on statistics' quasi-magical aura of neutrality—encapsulated nicely in the notion that statistics "speak for themselves"—to assert a hierarchical vision of Latin America's populations. Indeed, even as the producers of Latin America's early national censuses sought to deny any racial disadvantage in the pursuit of national progress, they presented racial statistics in ways that reinscribed racist presumptions about the kinds of human kinds that made up their aspiring nations.

CHAPTER 5 | Constructing Natural Orders

LATIN AMERICAN STATE BUILDERS heralded demographic censuses as essential tools for discerning the true condition of the nation. Nineteenth- and early twentieth-century census reports were held up as authoritative national portraits, providing unmatched insight into the national self. In the words of an Argentine census official: "Numbering, classifying, disaggregating [*descomponiendo*] men, its raw material, societies come to have plain consciousness of their weakness or their strength, substituting...the uncertain and hypothetical with the incontestable reality of the facts. [Censuses] are thus, for nations, like the useful and fecund words 'know yourself,' that Greek wisdom had written at the entrance to the Delphi temple."[1]

Yet national censuses did not simply describe "the incontestable reality of the facts"; they advanced as incontestable fact a particular perspective on reality. To produce statistical portraits of national populations, census officials had to make concrete decisions about how to count and classify populations. They also made choices about which results to report and how to report them. In making such decisions, they negotiated tensions among competing goals: the desire to conform to the prescribed international formula for taking a modern national census; the desire to confront racially determinist strains of social evolutionary science by documenting the regenerative potential of miscegenation; and the overriding desire to produce statistics that documented "national progress"– in part, by presenting the nation in a positive light for the rest of the world to see. The statistical tables contained in the published volumes of national census results reflected the negotiation of these pragmatic concerns, ideological currents, and symbolic aims.

---

[1] Argentina. Superintendente del Censo. *Primer Censo de la República Argentina*, III. This chapter draws in part on Loveman, M., "Whiteness in Latin America"; Loveman, M. "Census Taking and Nation Making in Nineteenth-Century Latin America."

The previous chapter showed how national censuses in nineteenth- and early twentieth-century Latin America were used to build the case for membership in the community of "civilized nations." Census reports described the distinct combinations of ethnoracial origins that made each Latin American population a unique people. Census reports also showed, against the dire predictions of racial determinists, that Latin American populations were undergoing a gradual process of racial "improvement." Pointing to the effects of selective processes, immigration, and racial mixture, census officials predicted the gradual decline or outright disappearance of Indian and African descendant populations. Defining national progress in racial terms, census officials from across the region predicted a demographically lighter, if not always explicitly whiter, national future.

Focusing on the same time period as the previous chapter, in this chapter, I turn from analysis of the explicit claims made with racial statistics in official census reports to scrutiny of the methods through which those statistics were produced. I argue that the process of producing racial data in late nineteenth- and early twentieth-century censuses both presumed and perpetuated tacit racist notions about human differences. Inscribed in the approaches used to generate racial data, these tacit racist assumptions helped to undergird and affirm census officials' explicit arguments about the demography of racial improvement.

The presumption of a natural hierarchy of races informed the creation of racial statistics from start to finish. The fundamental idea of inequality between the races shaped the design of census schedules, influenced the assignment of individuals to racial categories, informed the organization of statistical tables, and underwrote the selective inclusion of supplementary graphics and illustrations. Thus, beyond the explicit use of racial statistics to advance racist-inspired predictions of national progress, I show in this chapter how censuses reinforced racist beliefs implicitly, through the methods used to collect and display demographic data.

The steps involved in the production of official demographic data allowed for the translation and transmission of everyday ideas about race into official statements of demographic fact. Indeed, the production of official racial statistics necessarily drew upon prior beliefs about racial differences and hierarchies, among enumerators and those whom they enumerated. For this reason, the official reports of census results did not simply "construct race" from the top down. Acts of official statistical description selectively absorbed commonsense notions of race and packaged them as authoritative demographic observations. Presented as mere description, the statistical tables that displayed official census results reified Latin American populations as clearly bounded nations composed of particular and differentially valued ethnoracial kinds.

Collecting Racial Statistics

Contemporary theorists insist that race is a social relationship forged through a negotiated interaction between the "self" and "others." While this may be true in abstract terms, in practice there are many contexts in which racial ascriptions are made unilaterally and racial categories are taken to be natural and obvious divisions among human beings. For most of the history of modern census taking in the Americas, racial classifications were assigned to individuals by census enumerators. The use of self-identification in collection of racial and ethnic population data only became the internationally recommended and recognized standard in the 1940s; before then, it was standard practice for census enumerators to fill in household census schedules, including classification of individuals' race. Enumerators probably permitted literate household heads to fill in their own census forms in some contexts. Officially, however, the task of filling in the blanks on census questionnaires fell to hired agents of the state.

Given the nature of the work involved, enumerators were recruited from among sectors of the population that could read and write. In most parts of Latin America in the nineteenth and early twentieth centuries, this meant that census enumeration was done by local authorities such as notaries, teachers, and low-level government employees. Civic-minded volunteers from better-off families may have also joined the ranks. Though direct information about enumerators hired to take early censuses in the region is sparse, it is probable that the majority were lighter-skinned men. Unequal access to basic educational opportunities prevailed throughout most of the region, and inherited disadvantage and continued patterns of discriminatory behavior and policy disenfranchised many indigenous and African-descent individuals, along with most women regardless of background.[2]

Enumerators were typically supplied with a common set of written instructions to guide them in their data-collecting work. These instructions were usually cursory. Nonetheless, a close reading reveals implicit assumptions about the nature of individual traits and social relationships surveyed

---

[2] There is little research on census enumerators in nineteenth-century Latin America. On enumerators in early nineteenth-century Chile, see Jaramillo, "'Un Alto en el Camino." On enumerators in early twentieth-century Puerto Rico, see Loveman, M., "The U.S. Census and the Contested Rules of Racial Classification."

in the census. The absence of explicit instructions for collecting some kinds of information can also be telling. Such silences indicate that some queries were seen as sufficiently straightforward to eliminate the need for clarification. Together with the format of questions and the allowable responses, published enumerator instructions provide clues to underlying assumptions about the subjects of demographic investigation.

A review of all race and color queries found in the national censuses of Latin American countries from the nineteenth to the mid-twentieth century yields several insights into the tacit understandings of race that shaped the production of official statistics in this period. The first observation that stands out from examination of these queries is that enumerators were not usually provided with explicit guidance for deciding how to assign individuals to the appropriate racial category. The absence of explicit instructions in most cases suggests that race was presumed to be self-evident. This impression is reinforced by the fact that queries about race generally took the form of one-word prompts rather than full questions. The word *Raza* or *Color* would appear on the census form, followed by a blank line to be filled in with one of the officially allowable categories (for example, white, mestizo, Indian, or black).

The format of race questions in Latin American censuses suggests that race was not considered a matter of subjective identity or communal belonging, as it came to be defined in the censuses of some countries of the Americas toward the end of the twentieth century and beginning of the twenty-first.[3] Rather, race was construed as an objective individual attribute. For the most part, census enumerators classified individuals by race as if membership in a racial category were given by nature; as with sex or age, race was treated as something a person *just is*.

When they were included at all, enumerator instructions for race queries typically served only to clarify the allowable responses or indicate the proper shorthand to be used on the form. The specific terminology and number of categories that enumerators could choose from varied. The category set usually included some combination of "white" (blanco), "black" (negro), "Indian" (indio or indígena), and "mixed" (usually denoted with mestizo and/or mulato, but trigueño, pardo, and *mezclado* also appeared as official categories in some cases). A few censuses used the term "ladino" instead of or in addition to "white."[4] Some censuses also included *"amarillo"* (yellow or Asian) as an option, though this category was sometimes omitted from

---

[3] See chapters 6 and 7.

[4] For example, the 1880 Guatemalan census and the 1887 Honduran census.

the tables presenting results.[5] The inclusion of an "other" option in some censuses signaled recognition that the official category set was not comprehensive of all races that might be identified in national populations, while also implying the state's disinterest in the categorical identification of any specific racial kinds not already conceived as constitutive elements of the national population.

The primary racial categories in the majority of Latin American censuses were "white," "black," "Indian," and "mixed." The first three of these were generally considered to be unambiguous and easily discernible. There is not a single example from Latin American censuses between 1820 and 1940 in which there are clarifying comments for enumerators on how to identify whites, blacks, or Indians. At most, enumerators were provided with acceptable shorthand for reporting these categories (for example, "mark 'b' for *blanco*").[6] The presumed self-evidence of race made classificatory instructions superfluous. As Guatemalan enumerators for the 1921 Census were instructed matter-of-factly: "The characteristic marks of each race are well defined. For example, an individual of the yellow or black race is not easily confused with an Indian."[7]

The presumption of self-evidence often faltered, however, when it came to classification of mestizos. In some cases, enumerator instructions admitted the difficulty of identifying mixed-race individuals and offered some additional guidance for acceptable use of the category. For instance, enumerators for Peru's 1876 census received the following instructions:

> The column "*Raza*" has five subdivisions, the first for the *white* race, the second for the *Indian*, the third for the *black*, the fourth for the *mestiza*, and the fifth for the *Asian*. The first, second, third and fifth do not pose any difficulty whatsoever in the categorization of the individuals who belong to them. As for the *mestiza* race... it is to be understood that it includes all the mixtures [mezclas] without distinction.[8]

---

[5] Conversely, in a few instances tables reporting census results at the provincial level reported the number of amarillo individuals even though amarillo was not an allowable category according to official enumerator instructions. Such discrepancies speak to the disjuncture between official visions of the relevant racial kinds that make up the nation and the much broader array of ethnoracial distinctions informing social interactions in daily life.

[6] In this respect, instructions for racial classification on Latin American censuses mirrored those in the United States, where clarification for how to identify "whites" is also conspicuously absent from enumerator instructions (Nobles, *Shades of Citizenship*, 187–90).

[7] Instructions to enumerators, in: Guatemala. Dirección General de Estadística, *Censo de la Población... 1921*.

[8] Peru. Dirección de Estadística, *Resumen del Censo General*, XXXIII.

In essence, these instructions told enumerators that classification as *mestizo* was appropriate for any individual whose membership in one of the other categories was questionable or ambiguous. Similarly, in the 1920 Panamanian census, enumerators were instructed to include "under the generic denomination of *mestiza* everything that is situated between one race and another, making use of the general understanding of the term."[9] The Brazilian census of 1890, to take a final example, allowed enumerators to fill in the blank with the category of their choice; all responses other than "white," "black," and "caboclo" (which in this context referred to indigenous people[10]) were aggregated into a single, catch-all mixed category (mestiço).

In all these cases, enumerators were effectively instructed to resort to their commonsense understandings of racial groups and rules for membership to do their classificatory work. Of course, enumerators had to rely on their tacit knowledge of race to identify whites, blacks, and Indians as well. But only for categories denoting race mixture did census officials think it necessary to explicitly instruct enumerators to rely on their common sense.

In part, the additional directions to guide use of mixed-race categories stemmed from concerns about accuracy of racial classification. Census officials expressed concern about erroneous classification and provided specific instructions intended to minimize the possibility of mistakes. One possible source of error stemmed from the fact that colloquial racial terminology included many more categories than the restricted set of options allowed on census forms. To ensure reliable, standard responses, enumerators were sometimes admonished to adhere strictly to the official categories. For example, enumerators for Bolivia's 1900 census were instructed to use only the four official categories to describe respondents' race: blanca, mestiza, india, or negra. The instructions stated: "Be aware that in the statistical classification of races, only the four noted on the form will be accepted."[11] But the explicit instructions proved futile. In a letter to the Director of the Census, the official in charge of the enumeration of the city of La Paz explained apologetically that the category "yellow" had

---

[9] Panama. Dirección General del Censo, *Boletin Nº. 1*, 18.

[10] In all the tables presented in Brazil's 1890 census report, the Portuguese terms were accompanied by a French translation. The term *caboclo* was translated as "'Indiens." The effort to make the tables legible to European audiences was part of a broader campaign to attract European immigrants to Brazil in the years following abolition of slavery (in 1888). See Skidmore, *Black into White*; Loveman, M., "The Race to Progress."

[11] Bolivia, Oficina Nacional de Inmigración, Estadística y Propaganda Geográfica. *Censo General de la Población*, XXVII.

been spontaneously added by enumerators who did not know how else to classify the Chinese living in the capital city.[12]

Census officials also expressed concern about another potential source of error: the tendency of respondents to provide inaccurate information, due to ignorance, "social prejudice," or deceit. Thus, for example, enumerators for the 1921 Guatemalan census were instructed to note the race of each individual—ladino, Indian, "pure black" [*negro puro*], white, yellow ["child of Guatemalan and Chinese"] or "pure Chinese" [*Chino puro*] –without explicitly asking. Enumerators were told to classify people without their input because supposedly "in past enumerations this [asking individuals their race] has lead to the mistake of putting down *Ladinos* and *indios* [as opposed to more specific categories] and this should now be avoided in order to obtain more faithful classifications."[13] Not noted was the fact that enumerators' use of the dichotomous categories *ladinos* and *indios* in past censuses was in accord with their official instructions for those earlier counts. The 1880 Guatemalan enumerator instructions read: "to avoid confusion, [*raza*] is divided into *ladinos* by which denomination are included individuals of any race, and *indígenas* of the country."[14] In 1921, in contrast, enumerators were told to classify individuals into one of the six categories listed above; the tables included in the 1921 census reported results for five of these categories, omitting the category for "pure Chinese."[15] The use of more—and more conventional—race categories than in previous censuses made Guatemala's 1921 results appear more precise and "scientific" than in previous censuses. Interestingly, however, the 1921 census report *also* included tables that mirrored those from the 1893 census in juxtaposing only two categories: ladino and Indian. Thus, the shift to a larger set of racial categories in Guatemala's 1921 census in the interest of "more faithful" data supplemented, rather than replaced, a dichotomous understanding of the fundamental ethnoracial divide within Guatemala's population.[16]

---

[12] The letter, from the director of the "Comisión Central" to the Director of the National Office of Immigration, Statistics and Geographical Propaganda, is reproduced in Bolivia, Oficina Nacional de Inmigración, Estadística y Propaganda Geográfica. *Censo General de la Población* 155–7.

[13] Guatemala. Dirección General de Estadística, *Censo de Población de la república levantado el 28 de agosto de 1921*, LXXXII.

[14] Guatemala. Dirección General de Estadística, *Censo General de la República de Guatemala*, XIX.

[15] Guatemala's 1921 census is the only Guatemalan census that explicitly distinguishes "whites" and "ladinos" in the summary tables of the population; in all other national censuses, these are combined in a single category for statistical purposes.

[16] On the history of racial thought in 1880–1920 Guatemala, see Grandin, *The Blood of Guatemala*.

A professed concern with the reliability of racial statistics also prompted change in the categories enumerators were instructed to use in the 1890 census of Brazil. The 1872 census had used the categories "white," "black," "parda" and "caboclo" to describe the "raça" of the Brazilian population. In the 1890 census, the "white," "black," and "caboclo" categories remained unchanged, but the category "parda" was replaced with "mestiça."[17] In an official letter to the Minister of Interior in which he justified this change, the director of the General Directorate of Statistics (DGE) explained that mestiça was used because it was more "generic." While "parda,"only included "the product of the mixture (*crusamento*) of white and black," mestiça included these along with those resulting from mixtures involving "representatives of the indigenous race (*raça indigena*)."[18] The DGE's substitution of the more "generic" term was a concession to "social prejudice." The DGE director explained: "As was proven by the census of 1872, a very well known social prejudice frustrates the precise ascertainment of the ethnic fact (*facto éthnico*) that results from the fusion of the African element." Therefore, the letter continued, it was best to "include it together with [the fusion] that derives from cabocla origin, even though, in the interests of science, it would be more advantageous to distinguish them."[19] Since "mestiça" did not *necessarily* imply any African ancestry, it avoided the intimation of African origins and thus lower social status that was connected to the term "parda."

Enumerator instructions in Latin American censuses sometimes revealed a concern with accurate classification, but the extent of this concern never approximated the obsession over the possibility of racial misclassification seen in enumerator instructions in United States censuses during this period. The contrast between the mostly minimalist enumerator instructions throughout Latin America and the elaborate clarification provided to enumerators in the United States is revealing. In the 1870 and 1880 US censuses, enumerators were told to "Be particularly careful in reporting the class *Mulatto*. The word here is generic, and includes quadroons, octoroons, and all persons having any perceptible trace of African blood.

---

[17] Prior accounts of the history of racial classification in Brazilian censuses state that the mestiço category in the 1890 census referred only to the mix of blacks and whites (cf. Piza and Rosemberg, "Color in the Brazilian Census," 41). The archival sources reveal that the DGE actually defined the mestiço category more broadly.

[18] Official letter from Director of Brazil's General Directorate of Statistics to Minister of Interior, Officio n.667, July 12, 1890, p.4. National Archive of Brazil, Rio de Janeiro, GIFI 5C 272.

[19] Official letter from Director of Brazil's General Directorate of Statistics to Minister of Interior, Officio n.667, July 12, 1890, p.4. National Archive of Brazil, Rio de Janeiro, GIFI 5C 272. The justification for substituting "mestiço" for "pardo" was also included in the DGE's annual report in 1891 (Brazil. Ministerio do Interior. *Relatorio Apresentado ao Presidente da República,* Anexo E, 41).

Important scientific results depend on the correct determination of this class in schedules 1 and 2."[20] In the 1890 US census the mulatto category was disaggregated, and the instructions again emphasized the importance of accurate reporting: "The word 'black' should be used to describe those persons who have three-fourths or more black blood; 'mulatto,' those persons who have from three-eights to five-eighths black blood; 'quadroon' those persons who have one-fourth black blood; and 'octoroons' those persons who have one-eighth or any trace of black blood."[21]

The attempt to track "quadroons" and "octoroons" recalls the Spanish colonial practices of classifying *"castas"* (discussed in chapter 2). In contrast to this obsession with tracing "degrees of mixture" construed in explicitly biological terms, "mixed" categories in Latin American censuses served as catch-all categories, capturing individuals of mixed parentage along with anyone who did not clearly fit into the white/black/Indian/yellow classificatory scheme. The explicit directives to US enumerators to be on the lookout for traces of African blood and the lack of such directives to enumerators anywhere in Latin America, underscores that ideas of "purity" figured much more centrally in the social definition of whiteness in the United States than in most of Latin America in this period.[22]

The concern with capturing degrees of mixture evident in the 1890 U.S. census was short-lived; in 1900 the "mulatto," "quadroon," and "octoroon" categories were eliminated. "Mulatto" returned to the census in 1910 and 1920, but in 1930 it was removed again and "Negro" became an all-encompassing category for individuals showing any trace of "African blood."[23] The exclusion of a "mixed race" category for most of the twentieth century in US censuses stands in marked contrast to racial classification practices in Latin America during the same period. Additionally, while the racial

---

[20] On race classification in the US census, see Lee, "Racial Classifications in the US Census"; Goldberg, *Racial Subjects*; Anderson and Fienberg, *Who Counts?*; Nobles, *Shades of Citizenship*; Schor, *Compter et Classer*; Snipp, "Racial Measurement in the American Census." On the peculiarity of the system of official racial classification that took hold in the United States, see Davis, *Who Is Black?*; Dominguez, "Exporting U.S. Concepts of Race."

[21] Cited in Wright and Hunt, *The History and Growth of the United States Census*, 187.

[22] This is not to deny that ideas of "blood purity" informed—and continue to inform—ideas about race in the social thought and practices of some sectors of Latin American societies. The point here is that the weight placed on purity as a criterion for eligibility in the "white" census category was much greater in the United States.

[23] According to the 1930 enumerator instructions "A person of mixed white and Negro blood should be returned as a Negro, no matter how small the percentage of Negro blood. Both black and mulatto persons are to be returned as Negroes, without distinction. A person of mixed Indian and Negro blood should be returned a Negro, unless the Indian blood predominates and the status of an Indian is generally accepted in the community" (https://usa.ipums.org/usa/voliii/inst1930.shtml,item 151).

classifications included in US censuses proliferated over the course of the twentieth century, by comparison the number of categories in Latin American censuses remained quite stable over time.[24]

A final striking contrast in the official approach to racial data collection in the United States and Latin America in this period is that in the former, enumerator instructions stressed accuracy above all else, whereas in the latter, the desire for accuracy could at times be trumped by the desire to show respect for "honorable" families. The most explicit example of this comes from Peru's 1876 census, which included the following note of caution for enumerators:

> No warning would be sufficient to impress on the Enumerators the delicacy with which they should proceed with this question, without ever allowing themselves to ask the person concerned directly and making the annotation in his presence without letting him see. Of course, when dealing with absent individuals or with inscriptions based on the declarations of third parties, asking about race is inevitable; but in such unavoidable cases, [the enumerator] should proceed with extreme tact, so much so that, even dealing with absentees, if possible the Enumerator, on most occasions, should avoid the question, whether because he knows the person or because, when speaking of the person his race is casually mentioned, or finally, by logical deduction that ancestors and descendants belong to the same race, as when he's dealing with the son of whites or the parents of someone who is white; in which case the question would be unnecessary and insulting [*hiriente*].[25]

That asking about absent family members could be inherently insulting *when dealing with whites* reveals how the notion of family honor was bound to the idea of racial origins.[26] To avoid the "insult" of inquiring about race,

---

[24] The proliferation of racial categories in US censuses in the second half of the twentieth century reflects the direct connections between census data and the administration of post-Civil Rights era entitlement programs and antidiscrimination legislation (Skrentny, *The Ironies of Affirmative Action*).

[25] A less explicit version of this cautionary procedure for reporting individuals' "race" was reiterated in the instructions to enumerators for the 1940 Peruvian census. The instructions read: "Is [the individual] white, indian, black, yellow or mestizo?—It is not necessary to ask this question when the individual is seen; the Enumerator will record the data according to his personal judgment. Persons without a defined race such as white, indian, black or yellow will be reported as *mestizo*" (Peru. Dirección de Estadística, *Censo Nacional de Población y Ocupación*, 598).

[26] See Loveman, M., "Whiteness in Latin America." Notably, the insistence that enumerators prioritize the maintenance of honor over the accuracy of response was repeated for the question about civil status: "Here more than ever the Enumerator must deploy his talent for asking questions that preserve the honor of the interviewees; [the enumerator] must record the answer he receives, without

Latin American census takers were sometimes reminded to keep their racial classifications of the enumerated out of view, or to record individuals' race "in a discrete manner," as it was put to enumerators in the 1921 Guatemalan census.

In summary, analysis of methods for collecting racial population data in Latin American censuses in this period reveals a broad implicit consensus in the region on the view of race as an objective individual trait discernible through simple sight, at least most of the time. There is also an implicit recognition that embodied cues may not always be reliable indicators of racial category membership. The reality of biological and social mixture across generations complicated the task of racial classification on the census. For the most part, this complication was resolved through regular inclusion of an official "mixed" category on censuses. Such categories gave enumerators a legitimate way to deal with the inherent ambiguity involved in sorting populations that varied continuously along an array of phenotypic and social dimensions into discrete and mutually exclusive racial categories. In effect, official use of "mixed" categories on censuses subsumed and sublimated the full extent of the blurriness of racial distinctions on the ground. In the context of official census results, such categories presented those whose existence belied the clarity of racial boundaries as yet another clearly bounded racial type among others.

Yet the use of categories like "mestizo" to contain ambiguity had its limits. Enumerators had to exercise caution lest their use of the category inadvertently breach norms of social honor. The mere suggestion of racial impurity in certain families and regions could cause serious offense. Explicit directives to enumerators to proceed cautiously on this classificatory terrain revealed the extent to which prevailing social hierarchies in some areas continued to meld familiar honor with notions of racial purity; honor had a race, and that race was white.

Ultimately, the collection of racial data in Latin American censuses hinged on how enumerators chose to classify their fellow citizens. Even when written instructions were provided, enumerators had no explicit, practical guidance on how to actually sort the diverse array of human beings they encountered into the finite set of official racial categories. Not even in the accuracy-obsessed United States did enumerator instructions clarify

---

making observations, even if it appears to be false, because it is better to make minor errors [*errores no trascentales*] than to offend social conventions having to do with family secrets." (Peru. Dirección de Estadística, *Resumen del censo general de habitantes del Perú: hecho en 1876*, XXXIV. On race and honor in nineteenth-century Brazil, see Beattie, *The Tribute of Blood*.

the characteristics to be treated as reliable indicators of ancestry, which was supposed to determine category membership. In the absence of explicit classificatory rules, enumerators had to rely on their common sense understandings of what constituted tell-tale signs of racial difference. Thus, the work of racial classification on censuses was inherently interpretive and discretionary. The presumed self-evidence of race was reinforced by the default reliance on enumerators' tacit understandings of racial differences in the collection of official racial statistics.

Displaying Racial Statistics

Just as enumerators' implicit understandings of race systematically informed the collection of racial population data, census officials' tacit racial beliefs shaped how census results were publicly displayed. Census results do not magically present themselves. The masses of data collected by enumerators have to be aggregated, ordered, and packaged into the tidy rows and columns that comprise descriptive statistical tables. These tables crystallize in graphic form an array of decisions about how best to present official data. Statistical tables can thus be read for clues that reveal the assumptions and aspirations of their creators.[27]

The presentation of racial statistics in Latin American census publications suggests a broadly shared consensus about the natural order of racial hierarchy. Across countries and time, there is almost complete uniformity in listing the number of "whites" first, regardless of the numerical distribution of the population among racial categories. That this presentational choice seemed (and still seems) obvious speaks to the successful naturalization of the idea that the category "white" belongs at the top of any racial hierarchy. The publication of these statistical tables reinscribed this social fact as the natural order of things.

Of course, in the broader public spheres of individual Latin American countries this notion was sometimes contested. In the first decades of the twentieth century in particular, intellectuals, political elites, and social critics developed elaborate and nuanced arguments about the relative merits and deficits of different "races" and their potential contribution to national development. "Whites" were not left out of these debates. There were often disagreements

---

[27] See Goldstein, "What's in an Order?"; Zerubavel, *Social Mindscapes*; Hirschman, "The Meaning and Measurement of Ethnicity in Malaysia"; Monmonier, *How to Lie with Maps*; Starr, "The Sociology of Official Statistics"; Dirks, *Castes of Mind*.

about the relative worth of different kinds of "whites," disagreements that were analogous (though not identical) to those documented in historical scholarship on whiteness in the United States.[28] But despite the contested and complicated ideological terrain in which individual census volumes were produced, when it came time to draw the tables reporting numerical results, the near universal tacit consensus was that whites should be listed first. This tendency did not reflect a simple preference for alphabetical ordering; blancos preceded amarillos in vertical lists that included both terms. Nor did it correspond with numerical weight of different categories; mestizos often outnumbered blancos in reported census results. The tendency to list "white" first in statistical tables reflected the unstated but pervasive assumption that whites naturally belonged at the top of the racial hierarchy.

The most notable exception to this ordering trend proves the rule. In the 1921 Mexican census, the first after the 1910 Revolution, a summary table titled "Razas," lists "raza indígena" first, followed by "raza mezclada," "raza blanca," "all other races or unknown," and "foreigners, without distinction by race" (see figure 5.1).

Cuadro 3	RAZAS				
MEXICANOS DE NACIMIENTO		Hombres	Mujeres	TOTAL	Tanto por ciento
Raza indígena		2 060 984	2 118 465	4 179 449	29.16
Raza mezclada		4 134 989	4 369 622	8 504 561	59.33
Raza blanca		662 291	741 427	1 404 718	9.80
Cualquiera otra raza o que se ignora		73 564	70 530	144 094	1.00
Extranjeros, sin distinción de razas		70 987	30 971	101 958	0.71
	SUMAS	7 003 785	7 330 995	14 334 780	100.00

FIGURE 5.1 The Razas of Mexico, 1921.
SOURCE: Mexico. Departamento de la Estadística Nacional. *Resumen del censo general de habitantes, de 30 noviembre de 1921*, 62.

The Mexican Revolution, of course, extolled the indigenous past and laid the ideological foundations for the construction of the Mexican *raza cósmica* [cosmic race]; it was also virulently antiforeign, seeking to construct a new Mexican nationalism symbolically rooted in the glories of the indigenous past. The inversion of the "natural" order of racial categories was clearly a political act by those who produced the official statistics.[29]

---

[28] The dividing lines *within* the "white" category were often understood to be *racial* lines, as well as national and religious. See Kolchin, "Whiteness Studies"; Guglielmo, *White on Arrival*. On debates over the merits of different kinds of "whites" in Latin America, see especially Lesser, *Welcoming the Undesirables*; Skidmore, *Black into White*.

[29] In his analysis of census classifications in Malaysia, sociologist Charles Hirschman noted just such an inversion of the hierarchy of racial categories following independence from British imperial rule after World War II (Hirschman, "The Meaning and Measurement of Ethnicity in Malaysia").

And yet this deliberate disruption of the expected order of racial categories in the 1921 Mexican census serves to confirm the general rule, underscoring the extent to which the prioritization of whiteness was taken for granted in the presentation of racial statistics across most of the region.

The Guatemalan censuses also depart, nominally at least, from the general tendency of listing "white" first. "Ladino" is listed first in all censuses in which racial data are presented. In all but one of these, however, "whites" were included in the "ladino" category either in the initial collection of the data (as in the 1880 census), or in the official reporting of the data (as in the 1938 census). "White" was listed as a separate racial category only once, in 1921, and then it was listed fourth—after "ladinos," "indios," and "negros" (but before "amarillos"), even though it was the second most populous category.[30] Given the historical usage of "ladino" as a blanket term for "civilized" (i.e., not "indio"), the unusual placement of the "white" category in this particular context may indicate that it referenced primarily European immigrants and naturalized citizens.

The first category in official tables or lists generally signaled which racial type most approximated the desired or idealized national type.[31] Subsequent categories represented the other types that were officially recognized as component parts of the nation. The category listed last, in turn, could mark the least desired component of the national demographic mix. In some cases, the last category admitted a racial element within the national territory that did not figure in official narratives about the constitutive races that made up the nation. This was sometimes the case, for example, for the Asian or "yellow" category [amarillo]. An alphabetical ordering would have amarillos listed first in most tables. Instead, it tends to be listed either second to last or last in the cases where it appears at all.

This approach to organization of statistical tables is evident even in countries that did not include direct race queries on censuses. In Argentine census reports, for example, nationality statistics were arranged to

---

[30] Guatemala. Dirección General de Estadística, *Censo de la Población de la república levantado el 28 de agosto de 1921*, 466. Racial data were only reported for the *Municipio de Guatemala*. The national and foreign populations were cross tabulated by "race": "blancos" was the most populous category among foreigners (1,340 foreign "whites" compared to 1,162 foreign "ladinos") and the third most populous category among nationals (4,721 "whites" compared to 40,271 "ladinos" and 4,954 "indios"). "Blancos" were the second most populous in the general summary of the total population. In all three summary tables, the order remained the same.

[31] In his analysis of "vertical classification" across cultures, Schwarz (*Vertical Classification*, 94) notes the tendency for "the higher point in the vertical plain [to] be more worthy and desirable than the lower" (cited in Goldstein, "What's in an Order?," 5).

emphasize the Europeanness of the Argentine nation while downplaying the presence of Africans or Asians in the population. In a table describing the population of Buenos Aires by nationality, sex, and age, the various nationality categories of the population were grouped into two higher order categories, "Independent America" and "Europe," while "Africans" and "Asians" were listed separately, along with "unspecified," at the bottom of a vertical list (see figure 5.2).

Excluded from the two visually prominent metacategories, "Africans" and "Asians" appear as marginal or residual classifications. Another summary table from the same census lists nationality categories horizontally across the top, beginning with American nationalities in alphabetical order, followed by European nationalities in alphabetical order, and ending with the category "Africans." Although the logic of this ordering is not made explicit in the table, the effect is the placement of "Africans" (with no further disaggregation) at the far right hand side of the table—the farthest possible from the "Argentine" category.

Within category sets, the practice of lumping some categories together and splitting others apart are also revealing.[32] Guatemala's lumping of all non-Indians into a "ladino" category in most censuses is indicative of the fundamentally dichotomous nature of racial boundaries in that context. Whiteness was equated with being "civilized"; being civilized, in turn, was equated with not being an Indian. An additional example is provided by the Peruvian census of 1940, which combined "whites" and "mestizos" into a single category ("blanca y mestiza") to present the changes in the racial make-up of Peru's population since 1876 in graphic form (see figure 5.3).[33]

Such categorical lumping creates ambiguity. In effect, it graphically challenges the solidity of the line that—at the point of data collection—had supposedly distinguished "whites" and "mestizos." At the same time, the collapse of the categorical boundary between white and mestizo for purposes of presenting census results belies the belief that "whiter is better." The result is a graph that suggests a potentially much higher proportion of probable or possible "whites" than would appear to be the case if the categories were represented by separate colored bars.

---

[32] On lumping and splitting as cognitive processes, see Zerubavel, "Lumping and Splitting."

[33] A detailed analysis of the racial and scientific views of those who carried out Peru's 1940 census is provided by López, R., "Demographic Knowledge and Nation Building." For historical perspective on the Peruvian case, see Sulmont and Valdivia, "From Pre-Modern 'Indians' to Contemporary 'Indigenous People.'"

Tabla especial de la poblacion de la ciudad de

NACIONALIDADES		á 1 año V.	M.	2 á 5 V.	M.	6 á 10 V.	M.	11 á 15 V.	M.	16 á 20 V.	M.	21 á 30 V.	M.	31 á 40 V.	M.
AMERICA INDEPENDIENTE	Argentinos	3704	3565	6672	6136	7070	7668	5568	6358	3022	5811	4262	8240	2909	5543
	Bolivianos				1		2	1	1	9	3	26	13	11	2
	Brasileros	3	1	15	26	32	25	34	24	54	46	123	60	93	37
	Chilenos			1	1	5	4	9	13	46	30	96	32	65	23
	Norte-Americanos		1	2	6	7	6	15	8	47	13	239	20	128	11
	Orientales	48	25	150	129	266	221	414	325	620	449	1003	770	423	361
	Paraguayos	1	2	15	11	43	37	68	25	64	17	117	33	78	11
	Peruanos	1						2		4	3	13	2	7	6
	Otros Estados Americanos				2	1	1	3	2	4	4	15	15	13	7
EUROPA	Austriacos				2	3	1	3	4	46	2	241	17	109	11
	Alemanes	2	1	21	17	29	27	27	32	88	72	596	234	431	160
	Belgas			2	1	3		4	2	4	8	38	16	39	14
	Españoles	15	16	87	90	151	158	471	305	1604	496	3706	1035	2478	718
	Franceses	26	12	97	109	168	172	302	242	919	585	2810	1524	2229	1051
	Ingleses	9	2	28	20	45	46	71	67	192	132	809	368	453	166
	Italianos	82	75	559	524	954	818	1881	1026	2670	1629	9190	4063	7128	2612
	Portugueses	1	1	2		5	4	6	3	39	4	274	20	141	11
	Suizos	2	5	11	11	20	13	35	23	112	60	417	114	262	72
	Otros Estados Europeos	2	2	2	7	6	5	29	7	190	38	538	63	298	62
	Africanos			1	2	1	4		4	3	9	5	48	13	34	14
	Asiáticos							1			2		3		2	
	Sin especificacion		2					2	1	8		6		4	
	SUMAS	3896	3711	7666	8094	8812	9209	8949	8971	9753	9407	24870	10652	17635	10892

OBSERVACION—En la distribucion de las edades no fijamos los años segun el órden de las estadísticas y censos europeos, que es inconveniente y sugeto á errores.

Los europeos, por ejemplo, en general ponen en sus casillas así:—de 2 á 5 años, en seguida, de 5 á 10, despues de 10 á 15; y así, en este órden van siempre repitiendo la cifra antecedente.

Esto dá lugar á que los empadronadores confundan la colocacion de individuos que tienen la edad representada por el número repetido, poniéndoles unos en la primera columna de 2 á 5, y otros en la de 5 á 10., &.

FIGURE 5.2 The Nationalities of Argentina, 1869.

SOURCE: Argentina. Superintendente del Censo. *Primer Censo de la República Argentina . . . 1872*, 26.

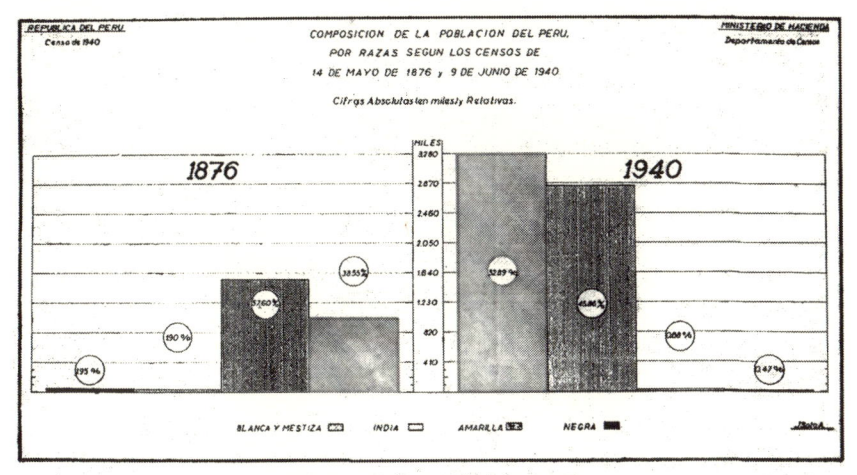

FIGURE 5.3 Changes in the Racial Composition of Peru, 1876 vs. 1940.
SOURCE: Peru. Dirección de Estadística. *Censo nacional de población y ocupación*, 1940. The tallest column in 1940 was "blanca y mestiza", at 52.89%, followed closely by "india" at 45.86%. In 1876, the "india" column was tallest, at 57.60%, followed by "blanca y mestiza", at 38.55%. The "amarilla" and "negra" columns were just under 2% in 1876, and under 1% in 1940.

The splitting of census categories can also be revealing, as in the 1872 Brazilian census where the division of pardos and negros according to slave or free status clearly indicated that "condition" was the more fundamental basis of distinction. In the census of 1890, two years after the final abolition of slavery in Brazil, pardos and negros who had previously been separated by a solid black line that demarcated slaves from free persons, were lumped together in common "racial" categories that effectively erased the once fundamental difference in their social status.[34]

Sudden changes in category sets, such as the addition or removal of categories, may suggest shifts in official views of race. For example, when the first national census of Cuba was taken under the direction of the US War Department in 1898, the "white" category that had been used in Spanish censuses of Cuba was split into "native-born whites" and "foreign-born whites." The change most likely reflected US Army officials' skepticism regarding the whiteness of whites born in Cuba; seeing the Cuban population through their North American racial lens, it evidently seemed necessary to distinguish "white whites" from "questionably white whites."[35]

---

[34] For a more detailed discussion of this case, see Loveman, M., "The Race to Progress."

[35] Anthropologist Virginia Domínguez documents an analogous preoccupation among "Protestant (American) whites" with respect to the "so-called (Creole) whites" in Louisiana around the same time (Domínguez, *White by Definition*).

Thus, census officials organized and displayed official census results in ways that revealed their beliefs about the differential value of component racial types in the population. The placement of categories in lists and tables was neither random nor governed by neutral ordering rules. Census officials made choices in the visual arrangement of census results, and these choices implied preferences for some kinds of human kind over others. Across the region and over the course of several decades, census officials typically listed what they saw as the most desirable racial categories first and the least desirable categories last. Through categorical lumping and splitting, they stressed the blurriness of boundaries between some racial categories and the solidity of boundaries between others. In these ways, the graphic display of racial statistics often subtly advanced ideas about natural racial hierarchy. The implicit reinforcement of racial ideologies through the organization of statistical tables helped to bolster, in turn, the explicit arguments about racial demographic improvement as the path to national progress.

Acts of Displacement

In making decisions about how to collect and display racial statistics, census officials not only revealed preferences for some racial categories over others, they also displaced some kinds of humans to the margins of their statistical portraits of the nation. In the census reports of many Latin American countries, for example, the existence of "uncivilized" indigenous peoples was noted in prefatory comments or parenthetical asides. Only occasionally were they included in tables that described the "general" population. This marginalization stemmed from a combination of ideological and practical reasons. Ideologically, since one aim of the census was to signal civilized-nation status, census officials sought to downplay the presence of "uncivilized" peoples in their midst. Practically, since census takers often could not physically reach indigenous populations, it was deemed inappropriate to include them in tallies of the officially enumerated population.

Census officials tended to differentiate between two basic kinds of Indians: "civilized" and "uncivilized." In distinguishing between the two, census officials tended to treat the accessibility of a population as diagnostic; the farther people lived from the institutional reach of the state, the less civilized they were in the eyes of state officials. Indeed, in several countries "uncivilized" Indians were, by definition, those who lived beyond enumerators' reach.

Latin America's nineteenth- and early twentieth-century statistics agencies lacked both the administrative capacity and legitimate authority to extract information from populations settled "outside civilization."[36] This state of affairs posed a dilemma for statistics agency officials. Aware that modern censuses should aspire to enumerate the entire population inhabiting the national territory, census officials lamented any gaps in coverage. Yet the limited infrastructural reach of most nineteenth- and early twentieth-century Latin American states meant some parts of the territory simply could not be canvassed, especially more remote areas where most unassimilated indigenous peoples lived.

Some census officials confronted this problem by openly conceding that certain tribes were not counted in the census. Such admissions usually appeared in portions of census reports devoted to disclosing administrative difficulties of census operations and resulting methodological shortcomings. Typical examples are the reports for the 1910 Honduran census, which clarified that "tribes of *sambos, payas* and *sumos* that inhabit the Mosquitia region and those of the *jicaques de yoro*" were not enumerated, and the 1880 Guatemalan census, which noted that three departments with a high percentage of indígenas were excluded.[37] A population table in Bolivia's 1854 census report contains a column for "indians, not counting the savages" (*indios sin contar los bárbaros*).[38]

Along with such straightforward disclosures, census officials sometimes dealt with the lack of returns from indigenous tribes by producing estimates of population numbers from these areas. Examples include Bolivia's 1854 guesstimate of "*tribus salvajes*," Chile's 1865 estimate of the population of Araucanía, and Costa Rica's 1864 and 1883 estimates of "uncivilized indians." Census officials took care to distinguish the numbers that came from the census from those that were mere estimates. In the 1926 Venezuelan census, for example, indigenous population counts were referred to as the "unspecified population" in contrast to the "specified" population who were actually enumerated. In twelve

---

[36] (Untaxed) Native Americas living in remote areas were also excluded from US censuses prior to the 1870s (and due to the role of censuses in determining political apportionment, slaves were discounted 2/5). Goyer & Domschke, *The Handbook of National Population Censuses*, 389; Nobles, *Shades of Citizenship*; Anderson, M. J., *The American Census*.

[37] Honduras. Dirección Nacional de Estadística, *Breve Noticia del empadronamiento general de casas y habitantes de la República de Honduras practicado el 18 de diciembre de 1910*, 4; Guatemala. Dirección General de Estadística, *Sexto Censo de Población*, I. In a historical review of the country's previous censuses, the 1950 Guatemalan census says that three departments "with a high percentage of indígenas, Totonicapán, Quetzaltenango and Huehuetenango, could not be enumerated."

[38] Delance, *Bosquejo Estadístico de Bolivia*, 153.

of thirteen national level summary tables published in the 1926 Venezuelan census, the population is divided into three types: men, women, and indígenas.[39] Notably, Venezuela's 1926 census did not include a query about race or indigenous origins. The indígena category referred to the "unspecified" or uncounted population; estimates of the size of the indigenous population were kept separate from tallies of the men and women actually counted in the census.

It seems that estimated numbers of "uncivilized" Indians were provided by local authorities or church officials residing nearest to territories inhabited by indigenous tribes. In some places, census officials made serious efforts to get as reliable estimates as possible. In the 1920 Nicaraguan census, for instance, enumerators were instructed to speak directly to caciques (Indian chiefs) to request estimated numbers of indígenas in nomadic tribes. Whatever their source, the estimated numbers of "uncivilized Indians" typically declined over time, providing support for pronouncements that Indians were destined to disappear as a distinct demographic element of the nation.

In a few cases, officials approached the task of counting indigenous peoples as a separate endeavor from the national census. Counts of indígenas were deemed useful, but not for the purpose of generating a statistical portrait of the nation. Put baldly, in the eyes of some census officials, Indians did not count as members of the nation, so it was not imperative that they be counted in a national census. Segregated counts and separated tables of indigenous peoples in the context of national censuses reflected their liminal status as not fully included in the national community, but not fully outside of it either.

In early twentieth-century Chile, for example, censuses of "uncivilized" indigenous populations were sometimes attempted, but separately from the national census. When indigenous peoples were enumerated as part of national census count in 1907, their schedules were printed in a different color so census staff could distinguish them from those used to survey the general population.[40] The very last table in Chile's 1907 census

---

[39] Venezuela. Dirección Nacional de Estadística y Censos Nacionales, *Quinto Censo Nacional de los Estados Unidos de Venezuela ... levantado en los días 31 de enero y 1, 2 y 3 de febrero de 1926*. In 1951 to 1952, Venezuela took a special census of the Indian population, which enumerated groups living near inhabited centers. Others were estimated. The totals were then added to the official total. "It was done in this fashion to separate this group from the total population, which consisted of only those directly enumerated" (Goyer and Domschke, *The Handbook of National Population Censuses*, 345).

[40] Chile. Comisión Central del Censo, *Censo de la República de Chile*, XXII. By way of comparison, a separate census schedule was also used to enumerate Native Americans in the US census of 1880, and a modified census schedule was employed in their enumeration in 1900 and 1910.

report presented results of the "Censo de los indios araucanos," with results broken down by province, department, subdelegation, and sex. Atypically, the census recognized a significant *increase* in the Araucanian population as well as noting the likelihood that numbers were underestimated in previous censuses. The introduction to the Araucanian census refers to the *"pueblos salvajes"* encountered by the Spanish on conquest and suggests that "while these peoples do not seem to be disappearing (*no parece en vias de estinguirse*), and their fusion with other ethnic elements has not been achieved in the desired proportion,...they no longer comprise...a nation with its defined frontiers, as was the case until a quarter century ago."[41] Thus the Chilean census agency associated mestizaje and social integration with advancement of Chilean nation building, while acknowledging that there remained resistance to this process by the Araucanian peoples.

Argentine national censuses did not generally pretend to include indigenous populations residing within the state's territorial borders. Census reports often included blanket estimates of "uncivilized" Indians in the national territory. But there was no place for indigenous peoples in the summary statistical tables that filled the published volumes of national census results. Only in special censuses of the *territories,* those regions still outside full and formal political inclusion in the Argentine nation-state, did questionnaires include a query that might admit the presence of indigenous peoples. The official schedule for Argentina's 1912 census of territories is reproduced in figure 5.4.

Argentina's 1912 census of the territories asked for individuals' pueblo. The official report for this census, in turn, presented separate numbers for the "enumerated indígena population."[42] The discussion of indigenous population statistics concluded with an assurance that the disappearance of a distinguishable indígena population within the nation was demographically inevitable.[43]

Thus, "uncivilized indians" were frequently relegated to the margins of published tomes of national census results. This statistical segregation seemed methodologically warranted given the principal aim of the official

---

[41] Chile. Comisión Central del Censo, *Censo de la República de Chile,* XXIII.

[42] The "pueblo" query may have been used to collect information about tribal identification in addition to information about "town" of residence. On the census schedule, it appears after other, higher-level administrative/jurisdictional specifications ("Department" and "District"), and it precedes the numbered questions that the enumerator was to ask the individual enumerated (see figure 5.4).

[43] Argentina. Dirección General de Territorios Nacionales. *Censo de Población de los Territorios Nacionales, República Argentina, 1912,* 34.

CONSTRUCTING NATURAL ORDERS | 189

He aquí la ficha:

CENSO DE LOS TERRITORIOS NACIONALES

1912

ESTA TARJETA SIRVE PARA UNA SOLA PERSONA

GOBERNACION de . . . .
DEPARTAMENTO. . . . .
DISTRITO . . . .
PUEBLO . . . .

1.—¿Cuál es su nombre y apellido? . . . .
2.—¿Qué edad tiene? *Meses.* . . . .
Años . . . .
3.—¿Es soltero, casado ó viudo? . . . .
4.—¿A qué nación pertenece? . . . .
5.—¿Qué religión tiene? . . . .
6.—¿Qué profesión, oficio, ó medio de vida tiene? . . .
7.—¿Sabe leer y escribir? . . . .
8.—¿Sabe sólo leer? . . . .
9.—¿Va á la escuela? . . . .
10.—¿Posee propiedad privada? . . . .
11.—¿Está vacunado? ¿Cuánto tiempo hace que se vacunó? . . . .

Firma del Censado   *Firma del Empadronador*

. . . .

Lugar y fecha . . . .

FIGURE 5.4 The Pueblos in Argentine Territories, 1912.

SOURCE: Argentina. Dirección General de Territorios Nacionales. *Censo de Población de los Territorios Nacionales*, 1914, 10.

reports: to present a "scientific" portrait of the nation based on information collected in the census. The fact that "uncivilized indians" had not actually been enumerated meant they could not legitimately be included in the presentation of census results without corrupting the scientific validity of the report. But the marginalization of discussions of *"tribus salvajes"* [untamed tribes] in census publications also reflected and symbolically reinforced their peripheral status in elite visions of modernizing Latin American nations.

Acts of Omission

Census officials sought to produce and package census results in ways that showed their nation in the most favorable light possible. Toward this end, officials often downplayed the presence of "uncivilized" or "undesirable" elements within the population. One way they did this was by displacing references to such elements, keeping them apart from the most prominently featured sections of official reports. Another way they downplayed undesirable elements in the nation was by denying the existence or relevance of certain categories of people altogether.

Including a query about race on the census brought the racial composition of the population into view; omitting such a query rendered racial distinctions within the population statistically invisible. The refusal to count certain kinds of individuals effectively "disappeared" them as categorically distinct components of the population. Such acts of administrative violence, which some analysts have termed "statistical ethnocide," both built upon and reified myths of national homogeneity.[44]

In Chile, most notably, officials claimed that the homogeneity of their population rendered queries on religion, race, or language irrelevant. Intriguingly, Chilean census officials arrived at this position only after first attempting a national census that classified citizens by ethnoracial "origins." Chile's 1813 census used a question on origins to reproduce the fundamental colonial-era distinction between whites and castas. Spanish and other Europeans were distinguished categorically from castas, who were subdivided into indios, mestizos, mulattos and negros.[45] Chile's 1813 census stands out as one case where colonial classification practices clearly influenced the content of the first (would-be) national census. This early instance of

---

[44] On "statistical ethnocide," see, for example, López, "Epílogos," 1077.

[45] Spanish and other Europeans were subdivided into American Spanish; European Spanish; Spanish from Asia, the Canaries, and Africa; and Foreign European. Jaramillo, "Un alto en el camino," 56.

official ethnoracial classification of citizens in postcolonial Chile also hints at how Chile's history of census classification might have been otherwise. Chile's postindependence state, however, lacked the capacity to actually complete the 1813 enumeration. A planned second attempt in 1824 was cancelled. By the time the 1835 census took place, the political context had changed, and Chilean officials explicitly rejected the question on "origins" used in the prior enumeration effort. From the 1835 census forward, Chilean census officials denied any need for questions about differences among citizens (they saw Indians as outside the boundaries of the national community, and thus dealt with their enumeration separately).

From the mid-nineteenth century, Chilean census official recognized that their omission of questions about religion and language, in particular, departed from recommendations made by "Mr. Quetelet" at the International Statistical Congress (ISC). In the context of Chile's 1865 census, a representative of the Chilean Central Statistical office explained, "It would be superfluous to ask for these data in Chile, seeing as belief as well as language are one among [Chile's] children."[46] The Chilean census did not need to inquire about race, the explanation continued, because unlike the United States, where the census distinguished the black slave population from the free population and the free persons of color, "happily in our country there exists a single race, free and equal as much in the color of their skin as in their political rights and obligations, which exempts us from the work of distinction that occupies long pages of the American Census."[47] Thus, the deviation from internationally recognized census taking standards was explained, and the presumption of Chilean religious, linguistic, and racial homogeneity justified the exclusion from the census of questions that might have generated data that proved otherwise. Diversity within Chile's population remained statistically invisible.

Argentine censuses also omitted queries about race. Like their Chilean counterparts, Argentine census officials minimized or denied the relevance of demographic diversity within the nation, then used this denial to justify the exclusion of census queries that could produce evidence to the contrary. Explaining the absence of a race query on the 1895 census, an Argentine census official wrote: "The Asiatic and African races clearly exist only in diminutive proportions, such that their influence with respect to the country's development [*transformación*] is null. The same can be

---

[46] Chile. Oficina Central de Estadística, *Censo General de la República de Chile*, viii.

[47] Chile. Oficina Central de Estadística, *Censo General de la República de Chile*, viii.

said with respect to the Indians."[48] In the 1914 census, in turn, the omission of a race question was explained by invoking the contrast to the United States. Echoing the comment in Chile's 1865 census, Argentina's census official noted the challenges of racial enumeration in the United States before noting that "happily in Argentina we don't have this serious reason for concern; here the race is completely white; we have blacks only as an exception."[49]

Argentine census reports did, however, admit to some diversity within the national population. As discussed in the previous chapter, Argentine censuses tracked the origins of the foreign-born population, and used the language of race to discuss the types and qualities of different streams of immigrants. Comparison of statistical tables that reported the racial composition of the immigrant population in two consecutive national censuses provides a striking example of how the display of descriptive statistics entailed acts of omission. While the table printed in Argentina's 1895 census registered the existence of a small number of immigrants of "raza asiatica" and "raza africana" (see bottom left of figure 5.5a), in the 1914 census, Asians and Africans were subsumed within a new category: "unspecified race" (see bottom left of figure 5.5b). Thus, the presence of nonwhite immigrants within the national population was statistically obscured.

The notion that Argentina and Chile were self-evidently homogenous nations was of course a nationalist fiction. In part, the successful creation and dissemination of this fiction owed to the selective omission by census officials of statistics that would have shown otherwise. The absence of census queries that could document internal diversity along racial, cultural, or linguistic lines ensured that census results would generate demographic portraits of homogenous peoples. Invoking the more "complicated" task of racial enumeration in the United States as a point of contrast, Chilean and Argentine census officials drew attention to a way in which they surpassed the United States in the race to progress: the demographic homogeneity—and whiteness—of their nations.

Outright denial of ethnoracial difference within the nation was less plausible in countries with large and visible indigenous, mestizo, or Afrodescendant populations. Yet even in these contexts, census officials often engaged

---

[48] Argentina. Segundo Censo de la República Argentina, II, XLVI, cited in Otero, *Estadística y Nación*, 361). See also Andrews, *The Afro-Argentines of Buenos Aires*. Argentina's 1895 Census Commission arrived at the decision to exclude a race query after a detailed discussion that focused on the presumed insignificance of the data for understanding national demographic trends, as well as concerns about the reliability of the data. See Otero, *Estadística y Nación*, 352.

[49] Argentina. Comisión Directiva del Censo. *Tercer Censo Nacional*, I: 174.

Población argentina por razas.

RAZAS	VARONES	MUJERES	TOTAL	PROPORCION POR MIL
Latina. — Hispana:				
Argentinos	1,452,952	1,497,432	2,950,384	746
Americanos de habla española	183,804	106,829	290,633	73
Latinos de otros idiomas	392,467	227,053	619,520	156
Total raza latina	2,029,223	1,831,314	3,860,537	975
Raza germánica	30,587	17,028	47,615	13
» anglo-sajona	15,154	8,046	23,200	6
» eslava	8,330	6,840	15,170	4
» escandinava	2,498	587	3,085	1
» asiática	310	104	414	—
» africana	290	164	454	—
Demás razas	2,527	1,909	4,436	1
TOTAL GENERAL	2,088,919	1,865,992	3,954,911	1000

FIGURE 5.5A The Racial Composition of the Argentine Population, 1895.

SOURCE: Argentina. Comisión Directiva del Censo. *Segundo Censo de la República Argentina, Mayo 10 de 1895.* Buenos Aires: Taller Tip. de la Penitenciaria Nacional, 1898.

RAZAS	VARONES	MUJERES	TOTAL	PROPORCION ⁰/₀₀
Latina:				
Argentinos	98.647	85.226	183.873	626
Americanos de habla española	23.565	15.994	39.559	134
Latinos de otros idiomas	34.113	15.540	49.653	170
Total raza latina	156.325	116.760	273.085	930
Raza Germánica	4.731	2.837	7.568	26
» Anglo Sajona	1.825	957	2.782	9
» Eslava	4.385	3.159	7.544	26
» Escandinava	33	3	36	—
Otras razas	866	157	1.023	4
Sin especificar	974	360	1.334	5
Total general	169.139	124.233	293.372	1.000

FIGURE 5.5B The Racial Composition of Argentina's Foreign-born Population, 1912.

SOURCE: Argentina. Dirección General de Territorios Nacionales. *Censo de Población de los Territorios Nacionales, República Argentina, 1912.* Ministerio del Interior. Buenos Aires: Imp. G. Kraft, 1914.

in selective omission of racial statistics to improve conformity of census results with official narratives of national identity and progress. Venezuelan censuses ignored the presence of Afrodescendant people within the population after abolition. Nineteenth-century historian José Gil Fortoul considered this a deliberate decision by elites who did not want blacks to be reminded of their painful experience as slaves.[50] The decision to make

---

[50] Fortoul, *El Hombre y la Historia,* cited in Wright, W., *Café con Leche,* 4.

Venezuelan censuses colorblind was formalized in 1926, with passage of a law that proscribed references to "color" in official statistics.[51] Such efforts appear to have extended to other government agencies as well: "For all intents and purposes, after emancipation took place the blacks simply disappeared from the official records of modern Venezuela."[52]

In countries with majority indigenous or *mestizo* populations, as well, officials often downplayed the presence of Afrodescendant populations. Census officials in Andean and Mesoamerican countries asserted the demographic insignificance of blacks or Asians, then relied on these assertions to justify excluding these categories from statistical representations of the nation. In the 1900 Bolivian census, for example, the official questionnaire asked about individual race and included a "black" category as an allowable response. The published census report included a table that reported the results, with the categories arrayed horizontally in order of their proportional share of the population (see figure 5.6a). On the next page of the report, a graphic representation of the results omitted blacks from the picture (see figure 5.6b). The text that preceded the image noted matter-of-factly: "the black population...has been omitted, since it is not of much significance for appreciating the data on the races."[53]

Guatemalan censuses from this period dealt with blackness in a similar way. In the 1893 Guatemalan census report, the existence of Afrodescendant individuals in the population was noted only to be immediately dismissed as demographically irrelevant:

> The territory that today constitutes the State of Guatemala was discovered by Pedro de Alvarado, on a mission given to him by Hernan Cortés, conqueror of Mexico. The indigenous families that Alvarado found were *quichés; cakchiqueles, zutuhiles, pocomanes, mames, lacandones* and other smaller groups; the first three were organized and offered the most resistance. When the African race was introduced with slavery, more so

---

[51] Charier, *Le Mouvement Noir au Vénézuela*, 26.

[52] Wright, W., *Café con Leche*, 4. Wright notes that "in government documents, court records, and national histories, blacks receive no attention, as such, and remain hidden from sight. Even their cultural contributions to Venezuelan society went unnoticed, for the most part, especially in the history texts used in the nation's schools" (4–5). Wright suggests that historians contributed to the official disappearance of Afro-Venezuelans by "overlooking the presence of blacks as a separate racial group following emancipation." See also Charier, *Le Mouvement Noir au Vénézuela*; Pollak-Eltz "Migration from Barlovento to Caracas" on race as a taboo subject in Venezuela.

[53] Bolivia. Oficina Nacional de Inmigración, Estadística y Propaganda Geográfica. *Censo General de la Población*, 31–2.

Población general de Bolivia, clasificada por razas

Departamentos	Población absoluta					Proporción por 100				
	Indígenas	Mestizos	Blancos	Negros	No especificados	Indígena	Mestiza	Blanca	Negra	No especificada
La Paz....	333,421	39,680	36,255	2,056	30,784	75.61	8.90	8.13	0.46	6.90
Cochabamba	75,514	169,161	60,605	161	22,722	23.04	51.54	18.46	0.04	6.92
Potosí.....	186,947	89,159	21,713	101	27,695	57.43	27.38	6.66	0.03	8.50
Santa Cruz.	94,526	44,248	59,470	930	10,418	45.11	21.11	28.37	0.44	4.97
Chuquisaca.	80,217	80,916	31,767	205	11,329	39.25	39.58	15.53	0.10	5.54
Tarija.....	51,670	39,377	8,184	206	3,450	50.25	38.25	7.95	0.20	3.35
Oruro......	58,607	14,309	7,774	35	5,356	68.09	16.62	9.03	0.04	6.22
El Litoral..	—	—	—	—	49,820	—	—	—	—	100.00
El Beni....	20,124	4,219	5,113	245	2,479	62.55	13.11	15.88	0.76	7.70
Terr. de Cls.	19,838	4,949	207	6	6,883	62.25	15.52	0.64	0.01	21.58
La República	920,864	486,018	231,088	3,945	170,936	50.91	26.75	12.72	0.21	9.41

En el diagrama siguiente, que es la representación gráfica del cuadro anterior, se ha suprimido la población negra y la no especificada, por no ser de mucha significación para apreciar el dato sobre las razas.

FIGURE 5.6A The Bolivian Population Classified by Race, 1900.

SOURCE: Bolivia. Oficina Nacional de Inmigración, Estadística y Propaganda Geográfica. *Censo general de la población . . . 1900*, 1902–04. [1973], 32.

in the north than in the south, this race was mixed with the rest, but without making an imprint on any region, due to their scarce number.[54]

The lack of any perceptible African influence on the nation was both asserted as fact and underscored through juxtaposition to the officially recognized components of the national mix: conquering Spaniards and specified indigenous tribes.

Another section of the same Guatemalan census report explained matter-of-factly: "The population total according to the census of 1892 is 1,364,678 inhabitants. The two principal groups are Ladinos and indios, the former being those who belong to the white race and the mixture of European and indígena. There are several other subdivisions that are not easy to specify, such as the not very perceptible group made up of the mixture of indígena and black, black and white, and the successions of these two."[55] The imperceptibility of peoples of African ancestry was both ensured and enshrined by the use of *ladino* as an umbrella category for anyone who was not indígena.

---

[54] Guatemala. Dirección General de Estadística. *Censo General de la República de Guatemala... 1893*, 11.

[55] Guatemala. Dirección General de Estadística. *Censo General de la República de Guatemala... 1893*, 14.

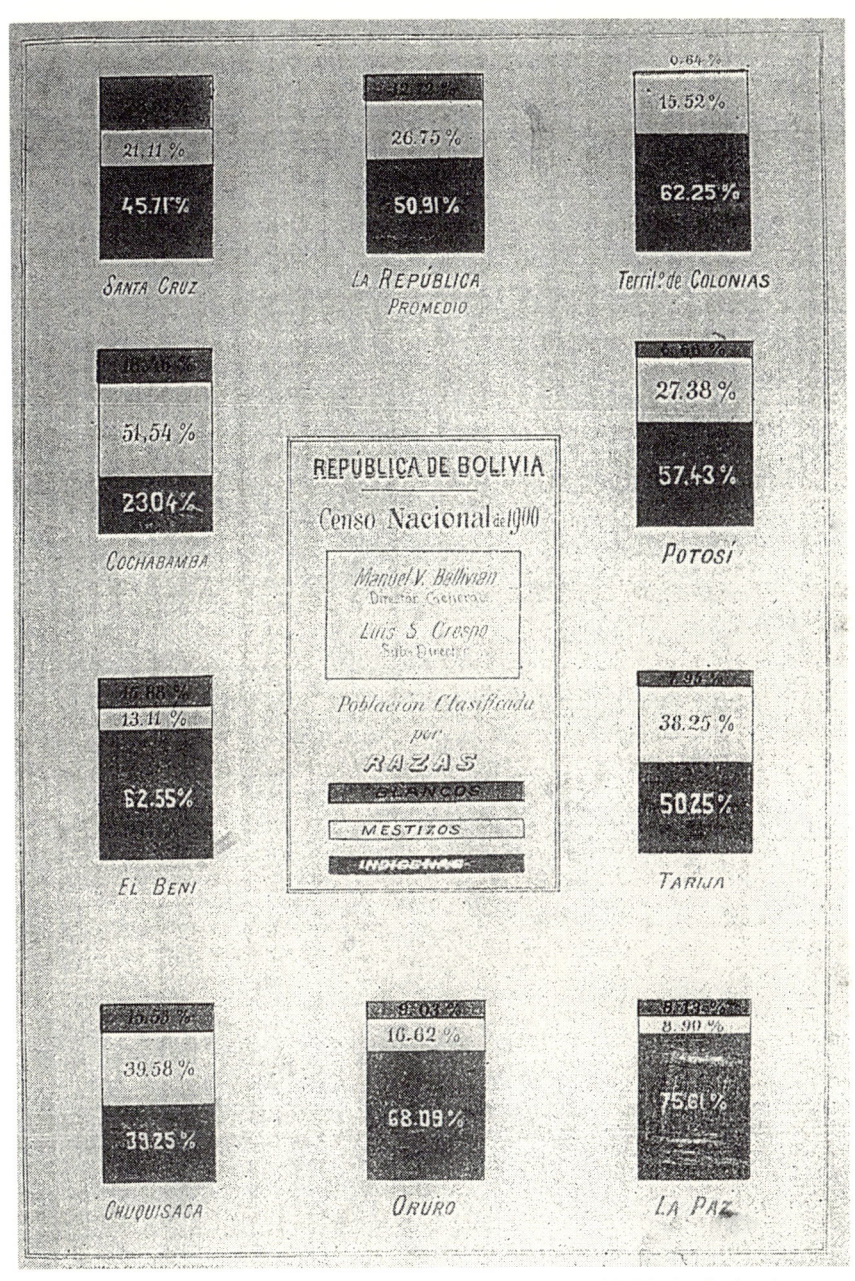

FIGURE 5.6B The Bolivian Population Classified by Race, with Blacks Omitted, 1900.
SOURCE: Bolivia. Oficina Nacional de Inmigración, Estadística y Propaganda Geográfica. *Censo general de la población de la República de Bolivia . . . 1900*, 33.

CONSTRUCTING NATURAL ORDERS | 197

Latin American census reports typically acknowledged at least some historical presence of Africans within the population. But in the collection and display of census data, officials found ways to minimize evidence of their contemporary demographic relevance. Sometimes these tactics were subtle and other times they were quite explicit. Either way, they helped obscure traces of African influence in some Latin American populations. The resulting demographic snapshots thus helped to advance idealized nationalist visions of white or progressively whitening populations.

Statistical images of racially vital and "progressing" nations were also bolstered by the way census officials dealt with the enumeration of Asians. Throughout much of Latin America in the late-nineteenth century, political and intellectual elites considered Asians, and especially Chinese, to be incompatible with emergent national types. Opponents of Asian immigration in the region invoked a wide range of arguments—from narrowly biological and racist to broadly cultural and moralistic—to support their contentions that such immigrants would inevitably form "yellow cysts" in the "national organism."[56] Nonetheless, Asian migrants were recruited as laborers to several Latin American countries in the late-nineteenth century, and were a visible minority in many rural mining towns, in railroad construction, and also in capital cities, especially before the wave of exclusionary immigration legislation specifically targeting Chinese swept across the continent in the early 1900s.[57]

Many countries that collected racial statistics in their early national censuses did not include a category for Asians. This was the case in Brazil, for example, where a "yellow" category was not added to the census until 1940 (and by then it primarily captured Japanese rather than Chinese immigrants and their descendants). In the Bolivian census of 1900, to cite another example, enumerators were explicitly instructed not to report any "races" other than "blanca," "mestiza," "india," or "negra." As a general rule, Asians were not included in the national imaginings of state-building elites in Latin America. They were never among the "formative races" featured in national "foundational fictions."[58] Perhaps not surprisingly, then, the demographic presence of Asians was often actively downplayed by census officials charged with producing statistical portraits of the nation.

Even when censuses included a category for Asians at the point of data collection, the category was often omitted from the summary tables

---

[56] Lesser, *Negotiating National Identity*.
[57] Fitzgerald and Cook-Martín, *Culling the Masses*.
[58] Sommer, "Irresistible Romance."

of census results. It is clear, for example, that enumerators for the 1912 Colombian census classified some individuals as "yellow" because tables reporting results at the departmental level sometimes included a column for amarillos. In national-level summary tables, however, amarillo is omitted.[59] Similarly, in the 1920 census of the Dominican Republic, enumerators used the category amarillo at the point of enumeration, but in the official published census results, amarillos were subsumed into the mestizo category, effectively eliminating them as a visibly distinct element in the national population.

The uneasy and reluctant acknowledgement of "yellow races" in the official statistical portraits of Latin American nations was also evident in the conspicuous silence about Asian immigrants in the narrative sections of census volumes devoted to extolling the contributions of immigrants to the nation. Assessments of the role of immigration in national development referred almost exclusively to European immigrants, as discussed in chapter 4. In a rare instance where attention was deliberately drawn to the numbers of Chinese immigrants, it was to provide reassurance that the total numbers were quite small. Demonstrating an orientation to international standards for comprehensive coverage in modern census taking, the first modern Panamanian census, taken in 1910, dutifully explained that the enumeration had not adequately counted the Chinese population, but that the fault for this defect lay with the "malicious" Chinese:

> We want to call attention to the enumeration of the Chinese. In our view, there are more subjects of the Celestial Empire in Panama than appear in the census, but the fault cannot be imputed to the enumerators but rather to the circumstance that, the immigration of the yellow race being prohibited by law since the year 1904, individuals belonging to that race, wanting to elude responsibilities, have maliciously hidden themselves with the object that the colony appear in the census with a smaller number than it really has. This is an incontrovertible fact....[60]

Still, the narrative continued, even counting all the Chinese who were involved in commerce and thus always in the street, "making their number appear greater than other nationalities, the total if all of them had been counted would only reach three thousand."[61]

---

[59] Colombia. Ministerio de Gobierno, *Censo General de la República de Colombia*, 82, 98).
[60] Panama. Dirección General de Estadística, *Boletín del Censo de la República de Panamá*, vi.
[61] Panama. Dirección General de Estadística, *Boletín del Censo de la República de Panamá*, vi.

The omission or marginalization of Asians in Latin American census reports both rested upon and reinforced the presumption of their insignificance to the demographic development of national populations. Census officials obscured the presence of Asians through the same sorts of practices used to downplay the relevance of other "undesirable" elements in the population. They omitted queries or categories that would render amarillos statistically visible; they relegated comments on Asian populations to peripheral sections of official reports; and they crafted positive portraits of national populations in formation in which Asian origin individuals had no recognized place.

Taken together, the array of subtle and not so subtle ways that census officials privileged certain racial categories over others in official published volumes of census results testifies to the influence of racist ideologies on the production of demographic knowledge. Census officials' racist beliefs and preferences were often explicitly elaborated and defended in the pages of official census volumes (as shown in chapter 4). But even when the desire for whiter populations was not expressed overtly, such preferences were often communicated indirectly. The idea of a natural hierarchy of racial kinds was taken for granted in the production of official census results. This foundational assumption was not only expressed between the lines; it was conveyed in the particular ways the lines of statistical tables were drawn, and in the ways that categories were ordered and labeled within those tables. Census officials' choices in collecting and arranging demographic data privileged some categorical distinctions within the population, while eliminating others from view.

Thus, the methods of data collection, organization, and display bolstered explicit narratives of ethnodemographic progress found in nineteenth- and early twentieth-century census publications. Census officials' predictions of national progress through racial "improvement" cited census results as if the numbers, being numbers, were inherently objective. But census counts were far from ideologically neutral. Whether deliberately or unselfconsciously, census officials' decisions about how to count and classify their populations reflected and reinscribed the fundamental racist belief in a natural hierarchy of human kinds. This belief informed the way census enumeration was conducted, the way returns were aggregated and displayed, and the way the final results were interpreted and framed for domestic and international audiences. Racial ideologies were deeply insinuated within the administrative practices of Latin America's central statistics agencies—the very agencies entrusted to produce objective, factual information about the condition of their respective populations.

Making the Nation Whole

The methods used to collect and visually display census results rank ordered different kinds of humankind, highlighting the demographic influence of some racial categories while downplaying the relevance of others. Census reports often showed Latin American populations divided into discrete, categorically different and unequal kinds. But ultimately, census reports subsumed internal categorical divides, however conceived, within clearly drawn external boundaries of the nation. Over and above their concern to document the ethnodemographic makeup and "progress" of their respective populations, census officials sought to document that their nations existed as clearly delineated and bounded entities—as modern nations among others.

The numbers and tables and texts bound together in leather volumes of national census results testified to the accomplishment of nationhood over and against the array of political and social divisions that threatened to undermine the consolidation of cohesive national communities. In the pages of official census results, state builders' aspirations for geographic, political, economic, and even ethnocultural integration could be presented not as a tenuous future possibility but as an already resolved matter of fact. After all, a census of the national population presupposed the existence of an identifiable and delimited national population to count.

Above all else, the official reports of national census results projected images of cohesive nations with clear external boundaries. The production of leather-bound tomes composed of official results from a national census was, in itself, an assertion that Latin American nations existed as such. The narrative text and statistical tables contained within, in turn, took the nation as their explicit referent population. At the front of each report was a summary table that described the total population of the nation. Such tables subtly yet forcefully instantiated the existence of a bounded national community. Whatever subdivisions were cross tabulated, they were all contained within the neat, solid boundaries of the nation as a whole. This had the effect of reifying the outer boundaries of the nation as given.

Summary descriptive tables presented the outer boundaries of the nation as obvious and unproblematic, eliding any trace of uncertainty or contestation. In the guise of mere description, such tables projected a confident image of national coherence and cohesion. The political underpinning of this vision was masked by the presumed neutrality of a simple table presenting presumably objective numerical data.

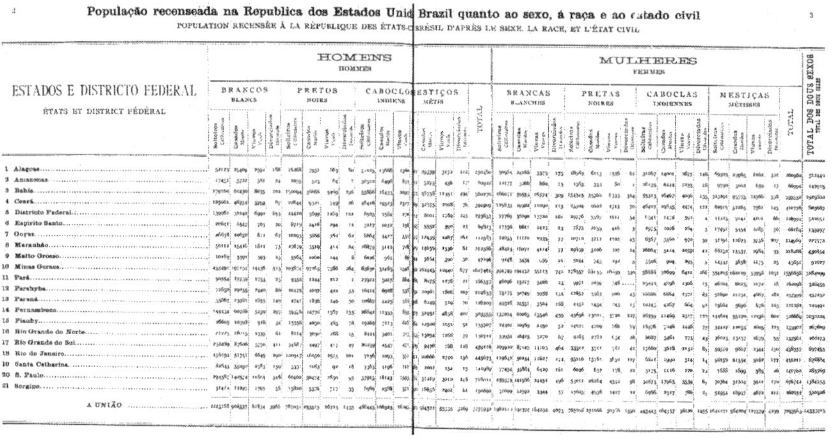

FIGURE 5.7 The Brazilian Population Postabolition, 1890.

SOURCE: *Synopse do recenseamento de 31 de dezembro de 1890*. Rio de Janeiro: Oficina da Estatística, 1898.

Exceptions to the typical presentational format bring into clear relief how standard summary tables worked to make tenuous and contested national boundaries appear unproblematic and self-evident. One example comes from Brazil's first general census, taken in 1872, before the final abolition of slavery in 1888 and the transition to a republic in 1889. The first and most prominent table in the 1872 census report described the aggregate numbers and characteristics of the entire *free* population of the Brazilian Empire. The second table, in turn, described the numbers and characteristics of the *slave* population.[62] While it not surprising that the preabolition census would distinguish free persons from slaves, the segregation of results into distinct tables on different pages conveyed that the two kinds of population enumerated in the 1872 census did not naturally belong together; they were not to be mistaken for a single people or nation.[63] In contrast, Brazil's census reports after abolition and the republican transition contain summary tables that bound census results for the population as a whole. As in the census reports of other Latin American republics, a single, unified summary table with clear and solid outer boundaries self-evidently "contains" the total population—in this case, the Brazilian nation (see figure 5.7).

The act of creating a single table to encapsulate all individuals within the claimed national territory was, in effect, a proclamation that the nation

---

[62] Brazil. Directoria Geral de Estatística, *Recenseamento da População*, "Quadros geraes."

[63] Side-by-side images of the pre- and postabolition tables appear in Loveman, M., "Census Taking and Nation Making in Nineteenth-Century Latin America," 339–341.

existed as an integral geographic, political, and demographic unit. Census officials could take geographic areas that remained contested, whether by competing states, autonomist political factions, or indigenous peoples, and make them appear in official reports as fully integrated into the national territory. A telling example of this comes from the 1895 Argentine census, which featured a table that portrayed each province as fully and equally incorporated into the nation. In an artistic variant on the conventional rectangular table format, the official charged with presenting the aggregate census results opted to make use of an Argentine national symbol, the sun (see figure 5.8).

The overall picture visually affirmed the direct and tight adhesion of each province and territory to the center. Disparities in the numerical weight of different regions notwithstanding, the symmetry of design implied the structural equivalence of each of the nation's parts in relation to each other and to the whole. At the same time, the clear attachment of each individual "ray" to the center, culminating in the "absolute" total of the Argentine population, elided the still very tenuous integration of some regions claimed by—but not yet materially or culturally integrated into—the Argentine nation-state. The accuracy of the numerical counts represented by the rays, in turn, are entirely secondary to the fact of their presentation as multiple pieces that together sum to a single, cohesive, and beautiful whole.

In Argentina as elsewhere, the summary tables that appeared at the front of national census volumes were followed by tables that reported selected cross tabulations. The national whole was thus sorted and re-sorted according to various individual characteristics such as marital status, religion, literacy, disability, nationality, language, or race. These cross-tabular breakdowns of the total populations were then repeated at smaller scales, in tables specific to regions, provinces, or cities. Whatever the scale and whichever the specific categorical distinctions in a given table, the particular appeared as a component of a larger, clearly delineated whole. The physical form and internal organization of the published volumes of national census results asserted the successful containment of all reported categorical divides within the dominant national frame.

Thus, even as they provided detailed numerical breakdowns of populations according to various kinds of distinction, Latin American censuses affirmed the primacy of the nation as the self-evident container for varied constituent parts. In this way, the publication of national census results helped to inscribe and reify the political and symbolic boundaries of Latin American nations that were still very much in formation. In the midst of ongoing struggles over the locus of political, cultural, and territorial

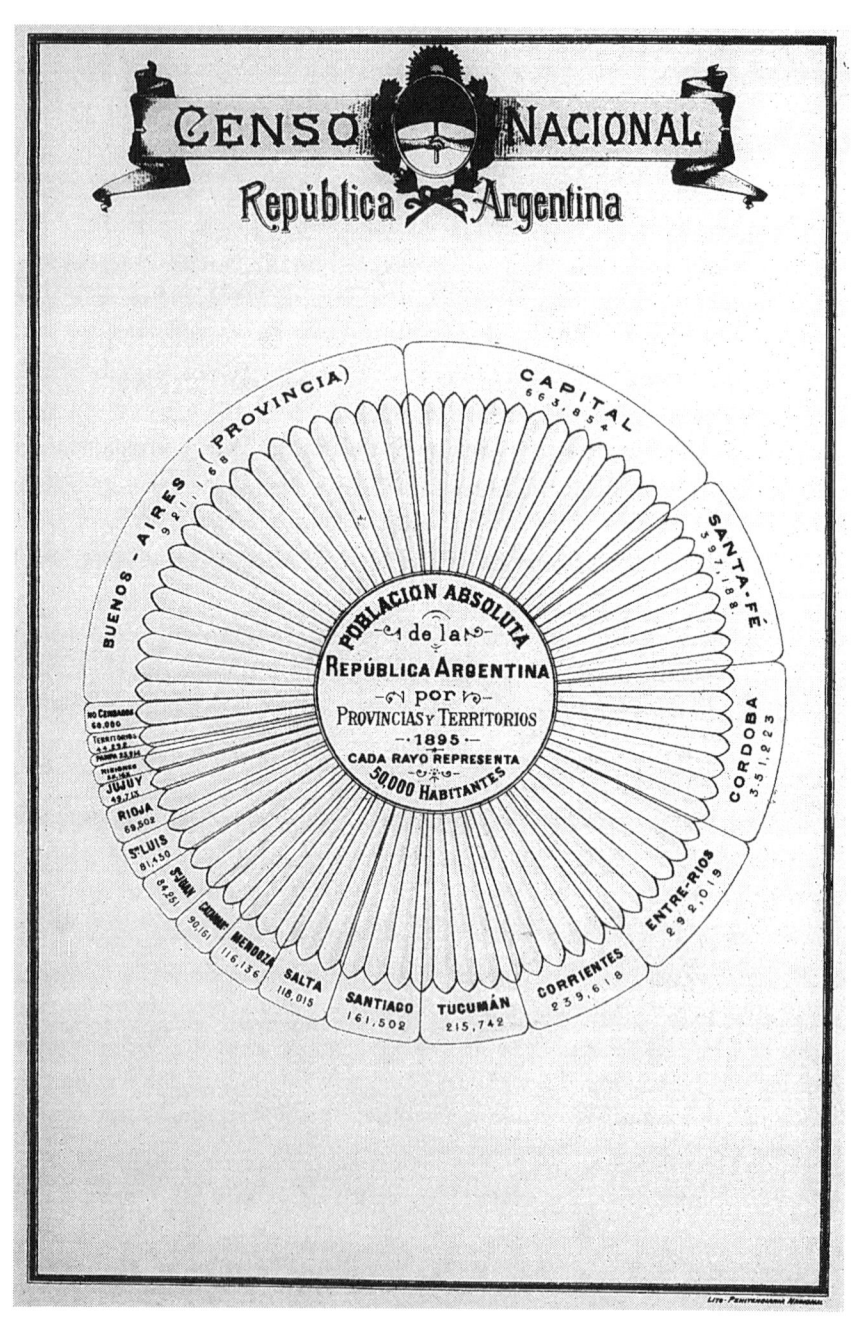

FIGURE 5.8 The Cohesive Argentine Nation, 1895.
SOURCE: Argentina. *Segundo Censo de la República Argentina, mayo 10 de 1895*, xxvii.

204 | National Colors

authority, national censuses pronounced nation-state consolidation as a foregone conclusion.

Considered as cultural products, late nineteenth- and early twentieth-century national census reports were masterpieces of nationalist reification. Censuses played a starring role in nationalist efforts to not only construct and define the boundaries and content of national communities, but to make those boundaries appear as already given and natural. Precisely because they were *not* considered cultural products, but scientific ones, census reports could advance nationalist depictions of the region's populations in the guise of providing objective descriptions. This work of reification was bolstered by the authority of the source, an authority that accrued to central statistics agencies in this period thanks to the growing prestige and international recognition of statistics as the ultimate science for advancing human progress.

Of course, the contribution of censuses to Latin American nation-state building and consolidation was not merely symbolic. The extraordinary administrative burden entailed in conducting a national census often stimulated the growth of "durable state structures"[64] and helped to extend the reach and depth of state power. In most countries, the effort involved in physically distributing census schedules to local authorities throughout the territory was itself a major feat, as was the coordination of return transport for thousands and thousands of manuscript census forms, not to mention the labor of tracking down returns from derelict or resistant municipal authorities, all this before manually compiling and distributing results. All these activities tended to enhance the infrastructural capacity of central governments—their ability to govern *through* societal networks, rather than merely ruling over them.[65] Thus, the enormous administrative labor involved in conducting national censuses gradually helped to reduce the gap between the statistical portraits of Latin American nations as clearly bounded, cohesive units, and the much messier and more contentious reality they claimed to portray.

As the twentieth century wore on, national censuses continued to testify to the self-evident existence of Latin American nations. Ongoing disputes over territorial boundaries and issues of regional autonomy notwithstanding, Latin American states gradually became consolidated. Modernizing elites trained their focus on the problem of national development. National censuses came to play an increasingly prominent role in elite public life,

---

[64] Tilly, *Coercion, Capital, and European States, AD 990–1992*.
[65] Mann, *The Sources of Social Power*. vol. 2, 59–61.

informing and helping to shape political debates over the nation's future.[66] Census officials, for their part, penned reports that focused less on asserting the existence and future promise of their nations, and more on identifying measures that revealed how national progress was coming to pass.

As they monitored statistics to assess the progress of their nations, the notion of "demographic progress" that had informed census officials' work in the first half of the twentieth century was called into question on the global scientific and political stage. Beginning in the 1930s and coalescing in the decade after World War II, the very concept of race together with the array of developmentalist theories that relied on it came under intense political and scientific scrutiny. Chapter 6 examines how Latin American census officials reconciled the international delegitimization of "race" as a scientific concept and "racial improvement" as a national ideal with their continued commitment to the pursuit of national development and progress.

---

[66] See, for example, Loveman, M., "The Race to Progress."

CHAPTER 6 | From Race to Culture

DURING THE LATE NINETEENTH and early twentieth centuries, national censuses were privileged venues to assert the inevitable racial improvement of Latin American populations. Census reports documented the growth of white and mestizo populations, while simultaneously registering the decline or disappearance of indigenous and Afrodescendant peoples. Official statistics told the tale in seemingly irrefutable terms: Latin America's populations were racially evolving, moving steadily forward on the path to a whiter, more modern, and more civilized future.

Aspirations for more homogenous and whiter national populations remained evident in Latin America's census reports into the second half of the twentieth century. Yet by the 1950s, most statistics agencies had stopped collecting official racial statistics. In place of direct queries about race, censuses inquired about a broadened range of ethnically coded cultural practices. "Culture" replaced "race" as the master category for measuring and interpreting diversity in demographic censuses throughout most of the region.

The shift away from the use of direct race questions on census schedules in the latter part of the twentieth century can be seen in table 6.1. For the nineteen Latin American countries under analysis, table 6.1 shows whether national censuses taken from the 1810s through the 1980s included a direct question about race or color. Clearly, there was substantial country-level variation in the timing and regularity of including questions about race on national censuses across this period. Just as clearly, there was a period from about 1870 to 1940 when race questions were regionally prevalent, followed by a period beginning around 1950 and then especially from 1960 to 1980, when race questions on censuses in the region all but disappeared.[1]

---

[1] Table 6.1 is based on information gleaned about each country from a combination of sources, including primary sources (copies of original census schedules and enumerator instructions), published census reports (official descriptions of methods of data collection), published statistics (from

TABLE 6.1   Race or Color Questions in Latin American Censuses, 1810s–1980s

	1810s	1820s	1830s	1840s	1850s	1860s	1870s	1880s	1890s	1900s	1910s	1920s	1930s	1940s	1950s	1960s	1970s	1980s
Argentina																		
Bolivia			?	R	R			?		R				R				
Brazil							R		R					R	R	R		R
Chile	R																	
Colombia											R							
Costa Rica												R		R				
Cuba				R		R	R	R	R	R	R		R	R	R		R	R
Dominican Rep.												R	R		R	R		
Ecuador																		
El Salvador							?	?	?	R			R					
Guatemala							R	R					R		R			
Honduras								R		R	R		R	R				
Mexico											R							
Nicaragua				R		R		R		?		R		?				
Panama												R	R	R	R			
Paraguay				R				?					?					
Peru		R				R								R				
Uruguay				R														
Venezuela																		

▨ = Census taken   R = Race or color question   ? = Census taken but no data on questions

Almost every Latin American country included a direct question about "race" or "color" on at least one national census in the first half of the twentieth century. Between 1900 and 1940, thirteen of the nineteen countries analyzed included such a question on at least one national census. The six exceptions include Ecuador, which did not take its first official national census until 1950; Paraguay, with insufficient information available about early censuses to determine if information about "race" was requested; and Argentina, Chile, Uruguay, and Venezuela. In these latter four cases census reports from the first half of the twentieth century devoted space to describing and discussing ethnoracial demographic trends *despite* the lack of census data.[2] During these decades, as the previous chapters revealed,

---

which the content of the census questionnaire can sometimes be deduced), and secondary sources (including surveys of census contents in particular periods and historical monographs on censuses in individual countries). The information contained in these various sources is mostly consistent, but in some cases there are inconsistencies across types of sources. For purposes of constructing table 6.1, primary sources held precedence in all cases for which such sources were available. When original documents could not be located, information comes from a combination of published census reports and secondary sources. In a handful of cases, a country took more than one census in a single decade: Bolivia (1831, 1835); Colombia (1912 and 1918); Cuba (1841 and 1846, both colonial censuses); Honduras (1881 and 1887; 1901 and 1905; 1910 and 1916; 1930 and 1935; 1940 and 1945); Uruguay (1841 and 1846; 1881 and 1887); Venezuela (1920 and 1926). For these cases, the cell for the decade in question is coded as "R" if either or both censuses taken in the decade included a race or color question. The same general rule applies for coding of these cells for other types of census questions in subsequent tables in this book.

[2] As described in chapters 4 and 5, Argentina used immigration statistics to discuss racial demographic trends. Venezuela and Chile relied on estimates or partial counts of indigenous populations conducted separately from national censuses.

Latin America's census reports often equated national progress with racial progress. Racial progress was typically equated, in turn, with "whitening" populations. Drawing on data from race questions along with other sources of information, census reports highlighted statistics that described trends in immigration, mestizaje, and racial differentials in rates of reproduction as key indicators of demographic "improvement."

In the second half of the twentieth century, the number of countries to include direct race queries declined, as did explicit efforts to use statistics to document so-called racial improvement of Latin American populations. In the 1950 census round, race questions were absent from the census schedules of all but five Latin American countries. In the 1960 round, only two countries, Brazil and the Dominican Republic, asked about race or color on the census. Cuba stands out as the only country in the region that never conducted a national census without a question about race or color. (In this respect, somewhat ironically, Cuba is the Latin American country most closely aligned with the United States).

Why did the majority of Latin American countries drop questions about race from their national censuses in the second half of the twentieth century? What were the consequences of this change for official statistical descriptions of Latin American populations? And what explains exceptions to the regional trend? In this chapter I address these questions based on an analysis of national censuses taken by nineteen Latin American states between the 1940s and 1980s. In addition to scrutinizing official explanations for the removal of race questions from censuses, I analyze changes in the international statistical field and broader scientific and political shifts leading up to and in the wake of World War II that influenced how Latin American officials portrayed their nations in numbers.

The analysis reveals that decisions to remove race from national censuses stemmed in part from professional concern with the quality of race data collected in the census. Census officials flagged race data as unreliable, and on this basis justified the omission of race questions from questionnaires. But the analysis also suggests that official explanations do not tell the full story. The regional trend to remove race from censuses only appeared in the context of broader scientific challenges to the concept of race, together with broader political challenges to the idea that national progress can or should.be defined in explicitly racial terms. Decisions to remove race from censuses in Latin America reflected shifts in international criteria for how to be a modern nation and promote national progress, as these shifts were refracted through domestic political and scientific fields.

As a direct consequence of removing race questions from censuses, the statistical picture of the kinds of humankind that make up Latin American populations changed. The adoption of census questions about an increasing array of cultural characteristics in lieu of questions about race altered which lines of difference were statistically visible within Latin American populations. Most glaringly, Afrodescendant populations disappeared from national statistical portraits throughout most of the region. Indigenous populations, in contrast, became *more* visible in censuses, though with the contravening aim of documenting and predicting their eventual disappearance as a distinct demographic component of the nation. The shift in focus from race to culture in Latin American censuses did not imply repudiation of evolutionary theories of social change. Demographic "progress" remained a touted goal, and measures of progress remained tied to the ideal of an increasingly "civilized" and homogenous population. What changed was the language used to discuss the goal of national homogeneity, the queries used to measure it, and the types of differences within populations made statistically visible as a result.

Official Explanations for Removing Race

Professed concerns about data quality figured centrally in official explanations for dropping race questions from national censuses. Census officials explained their specific concerns about the quality of race data in sections of census reports devoted to methods or in prefatory narrative comments. They lamented a combination of technical and social obstacles to collecting accurate data about race in the context of a national census.

Already in the early twentieth century, census officials in some countries had voiced concerns about the scientific validity of race data collected by enumerators. The most elaborate justification for dropping a race query from a national census appeared in Mexico's 1930 census report. Mexico had included a direct race question for the first time in its 1921 census. The official rationale for omitting the race query in 1930 is worth reproducing in full:

> Since Independence, through our terrible economic and social struggles, and even through simple national evolution, numerous indigenous groups have left the isolation in which colonial legislation and life maintained them, and by incorporating themselves into the other elements of our demography, they have lost their distinctive ethnic characteristics, including their language; and [indigenous] individuals have mixed with the individuals of

other indigenous groups, with mestizos, with criollos and with foreigners, and these new mestizajes have not left any legal or administrative trace, since our social stratification, particularly since the Revolution begun in 1910, has stopped obeying ethnic categories, in order to become subject to economic categories.

In these conditions, the data captured on raza, besides for carrying an antiscientific concept, have become progressively more false, to the point that they no longer deserve any credit whatsoever, since, except in exceptional cases, such as those presented by the groups that are still isolated from national life— among whom there are also sporadic mestizos, or the few families of the old Spanish or criollo nobility who continue the outdated custom of noting marriages in their genealogical tree—very few individuals have knowledge of the ethnic characteristics of their grandparents and none of their great-grandparents.

If the individuals enumerated cannot give accurate data about their raza or degree of mestizaje, it is absurd to rely on the a priori data of the enumerators, recruited throughout the country from among individuals of the most diverse culture and capacity.

In view of the before said, the Department of National Statistics, having consulted with the most competent specialists on this matter, decided to omit from the population census bulletins of 1930, the concept "raza."[3]

There is a tension between different lines of argument embedded within this official rationale for dropping the race question from Mexico's 1930 census. Initially, the explanation for removing race seemed to suggest that the concept of race just did not appear to be appropriate or useful for understanding Mexican society, especially since the 1910 Revolution made social stratification "subject to economic categories" rather than "ethnic" ones.[4] Yet Mexico's census agency had included a race question for the first time in 1921, in the first national census taken after the Revolution. Since the race question had been deemed relevant for the 1921 census, the invocation of the 1910 Revolution to justify the removal of the race question from the 1930 census rang hollow.

The official justification for dropping the race question from Mexico's 1930 census also pointed to concerns about the *validity* of racial statistics. These concerns are less easily dismissed as mere ideological ruse.

---

[3] Mexico. Departamento de la Estadística Nacional, *Censo de Población,* 54.
[4] Mexico. Departamento de la Estadística Nacional, *Censo de Población,* 54. The terminology of "race" and "ethnicity" are used interchangeably in this context.

Census officials considered themselves "men of science" and they took seriously their charge to produce technically robust and objective statistical data. The official explanation suggests Mexican census officials believed that, in principle, objective race data could be collected. It would not be problematic, for example, for geographically isolated Indians or for those criollo families obsessed with genealogy. And with more select and skilled enumerators, rather than the individuals "of the most diverse culture and capacity" they were able to recruit for the job, better information could potentially be collected from the rest of the population as well. The problem with collecting race data in Mexico, however, was that the classifications could not be trusted as *accurate* for the majority of the population. The inaccuracy of race data was attributed to extensive mestizaje combined with the limitations of intergenerational memory. Given these constraints, it was deemed better to side with "the most competent specialists" and to leave the race question off the 1930 census.

Census officials in other countries also registered their concern about the scientific integrity of race data collected through census enumeration. The director of Brazil's 1920 census justified the omission of a race query as follows: "the answers largely obscure the truth, especially with respect to mestiços, very numerous in almost all the states of Brazil and, ordinarily, the most uncooperative when it comes to making declarations related to the originating color of the race to which they belong."[5] This explanation was bolstered by a long footnote quoting an American expert on the subject, "the professor Mayo Smith, of Philadelphia," author of a book titled *Statistics and Sociology*. Brazil's census director quoted Smith's argument that "since it is obvious that clearly defined characteristics do not exist on which to base [our] statistical observations, the classifications and enumeration [of races and nationalities] are no more than mere conjecture."[6]

As in Mexico, the official rationale for omitting race from Brazil's 1920 census accepted the prevailing (and still prevalent) racialist wisdom that each individual has a *true* race. The problem lay in how to ensure accurate classification on the census. The official rationale conceded that census enumerators could not discern the truth with any confidence through simple observation. Nor could enumerators place faith in the information offered by the enumerated, not apt to be forthcoming about their racial origins in the face of social stigma. In an explanation to a colleague in another context, Brazil's census director concluded that asking about race in the census

---

[5] Brazil. Directoria Geral de Estatística, *Recenseamento do Brazil Realizado* ... 1920. 488–89.
[6] Brazil. Directoria Geral de Estatística, *Recenseamento do Brazil Realizado* ... 1920, 489n1.

would generate a false picture of Brazil's racial composition, overestimating the number of whites as those of mixed descent sought to escape the stigma of their true origins.[7] Brazil's census director thus defended the omission of a race question on scientific grounds even though he expected such a query would yield a "whitened" picture of Brazil's population—a goal that Brazil's census agency otherwise promoted.[8] Thus, official concern about the validity of race data cannot be dismissed as mere pretext for the removal of the race question from Brazil's 1920 census.[9]

In the few Latin American countries where direct race questions did not appear in nineteenth- and early twentieth-century censuses, officials also pointed to concerns about accuracy to justify the omission. In Argentina, for example, the director of the second national census, in 1895, explained that race was not requested for two primary reasons. First, the director claimed, the question was of little import to Argentina, given "the small numbers, in both absolute and relative terms, of blacks, mulattos, and civilized Indians."[10] The assertion that these populations were numerically insignificant served to justify the decision not to count them, which in turn generated census results that ratified the picture of Argentina as a racially homogenous country.[11] The second reason given for omitting the query was that "with the exception of pure blacks who cannot escape their classification, mulattos and Indians would have been counted in large part as whites, resulting in statistics that are inexact and inferior to reality."[12] As historian Hernán Otero observes, the ideological reasons for leaving race off the Argentine census were combined with motivations "of a technical order, stemming from a principle of methodological minimalism, attentive to obtaining those data whose reliability and validity was not in doubt."[13]

In a similar vein, though several decades later, Venezuelan census officials justified the absence of a race query on the 1940 census by underscoring the technical difficulty of obtaining accurate responses:

---

[7] See Vianna. "Raça e pesquisas estatísticas."

[8] Nobles, *Shades of Citizenship*, ch. 3.

[9] For a more extensive discussion of the omission of the race question from Brazil's 1920 census, see Loveman, M., "The Race to Progress."

[10] Argentina. Comisión Directiva del Censo. *Segundo Censo de la República Argentina,* II: XLVI. Cited in Otero, *Estadística y Nación*, 352.

[11] The symbolic violence inherent in this type of justification was discussed in chapter 5.

[12] Argentina. Comisión Directiva del Censo. *Segundo Censo de la República Argentina,* II: XLVI. Cited in Otero, *Estadística y Nación*, 352.

[13] Otero, *Estadística y Nación*, 352.

> Discrimination by race of the population has not been done because of the impossibility of obtaining a satisfactory racial identification due to the fact that the generative ethnic elements find themselves generally mixed in a form that is indiscernible by simple sight. A recommended scientific method, while inapplicable in a demographic census, would be to resort to certain hematological reactions that could demonstrate affinities of blood groups.[14]

The notion that a blood test for "certain hematological reactions" would rectify inaccuracies in racial classification based on "simple sight" affirmed the continuing acceptance of race as a biological fact, while acknowledging the impossibility of accurate classification through mere observation. As in Mexico and Brazil, race was still considered an inherited and innate trait of individuals, but it was no longer understood to be self-evident—raising insuperable obstacles for accurate classification by census takers. Echoing their Mexican and Brazilian counterparts, Venezuelan census officials stated that extensive race mixture made it impossible to ascertain individuals' true racial origins. Of course, the fact that many individuals would be identified as "mixed" was not in itself the methodological challenge; a "mixed" category could be—and was—routinely included in the set of allowable responses to race questions on Latin American censuses. Rather, the problem stemmed from the likelihood of respondent dissimulation about their "true" ancestry, in a context where social prejudice against African and Indian origins was as widespread as miscegenation.

Thus, census officials justified omitting race questions from censuses by raising doubts about the accuracy of responses. According to official explanations, race could be accurately determined in principle; but the procedures or knowledge necessary to discern individuals' "true race" were not available to census takers. The matter was framed as a decision to avoid collecting data of questionable validity. Census officials deemed the omission of race questions essential to maintaining the scientific integrity of the larger enumerative enterprise.

It is tempting to greet such official justifications for excluding race questions from censuses with skepticism. The professed concern with data quality can be parsed as convenient cover for less sanguine motivations, such as the desire to promote an image of the nation as racially homogenous by rendering minorities statistically invisible. The analysis in prior

---

[14] Venezuela. Dirección de Estadística, *VII Censo Nacional de Población*, "Notas Informativas," xxix. Curiously, the term *raza* appeared on a list of terminological definitions for items included in the 1941 census, despite the omission of race from the questionnaire.

chapters leaves little doubt that such ideological and often racist motives shaped the decisions of some census officials in this period.

Yet the evidence also makes clear that the directors of national statistics agencies were genuinely concerned about the scientific integrity of their work. They cared about their professional reputations as men of science. This was true from the outset of the modern census-taking enterprise in Latin America, and it became all the more so as the twentieth century wore on. Leading statistical figures in the region stayed abreast of developments in international census-taking standards, and they endeavored to promote the modernization of national statistics agencies in their respective countries.

Indeed, most of Latin America's central statistics agencies underwent significant modernizing reforms in the 1940s and thereafter. As a result, Latin American censuses conducted after World War II typically looked quite different from those taken in the late nineteenth and early twentieth centuries. Often with technical assistance from foreign experts, statistics agencies became larger and more bureaucratized. Hiring became more professionalized and the statistical expertise of staff improved. The adoption of new technologies for processing census returns began to enable faster collation, analysis, and reporting of results. As Latin America's statistical offices gained competency in updated survey and statistical methods, they began conducting more comprehensive and reliable demographic censuses.

One focus of the more general efforts to modernize statistics gathering infrastructure in Latin America was the content of census questionnaires, and in particular, the reliability, validity, and international comparability of the statistical data they generated. A clear example of this comes from Brazil, where a National Statistics Advisory Board (*Conselho Nacional de Estatística*) worked to advance the regional coordination of demographic data collection. In the early 1950s, the group produced a document devoted to the question of international comparability of data on "race or color" in censuses taken in the 1940s:

> Statistical investigation of the "race" or "color" of inhabitants is currently a controversial subject. There are those that express the view that, by its very nature, the determination of this attribute does not attend to the objective character of every statistical investigation. Others, for their part, while recognizing it to be difficult to determine, sustain that investigation [of race or color] is necessary due to the interdependence that exists between certain biological and social factors and the "racial" characteristics of a population.[15]

---

[15] Brazil. Conselho Nacional de Estatistica, Serviço Nacional de Recenseamento. "Métodos dos Censos de População das Nações Americanas," 69–71.

The report lamented the impossibility of international comparison of statistical data on race. It also noted that comparisons with European countries were not possible because neither France, nor Italy, nor England included a race question on their national censuses. Of greater concern, however, was the lack of consistency in the collection of racial data within the hemisphere. The report noted that within Latin America, some countries defined the "mestizo" category explicitly while others held it to be self-explanatory, making it impossible to know if identical criteria were used. The classificatory methods of the US census were identified as especially problematic. The United States was the only country to classify the descendants of a black parent and a parent of another racial group as black. In contrast, in Cuba, Costa Rica, El Salvador, Guatemala, Panama, and Peru such descendants were considered mixed.[16] The rule for classification as "black" in the United States, the report noted critically, made its race data totally incomparable to that of other countries in the region.

The Brazilian report suggested that "national pride and prejudice" undermined the collection of internationally comparable data: "With identical mixture of black and white stock an individual would be classified as 'white' in some countries and as 'black' or 'of color' in others; many Hindus of the purest Aryan ascendancy have blacker cutis than many American blacks." The report concluded that there was no clear way to resolve the issue of inconsistency of race data in the Americas: "In view of the difficulties that the investigation of racial composition offers, demonstrated, in part, by the discrepancies that exist between the censuses of the countries of the hemisphere, as briefly noted above, it appears impossible to arrive at any sort of satisfactory agreement with respect to this matter."[17]

While the existence and content of the Brazilian report testifies to their earnest concern about data quality and international comparability, by the time it was published in 1952, the problem of inconsistency in methods of racial enumeration was already essentially moot. In the 1960 census round, Brazil and the Dominican Republic were the only Latin American countries to include a direct race or color question on their national

---

[16] Brazil. Conselho Nacional de Estatística, Serviço Nacional de Recenseamento. "Métodos dos Censos de População das Nações Americanas," 71.

[17] Brazil. Conselho Nacional de Estatística, Serviço Nacional de Recenseamento. "Métodos dos Censos de População das Nações Americanas," 70.

census.[18] The Dominican Republic removed the question from its census in 1970. In a 2013 interview, the former director of the Dominican Republic's Department of Censuses and Surveys, Dr. Nelson Ramirez, recalled that the race question (along with the question on religion) was removed from the 1970 census on the recommendation of a technical adviser from the UN. Ramirez explained that the results from the race question used in prior decades were considered unreliable. The distribution of the population across categories exhibited "crazy changes" over time, reflecting the inconsistent and often euphemistic use of race terms in the country. Additionally, Ramirez noted that data on race from prior censuses "were not used for anything," which also argued for the omission of the question.[19]

In sum: Official explanations for the removal of race queries from censuses should not be accepted uncritically as the full story, but neither should census officials' professed concerns with the validity and reliability of the data they collect be denied. Technical, scientific, political, and ideological reasons for omitting race questions from national censuses were not mutually exclusive possibilities. Rather, as detailed in the next section, these motivations worked in combination to lead to the omission of race queries from nearly all Latin American census questionnaires in the latter part of the twentieth century.

Displacing Racial Determinism

Official decisions to remove race questions from national censuses partly reflected broad shifts in scientific thinking about race in this period. The abstention from direct racial classification in censuses was symptomatic of the more general decline in the scientific credibility of biological determinist strains of race theory. The influence of biological determinist theories of societal development began losing ground to cultural perspectives in Latin America in the 1920s and 1930s.[20] The science of eugenics remained extremely influential, but "softer" approaches that allowed for

---

[18] Cuba did not take a census in the 1960 round. The Brazilian census of 1970 omitted a question on "côr" (color) of the population, by decision of the military government (for an account of this decision, see de Azevedo, A., *Os Recenseamentos no Brasil*; Nobles, *Shades of Citizenship*). The question was reinstated in the census of 1980.

[19] Interview with Dr. Nelson Ramirez, Director, Centro de Estudios Sociales y Demográficos (CES-DEM), Santo Domingo, Dominican Republic, March 7, 2013. Interviewed by Martina Kunovic.

[20] See Stepan, *The Hour of Eugenics*; Barkan, *The Retreat of Scientific Racism*.

improving populations through education, sanitation, and cultural "betterment" began to prevail over rigidly biological determinist perspectives.[21] Latin American scientists and political elites actively debated questions such as whether inherited characteristics could be reformed through social interventions, whether acquired traits could be inherited, and whether the expression of hereditary group-based characteristics hinged on environmental triggers.[22] By the 1930s, most prominent Latin American scientists answered each of these questions in the affirmative.

The strains of eugenicist thought that dominated most Latin American scientific circles by the 1930s owed to diverse intellectual and political influences. Lamarckian theories of genetics, which allowed for the influence of environment on the process of intergenerational transmission of traits, resonated more broadly in Latin America than Mendelian approaches, with their emphasis on natural selection and biological determinism.[23] Latin American scientists were also receptive to the cultural anthropology of Franz Boas, who was a leading critic of racial-biological determinism and an early skeptic of the idea that race mixture was bad for the development of human populations. At the Second Pan American Scientific Congress, in 1915, Boas presented a paper in support of the idea that racial mixture could improve the traits of a population, echoing the arguments made by many Latin American scientists at the time.[24] By the 1920s, Boas was training Latin American students, some of whom would become preeminent scientific voices in the region. Among Boas' students were Gilberto Freyre of Brazil and Manuel Gamio of Mexico. Often considered the "fathers" of anthropology in their respective countries, Freyre and Gamio advanced distinct variants of the theory that nations could progress through ethno-cultural fusion of racially diverse populations.

The greater resonance of environmental over biological determinist strains of eugenicist thought in Latin America also owed partly to politics, both domestic and international. Within national political arenas, reformist politicians in the 1920s and populist regimes in the 1930s and 1940s embraced the idea that states could promote progress through public policies targeting health, sanitation, and education. Across the region, these decades saw the introduction of myriad programs that aimed to "modernize" or "civilize" populations through environmental and cultural "improvement."

---

[21] Bashford, "Internationalism, Cosmopolitanism, and Eugenics."
[22] For example, see Schwarcz, *O Espetáculo das Raças*.
[23] Stepan, *The Hour of Eugenics*.
[24] Boas, "Modern Populations of America."

International politics also played a role in creating fertile ground for the greater resonance of culturalist over biological determinist eugenics in early twentieth-century Latin America. Rejection of determinist strains of race science was partly a rejection of the ideological and political justifications for the United States' condescending and often outright racist treatment of Latin America in foreign affairs.[25] Indeed, the early rejection of hardline racial thought and legal racial segregation in Latin America took place partly in opposition to the embrace of such approaches in the early twentieth-century United States. On this front, Latin Americans sought to claim the higher ground.

Latin American scientists not only sought to demonstrate the potential of "positive" eugenics through "civilizing" reforms at home, they also worked to promote their views in international arenas. Latin Americans participated in the vibrant international epistemic community of eugenicists which flourished in the decades prior to World War II. At a series of international and regional conferences on eugenics, health, and sanitation, Latin American scientists joined global debates about the science of population improvement. Latin American delegates also pushed their views at congresses of the League of Nations and the Pan American Union, the first major international governmental organizations in the region. For example, Latin American delegates to international congresses were early opponents of racially selective immigration policies.[26] While they rejected the racially determinist justifications for such bans, however, they did not reject the more fundamental eugenicist notion that states should play an active role to continuously "improve" their populations. In lieu of "negative" eugenic policies that sought to influence processes of selection into populations, Latin American delegates advocated "positive" eugenic policies to create the environmental and social conditions needed to override the expression of undesirable inherited traits.

Latin American scientists helped call into question the scientific validity of biological determinist strains of race theory in the decades prior to World War II. In the wake of the war, the horrific evidence of state-directed genocide tipped the scales definitely against hardline eugenics as a scientific or political project. The scientific, political, and moral repudiation of core tenants of race science coalesced on the world stage with the creation of the United Nations Educational, Scientific, and Cultural Organization (UNESCO) in November of 1945. Among its first acts, UNESCO

---

[25] Loveman, B., *No Higher Law*.

[26] Fitzgerald and Cook-Martín, *Culling the Masses*, ch. 8.

organized a meeting of leading sociologists and cultural anthropologists from seven countries, including two from Latin America (Brazil and Mexico), to draft a statement on the status of race as a scientific concept.[27] The document was completed in 1950. It was subsequently published as *The Race Question* in 1952, complete with critical reactions and a second, revised statement on race that better represented the views of physical anthropologists and biologists.

The first UNESCO statement on race asserted a shared humanity ("mankind is one") and rejected as scientifically wrong theories that claimed innate racial inequality in mental capacities or potential. The statement also weighed in on debates over the consequences of intermarriage and miscegenation, pronouncing the lack of any evidence that race mixture led to "biologically bad effects." According to the report, research also proved that human beings are naturally cooperative rather than egotistical or chauvinistic. By implication, racism was not intrinsic or inevitable; it was learned—and could thus be unlearned.[28] The statement called for recognition that "for all practical purposes, 'race' is not so much a biological phenomenon as a social myth" responsible for "an enormous amount of human and social damage."[29]

Perhaps most significantly for understanding the shift in the classification practices of Latin American statistics agencies, the report also disparaged the widespread misuse of the term "race" to describe cultural groups of various kinds:

> To most people, a race is any group which they choose to describe as a race. Thus, many national, religious, geographic, linguistic or cultural groups have, in such loose usage, been called "race," when obviously Americans are not a race, nor are Englishmen, nor are Frenchmen, nor any other national group. Catholics, Protestants, Moslems and Jews are not races....

---

[27] The first UNESCO statement on race was drafted at the UNESCO House, Paris by the following experts: Professor Ernest Beaglehole, New Zealand; Professor Juan Comas, Mexico; Professor L.A. Costa Pinto, Brazil; Professor E. Franklin Frazier, United States of America; Professor Morris Ginsberg, United Kingdom; Dr. Humayun Kabir, India; Professor Claude Levi-Strauss, France; Professor M.F. Ashley-Montagu, United States of America (Rapporteur). UNESCO, *The Race Question*, 103.

[28] The belief that education could undo "errors" of racial prejudice informed the UNESCO-sponsored research project in Brazil, which aimed to discover how to replicate the harmonious race relations that supposedly obtained in that setting. The UNESCO researchers instead discovered systemic discrimination and interpersonal prejudice in Brazilian society, contradicting the presumptions that had motivated the research. Maio, "UNESCO and the Study of Race Relations in Brazil."

[29] UNESCO, *The Race Question*, 101.

People who live in Iceland or England or India are not races; nor are people who are culturally Turkish or Chinese or the like thereby describable as races.[30]

This list did not exhaust the ways that "race" was misused by nonspecialists, with potentially detrimental consequences. The UNESCO statement concluded that because "serious errors...are habitually committed when the term 'race' is used in popular parlance, it would be better when speaking of human races to drop the term 'race' altogether and speak of 'ethnic groups.'"[31]

The UNESCO statement is often credited for the widespread adoption of the term "ethnic group" instead of "race" in postwar research and writing on human variation. But while the terminological shift met with little resistance in most (but not all) scientific disciplines, it was not so simple to put an end to the race *concept.* Indeed, "race," which the principal author of the *The Race Question*, Ashley Montagu, had in earlier writing labeled "Man's Most Dangerous Myth,"[32] was reaffirmed as a valid biological category within the same document that labeled it "a social myth."

The first UNESCO report on race supposedly marked the triumph of universal humanism and cultural views of human difference over the notion of innate and hereditary differences between human races. Yet along with the affirmation of common humanity and declared absence of intrinsic inequalities, *The Race Question* asserted the biological existence of race. According to the UNESCO statement, "from a biological standpoint" a race could be "defined as one of the group of populations constituting the species *Homo sapiens*....These represent variations, as it were, on a common theme." Races were subgroups of humanity which shared "some concentrations, relative to frequency and distribution, of hereditary particles (genes) or physical characters, which appear, fluctuate, and often disappear in the course of time by reason of geographic or cultural isolation...." Notably, the UNESCO statement further clarified that "National, religious, geographic, linguistic and cultural groups do not necessarily coincide with racial groups: and the cultural traits of such groups have no demonstrated genetic connection with racial traits."[33] Thus, "races" existed

---

[30] UNESCO, *The Race Question*, 99.

[31] UNESCO, *The Race Question*, 99.

[32] Montagu, *Man's Most Dangerous Myth*.

[33] UNESCO, *The Race Question*, 99.

as biologically (genetically) clustered "populations"; but the boundaries of these populations did not neatly coincide with observable cultural boundaries of "ethnic" groups.

Many of the claims made in the first UNESCO statement on race were subsequently challenged by other scientists, resulting in a second statement that revealed broad and deep contention on the status of the race concept in postwar science.[34] Yet there was general agreement on a key point from the first statement: that lay usage of the term "race" was often erroneous and problematic. To avoid scientific error of classifying an ethnic group as a racial group qua "population," and to avoid the potential moral stigma of official racial classification in the postwar era, "ethnic group" gained ground as a scientifically and morally preferable alternative for describing and analyzing culturally or physically differentiable subgroups within national populations.[35]

How to Count Human Beings, Revisited

The aftermath of World War II shifted the terrain of ongoing scientific debates about the nature of human differences. This shift eventually translated into revised international conventions for census enumeration, which continued to influence the work of Latin America's statistical agencies in the postwar era.[36]

The international organizations that set the standard for how states should conduct modern demographic censuses up to the 1930s had left the question of racial enumeration off the table. The issue remained off the table during the interwar period, when the League of Nations took nominal responsibility for continuing the International Statistical Institute's efforts to advance international standardization of census methods. With the outbreak of World War II, efforts at international coordination

---

[34] The second UNESCO declaration on race, penned by physical anthropologists and biologists in response to the first, went even further to resurrect race as a valid scientific category, equating races with genetically distinct "populations" within the human species. The concept of race was thus constricted to apply to a narrower domain, but not rejected altogether. Foreshadowing early twenty-first-century discussions of race and genetics, the second UNESCO statement advanced the idea that "race" mapped onto genetically clustered populations in tandem with discursive insistence on a singular, common humanity. See Santos, "Da Morfologia ás Moléculas, de Raça a População."

[35] See Stolcke, "Sexo es para Gênero como Raça para Etnicidade?," 106; Martínez-Echazábal, "*Mestizaje* and the Discourse of National/Cultural Identity in Latin America," 110.

[36] See chapter 3 for a discussion of the influence of the international statistics regime on Latin American census enumeration prior to World War II.

of demographic statistics were once again disrupted. A planned meeting of the ISI in Washington, DC in 1939, intended to coincide with the centenary celebration of the American Statistical Association, was postponed indefinitely.

The absence of the ISI from the American event, and the obstacles to communication between the Americas and Europe during the war, became the official rationale for the creation of the Inter-American Statistical Institute (IASI) in 1940.[37] Under US leadership, and with collaboration from ISI members from Argentina, Brazil, Canada, and Mexico, the IASI sought to rectify the ISI's historical neglect of the Americas and to foster hemispheric coordination of statistics. The IASI held its inaugural meeting jointly with the World Statistical Conference in Washington, DC in 1947, followed by a second meeting in Bogotá, Colombia in 1950. A principal aim of the congresses was to contribute to the improvement and coordination of national censuses across the Western hemisphere in the 1950 census round (the 1950 Census of the Americas).

Surprisingly, the IASI congress proceedings remained silent on the questions of whether and how Western hemispheric states should collect ethnic or racial population data. At the opening plenary session of the second IASI congress, a member of the Executive Committee read aloud a "Program for improvement and coordination of statistics in the Western Hemisphere."[38] The statement called for improved statistical methods and techniques and better coordination of data collection across states so that statistics would serve both national and international needs. Evidence from census reports suggests that Latin American census officials were grappling with the challenges posed by racial and ethnic data collection in this period. Nonetheless, the detailed program of the second IASI Congress indicates that the topic did not make it onto the organization's agenda.[39]

The omission may have owed to the heavy influence of the United States in the IASI. The Americans would not have been eager to participate in a discussion of the US Census Bureau's scientifically indefensible racial classification practices, nor to provide more incentives for wartime enemies to broadcast the United States' hypocrisy on matters of race at home.[40] During the years the IASI met, the US's racist immigration

---

[37] Inter-American Statistical Institute, "Remarks of Stuart A. Rice."

[38] Second Inter-American Statistical Congress. "Summary, Participants, Program and Resolutions," 2.

[39] See Second Inter-American Statistical Congress. "Summary, Participants, Program and Resolutions."

[40] On the political and scientific battles over US Census Bureau classification practices during the 1940s–1980s, see Nobles, *Shades of Citizenship*; Schor, *Compter et Classer*.

policies became a target of criticism at other international scientific and hemisphere political conferences. Affronted by the stigma of racial and national exclusions in US immigration policy, Latin American delegates to the League of Nations and conferences of the Pan American Union in the 1920s and 1930s joined Asian delegates in pressuring the United States to drop race-based exclusions at its borders.[41] Directly confronted on its hypocrisy in the area of immigration policy, the United States may have used its leadership position in the IASI to minimize discussion of domestic racial classification. The IASI meetings prioritized efforts to coordinate statistical methods in other, less politically sensitive domains.

Authoritative guidance on the matter of how states ought to approach collection of racial or ethnic statistics in the post-WWII era came eventually from the United Nations. After the war, the UN took over the institutional role of promoting the international standardization of census-taking methods. Among the recommendations issued by the United Nations Preparatory Commission in 1945 was the establishment of a permanent statistical commission dedicated to working with states to coordinate and disseminate statistical activities.[42] In 1949, the United Nations published a handbook titled "Population Census Methods." The handbook did not include any reference to collection of data on race or ethnicity in national censuses. In 1959, however, the United Nations followed up with a publication titled "Principles and Recommendations for National Population Censuses." This time, the recommendations included guidelines, of a sort, for collecting racial and ethnic data on national censuses.

The UN recommendations acknowledged that states might want to collect racial statistics, while remaining agnostic on whether or not they should do so. Specifically, "race" was listed as an optional topic of inquiry under the heading of "Ethnic and Nationality Characteristics," which was listed under the more general heading of "Cultural Characteristics." Without advancing any specific recommendations, the UN publication identified a variety of characteristics that states might query under the generic heading of "Ethnic or Nationality Characteristics":

> The type of investigation of nationality or ethnic characteristics is dependent upon national conditions and needs. In different countries, ethnic groups are identified on various bases: country or area of origin, race, colour, lingual

---

[41] See Fitzgerald and Cook-Martín, *Culling the Masses*, ch. 8.
[42] Nixon, *A History of the International Statistical Institute, 1885–1960*, 42.

affiliation, religion, customs of dress or eating, tribal membership, or various combinations of these characteristics. In addition, some of the terms used, such as "race" or "origin," have a number of different connotations. The definitions and criteria applied by each country investigating any aspect of ethnic characteristics of the population must, therefore, be determined by the groups which it desires to identify. By the nature of the subject, these groups will vary widely from country to country, so that no internationally accepted criteria can be recommended.[43]

The UN's "Principles and Recommendations" marked a departure from the prewar international statistics regime in the explicit acknowledgement of "race" as a dimension of demographic difference of potential interest to states. For the first time since the creation of the international statistics regime in the 1850s, the organization recognized as the principal source for authoritative recommendations on demographic census methods lent legitimacy to the practice of official racial classification on national censuses. At the same time, however, the UN recommendations noted the unstable meaning of "race" across countries. While conceding that individual states may have use for such queries, it withheld affirmation of any intrinsic scientific value of racial data.

The postwar census guidelines reflected the prevailing scientific ambiguity and ambivalence on the status of the race concept vis à vis other categories used to demarcate human differences. "Race" was mentioned as one among other possible markers of "ethnic" difference, but there was no clarification of what counted as "race" for census purposes. The placement of "race" in a nominal list of several ways that "ethnic groups may be identified," after "place of origin" and before "colour," suggests "race" was construed as a self-evident marker. But it was not simply synonymous with "colour," since these were listed separately. "Race" was also singled out, along with "origin"—but not "colour"—as a potentially sensitive census query due to the "different connotations" it may carry. Ultimately, the UN guidelines abstained from issuing any

---

[43] The UN recommendations continued: "Because of the interpretative difficulties which may occur, it is important that where such an investigation is undertaken the basic criteria used should be clearly explained in the census report, so that the meaning of the classification will be readily apparent" (United Nations, *Principles and Recommendations for National Population Censuses,* 17). It is also interesting to note that the UN Population Commission decided at its fourth session *not* to include the subject of physical and mental handicaps in the list of recommended topics for 1950 censuses (United Nations, *Population Census Methods*, 175).

concrete direction for how states that opted to collect racial data should go about doing so.

The content of the UN's "Principles and Recommendations" with respect to ethnic and racial enumeration suggest that the issue was determined to be too sensitive and variable for standardization at the international level. At the same time, it is important to underscore that the explicit admission of this fact by the United Nations signaled a blanket endorsement for states to collect such statistics, or not, as they deemed suitable for their respective circumstances. It is possible that the US Census Bureau's commitment to continued collection of racial statistics influenced the UN position on this matter. Clearly, the UN's recommendations effectively sanctioned the existing state of affairs in the United States. By the time the UN recommendations were issued in 1959, only a few Latin American states still included direct questions about "race" on national censuses. The majority of Latin American states had already omitted race questions from their censuses in favor of questions about ethnically-coded cultural characteristics.

Racial Progress as Cultural Progress, and Vice Versa

The substitution of questions about various aspects of culture—such as language, clothing, and food—for questions about race in Latin American censuses was not a strictly linear development, nor was it universal. But in the latter half of the twentieth century (with anticipatory shifts earlier in some contexts), the general tendency in the region was to alter the evidentiary basis for discussing "difference" within the nation to measures of cultural attributes such as language and dress. On the surface, the change in terminology and types of questions suggested a paradigmatic shift from biological to cultural understanding of human variation and its consequences for development. Yet the transition from "race" to "culture" as the master category for analyzing human diversity in Latin American populations did not always entail a radical break from evolutionary social thought or its underlying racist premises. The idea of national progress was still tied to the idea of racial progress, even as racial progress was increasingly construed in cultural terms.

The case of Mexico's censuses is illustrative of this trend. Mexican census officials explained directly that questions about culture would replace the census question about race. The detailed explanation for removal of the race question from the 1930 Mexican census, cited earlier, continued with the announcement that in compensation for the omitted race question, two additional language questions had been added, supplementing the language questions used in the past. The aim of these new language questions, the official account explained, was to acquire "precise knowledge of the process of national integration...." To ensure that the public understood the significance of these data, the census director promised that "as complete ethnographic data as possible would be published in the preamble to each of the volumes corresponding to the censuses of the diverse entities of the Republic." Together with statistics on additional cultural indicators "such as for example the number, class, category, and use of residences," the new language data would thus provide "a more exact idea [*concepto*] of national reality" than could be gleaned from unreliable data on race.[44]

Clearly, the removal of the race question from Mexico's census did not remove census officials' interest in tracking the "the process of national integration." Nor did it alter the official conception of the direction of ethno-demographic change. In lieu of tracking growth in the number of "mestizos" at the expense of "Indians," as had been done in the prior census, the 1930 census would track growth in the number of Spanish speakers at the expense of speakers of only indigenous languages. The eventual forging of a homogenous, Spanish-speaking, mestizo national type was still the goal—as evidenced by the state-sponsored educational "missions" to teach Spanish literacy to Indians during this period.[45] As in prior decades, the boundary that demarcated "Indian" as a distinct type within the national population was depicted in the 1930 census as permeable, but in only one direction. National demographic progress was still understood to entail the absorption and eventual disappearance of distinctive indigenous populations. The shift to tracking culture instead of race on the census did not produce a true break with racialist evolutionary reasoning. The notion that a decline in distinct indigenous populations was a sign of demographic progress persevered.

Descriptions of human difference in terms of culture rather than biology turned out to be quite compatible with positivist, evolutionary perspectives on comparative societal development.[46] To some extent, biological-racial arguments were simply recast in cultural terms.[47] In making this

---

[44] Mexico. Departamento de la Estadística Nacional, *Censo de Población*, 54–5.

[45] Knight, "Revolutionary Project, Recalcitrant People."

[46] Santos, "Da Morfologia ás Moléculas"; Van Dijk, *Ideología, una Aproximación Multidisciplinaria*.

[47] Lourdes Martínez-Echazábal, "O Culturalismo dos anos 30 no Brasil e na América Latina"; Wade, *Race, Nature and Culture*.

discursive shift, the term and the concept of "mestizaje" proved extremely useful. A capacious construct, mestizaje could refer to either cultural or biological intermixture, or to both at the same time. Mestizaje could also reference both the mechanism and the outcome of national-demographic integration. Trafficking in the permissive blurring of meanings, leading Latin American writers idealized mestizaje as constitutive of their distinctive national identities, even as they celebrated how mestizaje dissolved differences to yield "improved" (meaning less Indian or black) populations. Undercurrents of biologistic logic and social Darwinian evolutionary thought coursed through the work of writers whose principal aim was to glorify the formation of mestizo national identities. This was true even of authors such as José Vasconcelos in Mexico and Gilberto Freyre in Brazil, who gained fame for supposedly breaking from the racial paradigm and supplanting it with a "cultural" approach.[48]

In the context of national censuses, officials in many Latin American countries embraced mestizaje as a respectable trope through which to continue equating national progress with the disappearance of internal diversity. Well into the latter part of the twentieth century, Latin American census officials treated mestizaje as both a pivotal mechanism and a critical indicator of national progress. Demographic homogeneity remained the ideal, even as it was increasingly described in ethnocultural rather than explicitly racial terms. The statistical measures of diversity changed. But the use of cultural indicators instead of direct race questions to track diversity within the population did not fundamentally alter census officials' visions of the demographic ideal to which their nations should aspire. Just as in previous decades, census officials read evidence of the decline or disappearance of distinguishable indigenous or Afrodescendant populations as a desirable demographic dynamic, en route to a "brighter" national future.

While in a growing number of countries the ideal national type was being recast as quintessentially "mixed" rather than white, in others the explicit preference for whiteness persisted well into the second half of the twentieth century. In these countries, the new culturalist idiom for describing and prescribing the disappearance of diversity was slower to catch hold. The report on the 1940 Panamanian census, for example, boasted that detailed racial data broken down by age groups made it possible "to evaluate... which

---

[48] Lourdes Martínez-Echazábal, "O Culturalismo dos anos 30"; Vasconcelos, *The Cosmic Race*; Freyre, *The Masters and the Slaves*.

race, from among the variety of the country's racial groups, seems to be the youngest and which race will be the most important in years to come."[49] The results revealed the impending demographic dominance of the white race. The 1940 Panama census also celebrated the introduction of a "new statistic": the number of women for every one hundred men ("information that has always appeared in the censuses of the most civilized countries"). When combined with data on the racial distribution, the report explained, information on the balance of sexes "sheds light on certain national problems such as migration, mestizaje, and the sufficiency of labor for certain occupations."[50] Thus, in 1940s Panama, racial data not only provided a vision of the nation's demographic future; it served to predict shortages for "certain occupations" within a racially conceived occupational structure.

The open celebration of whitening as a demographic trend also remained explicit in Brazil, where the introduction to the 1940 census report explained:

> If we admit that blacks and Indians are continuing to disappear, and that immigration, especially that of a Mediterranean origin, is not at a standstill, the white man will not only have in Brazil his major field of life and culture in the tropics, but be able to take from old Europe—citadel of the white race—before it passes to other hands, the torch of western civilization to which the Brazilians will give a new and intense light—that of the atmosphere of their own civilization.[51]

As in earlier Brazilian censuses, demographic movement toward a whiter population was portrayed as inevitable; the whitening trend both promised and signified a more "civilized" and prosperous national future.

By the 1950 census round, the few countries that still reported racial demographic trends did so in a less jubilant, more matter-of-fact tone—while still drawing attention to their putatively whitening populations. In Costa Rica, for instance, the 1950 census report noted that "in all the provinces the greatest percentage corresponds to the group of whites and mestizos and this is explained by the fact that Costa Rica is one of the Ibero-American

---

[49] Panama. Oficina del Censo, *Censo de Población*, 29.

[50] Panama. Oficina del Censo, *Censo de Población*, 29.

[51] The introduction was written by educational reformer Fernando de Azevedo (de Azevedo, *Brazilian Culture*, 40–41, cited in Skidmore, "Racial Ideas," 22–3).

countries in which the white race is predominant."[52] In Cuba, similarly, the 1953 census report explained that "since 1899 the white race grows at a more rapid rate than other races." To illustrate this growth, the report included a bar graph that showed an increase in Cuba's white population over time compared to the growth of "other," unspecified races. The bar graph, shown in figure 6.1a, did not actually provide clear evidence that the white share of the population had increased "at a more rapid rate than other races." The graph did, however, provide a clear picture of Cuba's population as consistently majority white. A subsequent pie graph, shown in figure 6.1b, depicted the change in Cuba's racial composition across three censuses (1899, 1943, and 1953). Eliding the fact of inconsistent classificatory practices across censuses, the pie graphs showed that the white share of the population had increased from 66.9 to 72.8 percent in just over five decades. The fact that the white share had dipped slightly in 1953 from a highpoint of 74.3 percent in 1943 was downplayed as the report called attention to the overall whitening trend.[53]

Thus, in the 1940s and 1950s, census officials in some countries continued to highlight statistics that purported to document the

GRÁFICO 21.—RAZA DE LA POBLACIÓN TOTAL DE CUBA: 1899 A 1953

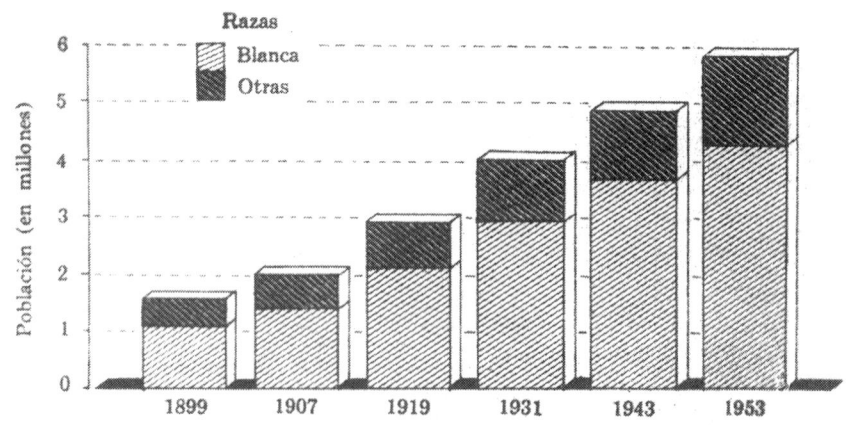

FIGURE 6.1A Whites and Others in Cuba's Population, 1899–1953.
SOURCE: Cuba. Oficina Nacional de los Censos Demográfico y Electoral. *Censos de población*, xxxvi.

---

[52] Costa Rica. Dirección General de Estadística y Censos. *Censo de Población de Costa Rica*, 33. The reason for the predominance of the "white race" is attributed to " the small number of the indigenous population that lived in our territory at the time of the arrival of the Spanish (according to Dr. Bernardo Augusto Theil, 27,000 indians)." The image of Costa Rica as a predominantly white population was of course bolstered by the unremarked categorical lumping of mestizos with whites.

[53] Cuba. Oficina Nacional de los Censos Demográfico y Electoral, *Censos de Población*, xxxvi.

GRÁFICO 22.—DISTRIBUCIÓN PORCENTUAL DE LA POBLACIÓN
TOTAL DE CUBA, SEGÚN RAZA: 1899, 1943 Y 1953

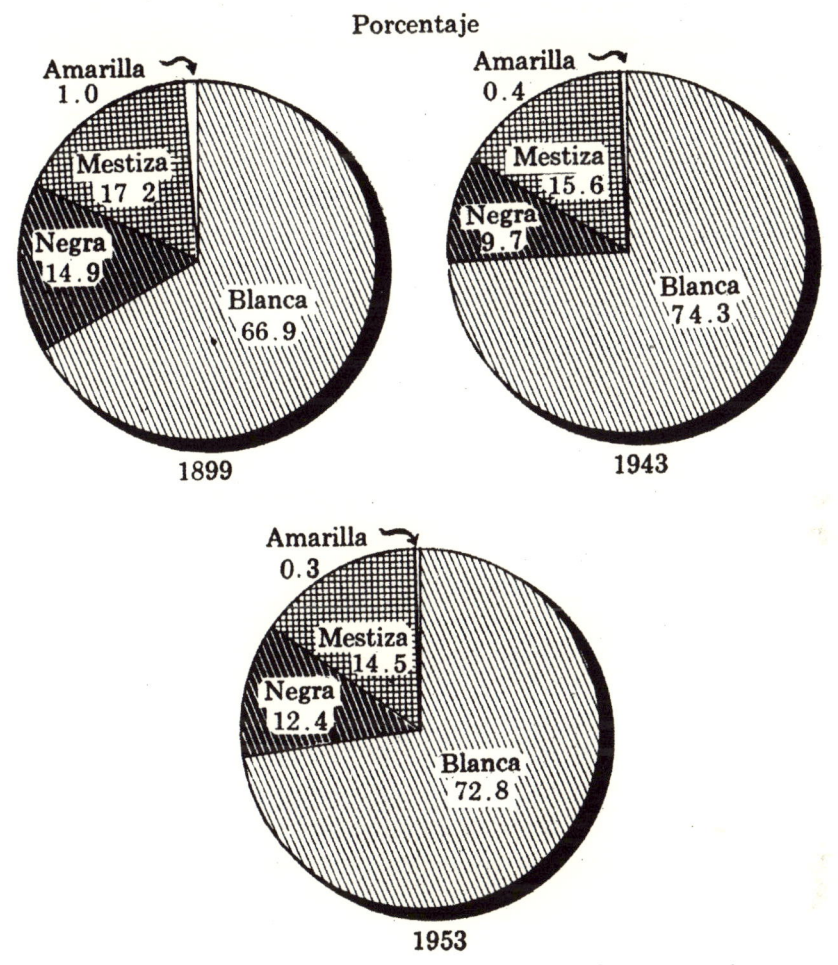

Porcentaje

1899: Amarilla 1.0, Mestiza 17.2, Negra 14.9, Blanca 66.9

1943: Amarilla 0.4, Mestiza 15.6, Negra 9.7, Blanca 74.3

1953: Amarilla 0.3, Mestiza 14.5, Negra 12.4, Blanca 72.8

FIGURE 6.1B The Racial Composition of Cuba's Population, 1899, 1943, and 1953.
SOURCE: Cuba. Oficina Nacional de los Censos Demográfico y Electoral. *Censos de población*, xxxvi.

demographic dominance of whites. In most of the region, however, census officials transitioned away from open celebration of "whitening" populations. Already by the 1930s, leading thinkers in some parts of the region had abandoned the illusion that uniform national types would eventually crystallize as white or quasi-white. Instead, they had increasingly embraced mestizaje as the defining and definitive character of their nations. The embrace of mestizaje as a nationalist ideal coincided with the rise of populist regimes in several countries, providing cultural reinforcement for political and economic policies that significantly broadened popular participation in electoral politics and formal market economies.[54] Along with populist promises to democratize polity and economy came the symbolic democratization of historically entrenched social hierarchies. State officials heralded mestizaje as both emblem and guarantor of racial egalitarianism. A thoroughly racially mixed people, the official stories explained, could not possibly sustain racial animosities or prejudices. Political leaders in a growing number of Latin American countries branded their nations racial democracies as a matter of demographic fact.

As mestizaje replaced whitening as the official national ideal in a growing number of countries, census officials stopped portraying the mestizo as evidence of a population in demographic transition. Instead, they redefined "mixture" as the inevitable and ideal demographic end state. As in earlier decades, however, the mestizo type was typically envisioned to be more European-like than not. In its various national incarnations, the mestizo usually bore symbolic stamps of non-European origins, while speaking and behaving in ways associated with "modern," "civilized," people—in other words, "whites." Thus, underlying the celebration of mixed national types, the ideological privileging of whiteness, and the tight association of European-ness with the very idea of modernity, remained essentially unscathed.

With explicitly racialist notions of national progress recast in cultural terms, census officials turned from racial statistics to cultural statistics as key measures of national progress. The implications for the production of demographic knowledge related to the ethnoracial diversity of Latin American populations were far-reaching. Most strikingly, the heterogeneity of indigenous populations within many countries became ever more apparent, while the very existence of Afrodescendant populations in much of the region was eclipsed from view.

Disappearing Indians

Many Latin American census reports from the mid-twentieth century documented the gradual disappearance of culturally distinct indigenous groups within national populations. The disappearance of Indians was parsed as an unequivocally positive development. National progress had become synonymous with modernization; and modernization, by definition,

---

[54] On populist regimes' embrace of national ideologies that celebrated mestizaje and racial democracy, see Andrews, *Afro-Latin America*.

meant movement away from the "primitive" past and toward a more "civilized" future.

Paradoxically, the use of censuses to track the demographic disappearance of Indians ended up accentuating their enduring and heterogeneous presence. An important consequence of the shift from race to culture as the master category for tracking difference within populations was that indigenous peoples gained visibility in the censuses of many Latin American countries. Census questionnaires for Andean and Mesoamerican countries, especially, included a variety of queries about cultural characteristics and behaviors. Questions about maternal and habitual language used in the household, diet, use of particular types of shoes or clothes, and household characteristics provided an array of data that testified to the diversity of indigenous populations even as they were marshaled to document indigenous peoples' gradual absorption into national societies.

Table 6.2a provides an overview of the statistical visibility of indigenous peoples in Latin American censuses from the 1810s to the 1980s. For

TABLE 6.2A Visibility of Indigenous Peoples in Latin American Censuses, 1810s–1980s

	1810s	1820s	1830s	1840s	1850s	1860s	1870s	1880s	1890s	1900s	1910s	1920s	1930s	1940s	1950s	1960s	1970s	1980s
Argentina																O		
Bolivia			?	O	O			?		O					O		O	
Brazil							O		O							O	O	
Chile	O									O		O	O	O				
Colombia											O							
Costa Rica												O			O			
Cuba																		
Dominican Rep.																		
Ecuador															O			
El Salvador						?	?	?	O			O						
Guatemala							O	O				O		O	O	O	O	O
Honduras							O		?	?		O	O	O				O
Mexico								O	O	O	O	O	O	O	O	O	O	O
Nicaragua			O		O		O		?		O		?	O				
Panama										O	O	O	O	O	O	O	O	O
Paraguay			O					?				?		O	O		O	
Peru		O				O								O		O	O	O
Uruguay				?														
Venezuela						O				O			O	O				O

▨ = Census taken O = Indigenous visibility ? = Census taken but no data on questions

TABLE 6.2B Approaches to Enumerating "Indians" in Latin American Censuses, 1810s–1980s

	1810s	1820s	1830s	1840s	1850s	1860s	1870s	1880s	1890s	1900s	1910s	1920s	1930s	1940s	1950s	1960s	1970s	1980s
Argentina																Ⓢ		
Bolivia			?	Ⓡ	Ⓡ			?		Ⓡ					⒧Ⓡ		⒧	
Brazil							Ⓡ		Ⓡ						⒧	Ⓟ		
Chile	Ⓡ									ⒸⒾ Ⓢ		Ⓢ	Ⓢ	Ⓢ				
Colombia												Ⓡ						
Costa Rica												ⓅⓇ			ⒾⓅ Ⓡ			
Cuba																		
Dominican Rep.																		
Ecuador															ⒸⒾ			
El Salvador							?	?	?	Ⓡ		Ⓡ						
Guatemala								Ⓡ	Ⓡ			ⒾⓅ Ⓡ		⒧Ⓡ	ⒸⒾ Ⓜ	ⒸⒾ Ⓜ	ⒾⓂ	ⒾⓂ
Honduras								Ⓡ		?	?		Ⓡ	Ⓡ	Ⓒ			⒧
Mexico									⒧	⒧	⒧	⒧Ⓡ	⒧	Ⓒ⒧	⒧	⒧	⒧	⒧
Nicaragua			Ⓡ		Ⓡ		Ⓡ		?		⒧	?	⒧					
Panama									Ⓡ	Ⓡ	Ⓡ	ⓇⓈ	Ⓢ	Ⓢ	Ⓢ	Ⓢ		
Paraguay			Ⓞ					?			?		⒧	⒧		⒧Ⓢ		
Peru	Ⓞ				Ⓡ							⒧Ⓡ		ⒸⒾ	⒧	⒧		
Uruguay			?															
Venezuela					Ⓞ					Ⓢ		Ⓞ	Ⓢ				⒧Ⓢ	

▓ = Census taken   ▒? = Census taken but no data on questions

Ⓒ = Indigenousness identified through customs
Ⓘ = Indigenousness identified through identity
Ⓛ = Indigenousness identified through language
Ⓜ = Indigenousness identified through group membership
Ⓡ = Indigenousness identified through race
Ⓢ = Separate indigenous census taken

each country and decade, table 6.2a shows whether a national census was taken and whether that census made indigenous peoples discernible as a distinct segment of the population. A number of different types of census questions served to make indigenous peoples visible in Latin American censuses, including questions about customs, identity, language, group membership, and "race" (where *indio* or *indigena* were listed as response options). Table 6.2a reports whether indigenous populations were made visible in censuses through any of these approaches. Table 6.2a also reports indigenous visibility if a country took a separate indigenous census in conjunction with a national census in a given decade.[55]

---

[55] Table 6.2a includes any query used by contemporaries to identify and count indigenous peoples, regardless of whether such queries technically did an adequate job of capturing such populations.

234 | National Colors

Table 6.2b provides more information about the specific ways that different countries tracked indigenous populations in censuses. For each country and decade, table 6.2b shows whether a national census included a question about indigenous customs (such as dress or diet), language, group membership (such as belonging to a named tribe), or "race." Table 6.2b also reports countries that took separate "Indian censuses" apart from national censuses (most notably, Chile, Panama, and Venezuela). These segregated counts are differentiated in table 6.2b (coded as "S") because they made indigenous populations statistically visible, but they did so outside the context of the national census.

As is evident in table 6.2a, the statistical visibility of indigenous peoples in the second half of the twentieth century was not, in itself, something new. In several Latin American countries, censuses had long classified and counted indigenous people as a distinct component of national populations. In the period from the 1810s through the 1940s, of the eighty-five censuses for which sufficient information on the content of the questionnaire is available, just under half (42/85) made indigenous populations statistically visible.[56] But the specific ways that "Indians" were identified and classified in censuses changed in the latter part of the century, in ways that made them both more statistically visible overall, and visible in more distinct ways, than in censuses in the past.

The shift from "race" to "culture" as the master frame for conceptualizing, classifying, and counting indigenous populations in Latin American censuses can be seen in table 6.2b. Prior to the 1950 census round, the majority of censuses that made indigenous people statistically visible did so exclusively through the use of a direct race question (that is, for example, a question that queried "*Raza?*" with "indio" or "indigena" as a response option among others). This was the case for twenty-one of the forty-two censuses taken prior to the 1950s in which indigenous populations were statistically visible (this does not include the cases in which, available sources make clear that Indians were counted but do not provide sufficient information to code the question type). In six additional cases, indigenous people were made statistically visible through a direct race question in combination with another type of question (such as a query

---

This means that table 6.2a errs on the side of suggesting more statistical visibility of indigenous populations rather than less.

[56] In twelve of the ninety-seven shaded cells from 1810–1940 in table 6.2a, available historical accounts or primary sources do not suffice to determine whether or not indigenous people were categorically distinguished by census-takers.

about mother tongue) or a separate indigenous enumeration conducted in conjunction with the national census. Three of the six censuses that used a race question in addition to some other means of enumerating "Indians" took place in the 1940 census round, anticipating the broader shift toward the use of varied queries to enumerate indigenous peoples in the second half of the century.

In contrast to the dominant approach before World War II, not one of the countries that counted indigenous peoples on a census during the 1950s relied exclusively on a race question to do so. In the 1950 census round, sixteen Latin American countries took national censuses and in nine of these indigenous peoples were counted (in another two cases, they were counted in separate indigenous censuses). Two countries, Bolivia and Costa Rica, retained versions of "race" questions to identify indigenous peoples, in addition to other types of questions. By the 1960 census round, direct race questions had altogether disappeared as a means to enumerate indigenous peoples in Latin America.[57] In the new normative context, Latin American states identified indigenous populations on the census via questions about culture, including an array of specific inquiries into language, customs, dress, diet, and even household characteristics and composition.

Census questions that targeted distinctively indigenous traits (or better, traits that scientists and census official construed as distinctively indigenous) made "indians" more visible in Latin American censuses. Yet a primary goal of such questions, ironically, was to generate data that would enable state officials to better track—and ideally, accelerate—the disappearance of indigenous peoples through their assimilation into the general population. Conceptual and methodological shifts notwithstanding, census officials' reading of data from queries about cultural characteristics tended to reveal considerable continuity of thought with the positivist, racial evolutionism of prior decades. Cultural indicators of indigeneity were often equated with the primitive past, while signs of assimilation were treated as evidence of the modern, mestizo present, en route to the nation's thoroughly civilized future.

A particularly striking example of the development of survey questions about cultural differences precisely to facilitate their disappearance comes from Mexico in the 1940s and 1950s. The famous anthropologist Manuel Gamio, who became director of the Mexican

---

[57] Direct questions about race or color to count indigenous people in the census would make a comeback in Brazil in the 1990s, as will be seen in chapter 7.

government's Department of Demography in the 1940s, argued that the existing questions about maternal language in Mexico's censuses should be supplemented with a battery of additional questions about cultural habits, including whether the individual "eats bread or tortillas; goes barefoot, in sandals, or in shoes; wears indigenous-style or European-style pants (*calzón* o *pantalón*) or dresses (*envuelto, enagua o vestido completo*); sleeps on the floor, in a hammock, a woven mat, or bed; the type of material of the home (adobe, simple plaster, stone, brick, wood, etc.);...owns a radio or sewing machine, etc."[58] With such data in hand, Gamio explained, one could identify cultural characteristics that are "purely Indian," "foreign" (European), and mixed indo-European, and then do an inventory of families' characteristics to identify those with the most "purely Indian" profiles. Official classification as "Indian" would be tied directly and exclusively to this inventory of cultural traits: "those with a high percentage of objects of Indian culture would thus be considered as Indian for administrative purposes, regardless of biological origin." These "Indian" families could then be targeted, Gamio reasoned, with benevolent indigenista policies that sought to eradicate "inefficient," "primitive," and "anachronistic" behaviors within the Mexican population.[59] Statistical description of "Indian" traits would bolster policy prescriptions for their targeted elimination.

In other countries as well, census officials used queries about mundane behaviors and living conditions to track the size and characteristics of indigenous populations. In the process, key indicators of "development" were rendered synonymous with cultural assimilation by Indians to a European/mestizo way of life. In Peru, for example, the 1961 census included a variety of detailed questions that served as proxies for whether or not an individual lived as an "Indian." Among the queries: "what type of floor is in this home?" ("improved" or "dirt"), "does this person chew coca leaves?" and "does this person go barefoot?" In an illustrative set of pie charts, shown in figure 6.2, those who wore proper shoes (*zapatos*) were distinguished from those who wore sandals (*huaraches*) or went barefoot (*descalzo*). As seen in figure 6.2, the two-toned graphic display of what Peruvians wore on their feet intimated that the nation was composed

---

[58] Gamio, "Las Caracteristicas Culturales y los Censos Indígenas," 18.

[59] Gamio, "Las Caracteristicas Culturales y los Censos Indígenas." Notably, even as he advocated for assimilation of Indians, Gamio worked to revive the production of "popular" arts and crafts (Brading, "Nationalism and State-Building," 103).

DISTRIBUCION PORCENTUAL DE LA POBLACION DE LA REPUBLICA, QUE USA Y NO USA ZAPATOS, SEGUN SEXO

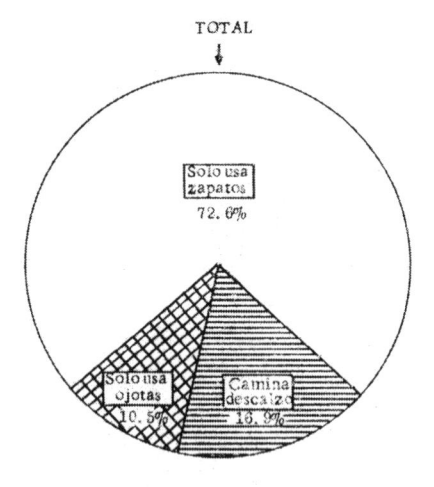

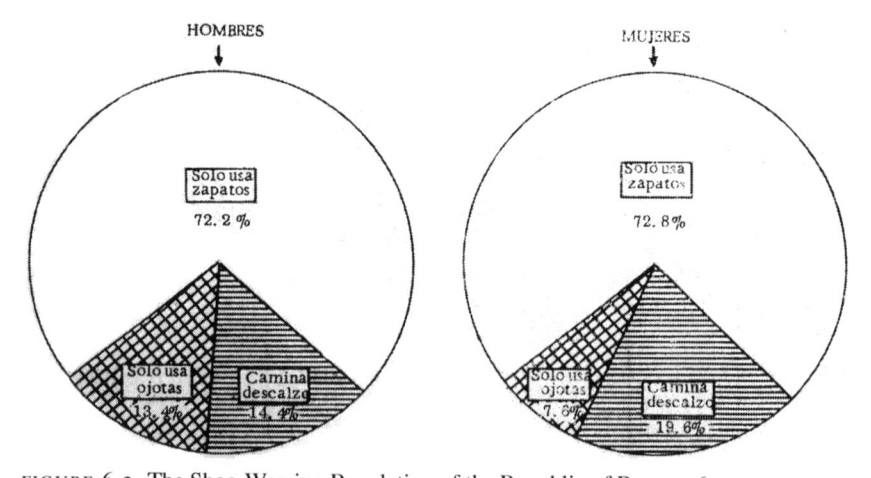

TOTAL
- Solo usa zapatos 72.6%
- Solo usa ojotas 10.5%
- Camina descalzo 16.9%

HOMBRES
- Solo usa zapatos 72.2%
- Solo usa ojotas 13.4%
- Camina descalzo 14.4%

MUJERES
- Solo usa zapatos 72.8%
- Solo usa ojotas 7.6%
- Camina descalzo 19.6%

FIGURE 6.2 The Shoe-Wearing Population of the Republic of Peru, 1961.
SOURCE: Peru. Dirección Nacional de Estadística y Censos. *Resultados del VI Censo Nacional de Población*, vol.1:5, 49.

of two basic "kinds" of people—those who do and do not wear civilized shoes—further stratified by sex.[60]

By treating impoverished living conditions as a proxy for indigenousness, census reports reified the idea that impoverishment was a defining

---

[60] Peru. Dirección Nacional de Estadística y Censos. *Resultados del VI Censo Nacional de Población*, vol. I:5, p.49.

characteristic of being an "Indian." The link between low social status and classification as "Indian" was made explicit in the 1973 Guatemalan census. Enumerators were instructed to consider the social status of the individual to determine whom to classify as indigenous: "The difficulty in formulating a precise definition of the indigenous population having been recognized by specialized organizations [*organismos especializados*], the criteria from the 1950 census have been adopted: to classify a person as indígena the social status [*estimación social*] of the person... is taken into account." Recognizing that this guideline may not always be sufficient for enumerators to make a determination, the instructions continued: "If there is doubt, as a last resort the person is to be asked if he is ladino or indígena."[61]

Census queries about cultural characteristics generated statistics that officials gleaned as indicators of the population's level of development. These measures of development were simultaneously measures of cultural assimilation by indigenous peoples into the national mestizo mass. As a result, the use of cultural characteristics to track "indianness" helped to solidify the strong association between impoverished living conditions, low social status, and "being Indian" in Latin America. In official census reports, the disappearance of indigenous people and the process of national development were often seen as one and the same dynamic.

Notably, this was the case even in countries that did not collect detailed cultural information on demographic censuses. In Venezuela, for example, the 1941 census did not include questions to identify indigenous peoples. Regardless, the official census report included an estimated number of "uncivilized Indians" remaining in the national territory.[62] In 1950, a separate indigenous census generated counts of "wild Indians" (*indios selvestres*). The first volume of published results from the 1950 national census described the methods used to identify "uncivilized indians":

> The findings of the special investigation of the indigenous population do not refer to the entire population that could be called "indigenous" on the basis of its more or less pure racial type, since without doubt a large number [of Indians] are incorporated into ordinary civil life and cannot be differentiated expressly [from the rest of the population]. Concretely, the results refer to

---

[61] Guatemala. Dirección General de Estadística, *VIII Censo de Población*.

[62] Vandellos, José A. "Ensayo de Demografía Venezolana," cited in Venezuela. Dirección General de Estadística y Censos Nacionales. *Octavo Censo General de Población*, page number illegible.

the indigenous population that maintains typically Indian characteristics in relation to their location, type of housing and customs, etc.[63]

By definition, culture, not "race" determined who got counted in Venezuela's special census of the indigenous population. The census director underscored that "the investigation did not include Indians that live incorporated into civil life, participating in the common regimen of life (*del régimen común de vida*).[64] The only type of "Indians" of concern to census takers were those not yet integrated into national society. And the point of collecting information about unincorporated "Indians" was precisely to hasten their disappearance into the mass of the population. This impetus is captured clearly in the official report: "[W]e took advantage of the occasion to collect sanitary, economic, and cultural information that would allow description of the exact situation of the Venezuelan Indian, in order to design measures aimed at improving their conditions of life and incorporating them progressively into civilization."[65] Thus, from the perspective of census officials, being an ethnoculturally distinguishable Indian and being part of civilization were mutually exclusive possibilities. The disappearance of Indians as a distinguishable type within the population figured as both aim and indicator of national development.

Latin American censuses from the post-WWII decades portrayed assimilation as a one-way street that moved Indians away from "primitive" practices associated with indigenous culture and toward "modern" practices associated with the "civilized" Euro-mestizo nation. The proliferation of census queries about cultural characteristics in the latter part of the twentieth century heightened the visibility of indigenous peoples within Latin American populations, but mostly with an eye to devising social policies that would hasten their absorption into the rest of the population. The modernizing aim was to make Indians disappear as a distinct type within Latin American nations.

---

[63] Venezuela. Dirección General de Estadística y Censos Nacionales. *Octavo Censo General de Población,* no page number (see description of indigenous census).

[64] Venezuela. Dirección General de Estadística y Censos Nacionales. *Octavo Censo General de Población*, page number illegible.

[65] Venezuela. Dirección General de Estadística y Censos Nacionales. *Octavo Censo General de Población,* page number illegible.

Disappeared Blacks

In stark contrast to the increased statistical visibility of indigenous peoples in Latin American censuses following World War II, Afrodescendant populations were eclipsed from view in national censuses throughout most of the region. Few countries retained direct race or color questions on national censuses after the 1940s (see table 6.1). And the use of cultural questions as a substitute did not typically capture behaviors or traits that differentiated Afrodescendants from others within national populations. Table 6.3 describes national censuses taken by Latin American countries from the 1810s to the 1980s in which Afrodescendant individuals are statistically visible as a distinct component of national populations.[66]

Table 6.3 reveals some general trends in the enumeration of Afrodescendant populations in Latin American censuses in the twentieth century; the table also draws attention to a few anomalous cases. Looking first at temporal trends, it is evident that Afrodescendant individuals were not identified in the majority of nineteenth-century censuses conducted in Latin America. They became more visible in censuses taken in the early part of the twentieth century, especially from the 1920s to the 1940s, for reasons analyzed in previous chapters. Between the 1940s and the 1960s, Afrodescendants all but disappeared from Latin American censuses. In the 1940 census round, more than fifty percent of Latin American countries

TABLE 6.3 Visibility of Afrodescendants in Latin American Censuses, 1810s–1980s

	1810s	1820s	1830s	1840s	1850s	1860s	1870s	1880s	1890s	1900s	1910s	1920s	1930s	1940s	1950s	1960s	1970s	1980s
Argentina																		
Bolivia			?	?				?										
Brazil							●		●						●	●	●	●
Chile	●																	
Colombia											●							
Costa Rica													●		●			
Cuba					●		●	●	●	●	●	●		●	●	●	●	●
Dominican Rep.													●		●			
Ecuador																		
El Salvador							?	?	?				●					
Guatemala													●		●	●		
Honduras											?	?		●				
Mexico																		
Nicaragua				●		●		●		?		●	●		?			
Panama											●	●	●	●				
Paraguay				●				?					?					
Peru		●				●								●				
Uruguay					●													
Venezuela																		

▨ = Census taken   ● = Afrodescent visibility   ▨? = Census taken but no data on questions

---

[66] A census with a question about "race" or "color" and/or with response options such as "negro," "preto," "mulatto," or "de color" shows up as a black circle in table 6.3.

that took a census (6/11) made Afrodescendants statistically visible. In the 1950 census round, the proportion of states that counted Afrodescendants on the census declined to one fourth (4/16). By the 1960 census round, only two countries included a question on their national census that enabled identification of Afrodescendants as a distinct subset of the population. In the second half of the twentieth century, Afrodescendants were (again) invisible in official statistics in most countries in the region.

Crosscutting the temporal trends, table 6.3 also reveals that the propensity to include questions about race or color on national censuses is tied to differences in the demographic histories associated with distinct regions of Latin America. Southern cone countries with relatively small African descendent populations routinely made them invisible in national censuses. Andean and Mesoamerican countries often identified Afrodescendant populations on at least one early twentieth-century census, but not thereafter. In Atlantic rim and Caribbean countries, which had proportionately larger populations of African slaves and their descendants, states were more likely to include questions about race or color across multiple censuses, and to retain them into the second half of the twentieth century. The association between region, demographic history, and the inclusion of race or color questions on censuses was not perfect; within each region, and across different historical periods, there were exceptions to the general rule. Ethnoracial demography was not determinative of census categories; but it was not irrelevant to them either.

The comparative overview provided by table 6.3 makes it possible to identify anomalous cases within regions, raising a number of previously unexplored questions about the comparative history of ethnoracial classification in Latin America. Venezuela stands out as a puzzling case. Among countries with a significant history of African slavery, Venezuela is unique in its consistent abstention from including race or color questions in national censuses. With respect to the visibility of Afrodescendant populations, Venezuela's censuses look surprisingly more like Argentina's than Brazil's.[67] Why would this be the case?

The Venezuelan historiography provides clues, but not a definitive answer. As noted in chapter 5, the historian José Gil Fortoul speculated in 1896 that Venezuela's national censuses purposefully omitted racial categories because elites did not want to remind blacks and their descendants

---

[67] While Venezuela's slave population was proportionately smaller than Brazil's, it was significantly larger than Argentina's. See Andrews, *Afro-Latin America*.

of the painful experience of slavery.[68] Fortoul deemed the omission appropriate because intermixture between whites, Indians, blacks, and mestizos meant that "concerns about color no longer have such a notable influence in social life, and even less in political life, where it is not rare to see the highest government positions occupied by people of color (who, it should be said in passing, do not show themselves to be inferior to whites of pure race with respect to their capacity to govern)."[69]

In subsequent decades, the notion that miscegenation had rendered racial distinctions in Venezuela socially and politically inconsequential became official dogma. Nationalist projects envisioned Venezuela as a racial democracy composed of a thoroughly racially mixed people—a "café con leche" nation.[70] The official line found support in social scientific and historical work that claimed miscegenation had been more extensive in Venezuela than elsewhere in the region, and that as a result, people of color had faced fewer barriers to political and social inclusion,[71] and no longer saw themselves as racially distinct.[72] The absence of official racial statistics throughout the nineteenth and twentieth centuries, meanwhile, ensured that racial distinctions and inequalities remained statistically imperceptible, contributing to the resilience of Venezuela's racial democracy myth.

Yet the Brazilian case challenges the argument that extensive miscegenation coupled with an official national ideology of racial democracy suffices to explain the historical omission of race questions from the census. As in Venezuela, the notion that the population was thoroughly mixed and thus did not discriminate based on race was central to Brazilian nationalist lore. Instead of abstaining entirely from official racial classification on the census, Brazil's nineteenth- and early twentieth-century census agency produced racial statistics precisely to document extensive miscegenation

---

[68] Fortoul, *El Hombre y la Historia*, 46. The omission was warranted, Fortoul suggested, because "individuals belonging to pure races comprise only a small fraction [of the population].... There are no blacks of appreciable number.... Without a doubt they will soon disappear, as a race, through mixture with the population of the interior. The tribes of independent Indians.... do not form, in reality, an essential part of the nation.... they are also condemned to disappear, whether through destruction in the case of war, or through absorption when those regions are colonized.... As for the colonial Spaniards, only a very few families remain in towns in the interior, where they have degenerated [due to inbreeding]."

[69] Fortoul, *El Hombre y la Historia*, 46.

[70] Wright, W., *Café con Leche*.

[71] Wright, W., *Café con Leche*, 9; Helg, "Race and Black Mobilization in Colonial and Early Independent Cuba," 54; Bermúdez and Suárez, "Venezuela," 248.

[72] Bermúdez and Suárez, "Venezuela," 248; Pollak-Eltz, "Migration from Barlovento to Caracas," 31.

and the demographic "whitening" of the population.[73] Comparison of Venezuela and Brazil underscores that neither ethnoracial demography nor national ideology directly determines how states classify their populations on the census.

The inclusion or exclusion of a race question from any given national census ultimately hinges on politics. This includes proximate struggles among scientists, political elites, and, in some contexts, domestic activists; it also includes the relative positions of domestic actors within broader transnational and international political and scientific fields that bear on census politics. The role of politics in shaping how states classify citizens on the census is especially clear in the two principal anomalous cases in the post-World War II period: Brazil and Cuba. These are the only two Latin American countries that continued to include a direct question about race or color on national censuses throughout the second half of the twentieth century (with the exception of 1970 in Brazil). Why did Brazil and Cuba retain these questions on their national censuses after the rest of the region—other than the United States—had retired them?

Brazil's continued use of race or color questions on national censuses in the decades after World War II is particularly curious. The international scientific and moral momentum weighed against retaining a direct race question on the census, and the Venezuelan model of pronouncing such a question superfluous in a supposed racial democracy was readily available. More than once during these decades, critics called into question the scientific validity and purpose of the "color" ("cor") query, nearly leading to its removal from the national census.[74] Critics not only pointed to technical and terminological misgivings, they also questioned the relevance of the data it generated for a society where racial distinctions (supposedly) did not matter since everyone was mixed. Yet arguments in favor of continuity in the census prevailed, and the color question remained in the national censuses in the 1940s through 1960s, and again from the 1980s through the 2010s.

In the 1970 census round, opponents of color classification in the census temporarily won the day. Brazil's democratically elected government was toppled by a military coup in 1964. The ensuing years witnessed severe repression of political opponents and concerted efforts to stifle dissent. Among the activities the military regime deemed subversive were efforts by academics and activists to draw attention to racial inequality in Brazilian society. In a move that both reflected and reinforced the dictatorship's

---

[73] Loveman, M., "The Race to Progress."

[74] See the account provided by Nobles, *Shades of Citizenship*, 98–110.

insistence that Brazilian society was a racial democracy, the color question was removed from the 1970 census. As in Venezuela, the claim that race was not relevant to understanding Brazilian society justified the omission of a census question that could have generated data that proved otherwise.

In the lead up to the 1980 census round, activists and sympathetic academics redoubled efforts to dispel the myth of racial democracy through a variety of means. Central to their efforts, they successfully lobbied the director of Brazil's statistics agency to reinsert a color/race query on the 1980 census. As suggested by political scientist Melissa Nobles, absent the organized pressure from academics and activists, Brazil's 1980 census would have been fielded without a color question (and Brazil would not show up as one of two outliers in the 1980s column of table 6.3).[75] The targeting of Brazil's census agency by activists concerned with racial inequality set an example that would be followed by several other countries in the 1990s and 2000s.[76]

The critical role of politics in shaping racial classification on national censuses also helps explain the other outlying case with respect to the visibility of Afrodescendant populations on national censuses in the latter part of the twentieth century. Cuba is the only Latin American country to retain a color question on each national census through the second half of the twentieth century. Indeed, in table 6.3, Cuba stands out as the only Latin American country that has never taken a national census *without* such a question.[77]

Cuba's twentieth-century census-taking history was profoundly shaped by its peculiar relationship to the United States. Cuba's first official national census, taken in 1899, was actually conducted by the US War Department (prior to this, Cuba's censuses were colonial censuses taken by Spain).[78] When Cuba became independent from Spain in 1898 and took charge of its own national censuses, it could have seized the opportunity to break with both the Spanish colonial and US traditions of official racial classification of citizens. Finding inspiration in the writings of Cuba's nationalist hero, José Martí, census officials might have declared racial statistics irrelevant for understanding the "raceless" Cuban nation.

---

[75] Nobles, *Shades of Citizenship*, 98–110.

[76] This issue is taken up in chapter 7.

[77] The US Census also included a race question throughout the nineteenth and twentieth centuries. See Schor, *Compter et Classer*; Nobles, *Shades of Citizenship*; Goldberg, *Racial Subjects*, ch. 3; Snipp, "Racial Measurement in the American Census"; Lee, "Racial Classifications in the US Census."

[78] Schor, *Compter e Classer*.

But this path was not taken. Instead, Cuba's early twentieth-century census officials collected and analyzed racial statistics with greater scrutiny than anywhere else in Latin America. Like their counterparts in several other countries in the region, Cuban census officials used racial statistics to document progress toward the whitening and "civilizing" of their population.[79]

The continued inclusion of color questions on Cuban censuses after the Revolution of 1959 is striking. In his first speech after taking power in January 1959, Fidel Castro brought the issue of racial inequality in Cuba into the spotlight. Among the "most immediate tasks" the provisional government identified was "a real and effective policy against race discrimination."[80] In a speech in March of 1959, a mere two months later, Castro named the elimination of racial discrimination as one of the four main aims of the Revolution: "One of the most just battles that must be fought, a battle that must be emphasized more and more... [is] the battle to end racial discrimination at work centers."[81] It was not long, however, before Castro declared the Revolutionary reforms successful and the issue resolved. Efforts to draw further attention to the matter were repressed. Yet unlike Brazil's military regime, which pronounced the racially egalitarian nature of Brazilian society with equal confidence and invoked it as justification for removing race from the census in 1970, in Castro's Cuba, the collection of racial statistics in national censuses continued without interruption.

Removing the color question from the census might have helped to enforce silence on racial matters on the island. But it would have also deprived the Castro regime of a valuable source of political ammunition in its ongoing ideological battles against the United States. The continued production of racial statistics made it possible to demonstrate, with the apparent objectivity of statistics, just how well the Revolution had fared in its project to eradicate racial inequality. Statistical tables showed the near absence of racial disparities in literacy, educational outcomes, and life expectancy, in sharp contrast to analogous statistical tables from the United States.[82] The continuous collection of racial statistics in Cuba provided the regime a legitimate and scientific means to track its progress on a central revolutionary goal. At the same time, the numbers also happened to hit at the Achilles' heel of the United States in the field of international

---

[79] De la Fuente, "Race, National Discourse, and Politics in Cuba," 46–9.
[80] Cited in de la Fuente, *A Nation for All*, 261.
[81] Cited in de la Fuente, *A Nation for All*, 263.
[82] For example, de la Fuente, *A Nation for All*, 310.

moral politics after World War II: its foundational hypocrisy and enduring reality of systemic racial inequality.[83]

While contingencies of domestic and international politics led Brazil and Cuba to retain questions about race or color on their national censuses in the decades after World War II, in the majority of Latin American countries, the presence and condition of Afrodescendant peoples became impossible to discern from national censuses in this period. The removal of race queries from census forms effectively "disappeared" Afro-Latin Americans from official demographic portraits of most countries in the region. The substitution of queries about cultural characteristics ended up highlighting indigenous diversity in several countries; it did not do the same for those of African origins. In most countries of the region, the shift from race to culture as master category for tracking diversity within the nation brought increased attention to indigenous populations while eclipsing Afrodescendants from view.

Conclusion: From Mestizaje to Multiculturalism

Census officials' open celebration of whitening or mestizaje as demographic ideals did not disappear by the mid-twentieth century, but it did become more subdued as the twentieth century wore on. In the wake of World War II, the pursuit of racial progress as an explicit demographic goal was no longer politically or morally legitimate. In the international scientific field, critics of biological determinist theories gained the higher ground. With the increasingly professionalized, bureaucratic-scientific statistics agencies in each Latin American country, the scientific validity of race data collected in social surveys was repeatedly called into question. In the field of politics, in turn, state classification of citizens by race or color came under increased scrutiny. At the same time, the legitimacy of state interest in discerning *cultural* divides within their populations became internationally validated and institutionally enshrined.

By the end of the 1940s, the lingering tendencies of some census officials to champion explicitly the whitening of their populations lost any remaining legitimacy. This was not the case, however, for the underlying ideal of forging a racially, ethnically, and culturally homogenous nation. The fundamental nationalist principle of "one nation, one state" remained

---

[83] Winant, *The World Is a Ghetto*, ch. 7.

intact. Thus, the gradual disappearance of racial or cultural differences within the population continued to be welcomed, and actively pursued, by political and intellectual leaders in the region.

Nationalist intellectuals and political leaders throughout Latin America championed the view that demographic homogeneity bolstered national unity and strength. The notion that Latin American populations had already become or would soon emerge as distinctive, unified, internally homogenous types endured. The specific conception of the formative elements of uniform national types varied, of necessity, from country to country. In some countries, like Argentina, Chile, Costa Rica, and Uruguay, the process of demographic homogenization continued to be treated as a fait accompli, with the national type envisioned as a Latin shade of white. In others, like Brazil, Mexico, and Venezuela, homogeneity was projected to result from widespread intermixture; regardless of skin tone or ethnic background, everyone was—or was soon to be—quintessentially mixed (if preferably in the direction of whiteness). In Andean countries like Peru and Bolivia, meanwhile, the prospect of national ethnoracial uniformity appeared ever more elusive; regardless, their postwar national censuses tracked the cultural assimilation of indigenous peoples for evidence of slow but steady progress toward a more homogenous and more "Hispanic" (less "Indian") demographic future.

Crosscutting these different conceptions of the particular composition of the ideal national type ran a shared acceptance of a single core idea: that sameness was better than difference. Throughout the region, homogenization of national populations remained the overarching demographic goal. In the census reports of some countries, this aim was implicit; in most, however, census officials wrote explicitly of the desirability of assimilation or mestizaje as a means to absorb distinct indigenous, Afrodescendant, or other groups within the nation.

The nationalist ideals projected in official census reports often reflected prevailing elite views of the ideal demographic trajectory of the nation. While these demographic preferences may have been pervasive among those who wielded state power, the view that assimilation and homogenization could be read as a measure of national progress was never entirely hegemonic. Countervailing views existed within elite circles, and also, not surprisingly, among the "popular" classes. Indeed, dissenting voices in most countries echo back through decades, some would argue centuries.

Race or color-conscious activism has a very long and deep history in Latin America. But those who carried this torch through the twentieth century often met with stiff resistance if not outright repression. From the 1970s and with increasing intensity in the 1980s, activists in some countries began to carve out public spaces for registering their disapproval of official national and racial ideologies. The transition back to democratic rule throughout most of the region by the mid-1980s opened new spaces for dissent. A growing number of new or old-but-reinvigorated organizations and movements promoting racial and ethnic consciousness emerged throughout the region. Many of these focused directly on exposing entrenched racism in their societies, in part by decrying national ideologies premised on the negation of enduring ethnic or racial differences within the nation. In country after country, the national census became a central target of criticism for its historic and contemporary contributions to perpetuating such national myths.

As I describe in chapter 7, the concluding decades of the twentieth century unleashed a historic shift in how Latin American states classify citizens on censuses. Breaking with the long history of presuming and celebrating the eventual disappearance of indigenous and Afrodescendant populations, contemporary Latin American censuses increasingly underscore enduring ethnoracial diversity within the nation. The introduction of new census questions about racial or ethnic group membership in a growing number of Latin American countries represents a historic break from census-taking tradition in the region, on more than one front. Symbolically, the new census queries in many countries signify a rejection of the racially evolutionist vision of national progress as synonymous with annihilation of undesirable "difference" in the population. Politically, the addition of these queries in several countries signifies an unprecedented democratization of the census, which remains the preeminent bureaucratic and technological instrument for production of official facts about the population. For the first time in the history of census taking in several countries of the region, as chapter 7 details, the enumerated have won a seat at the table to debate the questions and categories states use for their enumeration.

CHAPTER 7 | "We All Count"

BY THE END OF the twentieth century, the view that national progress could be measured by the decline of ethnic and racial minority populations began to erode. A growing chorus of critics, both domestic and international, called into question the ideal of modern nation-statehood to which earlier generations of state officials had aspired. Under the combined and often coordinated pressures of local social movements and international organizations and conventions, the normative preference for national integration via the annihilation or absorption of ethnocultural difference finally began to give way.[1] It was replaced by a growing recognition that states should acknowledge diversity and address ethnoracial inequality.

Official recognition of internal diversity was especially forthcoming in internationally visible forums.[2] Among these forums, national demographic censuses continued to hold a privileged place. From the 1990s, countries that had rarely or never included questions about ethnoracial differences on national censuses began to include explicit questions about ethnic or racial identity or origins. Latin American census agencies

---

[1] The recent shift away from assimilationist nationalisms was presaged in some countries by *neo-indigenista* projects that emerged in the 1980s. In Ecuador, for example, a *neo-indigenismo* emerged that departed from indigenismo's traditional emphasis on integration and assimilation: "Rather than emphasize integration, new indigenism stressed the autonomy and validity of multiple indigenous cultures, and the importance of respect for difference." Radcliffe and Westwood, *Remaking the Nation*, 69–70.

[2] Banton, "International Norms and Latin American States' Policies on Indigenous Peoples." In his consideration of the formal reports submitted by Latin American signatories to the International Convention on the Elimination of All Forms of Racial Discrimination from the 1970s to the 1990s, Michael Banton documented a pronounced shift toward official recognition of "pluricultural" and "pluriracial" national societies in the region. Several countries also amended their constitutions to reflect this altered official vision of the national population, incorporating the language of minority group rights and promising entitlements such as free public education in indigenous languages.

transmitted refashioned images of national populations. Demographic projections of ethnoracially homogenous or gradually homogenizing citizenries gave way to demographic portraits of multi-racial, multi-ethnic, multi-lingual societies. Reversing the longstanding insistence on the blurriness or irrelevance of ethnoracial distinctions, Latin American censuses began to document the existence of discrete ethnoracial groups co-existing within the territorial boundaries of the state. According to the latest census results, Latin American societies are no longer ethnoracial melting pots. They are now (once again) ethnoracial mosaics.

What explains the resurgence of official ethnoracial classification in Latin American censuses? In this chapter, I trace the introduction of new census questions across the region since the 1980s and demonstrate that national statistics agencies added new questions to capture ethnoracial diversity in response to the demands, often coordinated, of domestic social movements and international organizations. In a few countries, domestic activists took the lead and reached out to regional and international development agencies as willing partners in campaigns to reform the census. In most countries, however, the roles were reversed: representatives of international and regional development agencies pressured states to introduce new census questions and encouraged domestic activists to participate in projects that included census reform.

In the late 1980s and early 1990s, activists on behalf of marginalized populations in a few Latin American countries set their sights on the national census as a strategic battleground in the larger struggle for recognition, rights, and redress. Grassroots mobilization to demand visibility of ethnic and racial populations on national censuses found sympathetic allies within international development agencies and financial institutions. By the early 2000s, major regional and international development organizations had identified the elimination of ethnic and racial inequalities as a strategic development goal. They called for the collection of more and better racial and ethnic population data to further this aim. Through a combination of carrots and sticks, development agencies and key international lenders such as the World Bank gradually translated recommendations for census reform into a quasi-mandate. By the 2010 census round, virtually all countries in the region—even those without significant domestic pressure for change—had introduced new questions about racial or ethnic origins on their national censuses.

The resurgence of official ethnoracial classification in censuses since the 1990s coincides with an extraordinary moment of renegotiation in the relationships between states, ethnic minorities, and broader publics in Latin

America. The production of official ethnoracial statistics has become both a critical stake and a powerful tool in unfolding struggles over the relationship between states and historically marginalized populations in the region. In this chapter, I provide a descriptive overview of changes to ethnoracial data collection in Latin American censuses between the 1980 and 2010 census rounds and analyze the confluence of domestic and international processes that brought these changes about. The analysis reveals that most Latin American states have embraced official ethnoracial classification in response to shifts in international norms for what defines a modern nation and to international development organization criteria for how to promote national progress.

Recognizing Diversity in National Censuses, 1980–2010

The final decades of the twentieth century and the first decade of the twenty-first witnessed major changes to ethnoracial enumeration in Latin American censuses. In the 1980 census round, only three countries (Brazil, Cuba, and Guatemala) included a direct question about race or ethnic group membership on their national census (a few other countries included questions that asked about ethnoracial difference indirectly, through questions about language for example). By the 2010 census round, every Latin American country except one (the Dominican Republic) included, or had publicly committed to include, at least one direct query to capture indigenous and/or Afrodescendant individuals.

Ethnoracial distinctions within Latin American populations became more visible in national censuses between 1980 and 2010. In the first decades of the twenty-first century, the inclusion of census queries that made ethnoracial populations statistically visible had become the new norm. The overarching trend toward increased visibility of ethnoracial minority populations in Latin American censuses was accompanied by considerable variation in the specific types of questions added to census forms. Some national statistics agencies added new census queries to supplement prior methods of acquiring data about minority groups. Others added queries that made particular minority populations statistically visible in the context of a national census for the first time.

Table 7.1a provides an overview of the increased attention to enumeration of indigenous and Afrodescendant populations in Latin American censuses by country. Table 7.1b describes the varied types of questions that were used to capture ethnoracial diversity within national populations in censuses from the 1980s through the 2010s.

TABLE 7.1A Visibility of Afrodescendant and Indigenous Peoples in Latin American Censuses, 1980s–2010s

	1980s	1990s	2000s	2010s
Argentina			○	●○
Bolivia		○	○	●○
Brazil	●	●○	●○	●○
Chile		○	○	○
Colombia		●○	●○	●○
Costa Rica			●○	●○
Cuba	●		●	●
Dominican Rep.				
Ecuador		○	●○	●○
El Salvador			●○	
Guatemala	○	○	●○	●○
Honduras	○		●○	●○
Mexico	○	○	○	●○
Nicaragua		○	●○	●○
Panama	○	○	○	●○
Paraguay	○	○	○	●○
Peru	○	○	○	●○
Uruguay				●○
Venezuela	○	○	○	●○

● = Afrodescent visibility
○ = Indigenous visibility
▧ = Census taken

It is clear from a simple glance at Table 7.1a that indigenous and Afrodescendant populations became more visible in Latin American censuses between the 1980 and 2010 census rounds. In the 1980s, indigenous people were distinguished from the rest of the population in just under half of the countries that took a national census in the decade (7/16). In the 1990s, indigenous people were statistically visible in three-fourths of the censuses conducted (12/16). By the 2000 census round, sixteen of nineteen countries (84 percent) included at least one question that aimed to capture the presence of indigenous peoples. By the 2010 census round, twelve of fourteen countries that had carried out the census by 2013 made indigenous people statistically visible, and five countries that had not yet carried out the census planned to include such queries in their next census. In total, indigenous peoples would be distinguishable in the census results of seventeen of nineteen countries (90 percent) in the 2010 census round.

The increased visibility of Afrodescendant populations in Latin American censuses between the 1980s and the 2010s is even more striking. As can be seen in Table 7.1a, during the 1980s and 1990s, only three of nineteen countries (16 percent) took a national census in which Afrodescendants

"WE ALL COUNT" | 253

TABLE 7.1B Approaches to Enumerating Afrodescendant and Indigenous Peoples in Latin American Censuses, 1980s–2010s

Country	1980s	1990s	2000s	2010s
Argentina			(A) (M)	(A)(I) / (A)(I)
Bolivia		(L)(S)	(L)(M)	(M) / (L)(M)
Brazil	(P)	(P)(R) / (P)(R)	(P)(R) / (P)(R)	(P)(R) / (P)(R)(I)(P)(R)
Chile		(M)	(M)	(L)(M)
Colombia		(M) / (M)(S)	(C)(I)(M)(P) / (C)(I)(L)(M)(P)	● / ○
Costa Rica			(M) / (M)	(I) / (I)(L)(M)
Cuba	(P)		(P)	(P)
Dominican Republic				
Ecuador		(S)	(I) / (I)(L)(M)	(C)(I) / (C)(I)(L)(M)
El Salvador			(I) / (I)(L)(M)	
Guatemala	(I)(M)	(C)(I) / (L)(M)	(M) / (I)(L)(M)	● / ○
Honduras	(L)		(M) / (M)	(I)(M) / (I)(M)
Mexico	(L)	(S)	(I)(L)(M)	● / (C)(I)(L)
Nicaragua		(S)	(M) / (L)(M)	● / ○
Panama	(S)	(I)(M)	(I) (M)	(I) / (L)(M)
Paraguay	(L)(S)	(M)(L)	(I)(L)(M)(S)	(C)(I)(P) / (I)(L)(M)(S)
Peru	(L)	(L)(S)	(L)	(S) / ●
Uruguay			(A)	(A)
Venezuela	(L)(S)	(S)	(L)(M)(S)	(A)(C)(I)(P) / (L)(M)(S)

☐ = Census taken
(A) = Afrodescent identified through ancestry
(C) = Afrodescent identified through customs
(I) = Afrodescent identified through identity
(M) = Afrodescent identified through group membership
(P) = Afrodescent identified through physical appearance
(R) = Afrodescent identified through race
(S) = Separate census of afro-descendent population taken
(A) = Indigenousness identified through ancestry
(C) = Indigenousness identified through customs
(I) = Indigenousness identified through identity
(L) = Indigenousness identified through language
(M) = Indigenousness identified through group membership
(P) = Indigenousness identified through physical appearance
(R) = Indigenousness identified through race
(S) = Separate indigenous census taken

could be differentiated from the rest of the population.[3] In the 2000 census round, nearly half (9/19) of all Latin American countries did so. By the 2010 census round, eleven of fourteen countries that had carried out the census by 2013 included queries that made Afrodescendant populations discernible in official census results, and such queries were expected to be included in the proximate censuses of six additional countries. Assuming no abrupt change in plans in those countries, Afrodescendant people

---

[3] In Brazil and Cuba, this continued their established practice of identifying those of African descent on the census using a direct question about race or color. In the Colombian case, discussed in more detail later in this chapter, a new census question in the 1990s broke with decades of statistical invisibility for Afrodescendant people in the country.

would be counted in seventeen of nineteen countries (84 percent) in the 2010 census round.[4]

Table 7.1b shows that not only did more Latin American states differentiate indigenous and Afrodescendant peoples on national censuses in the first two decades of the twenty-first century than in any previous decade, they also used a greater variety of approaches to identify them than in the past. The black and white circles in Table 7.1b contain letter codes that signify different conceptual bases for identification as indigenous or Afrodescendant. When a cell has more than one white or black circle, this means that more than one question was asked to capture these populations in different ways, or that a single question invoked more than one conceptual understanding of what makes someone indigenous or Afrodescendant. The trend over time is toward the use of census questions that identify indigenous and Afrodescendant peoples using multiple criteria.

Table 7.1b also shows that from the 1990s onward, new types of questions started to appear on censuses alongside or in lieu of the types of questions used to identify ethnoracial diversity in the past. Historically, as seen in earlier chapters, the most common approach to identifying indigenous and Afrodescendant peoples in Latin American censuses was via a direct question about "race" or "color." In some Andean and Mesoamerican countries, direct race questions were supplemented with other approaches to identifying indigenous people, such as questions about maternal language. After World War II, direct race questions disappeared from the censuses of nearly all countries in the region, as discussed in chapter 6. Brazil and Cuba, the two historical outliers for the post–World War II years, continued to include "race" or "color" questions right through the second half of the twentieth century. But most Latin American states relied on questions about cultural characteristics to identify indigenous peoples in national censuses, while Afrodescendant peoples became largely invisible in official census results in the region. Around the turn of the twenty-first century, a new type of question started to appear. Latin American censuses began to identify indigenous and Afrodescendant people through questions that asked

---

[4] Mexico conducted a national census in 2010 that made indigenous peoples visible but not Afrodescendants. In 2013, Mexico announced plans for another census in 2015 that would enumerate Afrodescendants. Census officials in Guatemala, Nicaragua, and Colombia made public commitments, reported in the media, that their next census would include versions of questions that had made indigenous and Afrodescendant peoples visible in the prior census. Media reports from Peru indicated the likely inclusion of a question to allow identification as Afro-Peruvian on the census planned for 2017. El Salvador had not released any information about plans for the next census as of September, 2013.

about individual identity, membership, or feelings of belonging to a distinct ethnoracial group.

Whether explicitly or implicitly, such questions conceded the fundamentally inter-subjective basis of ethnoracial distinctions, marking a break with objectivist understandings and measures that had prevailed in the past (including questions about race or color and questions about cultural practices). To be sure, several countries retained such "objective" measures of ethnoracial difference alongside queries that asked about individual identity. But the momentum in this period was toward the use of questions that made self-declared identity or membership a sufficient basis to be counted as indigenous or Afrodescendant on the census.

Table 7.2 reports the specific questions included on Latin American census schedules in the 2000 and 2010 census rounds to capture ethnoracial diversity within national populations. Beneath the general regional consensus that states should now count indigenous and Afrodescendant populations on national censuses, it is evident that Latin American governments diverged widely in their specific approaches to ethnoracial enumeration.

TABLE 7.2 Questions about Ethnoracial Diversity in Latin American Censuses, 2000s–2010s

Argentina

2001	*Is there any person in this household who identifies as descendant of or belonging to an indigenous people [pueblo]?*
	Yes; No
	[If "Yes"]: To which people [pueblo]?
	Chané; Chorote; Chulupi; Diaguita Calchaqui; Huarpe; Kolla; Mapuche; Mbyá; Mocoví; Ona; Pilagá; Rankulche; Tapiete; Tehuelche; Toba; Tupí Guaraní; Wichí; Another indigenous people [pueblo]; Don't know
2010	*Are you or any person in this household afrodescendant or have afrodescendant or African-origin ancestors (father, mother, grandparents, great-grandparents)?*
	Yes; No; Don't know
	[If "Yes"]: Indicate which person
	[open to specify]
	Is any person in this household indigenous or descendant from indigenous (native or aboriginal) peoples [pueblo]?
	Yes; No; Don't know
	[If "Yes"]: Indicate which person
	[open to specify]
	[If "Yes"]: Indicate which peoples [pueblo]
	[open to specify]

Bolivia

2001   *Do you consider yourself as belonging to any of the following native or indigenous peoples [pueblos]?*
Quechua; Aymara; Guaraní; Chiquitano; Mojeño; Other native [open to specify]; None
What languages do you speak? (Choose more than one if appropriate)
Quechua; Aymara; Castellano; Guarani; Foreign language; Doesn't speak; Other native language [open to specify]
What was the language in which you learned to speak as a child?
Quechua; Aymara; Castellano; Guarani; Other native language; Foreign language; Doesn't speak

2012   *As a Bolivian, do you belong to any nation or native peasant indigenous people [pueblo indigena originario campesino] or [are you] Afro-Bolivian?*
Yes; No; I am not Bolivian
[If "Yes"]: To which?
[open to specify] The following options provided to the enumerator, but instructed not to be read: Afro-Bolivian; Araona; Aymara; Ayoreo; Baure; Canichana; Cavineño; Cayubaba; Chácobo; Chipaya; Chiquitano; Ese Ejja; Guaraní; Guarasugwe; Guarayo; Itonoma; Joaquiniano; Kallawaya; Leco; Machineri; Maropa; Mojeño; Moré; Mosetén; Movima; Murato; Pacahuara; Quechua; Sirionó; Tacana; Tapiete; Tsimane/Chiman; Weenayek; Yaminagua; Yuki; Yuracaré; Yuracaré—Mojeño
What languages do you speak? (Note in order of importance)
[open to specify]
What was the first language in which you learned to speak as a child?
[open to specify]; Doesn't speak

Brazil

2000   *Your color or race is:*
White; Black; Yellow; Parda; Indigenous

2010   *Your color or race is:*
White; Black; Yellow; Parda; Indigenous
Do you consider yourself indigenous?
Yes; No
[If "Yes"]: What is the ethnic group or people [povo] to which you belong?
[open to specify]
Do you speak any indigenous language in your household? (This includes if the language is spoken with signs.)
Yes; No
[If "Yes"]: Which one? (Specify indigenous languages—up to two languages)
[open to specify two answers]

(cont.)

TABLE 7.2 (*Continued*)

Chile

2002   *Do you belong to any of the following native or indigenous peoples [pueblos]?*

Alacalufe (Kawashkar); Atacameño; Aimara; Colla; Mapuche; Quechua; Rapa Nui; Yámana (Yagán); None of the above

2012   *Do you consider yourself as belonging to any indigenous (native) people [pueblo]?*

Yes; No

[If "Yes"]: Which one?

Mapuche; Aymara; Rapa Nui; Likan Antai; Quechua; Colla; Diaguita; Kawésqar; Yagán o Yámana; Other [open to specify]

In what languages can you maintain a conversation? (You can mark more than one option)

Can't speak; Spanish; Mapudungún; Aymara; Quechua; Rapa Nui; English; Other

Colombia

2005   *According to your culture, people [pueblo] or physical traits, ____ is or recognizes himself/herself as:*

Indigenous; Rom; Raizal from the San Andrés and Providencia Archipelago; Palenquero from San Basilio; Black, mulatto, Afro-Colombian or Afrodescendant; None of the above

[If "Indigenous"]: To which indigenous people [pueblo] does s/he belong? (Write the name of the people [pueblo])

[open to specify]

Does ____ speak the language of his/her people [pueblo]?

Yes; No

Costa Rica

2000   *Does ____ belong to the culture...*

Indigenous; Afro-Costa Rican or black; Chinese; None of the above

2011   *Does ____ consider himself/herself... [This question is skipped if the person identifies as indigenous]*

Black or Afrodescendant; Mulatto; Chinese; White or Mestizo; Other, None

Does ____ consider himself/herself indigenous?

Yes; No

[If "Yes"]: To which indigenous people [pueblo] does ____ belong?

Bribri; Brunca or Boruca; Cabécar; Chorotega; Huetar; Maleku or Guatuso; Ngöbe or Guaymí; Teribe or Térraba; From another country; No people [ningún pueblo]

Does ____ speak any indigenous language?

Yes; No

Cuba

2002   *What is his/her skin color? (Mark only one)*
        White; Black; Mestizo or Mulatto
2012   *What is his/her skin color (Mark only one)*
        White; Black; Mestizo or Mulatto

Dominican Republic

2002   *No question made Afrodescendant or indigenous populations visible on this census.*
2004   *No question made Afrodescendant or indigenous populations visible on this census.*

Ecuador

2001   *How do you consider yourself?*
        Indigenous; Black (Afro-Ecuadorian); Mestizo; Mulatto; White; Other
        [If "Indigenous"]: To which Indigenous Nationality or Indigenous People [Pueblo] do you belong?
        [open to specify]
        What language do you speak?
        Only Spanish; Only Native Language; Only Foreign Language; Spanish and Native Language; Other [open to specify]
        [If "Native Language" or if "Spanish and Native Language"]: Which Native language?
        [open to specify]
2010   *How does ____ identify himself/herself according to his/her culture and customs?*
        Indigenous; Afro-Ecuadorian/Afro-descendant; Black; Mulatto; Montubio; Mestizo; White; Other
        [If "Indigenous"]: To which nationality or indigenous peoples does ____ belong?
        [open to specify] The following options provided: *Nationalities*: Achuar; Awa; Cofan; Chachi; Epera; Waorani; Kichwa; Secoya; Shuar; Siona; Tsáchila; Shwar; Zápara; Andoa. Peoples [*Pueblos*]: Pasos; Natabuela; Otavalo; Karanki; Kitukara; Panzaleo; Chilaleo; Salasaka; Kisapincha; Tomabela; Waranka; Puruhá; Kañari; Saraguro; Paltas; Manta; Huancavilca
        What language(s) do/did ____'s father and mother speak normally?
        Indigenous; Castellano/Spanish; Foreign language; Doesn't speak
        What language(s) does ____ speak?
        Indigenous; Castellano/Spanish; Foreign language; Doesn't speak
        [If "Indigenous"]: What indigenous language does ____ speak?
        [open to specify] The following options provided: Achuar; Andoa; Awapit; A'ingae; Cha'palaa; Zia pedee; Kichwa; Paicoca; Shuar; Tsalfiqu; Shiwiar; Waotededo; Zapara

El Salvador

2007   *Are you...?*
        White; Mestizo (mix of white and indigenous); Indigenous; Black (of race); Other

(cont.)

TABLE 7.2 *(Continued)*

[If "Indigenous"]: If you are indigenous, to which group do you belong?
Lenca; Kakawira (Cacaopera); Nahua-Pipil; Other [open to specify]
Do you speak any other language in addition to Spanish?
Yes [open to specify]; No

Guatemala

2002 *Are you indigenous?*
Yes; No
[If "Yes"]: To which ethnic group (people [pueblo]) do you belong?
Achi; Akateko; Awakateko; Ch'orti'; Chuj; Itza; Ixil; Jakalteko (Popti'); Kaqchikel; K'Iche'; Mam; Mopan; Poqomam; Poqomchi'; Q'anjob'ai; Q'eqchi'; Sakapulteko; Sipakapense; Tektiteko; Tz'utujil; Uspanteko; Xinka; Garifuna; Ladino; Spanish Language; None; Other
What is the language in which you learned to speak?
Achi; Akateko; Awakateko; Ch'orti'; Chuj; Itza; Ixil; Jakalteko (Popti'); Kaqchikel; K'Iche'; Mam; Mopan; Poqomam; Poqomchi'; Q'anjob'ai; Q'eqchi'; Sakapulteko; Sipakapense; Tektiteko; Tz'utujil; Uspanteko; Xinka; Garifuna; Ladino; Spanish Language; None; Other
What other languages do you speak?
Achi; Akateko; Awakateko; Ch'orti'; Chuj; Itza; Ixil; Jakalteko (Popti'); Kaqchikel; K'Iche'; Mam; Mopan; Poqomam; Poqomchi'; Q'anjob'ai; Q'eqchi'; Sakapulteko; Sipakapense; Tektiteko; Tz'utujil; Uspanteko; Xinka; Garifuna; Ladino; Spanish Language; None; Other

Honduras

2001 *What population group do you belong to?*
Garífuna; English Black; Tolupán; Pech (Paya); Misquito; Lenca; Tawahka (Sumo); Chortí; Other

2013 *Do you self-identify as:*
Indigenous; Black; Afro-Honduran; Mestizo; White; Other [open to specify]
[If "Indigenous"; "Black"; "Afro-Honduran"]: What native or indigenous peoples [pueblo] do you belong to?
Maya-Chorti; Lenca; Misquito; Nahua; Pech; Tolupán; Tawahka; Garifuna; Black that speaks English; Other [open to specify]

Mexico

2000 *Ethnic belonging: Is* (name) *náhuatl, maya, zapoteco, mixteco, or member of any other indigenous group?*
Yes; No
Indigenous language: Does (name) *speak any indigenous dialect or language?*
Yes; No
[If "Yes"]: Which indigenous dialect or language does (name) *speak?*
[open to specify]

2010 *According to* (name)*'s culture, does s/he consider himself/herself indigenous?*
Yes; No

Does (name) *speak any indigenous dialect or language?*
Yes; No
[If "Yes"]: Which indigenous dialect or language does (name) *speak?*
[open to specify three languages]
Does (name) *understand any indigenous language?*
Yes; No

Nicaragua

2005   *Does _____ consider himself/herself as belonging to an indigenous people [pueblo] or ethnic group?*
Yes; No
[If "Yes"]: To which of the following indigenous peoples [pueblos] or ethnic groups does _____ belong?
Rama; Garifuna; Mayangna Sumu; Miskitu; Ulwa; Creole (Kriol); Mestizo from the Caribbean Coast; Xiu-Sutiava; Nahoa-Nicarao; Chorotega-Nahua-Mange; Cacaopera-Matagalpa; Other; Doesn't know
[If "Rama"; "Garifuna";"Mayangna Sumu"; "Miskitu"; "Ulwa"; "Creole (Kriol'); "Mestizo from the Caribbean Coast"]: Does _____ speak the language of the indigenous people [pueblo] or ethic group to which s/he belongs?]
Yes; No

Panama

2000   *Do any indigenous people live here?*
Yes; No
[If "Yes"]: Who?
[checks circle for the corresponding person]
[If "Yes," for each person]: To which indigenous group does s/he belong?
Kuna; Ngöbe; Bugle; Teribe; Bokota; Emberá; Wounaan; Bri Bri; None

2010   *Does any person in this household consider himself/herself black or Afrodescendant?*
Yes; No
[If "Yes"]: Who?
[checks circle for the corresponding person]
[If "Yes," for each person]: Do you consider yourself...?
Colonial black; West Indian [Antillano] black; Black; Other [open to specify]; None
Does any indigenous person live here?
Yes; No
[If "Yes"]: Who?
[If "Yes," for each person]: To which indigenous group does s/he belong?
Kuna; Ngäbe; Buglé; Naso/Teribe; Bokota; Emberá; Wounaan; Bri Bri; Other [open to specify]; None

(cont.)

TABLE 7.2 *(Continued)*

Paraguay

2002   *A separate indigenous census was carried out (in addition to the questions asked below).*
Is there any person in this household who considers himself/herself indigenous or belonging to an indigenous ethnic group?
Yes; No
[If "Yes"]: (Note in one line the name, surname, age, and ethnicity [la etnia] to which they belong for each person who has identified as indigenous)
[open to specify] The following options provided: Aché ñe'e; Angaité; Ava-guarani ñe'e; Ayoreo; Enlhet norte; Enxet Sur; Guarani occidental ñe'e; Maká; Manjui; Maskoy; Mbya ñe'e; Nivaclé; Nandeva ñe'e; Pai ñe'e; Sanapaná; Toba; Toba-qom; Tomárâho; Ybytoso
What languages does ____ speak? (You can mark more than one)
Guaraní; Castellano; Portuguese; German; English; French; Doesn't speak; Indigenous [open to specify)]; Other language [open to specify]
To speak to one another, the people in this household usually use ...
Guaraní; Castellano; Portuguese; German; English; Indigenous [open to specify]; Other language [open to specify]

2012   *A separate indigenous census was carried out (in addition to the questions asked below).*
According to your physical traits, culture, or traditions, does any person in this household consider himself/herself afrodescendant or kamba?
Yes; No
[If "Yes"]: (Note in one line the name and surname for each person who has identified as Afrodescendant or kamba)
[open to specify]
Does any person who lives in this household consider himself/herself indigenous or belonging to an ethnic group (indigenous peoples) [pueblo indígena]?
Yes; No
[If "Yes"]: (Note in one line the name, surname, and ethnicity [la etnia (pueblo)] to which they belong for each person who has identified as indigenous)
[open to specify] The following options provided Aché ñe'e; Angaité; Ava-guarani; Ayoreo; Enlhet norte; Enxet Sur; Guarani occidental; Maká; Manjui; Maskoy; Mbya; Nivaclé; Nandeva; Pai Tavytera; Sanapaná; Toba; Qom; Tomárâho; Ybytoso
What languages does (name) speak? (You should register only one response in each column (three columns provided: first language, second language, third language)
Guaraní; Castellano; Portuguese; German; English; French; Doesn't speak [in the first column]/No other language [in the second and third columns]; Indigenous [open to specify]; Other language [open to specify]
To speak to one another, the people in this household usually use...
Guaraní; Castellano; Castellano and Guarani; Portuguese; German; Don't speak; Indigenous [open to specify]; Other language [open to specify]

Peru

2007   *A separate indigenous census was carried out (in addition to the question asked below).*
The language with which you learned to speak was...
Quechua; Aymara; Asháninka; Other native language [open to specify]; Castellano; Foreign language; Deaf/mute

Uruguay

2004   *No question made Afrodescendant or indigenous populations visible on this census.*

2011   *Do you believe yourself to have ancestry...?*
Afro or Black; Asian or Yellow; White; Indigenous; Other [Yes or No for each response]
[If they marked "yes" for more than one]: Which one do you consider to be the main one?
Afro or Black; Asian or Yellow; White; Indigenous; Other; None

Venezuela

2001   *A separate indigenous census was carried out (in addition to the questions asked below).*
Do you belong to any indigenous people [pueblo]?
Yes; No
[If "Yes"]: Which one?
[open to specify]
Do you speak the language of that people [pueblo]?
Yes; No

2011   *A separate indigenous census was carried out (in addition to the questions asked below).*
According to your physical traits, family ancestry, culture and traditions, you consider yourself to be: [This question is skipped if the person identifies as indigenous]
Black; Afrodescendant; Brown [Morena/o]; White; Other [*Which one?* [Open to specify]]
Do you belong to any indigenous people [pueblo] or ethnic group?
Yes; No
[If "Yes"]: Which one?
[open to specify]
[If "Yes"]: What language(s) do you speak? (Allow more than one answer)
The languages of your Indigenous People [Pueblo] or Ethnic Group; Castellano; Other language [open to specify]
[If "Yes"]: Do you know how to read and write in the language of the indigenous peoples [pueblo] or ethnic group to which you belong?
Yes; No

As can be seen in Table 7.2, the types of questions used to identify and count those of indigenous and African ancestry varied widely across the continent. There was no uniformity in the format, wording or allowable response options across countries. Questions used to count Afrodescendant populations ranged from a question that asked "Your color or race is...?" in Brazil, to a question that inquired about culture, group membership, or physical appearance in Colombia ("According to your culture, people [pueblo] or physical traits, [this person] is or recognizes himself/herself as..."), to a question that asked about ancestry in Argentina ("Are you or any person in this household afrodescendant or have afrodescendant or African-origin ancestors (father, mother, grandparents, great grandparents?)").[5] In a few cases, a question about belonging to an indigenous or ethnic group was used to capture specific, named subsets of the Afrodescendant population. For instance, Nicaragua's 2005 census asked, "Does [this person] consider himself/herself as belonging to an indigenous people [pueblo] or ethnic group?" Those who answered "Yes" could choose from a list of options that included "Garifuna" and "Creole (Kriol)." Thus, Afrodescendant Nicaraguans could be recognized as such only through claimed membership in a specific "ethnic" category.

Approaches to enumerating indigenous people also varied, and often combined objectivist understandings of indigeneity (for example, questions about language) with subjectivist understandings (for example, questions about identity or feelings of belonging to a community).[6] In some countries with long traditions of counting indigenous peoples in national censuses, new approaches to their enumeration fractured indigenousness into a greater array of categorically distinct subsets of the population than had ever before been recognized by the state, reaching back as far as the colonial period. Bolivia's 2012 census, for example, recognized thirty-seven distinct indigenous identities.[7]

---

[5] According to Argentina's national statistics agency, the addition of the query about Afrodescent on the 2010 census responded "not only to international conventions, but [also] to a longstanding debt owed to certain sectors of the Argentine population." Argentina. Instituto Nacional de Estadísticas y Censos. "Afrodescendientes." http://www.censo2010.indec.gov.ar/index_afro.asp.

[6] Peyser and Chackiel, "La identificación de poblaciones indígenas"

[7] The census recognized more indigenous identities than are recognized in the constitution. Part of the political rationale for this change to the census was to make the country seem more indigenous than mestizo, an agenda advanced by president Evo Morales. The absence of a "mestizo" response category on the 2012 census became the focal point for a backlash against Morales' indianist political vision. Valdez, "Bolivia's Census Omits 'Mestizo' as Category." See also Regalsky, "Bolivia: Indigenous Identities and Collective Subjects in the Andes."

The varied approaches to ethnoracial enumeration partly reflect distinct historical traditions, institutional legacies, and contemporary political struggles in each country. But the heterogeneity of approaches to capturing diversity on the census also reflects the complexity of the phenomenon that census agencies seek to measure. Racial and ethnic categories and identities are connected to history, culture, and language in ways that make responses on surveys highly contingent on how questions are constructed and phrased. Census officials are increasingly aware of this fact, and they struggle to reconcile this recognition with their professional mission to produce valid, reliable, and accurate demographic data. This challenge is further complicated, from the perspective of census agency officials, by the historically novel imperative to appear at least somewhat responsive to the concerns of those whom the census aims to classify and count.[8]

The surge of attention to the enumeration of indigenous and Afrodescendant populations across nearly all Latin American countries in the 2000 and 2010 census rounds is clearly not a coincidence. Breaking from decades-long traditions of using the national census to document either the absence or the gradual disappearance of ethnoracial distinctions within the nation, Latin American census agencies have shifted gears to document—and, in some cases, to help promote—the persistence of discrete ethnoracial groups. Especially when considered in light of nineteenth- and twentieth-century census-taking history in the region, the sudden turn to highlighting ethnoracial difference within national populations is striking. Why and how did this dramatic reorientation of census agency priorities come about?

Democratization and Diversification

A critical precursor to the recent census changes across Latin America was the broad and multifaceted push for democratization throughout the region in the 1980s. From the mid-1960s into the 1970s, most of Latin America fell under authoritarian rule. Citizens of formerly democratic polities suffered a range of assaults on basic freedoms and rights, ranging from constraints on free speech and assembly to arbitrary arrest and torture to disappearance and assassination by state or parastate forces. In some countries, state repression targeted those defined as leftist subversives,

---

[8] I discuss the increased pressure for census agencies to engage with and be accountable to the populations they count in the concluding chapter.

organizers, or dissidents; in others, entire communities, including indigenous and ethnic communities, were targeted, ostensibly to wipe out sympathizers who might offer support to insurgents. The experience of living under dictatorship differed profoundly across the region; the chill and violence of state repression—and in some contexts the armed response—bore unevenly on different subgroups within Latin America's populations.[9]

Over the course of the 1980s, most of Latin America shifted back toward formally democratic government. Just as the duration and severity of authoritarian rule varied across the region, so too did the timing, pace, and substantive depth of the "transitions to democracy" that ensued. Democratic reforms were piecemeal. They were slow. And often, they stopped short of measures needed to fully institutionalize and consolidate democratic governance.

Gradual, faltering, and incomplete as they often were, the democratic reforms of the 1980s created space for citizens to voice collective dissent and demand additional reforms. It was not democratization per se that made states embrace official recognition of ethnoracial communities. Earlier in the twentieth century, periods of democratic opening and expansion of popular politics had resulted, for example, in aggressive integrationist policies (various renditions of indigenismo) as well as racially exclusionary immigration policies.[10] In the early twenty-first century, in contrast, democratization combined with the emergence of new types of collective political claims making to yield very different results.

A broad range of new—or newly politicized—collective actors emerged to engage the political process and make claims on the state. Citizens mobilized as women, as victims of human rights abuses, as gays and lesbians, as environmentalists, and as members of indigenous and Afrodescendant communities, among others. Although they are often designated as "new" social movements in scholarly accounts (to distinguish them from class-based movements of the past), the notion that these new social movements were historically novel in advancing claims based on "identity" is misleading. The mobilization of most of these groups was just as much about material conditions and demands as about collective recognition, in much the same way that class-based movements have relied historically on collective identities and loyalties

---

[9] See Menjívar and Rodríguez, *When States Kill*; Loveman, B., *For la Patria*, ch. 8; Corradi, et. al., *Fear at the Edge*.

[10] Fitzgerald and Cook-Martín, *Culling the Masses*.

to struggle for material gains.[11] Particularly in the case of indigenous and Afrodescendant groups, "identities" and "interests" tended to be inextricably intertwined. What was new, however, was the extent to which these collective actors made claims that were grounded in, rather than incidental to or despite, their membership in ethnoracially defined categories or communities.

Spurred in part by neoliberal reforms that undercut institutional and economic arrangements that had sustained the livelihoods of many poor and rural populations, indigenous and Afrodescendant organizations mobilized to demand recognition, rights, and redress.[12] In targeting national states, activists drew on discursive and material resources from the transnational political fields of indigenous and human rights that developed in the second half of the twentieth century.[13] Harnessing international norms and conventions to the agendas of domestic constituencies, Latin American activists pushed for constitutional reforms, new collective rights and forms of autonomy, policies to combat racial discrimination, and official recognition of ethnoracial diversity within the nation.

Not surprisingly, the intensity and resonance of domestic mobilization around issues of racial and ethnic inequality varied, as did the responsiveness of different Latin American governments to activists' demands. Governments also differed in their response to claims by indigenous versus Afrodescendant organizations; in most countries, campaigns on behalf of the latter faced stiffer resistance and successes were thus harder won.

From Mestizaje to Multiethnicity

Owing to the combination of domestic social pressures and the consolidation of an international human rights regime that espoused protection of minority rights among its central tenets, by the 1990s most Latin American governments had made significant rhetorical concessions to the idea of

---

[11] Escobar and Alvarez, eds., *The Making of Social Movements in Latin America*; Eckstein and Garretón Merino, *Power and Popular Protest*.

[12] On the emergence of indigenous movements in the 1980s, see Yashar, *Contesting Citizenship in Latin America*; Sieder, *Multiculturalism in Latin America*; Stavenhagen, "Indigenous Peoples and the State in Latin America."

[13] On the connections between domestic activism, international human rights organizations and the rise of indigenous rights regimes, see Van Cott, *The Friendly Liquidation of the Past*.

enduring ethnoracial diversity within the nation.[14] Amended constitutions announced the multiethnic or pluricultural nature of Latin American nations. For example, the 1985 Guatemalan Constitution, promulgated after a civil war that included incidents of ethnocide, proclaimed that "The Guatemalan nation is one and solidary; within its unity and territorial integrity, it is pluricultural, multiethnic and multilingual" (Art.1). Additional amendments in 1998 elaborated on the rights and guarantees afforded for the protection of diversity. The 1991 Colombian Constitution declared that "The State recognizes and protects the ethnic and cultural diversity of the Colombian Nation" (Art.7). The 1994 Bolivian Constitution, in turn, defined the nation as "multiethnic and pluricultural" (Art.1), as did the 1998 Ecuadorian Constitution.[15] The preamble to the latter announced that Ecuador "proclaims its will to consolidate the unity of the Ecuadorian nation in recognition of the diversity of its regions, peoples (*pueblos*), ethnicities and cultures." The 1993 Peruvian Constitution declared that "The State recognizes and protects ethnic and cultural plurality of the Nation" (Art.2), while the 1987 Nicaraguan Constitution stated that "the Nicaraguan *pueblo* is multiethnic in nature" ("es de naturaleza multiétnica") (Art 8). As of 2013, only six Latin American countries had not reformed their constitutions to explicitly recognize the cultural or ethnic diversity of the population that comprised the nation.[16]

In several countries, constitutional recognition of diversity included explicit legal protections or guarantees for minority populations. Nearly all countries included some form of recognition of communal property rights and limited forms of political autonomy for indigenous communities and in some countries (Brazil, Colombia, Ecuador, Guatemala, Honduras, and Nicaragua) for Afrodescendant communities as well. Customary law received constitutional sanction in several countries (including Bolivia, Colombia, Ecuador, Guatemala, Mexico, Nicaragua, Panama, Paraguay, Peru, and Venezuela). Many

---

[14] Van Cott, *The Friendly Liquidation of the Past.*

[15] Albo and Barrios, *Por una Bolivia Plurinacional e Intercultural con Autonomías*; de Sousa Santos, *La Reinvención del Estado y el Estado Plurinacional*; García Linera, "Estado Plurinacional."

[16] The six countries are Chile, Costa Rica, Cuba, the Dominican Republic, El Salvador, and Uruguay. In 2004, a proposal to reform Chile's constitution to recognize indigenous peoples failed to secure enough votes in Congress due to the requirement of a supramajority for constitutional reforms (53 in favor, 26 against, and 24 abstentions). González, "Indígenas-América Latina." Although they lack constitutional recognition, indigenous peoples in Chile, Costa Rica, and El Salvador are recognized in targeted national legislation, such as Chile's *Ley Indígena* (Chile. Ministerio de Planificación y Cooperación. *Ley Indígena*. Ley Nº 19.253, Published 05.10.1993, Last modified 13.11.1998, Ley 19.587). By 2013, in Latin America, only Cuba, the Dominican Republic, and Uruguay refrained from legal recognition of indigenous peoples.

countries' constitutions also guaranteed, or at least promised to support, bilingual education for certain populations (Argentina, Bolivia, Brazil, Colombia, Ecuador, Guatemala, Mexico, Nicaragua, Paraguay, Peru, and Venezuela). In addition to positive rights, constitutions promised protection from discrimination, usually through generic equality before the law clauses, but in some cases (Brazil and Colombia) bolstered by explicit prohibitions against ethnic or racial discrimination. Over the course of the 1990s and 2000s, many governments in the region expanded on vague constitutional provisions with new laws targeting specific educational, health, occupational, or property issues related to particular populations.[17]

Changes to Latin American constitutions and law with respect to ethnic and racial minorities since the 1990s reveal a clear shift in the official stance of most governments away from the ideal of color-blind integration. In lieu of celebrating mestizaje, a growing number of Latin American countries now celebrate multiethnicity. Political scientist Deborah Yashar points to the significant role of indigenous social movements in pressuring national states to implement reforms. She traces the rise of mass indigenous movements to unintended consequences of neoliberal reforms in the previous decade. Structural adjustment policies undermined corporatist political ties and undercut the livelihoods and local autonomy of indigenous communities, spurring mobilization.[18] Other scholars suggest that politically fragile transitional governments responded to claims for ethnic-based rights as a relatively low-cost way to shore up legitimacy and consolidate democratic rule.[19] A stronger version of this argument suggests that states acted strategically in extending culturally based rights to segments of the population to divert and dilute potentially more radical and broad-based demands.[20] While analysts may disagree on the underlying reasons for the wave of multiculturalist reforms in Latin America, there is broad agreement on at least one critical point: for states that had

---

[17] Useful overviews of multicultural constitutional and legal reforms in Latin America include: Inter-American Dialogue "Race Reports"; Sieder, ed., *Multiculturalism in Latin America*; Aparicio, *Los Pueblos Indígenas y el Estado*; Barié, *Pueblos Indígenas y Derechos Constitucionales en América Latina*; Sánchez, ed., *Derechos de los Pueblos Indígenas en las Constituciones de América Latina*; Van Cott, *Indigenous Peoples and Democracy in Latin America*; Van Cott, *The Friendly Liquidation of the Past*, ch. 9; The Georgetown University, *Political Database of the Americas*; Inter-American Development Bank, "Legislación Nacional por País."

[18] Yashar, *Contesting Citizenship in Latin America*; Brysk and Wise, "Liberalization and Ethnic Conflict in Latin America"; and Yashar, "Democracy, Indigenous Movements, and the Postliberal Challenge in Latin America."

[19] Van Cott, *The Friendly Liquidation of the Past*.

[20] Hale, "Does Multiculturalism Menace?"

invested for decades in the cultivation of mestizo nationalism or myths of racial democracy, the embrace of a multicultural national identity marked a momentous symbolic break with the past.

Yet throughout the region, a large gulf continued to separate the official rhetoric from the reality. As an Inter-American Dialogue report noted, "Recently, many countries have made amendments to their constitutions to include clearer references to the multicultural character of the state as well as stronger anti-discrimination laws. Still, many such amendments are merely symbolic. They recognize the universal rights of historically marginalized populations but do not include mechanisms to guarantee such rights."[21] Constitutional promises notwithstanding, few governments provided effective tools or sufficient resources to implement, monitor, and enforce rights and protections for minority populations.[22]

Moreover, in moving from official discourse to political practice, governments often revealed preferences for recognition of some kinds of diversity more than others. Policies focused on the rights and well-being of indigenous communities proliferated more readily than policies focused on Afrodescendant populations. The situation of minority populations resulting from voluntary migration, meanwhile, was generally left out of the discussion altogether.

There are numerous examples of successful mobilization by indigenous groups across Latin America in the 1990s and 2000s. In Argentina, for example, Mapuche groups from the southern region successfully lobbied the national state to demand greater political autonomy from provincial government; in the process, they chiseled away at the popular notion that there are no indigenous peoples remaining in Argentina.[23] In Bolivia, to cite perhaps the most dramatic instance of successful indigenous mobilization in this period, the indigenous movement became channeled into national political organization that resulted in the election of the first self-identified indigenous president of the country, Evo Morales, on December 18th, 2005. Even in Venezuela, which political scientist Donna Lee Van Cott characterized as a "'least likely' case of marginalized groups obtaining constitutional rights," indigenous movements won collective recognition and rights

---

[21] Inter-American Dialogue, "Constitutional Provisions and Legal Actions Related to Discrimination and Afro-Descendant Populations in Latin America," 3.

[22] Hooker, "Indigenous Inclusion/Black Exclusion," 5.

[23] Richards, *Pobladoras, Indígenas, and the State*; Warren, "A Nation Divided"; Barrientos, "Are There Still 'Indians' in Argentina?"

"comparable or superior to those obtained in neighboring countries with more consolidated movements."[24]

Indigenous movements gathered adherents and political capital in contexts where they were already officially recognized as a constitutive force in the forging of the nation. As previous chapters revealed, most Latin American states had cultivated official national identities that granted visibility to indigenous peoples within the nation—if primarily as demographic contributors to the mestizo ideal. In many countries, meanwhile, the presence of Afrodescendant peoples within the nation was either denigrated or outright denied. An enduring ideological preference for indigenous over African ancestry remained evident in popular culture across most of Latin America as the twentieth century came to a close.

Indigenous movements could leverage states' prior recognition of Indian communities and territories. Whether in national laws or de facto administrative practices, most Latin American states already acknowledged the existence of distinct indigenous communities within the nation. In the nineteenth and twentieth centuries, most national states had created specialized agencies for dealing with "Indian affairs." Further, many of the indigenous communities at the forefront of contemporary mobilizations had deep histories of communal organization, including prior episodes of sustained collective action targeting local, provincial, or national governments. These histories provided institutional, organizational, and cultural resources for building movement coalitions and effectively framing movement demands. When political crises in the 1990s elicited calls among elites for institutional reform, indigenous social movements in many countries were well positioned to pry open small fissures in political opportunity structures to press for more radical institutional change.[25]

Indigenous movements in Latin America also benefited from the prior existence of an international human rights regime with conventions focused explicitly on the rights of indigenous peoples. The mass social movements of the 1950s and 1960s—including the US Civil Rights movement, the First Nations movements, and decolonization movements in Africa and Asia—precipitated the creation of international indigenous organizations that successfully pushed for revisions to international human rights law through the institutions of the United Nations.[26] As legal scholar Luis

---

[24] Van Cott, "Andean Indigenous Movements and Constitutional Transformation," 50.

[25] Tarrow, *Power in Movement*; Van Cott, "Andean Indigenous Movements and Constitutional Transformation," 50.

[26] Rodriguez-Piñero, *Indigenous Peoples, Postcolonialism and International Law*, 260–261; Brysk,

Rodríguez-Piñero explains, "The political discourse of the international indigenous movement was founded on a critical reformulation of the bases of international law that did not recognize the legal personality of indigenous peoples and relegated them to a predicament of internal colonialism within their own territories."[27] Over the course of the 1970s and 1980s, the demands of international indigenous organizations were incorporated into several international human rights declarations and conventions.[28] With UN sponsorship, international indigenous organizations also crafted separate statements on the rights of indigenous peoples, such as the *1977 Draft Declaration of Principles for the Defense of Indigenous Nations and Peoples of the Western Hemisphere*. The UN established a Working Group on Indigenous Populations in 1981, which in 2002 became the UN Permanent Forum on Indigenous Issues.

The indigenous movements that emerged in Latin America in the 1980s and 1990s operated in a transnational political field with established activist networks linked to the international human rights legal regime. Domestic movements leveraged international conventions and networks to pressure national states for reforms.[29] An especially visible example of this dynamic centered on the ratification, in 1989, of International Labor Organization Convention 169 (ILO 169), concerning the rights of Indigenous and Tribal Peoples in Independent Countries. ILO 169 evolved from a previous accord (ILO 107) that was crafted without participation from indigenous peoples and espoused an explicitly integrationist perspective. In contrast, ILO 169 commits signatory states to recognize "the aspirations of [indigenous] peoples to exercise control over their own institutions, ways of life and economic development and to maintain and develop their identities, languages and religions, within the framework of the States in which they live."[30] The convention stakes out broad rights and protections for indigenous peoples, including articles pertaining to collective land rights, control of natural resources, use of customary law, freedom from discrimination, and rights to participate in decisions that affect their livelihoods and cultural sustainability, among others.[31]

From Tribal Village to Global Village; Niezen, *The Origins of Indigenism,* 29–52; Wilmer, *The Indigenous Voice in World Politics,* 127–61.

[27] Rodriguez-Piñero, *Indigenous Peoples, Postcolonialism and International Law,* 261.

[28] Rodriguez-Piñero, *Indigenous Peoples, Postcolonialism and International Law,* 262, n. 20.

[29] See Sikkink and Keck, *Activists Beyond Borders;* Tsing, "Indigenous Voice"; cf. Olzak, *The Global Dynamics of Ethnic and Racial Mobilization.*

[30] International Labour Organization, *Convention No. 169,* preamble.

[31] For the full text of Convention 169, see International Labor Organization, *Convention No. 169;* Anaya, *Indigenous Peoples in International Law,* 59.

TABLE 7.3 Latin American Signatories to ILO 169 (1989)

COUNTRY	YEAR OF RATIFICATION
Mexico	1990
Colombia	1991
Bolivia	1991
Costa Rica	1993
Paraguay	1993
Peru	1994
Honduras	1995
Guatemala	1996
Ecuador	1998
Argentina	2000
Brazil	2002
Venezuela	2002
Chile	2008
Nicaragua	2010

Not ratified as of October 2013: Cuba, Dominican Republic, El Salvador, Panama, Uruguay.

Mexico ratified ILO 169 in 1990, becoming the first Latin American country to do so. Colombia and Bolivia followed in 1991, as did several other Latin American countries later in the 1990s. As of 2013, all but five Latin American states considered in this analysis had ratified ILO 169.[32] Table 7.3 shows the year of ratification of ILO 169 by Latin American signatories.

Although prominent organizations in the international indigenous movement initially rejected ILO 169 in protest against the limited channels for their direct input into its formulation, indigenous activists ultimately embraced the convention as a powerful political and legal tool for advancing claims against individual states.[33] In Latin America, the existence of ILO 169 directly influenced constitutional reforms in several countries, provided a legal framework for negotiation of collective land rights and political autonomy (e.g., Bolivia, Colombia, and Ecuador), influenced judicial decisions (e.g., Colombia, Costa Rica, and Venezuela), and informed peace accords involving relations between states and indigenous peoples (e.g., Guatemala and Mexico).[34] Domestic

---

[32] Five of the nineteen Latin American countries considered in this analysis had not ratified ILO 169 as of October 1, 2013: Cuba, Dominican Republic, El Salvador, Panama, and Uruguay.

[33] Rodriguez-Piñero, *Indigenous Peoples, Postcolonialism and International Law*, 317–8, 325–6; Banton, "International Norms."

[34] Rodriguez-Piñero, *Indigenous Peoples, Postcolonialism and International Law*, 326–7, nn. 180–85; Van Cott, *The Friendly Liquidation of the Past*, 266–8. Illustratively, according to anthropologist Andrew Canessa, "ILO 169...has proved to be an important legal basis for defining indigeneity and

activists leveraged the existence of ILO 169, as part of the broader international indigenous rights regime embedded within the international human rights regime, to make claims on national states and hold them accountable through legal means for treaty commitments made in international regimes.

Over and above its direct use as a legal instrument in numerous contexts, ILO 169 became a significant normative and political resource for indigenous movements in several countries. Especially where indigenous movements were weaker or lacked strategic allies within ruling political parties, the existence of ILO 169 became a critical source of symbolic leverage in efforts to wrestle unlikely gains from recalcitrant states. Illustratively, the Venezuelan indigenous movement pressed successfully for major constitutional reforms by arguing "that Venezuela's was the most backward constitution in the hemisphere with respect to indigenous rights" and that their claims "were identical to ones ratified by neighboring states and protected by international law."[35] The fact that all of Venezuela's neighbors had already signed on to ILO 169 became a means to shame the Venezuelan government while legitimizing the claims of Venezuela's indigenous organizations as moderate demands, in keeping with established international norms and law. More broadly, the existence of the international indigenous movement and the international rights regime it managed to construct dramatically shifted the political terrain on which Latin America's indigenous movements confronted national states from the 1990s forward.

Afrodescendant communities in Latin America, in contrast, struggled for rights and recognition in the absence of an international legal framework analogous to the international indigenous rights regime. The specific situation of Afrodescendant populations in Latin America did not really break through as a priority in the international arena until the 2000s.[36] A key turning point was the 2001 World Conference against Racism in Durban.[37] Capitalizing on momentum from the conference, activists garnered unprecedented support from international issue networks and development agencies. Increased visibility of Afrodescendant concerns

---

has grealy [sic] influenced the Bolivian definition of indigeneity in the Law of Popular Participation (1993) (Article 1)," Canessa, "Who Is Indigenous?," 203.

[35] Van Cott, "Andean Indigenous Movements," 61.

[36] Black movements mobilized much earlier than the 2000s in several Latin American countries, but usually with limited visibility beyond a particular city or region. For an overview of Afrodescendant movements in individual Latin American countries up to 2000, see Andrews, *Afro-Latin America*, chaps. 5, 6; Rahier, ed., *Black Social Movements in Latin America*.

[37] United Nations. "World Conference against Racism, Racial Discrimination, Xenophobia and Related Intolerance." On the broader significance of the conference, see Banton, *The International Politics of Race*.

in international forums proved decisive for escalating pressure on individual national governments to take action.[38] Since the late 2000s, historical deprivations and contemporary discrimination experienced by those of African descent has become a high-profile priority for development agencies and human rights organizations. In 2012, discussions were underway to create a Permanent Forum for Afrodescendant Issues within the UN institutional framework, to parallel the Permanent Forum already in existence for indigenous peoples. But entering the second decade of the twenty-first century, Latin American Afrodescendant movements lacked international conventions or norms equivalent to those available to Indigenous peoples to legitimate and leverage claims vis-à-vis national states.

Despite the absence of a consolidated international Afrodescendant rights regime, Afrodescendant activists have won legal recognition and special rights within national legal institutions in some countries. Afrodescendant movements have had the greatest success in making collective claims on Latin American states where they have followed an "indigenous strategy" in defining their communities and identifying their needs. In a few countries, including Brazil, Colombia, Guatemala, Honduras, and Nicaragua, Afrodescendant activists advanced claims for special economic, political, or cultural rights based on claims of cultural distinctiveness and historic residence in specific geographic regions. In Brazil, for example, the 1988 constitution provided for legal recognition of collective land claims by *quilombolas* (residents of rural communities composed of descendants of runaway slaves), extending rights traditionally reserved for indigenous communities.[39] In Colombia, the 1991 Constitution and Federal Law 70 (1993) recognize collective land rights for certain Afro-Colombian communities, modeled on legal recognition of collective rights for indigenous peoples.[40] In Nicaragua, the 1995 Constitution guarantees the "Atlantic Coast communities" forms of autonomy that parallel guarantees for indigenous populations, as well as the "preservation of their cultures and languages, religions, and customs."[41]

---

[38] Paschel and Sawyer, "Contesting Politics as Usual."

[39] French, *Legalizing Identities*.

[40] Blanco, "Logros y Contradicciones de la Jurisdicción Especial Indígena en Colombia," 61–2; Cottrol, "Coming into their Own?"

[41] Nicaragua Const., art. 180 and 181. http://www.ineter.gob.ni/Constitucion%20Politica%20de%20Nicargua.pdf. For an overview of laws related to Latin American Afrodescendant populations as of 2004, see Inter-American Dialogue, "Constitutional Provisions and Legal Actions Related to Discrimination and Afro-Descendant Populations in Latin America," 5.

Despite some noteworthy successes, Afrodescendant activists faced uphill battles to win concessions from Latin American states. As political scientist Juliet Hooker notes, "Even when Afro-Latinos were granted collective rights,... in almost no instances did they gain the same rights as indians. In fact, there are only three countries in Latin America where indians and Afro-Latinos have exactly the same collective rights: Honduras, Guatemala and Nicaragua. Moreover, only a small subset of Afro-Latinos—generally rural communities descended from escaped slaves—has been able to win collective rights under Latin America's multicultural citizenship reforms."[42] The important victories of some specific communities notwithstanding, the more common story for Afrodescendant Latin Americans is that efforts to secure collective protections or legal rights have faltered.

In most of Latin America, multiethnic policies were conceptualized and operationalized in ways that ruled out claims making by Afrodescendant populations.[43] Such policies recognized minority communities as legitimate claimants based on their cultural distinctiveness from majority populations and their historic (preferably precolonial) geographic roots in specific areas of the national territory. The vast majority of Afrodescendant individuals in Latin America did not have the requisite characteristics—as defined by state actors and academic cultural experts—to qualify them for differential treatment under the law. For the vast majority of Afrodescendant peoples in Latin America, state recognition as a legally protected minority was not forthcoming.

Activists thus focused their sights on other goals, including passage or enforcement of antidiscrimination laws, campaigns against racist media, consciousness raising, school curriculum reform, and affirmative action policies. Yet even the pursuit of equal recognition and treatment under the law met with resistance in most contexts, not only from states, but also from ostensible allies. The challenge of mobilizing for racial equality was amplified in some contexts by the fact that many Afrodescendant individuals in whose name activists claimed to speak remained reluctant to identify with the cause.[44]

Legal proscriptions against explicit racial or ethnic discrimination in hiring or other domains gained steam in a few contexts, contributing

---

[42] Hooker, "Indigenous Inclusion/Black Exclusion," 2; Brazil, Colombia, Nicaragua and Honduras have recognized land rights for descendants of fugitive slave communities. Cottrol, "Coming into Their Own?"

[43] Hooker, "Indigenous Inclusion/Black Exclusion."

[44] Hanchard, *Orpheus and Power*; Marx, *Making Race and Nation*; Andrews, *Afro-Latin America*; Nobles, *Shades of Citizenship*; Telles, *Race in Another America*; Wade, *Blackness and Race Mixture*.

to gradual cultural shifts in the awareness of racism as a social issue. In Brazil, for instance, the 1988 constitution gave teeth to antidiscrimination laws by making racial discrimination a criminal act with severe penalties. Some scholars argue that Brazil's strong enforcement provisions ultimately backfired; the consequences for racial discrimination were so severe that prosecutors proved unwilling to use the law except in extraordinary circumstances.[45] Nonetheless, efforts to attach legal consequences to racist acts marked a rupture with deeply rooted historical customs in the region, signaling a historic opening for cultural change. By the 2000s, activists had exploited this opening, winning over politicians to their cause and successfully pushing for the introduction of affirmative action in key government agencies and subsequently in public universities around the country.[46]

In other countries as well, movements that sought to raise awareness of racism and combat racial and ethnic inequality gained momentum in the 2000s, adapting their strategies to particular contexts and often advancing claims simultaneously on legal, political, and cultural fronts.[47] In Colombia, activists based in major cities challenged the state's selective recognition of Afrodescendant communities in specific territories and worked to make the problems of racial discrimination and inequality a topic of national political debate.[48] In Guatemala, Garifuna organizations leveraged their combined indigenous and Afrodescendant ancestry to claim recognition and rights from the state as an indigenous people, and development funds from international lenders targeted for Afrodescendant people.[49] In Ecuador, activists translated initial demands for cultural recognition into a political movement that fought successfully for collective rights, redistributive policies, affirmative action, and institutionalized representation within the state.[50]

By the first decades of the twenty-first century, indigenous and Afrodescendant social movements in Latin America thus ranged from local, intermittent campaigns focused on proximate issues or tangible goals, to

---

[45] For a discussion of the limited use of Brazil's antidiscrimination law, see Guimarães, *Racismo e Anti-racismo no Brasil*.

[46] Htun, "From 'Racial Democracy' to Affirmative Action."

[47] Reiter and Simmons, *Afro-Descendants, Identity, and the Struggle for Development in the Americas*.

[48] Paschel, "The Right to Difference"; Rahier, ed., *Black Social Movements in Latin America*.

[49] Agudelo, "The Afro-Guatemalan Political Mobilization." On Garifuna mobilization in other Central American countries, see Minority Rights Group, *No Longer Invisible*. On the Garifuna as both indigenous and Afrodescendant, see Cunin, *Mestizaje, diferencia y nación*.

[50] de la Torre and Sanchez, "The Afroecuadorian Social Movement." de la Torre and Sanchez note that the price of these successes was the demobilization of the Afro-Ecuadorian movement. They argue that the movement was successfully coopted by the state.

sustained national mobilizations that ushered in historic new leadership with radical visions for social change.

Targeting the National Census

Calls for census reform crystallized as one concrete objective of the much broader campaigns for ethnic and racial equality that emerged in Latin America in the 1990s and early 2000s. Initially a low-profile issue, the question of how states categorize populations on national censuses became a focal point for contact and negotiation between social movement activists, government officials, and representatives of regional and international development agencies. National censuses became strategic targets of campaigns that sought cultural recognition and economic redress for indigenous or Afrodescendant populations. Activists targeted the census as a highly visible stake in the symbolic struggle to redefine the cultural value of ethnic and racial difference within the nation. Activists also targeted the census as a key pragmatic opportunity in the struggle to reconfigure historically entrenched relations of economic exploitation and ethnoracial discrimination.

Campaigns to reform national censuses sought in part to counteract the social invisibility of many ethnic and racial minorities in Latin America. This invisibility, activists claimed, resulted in no small part from the historic neglect or mistreatment of ethnic or racial groups by national statistics agencies. The addition of new queries and categories to censuses was seen as a means to address the "blindness" afflicting majority populations with respect to the ethnic or racial diversity of their nations.

To be named and counted on the national census was to win official recognition of the social existence of a collective identity or community. Official recognition, in turn, allowed new claims to be made on behalf of the named collective. The state's power to fortify the social existence of groups by naming and counting them was not lost on activists. The census became a prime target in struggles to advance the living conditions of indigenous and Afrodescendant communities because official classification was seen as key to undermining the symbolic violence of the past and opening up new avenues for effective claims making in the future.

Activists also targeted the national census because of the practical and political value of data that could speak to the material conditions of minority populations. In most Latin American countries, national censuses remain the primary source of statistical information about the population. Even in countries that now conduct annual or biannual household surveys, the national census provides a critical data source on a range of issues and serves as a baseline comparison for smaller-scale surveys. The inclusion of new questions on racial or ethnic group membership promised to generate more and better data to document inequalities. In some contexts, census officials acknowledged the specific political import of generating new ethnic and racial statistics for the design or monitoring of domestic policy initiatives that targeted specific groups. Illustratively, Argentina's statistics agency explained on its website that the new question on Afrodescent on the 2010 census would aid "the elaboration of future studies and investigations... with an eye to the realization of targeted public policies."[51]

The implementation of census reforms came earlier to some Latin American countries than others, with the timing of reform closely related to the intensity and focus of domestic social activism on this issue. Afro-Brazilian activists set an early example for the region. Together with allied academics, Afro-Brazilian activists successfully pressed the Brazilian statistics agency, the Instituto Brasileiro de Geografía e Estatística (IBGE), to restore a race/color question to the 1980 census.[52] Social scientists used the data that resulted to produce studies that documented race/color inequality in Brazilian society. The IBGE itself also began to produce reports that analyzed disparities in key social and economic outcomes. Taken together, these studies marshaled statistical evidence that directly challenged Brazil's myth of racial democracy; the growing body of research exposed race/color inequality that could not be reduced to differences in education or occupation. By the 1990s, the accumulation of statistical analyses helped motivate and justify activists' calls for targeted social programs to combat racial inequality. When sociologist Fernando Henrique Cardoso became Brazil's president in 1995, he placed the fight against racial inequality on the national agenda. The Cardoso government (1995–2002) introduced a range of policies, including affirmative action in government hiring within some ministries, which were subsequently expanded under the presidency of Luis Ignacio Lula da Silva (2003–2010).

Inspired in part by the success of Afro-Brazilian activists, beginning in the early 1990s, Afro-Colombian and indigenous organizations lobbied the national statistics agency, the Departamento Administrativo Nacional de

---

[51] Argentina. Instituto Nacional de Estadísticas y Censos. "Afrodescendientes," http://www.censo2010.indec.gov.ar/index_afro.asp.

[52] According to political scientist Melissa Nobles, "IBGE at first designed the 1980 census without the question but changed its decision in response to lobbying." For more on this episode, see Nobles, *Shades of Citizenship*, 116–19.

Estatística (DANE), to add new queries to Colombia's national census.[53] Activists called for new census queries on ethical grounds. They argued that the statistical invisibility of Colombia's indigenous and Afrodescendant populations in the national census perpetuated cultural violence against these segments of the Colombian population. The addition of new census questions was required, activists explained, to ensure that indigenous and Afrodescendant populations garnered official recognition of their existence, protection of their rights, and redress for their historical marginalization.[54]

Activists' demands for census reform were bolstered by the shifting stance of the Colombian state on the issue of recognition of domestic minority populations. Colombia became a signatory to ILO 169 in 1991 and new data were required for compliance. Signatories to ILO 169 are expected to track and report numerous indicators of indigenous peoples' well-being in comparison to the general population. States require data on socioeconomic conditions, education, health, land tenure, working conditions and employment, impacts of large development projects, infrastructure, and human rights violations.[55] The Colombian state also needed information about the size of indigenous reserves (*resguardos*) to carry out planned decentralization. Constitutional reforms granting special rights to Afro-Colombian communities, in turn, made it desirable to collect new information about the size and situation of these communities. Thus, momentum toward democratization domestically, growing pressure for official recognition of diversity internationally, and the specific targeted demands of indigenous and Afrodescendant organizations converged to usher in a historic change to Colombia's national census. Building from their success, Afro-Colombian activists and their allies within DANE set their sights on empowering their counterparts in other Latin American countries to introduce analogous reforms.

By the early 2000s, pressure to adopt new census queries had disseminated across Latin America through the deliberate and coordinated efforts of domestic activists, their census agency allies, and regional and international organizations. Bottom-up activism put the issue of statistical visibility of minority populations on political agendas in a growing number of Latin American countries. In most cases, however, the appeals of domestic activists did not suffice to convince census agencies to introduce new questions on national censuses. It was the convergence of such appeals with

---

[53] Buvinić and Mazza, *Social Inclusion and Economic Development in Latin America;* Mesa, "Who Counts Indigenous People."
[54] Paschel, "The Right to Difference."
[55] Rodriguez-Piñero, *Indigenous Peoples, Postcolonialism and International Law.*

new initiatives and demands from regional and international organizations that ushered in census reforms across much of the region.

International Influence on National Census Reforms

The majority of Latin American countries introduced new questions about ethnoracial origins and identities on national censuses in response to pressure from regional and international organizations. Initially, the pressure from these organizations was indirect and diffuse, operating primarily through support for domestic activism and research around this issue. When some Latin American states proved insufficiently responsive to such indirect measures, international organizations adopted more direct and targeted approaches to instigating census reforms in the region.

Before describing how international organizations helped usher in the resurgence of official ethnoracial classification in Latin American censuses, it bears asking why they bothered to do so. International development agencies and lending institutions had longstanding interests in the improvement of general data collection infrastructure in the region. But their sudden and particular concern with whether and how Latin American states collected data about ethnoracial distinctions within national populations was without historical precedent.

The interest of international organizations in Latin American census taking per se was not a new development. As discussed in chapter 3, since the nineteenth century, international scientific organizations, such as the International Statistical Institute, had worked toward the goal of census modernization and standardization across countries. In the mid-twentieth century, the UN became deeply involved in efforts to improve the capacity and coordination of census taking activities throughout the world. The United Nations Population Fund (UNFPA) helped finance and coordinate census operations in several Latin American countries from the 1960s to the 1980s. Numerous other UN agencies and multilateral organizations became involved in Latin American census operations in subsequent decades.[56] By 2010, the list of organizations involved in census-related loans, grants, or technical cooperation agreements with Latin American census agencies included the World Bank, the

---

[56] A few countries have tried to retain financial autonomy for census operations. For example, according to a representative from Mexico's national statistics agency, "Because the censuses are matters of national interest, they are financed with resources of the Federal Government, which requests from Congress a special appropriation in the budget to carry out the census project." Email to author, April 2005.

InterAmerican Development Bank (IDB), the European Union, the national governments of Japan, Sweden and the United States, the US Census Bureau, and at least ten different UN agencies.[57] The level of direct substantive and financial involvement by international organizations in national census operations in much of Latin America reached unprecedented levels at the turn of the twenty-first century.

International development banks and regional economic organizations began to focus sustained attention on data gathering infrastructure in Latin America in the 1990s. In 1996, the IDB, World Bank, and Economic Commission on Latin America and the Caribbean (ECLAC) organized the "Program for Improvement of Household Surveys and Measurement of Living Conditions in Latin America." The central aim of the program was to improve the technical capacity of statistics agencies in the region.[58] Major grants and loans to several Latin American governments followed, providing support for improvements of census operations, including capacity building, methods training, and infrastructure development. These funding sources were welcomed by Latin American census agencies confronting severe budgetary shortfalls for financing ongoing census operations.[59]

In the 2000s, international development banks' support for efforts to improve the general data collection capacity of Latin American states segued into support for initiatives to improve collection of data about ethnic and racial minority populations in particular. Development banks' interest in the addition of race or ethnicity questions to Latin American censuses emerged at a moment of heightened public criticism of their longstanding neglect of racial and ethnic dimensions of poverty in the region. In the wake of the first World Social Forum in January 2001 in Porto Alegre, Brazil, and in anticipation of the UN World Conference against Racism to be held later that year in South Africa, critics decried the failure of major development banks to directly confront racial inequality in Latin America. The World

---

[57] This list is not comprehensive. The financing and coordination of various stages of census operations in different Latin American countries has become incredibly complex in recent decades, making it difficult to track all sources of funding and technical support. Bilateral agreements between statistics agencies of particular countries and international development banks, UN agencies, and other organizations vary in number and terms, across countries and across censuses. See, for example, the list of thirteen international cooperation agreements in effect for the 2010 Census of the Dominican Republic: Dominican Republic. Oficína Regional de Estadística. "Cooperación Internacional." http://www.one.gob.do/index.php?module=articles&func=view&catid=212

[58] Inter-American Development Bank, "BID, Banco Mundial y Colombia Auspician Seminario Internacional Sobre Factores Raciales y Étnicos en Censos de América Latina."

[59] Chackiel, *Censuses in Latin America*. Chackiel discusses the challenges of financing contemporary censuses in Latin America.

Banks' 2000/2001 World Development Report did not help matters. It was the first such report in ten years to focus on poverty, and it included analyses stratified by gender, but not race or ethnicity. This omission sparked outrage from many quarters. An IPS-Interpress headline summed up the response: "World Bank Lambasted for Ignoring Racial Dimension of Poverty."[60]

In this climate, the international development banks began to issue official statements in support of calls to improve ethnic and racial data collection in Latin America. Spokespersons for the development banks did not draw attention to the historical novelty of their concern about ethnoracial inequality in the region. Instead, they explained that greater attention to ethnic and racial disparities in the region was necessary to fulfill their traditional institutional goals. For example, a World Bank newsletter reported that the bank became involved with the issue of racial and ethnic data collection as an offshoot of its programs to combat poverty in Latin America:

> As the Bank expands its work on poverty reduction strategies and increases its outreach to civil society, it has become clear that there is a need to improve the data-collecting tools to more accurately reflect the poverty-stricken states of historically excluded groups in Latin America and the Caribbean. After several meetings with nongovernmental organizations (NGOs) representing the Afro-Latin communities, the LCR [Latin American and Caribbean region] vice president sent out letters to the heads of statistical offices in selected countries encouraging them to include questions on race and ethnicity in their national censuses.[61]

The World Bank also emphasized the critical need for better racial and ethnic statistics to inform its operations in Latin America going forward:

> The need to have more reliable demographic and socio-economic data on all groups within Latin American and Caribbean society is important in order to design more effective investment operations and provide development services to racial, ethnic, and other vulnerable groups. There is therefore an urgent need for better census and statistical data, not just to understand the scope of the poverty, race, and ethnicity nexus but also to design operations, in collaboration with borrower countries, that will alleviate poverty and bring an end to social discrimination and marginalization.[62]

---

[60] Mutume, "Development." http://www.ips.org/socialforum/0122/worldbank.htm
[61] World Bank, "The 'Todos Contamos' Workshop," 6.
[62] World Bank, "The 'Todos Contamos' Workshop," 6.

The development banks' support of ethnic and racial data collection confirmed a new consensus among major multilateral development agencies: national states should collect statistics about racial and ethnic minority populations.[63] This new consensus crystallized in the International Convention on the Elimination of all Forms of Racial Discrimination (ICERD) and the Action Plan from the World Conference against Racism in Durban, which "Urges states to collect, compile, analyse, disseminate and publish reliable statistical data at the national and local levels and undertake all other related measures which are necessary to assess regularly the situation of individuals and groups of individuals who are victims of racism, racial discrimination, xenophobia and related intolerance."[64] Over the next several years, various agencies within the UN, as well as the World Bank, the IDB, and an array of governmental and nongovernmental organizations sought to encourage Latin American states to comply with this recommendation.

Forms of International Influence

International organizations helped usher in the new era of official ethnoracial classification in Latin America by pressuring national statistics agencies to adopt reforms. This pressure came in varied guises: from discursive to material, diffuse to targeted, normative to coercive. Different forms of international influence operated simultaneously and in different configurations across contexts and over time. In some countries, international pressure bolstered data collection initiatives that were already on domestic agendas. In others, international organizations effectively introduced agendas for reform. In all cases, new international expectations for data collection in Latin America played a role in shaping domestic political battles over the content of national censuses.

The process by which nearly all Latin American states embraced official ethnoracial classification on their national censuses in little more than a decade was not one of neutral diffusion of international models or norms. New international expectations for how states should count and classify their populations influenced domestic politics of census taking

---

[63] The extent to which this new consensus of multilateral development agencies extended to other parts of the world remains a topic for future research. A suggestive point of departure is provided by Morning, "Ethnic Classification in Global Perspective"; Simon, "Collecting Ethnic Statistics in Europe."

[64] United Nations, "World Conference against Racism, Racial Discrimination, Xenophobia and Related Intolerance," 37–8.

in Latin America via specific types of power-laden relationships between domestic and international actors. For purposes of exposition, I identify three specific mechanisms of international organizations' influence on ethnoracial census enumeration in Latin America and provide illustrative examples of each.

First, international organizations influenced domestic agendas for census reform indirectly through *support of domestic activists*. Beginning in the 1980s, international non-governmental organizations provided discursive and institutional support to domestic actors who pressed for census reforms as a small part of broader campaigns to draw attention to racial inequality in their societies. Such support was especially important in the two countries—Brazil and Colombia—where domestic activists were at the forefront of targeting national statistics agencies with demands for change. During the 1990s, for example, funding from organizations such as the Ford Foundation bolstered the efforts of Brazilian and Colombian activists who drew attention to census categories as part of broader efforts to increase the visibility of Afrodescendant populations in their countries.[65] Some of these activists went on to play a decisive role in creating a regional network of stakeholders to push for census reforms throughout Latin America.

In addition to endorsing census reforms indirectly, through back-stage support of domestic activists who took up the cause, international organizations also facilitated the region-wide return of official ethnoracial classification through more direct means. A second and much more significant mechanism of international organizations' influence was *direct logistical support and public advocacy* for the introduction of new questions on Latin American censuses. Over the course of the 2000s, major international development organizations and lending institutions with ties to the region became vocal proponents of improved ethnic and racial data collection in Latin America. Their rhetorical advocacy was coupled with material support for professional conferences that sought to eliminate both political and "technical" obstacles to ethnoracial data collection in the region. Referring back to Table 7.1a, this is the period when several states adopted questions that made Afrodescendant people statistically visible on the census; it is also the period when indigenous

---

[65] Nobles, "Responding with Good Sense." In an interview in 2005, Nobles noted how Brazilian activists who planned to mount a campaign focused on racial classification in the census sought and received assistance from the Ford Foundation. Nobles, "The Politics of Counting," http://web.mit.edu/shass/soundings/issue_05s.

people were made statistically visible through a greater variety of questions than in the past.

In the early 2000s, international organizations sponsored a series of regional conferences and technical workshops that focused specifically on the issue of ethnoracial data collection by Latin American governments. The first major international conference of this kind took place in Cartagena, Colombia in 2000. The conference, titled "Todos Contamos" (We All Count), was hosted by the Colombian census agency (DANE) and cosponsored by the World Bank and the IDB. The conference was timed to anticipate the UN World Conference against Racial Discrimination, Racism, Xenophobia, and Related Intolerance (UNWCAR) that would take place in Durban, South Africa, in September of 2001.[66] The central aim of the "Todos Contamos" conference, as a press release issued by the IDB explained, was "to identify strategies to promote the inclusion of ethnic and cultural diversity on the censuses of Latin America and the Caribbean."[67]

Letters of invitation were sent to statistics agency personnel across Latin America. Organizers also invited representatives of indigenous and Afrodescendant nongovernmental organizations from several countries. According to a follow-up report by two IDB employees, "The two-day work-shop covered three major themes that were discussed in three working groups: (1) concepts and methodologies related to determining ethnicity in national censuses; (2) variables to assess the socioeconomic status of ethnic and/or racial groups; and (3) the participation of community groups in the design and implementation of the methodologies."[68] The conference provided an opportunity for stakeholders from across the region to share information about the obstacles to better ethnic and racial data collection in each country, and to brainstorm about possible ways forward.

The "Todos Contamos" conference spurred several Latin American countries to begin laying the groundwork for the addition of new queries to their national censuses. As a report issued by the Canadian Foundation for the Americas (FOCAL) noted, "The conference sparked a positive reaction, and ten countries in the region included questions about racial or ethnic self-identification in their censuses over the next two years."[69] A report from the US Congressional Research Service also credited the

---

[66] Márquez et al., "Outsiders?"

[67] Inter-American Development Bank, "BID, Banco Mundial y Colombia Auspician Seminario Internacional."

[68] Buvinić and Mazza, eds., *Social Inclusion and Economic Development in Latin America*.

[69] Canadian Foundation for the Americas, "Report from the March 2nd 2006 Ottawa Roundtable."

"Todos Contamos" conference with the introduction of race questions on censuses throughout Latin America.[70]

The World Bank and IDB funded a followup conference, "Todos Contamos II," in Lima, Peru in 2002. The Peruvian statistics agency (INEI) hosted the conference, which was attended by participants from eighteen Latin American countries, organized in four-person "country teams." Each team was composed of a representative from the country's national statistics agency, an autonomous indigenous organization, a national organization of Afrodescendants, and a "government representative from the social policy sector."[71] The participants reviewed each country's progress on specific goals since the first conference in 2000. They noted that efforts to incorporate new queries about indigenous peoples had been more successful up to that point than attempts to add queries about Afrodescendants. Attendees were encouraged to continue efforts to expand ethnic and racial data collection in the region. Discussion also focused on the use of new data for design and evaluation of public policies that targeted Afrodescendant and indigenous populations.[72]

The agenda mapped out at the "Todos Contamos" conferences garnered support from several Latin American governments and regional organizations, which sponsored the continuation of efforts at census reform over the next few years. For example, from 2003 to 2005, ECLAC partnered with the World Bank to organize working groups focused on incorporating racial self-identification questions on household surveys in Argentina, Colombia, Ecuador, Honduras, and Peru. The working groups included census agency personnel, independent researchers, and representatives of Afrodescendant community organizations in each country. In addition to developing new survey modules to collect data on racial identification, the working groups sought to draw attention to racial inequalities by advancing analyses of educational and living conditions that go "beyond the averages" ("más allá de los promedios"). The groups also organized educational campaigns to raise awareness among targeted populations of the benefits of survey response and the importance of "accurate" self-identification.[73]

The agenda of the "Todos Contamos" conferences earned public endorsements from influential hemispheric policy institutes, such as the Inter-American

---

[70] Seelke, "Afro-Latinos in Latin America and Considerations for US Policy," 8.

[71] Mazza, "Todos Contamos II."

[72] Mazza, "Todos Contamos II"; Peru. Instituto Nacional de Estadística e Informática. "Analizaron recolección de información sobre poblaciones indígenas y afrodescendientes."

[73] Sánchez and García, "Los Afrocolombianos."

Dialogue, an organization of regional leaders based in Washington, DC. In 2002, the Inter-American Dialogue called for Latin American governments to add new queries to national surveys: "we join others, such as the *Todos Contamos* project sponsored by the World Bank and the Inter-American Development Bank, in encouraging the countries of Latin America to recognize and count their Afrodescendant populations."[74]

The Inter-American Dialogue formed part of the Inter-Agency Consultation on Race in Latin America (IAC), a coalition of international development agencies created in 2000 with the goal of sharing information and coordinating plans across agencies related to projects that target racial inequality.[75] Other IAC members included the World Bank, the IDB, the Pan-American Health Organization, the InterAmerican Foundation, the Ford Foundation, and the Rockefeller Foundation, with other international agencies, private NGOs, and foundations coming on board in later years.[76] According to the Inter-American Dialogue, the IAC was formed to address the fact that "With few exceptions, Latin American governments and international aid organizations (multilateral, bilateral, public and private) have largely ignored race in designing and implementing programs, even though it is obvious to even the most casual observer that race is a key factor in the distribution of income, wealth, and social services in the region. Data on race is still scarce and unreliable in most of Latin America, and there have been few serious efforts to study the needs and challenges confronting Afro-Latin Americans."[77] Through annual conferences, reports, and newsletters, IAC members sought to develop and share strategies to heighten awareness of racial inequality in Latin America, including efforts to improve data collection throughout the region.

Adding to the pressure on Latin American states to collect ethnoracial population data, the United Nations coordinated specialized working groups and committees focused on the issue in global perspective. For instance, as an outgrowth of the Permanent Forum on Indigenous Issues, the UN organized an International Expert Workshop on Data Collection and Disaggregation for Indigenous Peoples in January 2004. The workshop brought together "36 experts from the United Nations system and other intergovernmental organizations, Governments, indigenous organizations

---

[74] Inter-American Dialogue. "Afro-Descendants in Latin America," 2.

[75] The creation of the IAC was motivated by discussions at a regional meeting in Santiago, Chile, in preparation for the UN Conference against Racism in South Africa.

[76] Inter-American Dialogue, "Afro-Descendants in Latin America," 4.

[77] Inter-American Dialogue, "Afro-Descendants in Latin America," 6.

and academics...including many statisticians."[78] The discussions focused on the challenges of designing survey questions that allow for international comparability of statistics while also meeting the needs of specific indigenous communities. Ultimately, the working group advocated for approaches that respect principles of self-identification and that maximize participation of indigenous peoples in all stages of survey research, from questionnaire design to data collection, analysis, and dissemination.[79]

The UN partnered with regional organizations to disseminate information about emerging expectations for data collection and to facilitate communication and knowledge sharing across Latin American statistics agencies. The Population Division of ECLAC (the Centro Latinoamericano y Caribeño de Demografía [CELADE]), for example, helped organize working groups and regular conferences that brought together stakeholders for discussions about collecting racial and ethnic identity data on censuses. In 2005, CELADE and the Indigenous Fund held a workshop with sponsorship from the French government and the UN Population Fund (UNFPA) that brought together experts from across Latin America to share best practices and lessons learned about methods of generating ethnic statistics for use in public policy.[80] In 2008, CELADE coordinated another conference with representatives from UNICEF, UNFPA, the Statistical Conference of the Americas census group, the Pan American Health Organization and the Fund for the Development of Indigenous Peoples of Latin America and the Caribbean, along with representatives of national statistics agencies, academics, and indigenous and Afrodescendant organizations, to discuss preferred approaches to classification of Afrodescendant and indigenous peoples in the 2010 census round.[81]

Regional organizational support for the cause of racial and ethnic data collection also came from the Organization of IberoAmerican States (OEI), which helped coordinate a conference in Colombia in 2008 that produced the symbolically important Cartagena Declaration (*Declaración de Cartagena*). The OEI collaborated with Colombia's Ministry of Culture to hold the first international conference dedicated to the construction of a regional political project to advance the

---

[78] United Nations. Department of Economic and Social Affairs, "Workshop on Data Collection."

[79] United Nations. Department of Economic and Social Affairs. "Workshop on Data Collection."

[80] Economic Commission for Latin America and the Caribbean, Population Division (CELADE). International Seminar, "Pueblos indígenas y afrodescendientes de América Latina y el Caribe."

[81] Economic Commission for Latin America and the Caribbean. "Biennial Programme of Regional and International Cooperation Activities of the Statistical Conference of the Americas of ECLAC, 2007–2009."

well-being of Afrodescendant peoples throughout Latin America.[82] The conference culminated with the unveiling of the Cartagena Declaration, a statement of official recognition of Afrodescendant communities in the Americas and solidarity with their distinctive struggles throughout the region. Representatives of twelve Latin American governments signed on to the Declaration, committing to numerous action items on behalf of Afrodescendant communities. Among the commitments was a promise to "Promote, within the framework of this declaration, a campaign to raise awareness in the different countries, encouraging self-recognition and affirmation of the values and the cultural and spiritual heritage of the Afrodescendant population. And to recommend that governments include a variable about 'ethnic belonging', by self-identification, on demographic censuses and surveys of household and quality of life."[83]

Thus, over the course of the 2000s, the goal of collecting more and better ethnoracial population data in Latin America gained backing from major players in the international development field. International expectations for the content of a modern national census had changed: color-blind census counts were no longer legitimate. These new expectations were communicated to Latin American governments via public pronouncements of new norms by major international development agencies and lending institutions.[84] They were also communicated to Latin American statistics agencies in a more targeted fashion, via a growing number of specialized conferences and workshops that redefined the proper scope and methods of counting and classifying populations.[85]

The pressure exerted by international organizations on Latin American governments via public advocacy and direct logistical support for improved ethnoracial data collection was bolstered significantly by a third mechanism

---

[82] The conference was called: *Primer Encuentro Iberoamericano "Agenda Afrodescendiente en las Américas."*

[83] Organización de Estados Iberoamericanos, "Declaratoria de Cartagena—Agenda Afrodescendiente en las Américas" http:www.oei.es/afro03.php.

[84] In the terms coined by sociologists Paul DiMaggio and Walter Powell, this was a *coercive* mechanism of institutional change; it resulted from "both formal and informal pressures exerted on organizations by other organizations upon which they are dependent and by cultural expectations in the society within which organizations function." DiMaggio and Powell, "The Iron Cage Revisited," 150.

[85] In DiMaggio and Powell's terms, this was a form of *normative* pressure for institutional change, relying on the cultivation and intensification of professional networks to elaborate and spread a new norm and methods for tracking diversity on national surveys. DiMaggio and Powell, "The Iron Cage Revisited," 152.

of influence. International development agencies and multilateral lending institutions increased states' need for ethnoracial statistics by introducing *new organizational goals and evaluation procedures* for development projects. International organizations redefined their objectives and operating practices in ways that effectively compelled Latin American statistics agencies to adopt new practices as well. Most significantly, the major international development organizations redefined "development" to include the protection of "cultural liberty" and the amelioration of ethnoracial inequality as explicit goals. In line with this broadened mission, they modified data requirements for new project proposals to include assessments of differential benefits or harms to ethnic and racial subpopulations.

In the early 2000s, international development agencies and banks broadened their definition of "development" to explicitly include reduction of ethnic and racial inequality as a goal. In 2003, the IAC convened a meeting with delegates from the major international development agencies to identify strategies "to make sure issues of race and ethnic equality were included in the MDGs (Millennium Development Goals)."[86] The idea of using MDGs as benchmarks for monitoring the progress of ethnic and racial minorities across Latin America was embraced by the World Bank, the IDB, and UN development agencies, among others. Despite the fact that significant progress toward achieving MDGs remained illusory in many countries of the region, the decision to include the reduction of ethnoracial inequality as an explicit goal institutionalized demand for official ethnoracial statistics. The constituencies for such data grew as activists, members of nonprofit organizations, scholars, and policy makers sought ways to disaggregate populations by race or ethnicity in data used to assess progress toward MDGs across countries and over time.[87]

Beyond adding an ethnoracial dimension to the evaluation of traditional development indicators, international development agencies reformulated the definition of "development" to encompass the preservation—or even cultivation—of ethnoracial diversity. In the wake of the Durban conference in 2001, the United Nations Development Programme (UNDP) officially adopted a broadened understanding of "human development" that included the right to enjoy "cultural liberty."[88] The UNDP Human Development

---

[86] Inter-American Dialogue, "Constitutional Provisions and Legal Actions Related to Discrimination and Afro-Descendant Populations in Latin America," 12.

[87] See, for example, Telles, "Race and Ethnicity and Latin America's United Nations Millennium Development Goals."

[88] Sen, *Development as Freedom*.

Report for 2004 argued that enhancement of cultural liberty should be an explicit development goal, alongside traditional concerns such as access to health and education or pro-poor economic growth:

> People must also be free to be who they are and to choose their cultural identity accordingly—as a Thai, a Quaker, a Wolof speaker, a South African of Indian descent—and to enjoy the respect of others and live in dignity. They must also be free to make cultural choices without penalty, without being excluded from other choices—for jobs, schooling, housing, healthcare, political voice and many other opportunities critical to human well-being. They must be allowed to choose multiple identities—as Thai and Muslim, for example, or as Wolof and Senegalese.[89]

The UNDP report advocated for improved measurement of culturally based exclusion or oppression, starting most fundamentally with the inclusion of better questions about "cultural identities" on national censuses and other surveys.[90]

In the mid-2000s, international development organizations began to introduce new policies and procedures that formalized organizational demands for ethnoracial population data. An innovative organizational practice developed at the Ford Foundation in the 1990s became an inspiration and model for international development agencies working throughout Latin American in the 2000s. As an extension of its commitment to support projects by and for Afrodescendant communities in Latin America, the Ford Foundation introduced the idea of requiring a "Racial Impact Statement" (RIS) on all grant applications in the region: "The RIS would require applicants (be they government or civil society organizations) to collect and provide solid data and a narrative explanation of the ways in which a given funded project would positively and negatively affect different racial groups."[91] By making all grant proposals "provide solid data" to explicitly address disparate impacts or benefits of a project, the Ford Foundation drew attention to the paucity of good data that differentiated populations by race or ethnicity in Latin America.[92] In 2003, the IAC endorsed the use of RIS or similar practices by all

---

[89] UNDP, "Human Development Report 2004," 28.
[90] UNDP, "Human Development Report 2004," 31.
[91] Inter-American Dialogue, "Afro-Descendants in Latin America," 8.
[92] Some analysts criticized the Ford Foundation for relying on organizational practices that impose a North American conception of race on Latin American racial dynamics. The RIS, with its requirement for statistical measures of disparity between clearly defined ethnic and racial groups, typifies such practices. See Bourdieu and Wacquant, "On the Cunning of Imperialist Reason." For a defense

major development agencies working in the region.[93] As community groups, NGOs, researchers, and development agency personnel attempted to comply with the RIS requirement they would become acutely aware of data deficiencies across social sectors and sometimes entire countries, bolstering support for new data collection initiatives and reforms.

In the latter half of the decade, the multilateral development banks upped the stakes significantly by making ethnoracially differentiated population data a standard requirement for new project proposals. In 2006, the IDB adopted a new "Operational Policy on Indigenous Peoples and Strategy for Indigenous Development" which advanced a "proactive approach" to "development with identity" for indigenous peoples. The policy required all projects funded through the IDB to take into account a number of factors affecting indigenous peoples. This approach was subsequently extended to Afrodescendant communities as well. According to the IDB website (in 2013): "The IDB proactively promotes social inclusion of African descendant communities and indigenous peoples as stakeholders in the development of Latin America and the Caribbean, through direct investments and the application of safeguards in IDB projects."[94]

In addition to raising data requirements for a range of IDB-funded development projects within a country, the new "safeguards" applied to loans made for census operations themselves. In the 2000s, several Latin American countries relied on loans from the IDB, the World Bank, and other institutions to finance census operations. Through the banks' prioritization of ethnic and racial data collection, these loans translated into clear (if not always explicit) pressure to include questions about ethnic or racial identification on national censuses. Illustratively, Nicaragua received an IDB loan "to support the 2005 census, the continuity of household surveys and the strengthening of the Nicaraguan Statistics and Census Institute (INEC). A key goal is to generate timely, accurate and reliable data on the population and its living standards, with particular attention to racial and ethnic minorities."[95] While the obligation to generate ethnic and racial population data may not have been a formal condition of the loan, the expectation was nonetheless clear.

---

of the Ford Foundation's approach to combating ethnic and racial inequality in Latin America, see Telles, "US Foundations and Racial Reasoning in Brazil"; French, "The Missteps of Anti-Imperialist Reason," Hanchard, "Acts of Misrecognition."

[93] Inter-American Dialogue, "Afro-Descendants in Latin America," 8.

[94] Inter-American Development Bank, "Gender and Diversity."

[95] Inter-American Development Bank, "IDB Approves $6,550,000 Loan to Nicaragua for Census and Statistics System."

In sum, during the first decade of the twenty-first century, international development organizations and lending institutions made it a priority to persuade Latin American states to produce more and better ethnic and racial statistics. This priority was communicated directly to government agencies and indirectly, via financial support for domestic groups that pressed for census reform. This priority was also communicated through advocacy for improved ethnic and racial statistics, sponsorship of regional workshops and conferences on how to introduce new questions on Latin American censuses, and the adoption of new organizational practices and reporting requirements for development-related grants and loans. Having identified ethnoracial inequality as an enduring obstacle to development, international agencies sought to bolster Latin American states' will and capacity to produce official ethnoracial statistics in order to measure disparities and monitor change. The coordinated international efforts succeeded in ushering in a region-wide resurgence of official ethnoracial classification in Latin America.

Of course, this does not mean that the World Bank-sponsored conferences, the broad endorsement of their agenda by the major international development agencies, or the adoption of new data requirements for grants and loans unilaterally dictated specific changes to national censuses in every Latin American country. The often-contentious dynamics and uneven pace of reform in individual countries reflected domestic political struggles as well as the differential influence of international organizations on the parties involved. What is clear, however, is that in the wake of the first "Todos Contamos" conference and in the years that followed, the normative international expectation for what a national census should cover shifted decisively in favor of including questions about race or ethnicity. Also clear is that through specific conduits of influence—support for domestic activists, public advocacy and sponsorship of programmatic conferences, and the adoption of new organizational procedures and practices—international organizations pressured Latin American governments to adopt census reforms and facilitated their implementation. International organizations accelerated the emergence of a new era of official ethnoracial classification on national censuses in Latin America.

Holdouts and Harbingers

By the second decade of the twenty-first century, it had become difficult for Latin American states to *not* classify their populations by race or ethnicity on censuses. As recently as the 1990s, taking a national census that to distinguish indigenous peoples in the census, nor has there been any significant international or domestic pressure for them to do so.

In the Dominican Republic, recent censuses do not identify either indigenous or Afrodescendant individuals. The absence of a census question on indigenous peoples has not yet become a focus of debate; as in Cuba, the historiography of the Dominican Republic generally assumes that Indians who survived the conquest disappeared through assimilation long ago.[99] The absence of a question about race more generally, however, has sparked significant controversy.

In the leadup to the 2010 census, at an international meeting of statistics officials in Santiago, Chile, activists publicly challenged Francisco Cáceres Ureña, the director of the Dominican Republic's 2010 census, on the need to add a question about race. Ureña rejected their appeals and the 2010 census was undertaken without such a question. In an interview in 2013, Ureña, who self-identifies as black, offered an explanation for this decision.[100] First, he noted that the activists in Santiago did not provide any reason to include the question, beyond insisting that it was necessary for blacks to "be included." Yet in the Dominican Republic, Ureña explained, "we are black"; the group that is the minority elsewhere is the majority in the Dominican Republic. Second, Ureña pointed to the impossibility of collecting reliable data on race in the census through either self- or enumerator identification. In the Dominican Republic, he explained, individuals would not choose to identify as black on the census if given other options. He noted that Dominicans often assumed that those with an education or a prestigious occupation cannot be black. There is also strong anti-Haitian sentiment that leads Dominicans to identify with other categories to maximize distance from this stigmatized "other." Given the ideological biases of the Dominican population, Ureña suggested, including a race question on the census would end up making blacks less, not more, visible. In sum: The director of the Dominican Republic's 2010 census resisted pressure to add a race question on the grounds that it would generate a fictitiously "whitened" picture of the country. It remains to be seen whether the Dominican Republic's statistics agency will resist the mounting international pressure to incorporate a race question in the next census round.

---

[99] Curiously, the term *indio* is widely used in the contemporary Dominican Republic. Until recently, it was used as an official category on individual identification cards. But *indio* is not used to refer to Indians. Rather, it is typically employed as a euphemism for individuals who in other parts of Latin American would be called mestizo or mulatto. See Simmons, "'Somos Una Liga'"; Howard, *Coloring the Nation*; Roth, *Race Migrations*.

[100] Interview with Martina Kunovic, June 27, 2013.

The Chilean case in turn, illustrates how the new international norm of multicultural nationhood, combined with international organizations' focus on censuses as a site for the norm's realization, set significant constraints on how government officials could legitimately respond to calls for reform. In the leadup to the 2012 census, Afro-Chilean activists lobbied the Chilean National Statistics Institute (INE) to add a new question to the national census that would allow self-identification by those of African descent. They wanted to be classified in order to be counted as a distinct group within the nation. The INE rejected their appeals, citing the high cost of adding new questions to the national census and the very small numbers of Afrodescendant Chileans. In response, representatives of organizations belonging to the Afro-Chilean Alliance charged the INE with racist exclusion. They threatened to denounce the Chilean government to a long list of international organizations, including the UNDP, UNESCO, UNICEF, and ECLAC, among others.[101] The INE director balked and offered a compromise position: a separate regional survey of Afrodescendants that was "officially linked to the census" and would "visibilize" Chile's population of African descent in official statistics for the first time.[102]

The INE's proposal fell far short of activists' desired outcome. Afrodescendants would not get their own question or response category on the census, or even on the regional survey. Instead, the INE agreed to train census enumerators in the northern region, where Afrodescendant Chileans are concentrated, to identify Afrodescendants "indirectly." Afrodescendant Chileans could be counted in the survey by responding "yes" to the question that asked if the individual is indigenous or *originario* and then writing in "afrodescendiente" under "other." The INE director took pains to insist that these steps counted as official recognition of Afro-Chileans by the Chilean state: "The INE is the official statistical agency of Chile and if this institution takes the census and will also conduct this study in connection with the census, then obviously the recognition of the Afrodescendant pueblo is a recognition by the INE and thus, it is understood, by the Government of Chile."[103]

---

[101] A firsthand account of a meeting between representatives of Afro-Chilean organizations and the Director of Chile's INE described the INE's justifications for excluding the query (for example: "each new query costs one million dollars") and activists' response, including the threat to denounce Chile's government to international organizations. See: http://afrochileno.blogspot.com/"Afrochilenos... hacia la inclusión y el reconocimiento." For more information about this episode, see: Estrada, Daniela. "Afro-Chileans Seek Recognition in Census"; Francisco, "Chile: afrodescendientes quieren hacer parte de las estadísticas"; Castillo Olivares, "INE realizará estudio sobre los afrodescendientes"; INCIDE, "Ley Antidiscriminación: Caso Lumbanga."

[102] INCIDE, "Ley Antidiscriminación: Caso Lumbanga."

[103] Castillo Olivares, "INE realizará estudio sobre los afrodescendientes."

While Chile's statistics agency ultimately resisted the pressure to add a direct question about African descent on the 2012 census, the compromise accommodation nonetheless revealed a significant concession to activists' demands in light of new international expectations. Moreover, the INE's rather contorted compromise plan, and in particular the effort to ensure that this plan be recognized by Afro-Chileans as a legitimate form of official recognition by the Chilean state, testifies to the pervasive influence of the new international norms even in those countries that have been most resistant to reforms. Faced with demands by a geographically concentrated and (presumed) numerically small subpopulation for a census question of their own, the INE's director recognized that a simple "no" would not suffice. Gone were the days when Chile's self-evident homogeneity could be invoked to explain why a census question to capture Afrodescendant peoples was irrelevant.[104] In 2012, the idea that the Chilean state should officially recognize Afrodescendant individuals within the national population—however small their absolute numbers relative to the whole—was no longer (publically) in dispute. Thus, even as the INE refused to add a new question to the census, with the compromise position the official story of Chilean nationhood nonetheless underwent a significant revision.

As in Chile, so in the rest of Latin America: National censuses no longer described populations as either inevitably homogenizing or already homogenous. According to early twenty-first-century censuses in the region, Latin American nations were now (and now had always been) multiethnic, multicultural, and multiracial. While some Latin American census agencies embraced their new commitment to ethnoracial data collection more reluctantly than others, by the 2010 census round, nearly all of them had accepted the agenda of collecting information about self-identified racial or ethnic group affiliation. Once the transition to official ethnic or racial enumeration was made, government officials appeared to champion the change. For twenty-first-century Latin American states, classifying diversity and counting difference had become both a signal of up-to-date membership in the club of civilized nations, and a means to the continued pursuit of national progress.

---

[104] The official explanation for refusing to add a question about Afrodescent in Chile's 2012 census was a far cry from the official explanation offered for an analogous omission 150 years prior. As noted in chapter 5, the official rationale for excluding a race question from Chile's 1865 census rested on the self-evident racial homogeneity of the population: "happily in our country there exists a single race, free and equal as much in the color of their skin as in their political rights and obligations, which exempts us from the work of distinction that occupies long pages of the American Census." Chile, Oficina Central de Estadística, *Censo general de la República de Chile levantado el 19 de abril de 1865*, viii.

It is tempting to conclude this chapter by designating Latin America's early twenty-first-century censuses as those in which the victims of centuries of symbolic violence finally got their day: The invisibilized have made themselves visible, the presumed-assimilated have declared themselves unassimilable. Such a narrative might not overstate the momentous transformation of Latin American censuses into sites for documenting enduring diversity rather than projecting its inevitable elimination. Such a triumphalist conclusion would, however, require willful neglect of the ongoing challenges and tensions surrounding the politics of official ethnoracial classification in contemporary Latin America.

The 2010 census round was not some kind of multiculturalist end-of-history moment. The complex and contested histories of Latin American states and their ethnoracial others continue to unfold. Some observers caution that Latin American statistics agencies' willingness to recognize the existence and demands of ethnoracially defined subgroups within national populations could be short lived. According to sociologist Edward Telles, there is no guarantee that recent gains in racial and ethnic data collection in the region will be sustained: "While much progress has been made in collecting race data, these efforts are far from having become institutionalized. Longterm commitments are questionable at this point as the new questions and modules or the lessons learned from these experiences often are not incorporated in planning for subsequent surveys and censuses. There is a temptation to return to the old order of collecting demographic information."[105] Pointing to the Brazilian case as a positive example, Telles suggests that an enduring commitment to racial or ethnic data collections hinges not only on financial support and technical expertise, but especially on "political willingness" and continued "encouragement" from civil society.

Much more than ever before, however, the political will to collect racial and ethnic statistics in many Latin American countries hinges on evolving priorities of international organizations. It remains an open question whether the broad international consensus documented in this chapter—that official ethnoracial data collection is an unequivocally good and necessary state practice in Latin America—will endure. In some countries, including Bolivia, Brazil, and Colombia, domestic constituencies and their representatives within the state are currently positioned to sustain and extend data collection initiatives. If international development agencies

---

[105] Telles, "Race and Ethnicity."

shift priorities and resources away from these projects, the efforts would definitely be hampered, but probably not derailed. In many other countries, it is questionable whether projects to improve collection of ethnoracial statistics would survive in the absence of sustained international development agency pressure and resources. By demonstrating the "political will" to allow census reforms, national governments in countries like Argentina, Ecuador, and Peru garnered new resources for census operations while appearing responsive to new international norms and "civil society" demands. The affinity between the goals of domestic social movements of indigenous and Afrodescendant peoples and the priorities of international development organizations allowed states to bolster legitimacy on both domestic and international fronts, at minimal cost to other priorities. Absent symbolic and material benefits from international development organizations, however, the political will to devote limited resources to ethnic and racial data collection—and to the broader goal of eliminating ethnoracial inequality—might evaporate in much of the region.

Indeed, public backlash against the reincarnation of official ethnoracial classification in Latin American appears to be growing.[106] Critics of the multiculturalist turn in many Latin American countries decry the "racism" inherent in particularist ethnoracial identifications and the policies that they enable and inform. Appealing to the color-blind promises of Latin America's liberal tradition (in its ideal, not realized, form), they insist on the social value of the "inclusionary" *mestizo* nationalisms of the past as a foundation for national solidarity and cohesion.

Of course, the notion that official ethnoracial classification of Latin American populations marks a radical departure from historical tradition is misguided. For most states in the region, the practice of classifying citizens by race is not entirely new. As I have shown in this book, official ethnoracial classification has deep roots in Latin America. In the concluding chapter, I assess the contemporary politics of official ethnoracial classification in Latin America in light of the centuries-long history of official ethnoracial classification on censuses documented in this book. Situating twenty first-century state projects to classify and count diversity in relation to analogous efforts from the sixteenth through the twentieth centuries exposes both continuity and change in why and how Latin American states engage in official ethnoracial classification of their populations.

---

[106] I discuss the rising backlash in some countries against official ethnoracial classification of citizens in the concluding chapter.

CHAPTER 8 | Conclusion
The International Politics of Ethnoracial Classification

THE POLITICS OF OFFICIAL ethnoracial classification in Latin America are likely to escalate as the twenty-first century unfolds. Questions about indigenous and Afrodescendant identification on early twenty-first-century censuses will yield a bumper crop of official ethnoracial statistics. Together with information gleaned from the growing number of supplementary household surveys in the region, these data will change the basic descriptive picture of Latin American populations. Results from official surveys have already made many ethnoracial distinctions statistically visible for the first time; they have also exposed ethnoracial dimensions of inequality. With analyses of these new statistics in hand, policy makers, researchers, activists, and others are working to reshape understandings of the region's principal social problems and their prescribed solutions.[1]

As in the past, so in the early twenty-first century, the national census is both a symbolic site where the nation is defined and a political tool for charting the path toward future national prosperity. In contemporary political struggles to redefine Latin American nations as plurinational and multicultural, the national census is a valued prize in battles for official recognition and political representation of particular ethnoracial groups. The census continues to play a critical role in the production of basic knowledge about the region's populations. The categories used to count and classify the population determine the official statistical picture of the kinds of human beings who comprise a given nation. Across Latin America, new census questions and categories are revising earlier statistical portraits of homogenizing populations, replacing them with pictures of multicultural and pluriethnic nations.

---

[1] Garavito et al., *Raza y Derechos Humanos en Colombia*, exemplifies this new wave of research.

The census in twenty-first century Latin America is not only a symbolic stake in the politics of recognition, it is also a strategic instrument in the politics of distribution. For those engaged in political battles to define the priorities and future course of national development, census data can be a critical resource. The questions and categories used to collect demographic information set constraints on what is knowable, statistically, about a given population. Categories of citizens who are officially counted can leverage official statistics to anchor specific demands for representation, rights, or redress.

The politics of official ethnoracial classification in contemporary Latin America are thus deeply implicated in the broader politics of diversity, development, and the relationship between them. In this conclusion, I offer preliminary reflections on the twenty-first century politics of official ethnoracial classification in Latin America in light of the centuries-long history of such practices analyzed in this book. I begin with a brief review of the core historical arguments made in previous chapters, identifying both continuity and change in Latin American states' motives and methods of engaging in ethnoracial classification of their populations. In some respects, twenty-first-century initiatives to classify and count ethnoracial diversity within Latin American populations are reminiscent of analogous efforts to do so in the past. In other respects, however, the new era of official ethnoracial classification in Latin American breaks decisively with historical precedent. Latin American governments have resurrected the practice of official ethnoracial classification, but they have done so with revised methods and new purpose. In these final pages, I note how new facets of census politics in Latin America—in particular, efforts to democratize the process of data production, create constituencies for new census categories, and reconcile commitments to ethnoracial diversity and equality with the continued pursuit of national development—have opened up new spaces of political contestation over how and toward what ends states engage in official ethnoracial classification of citizens.

Official Ethnoracial Classification in Historical Perspective

States in Latin America have a long history of engaging in official ethnoracial classification in censuses of their populations. Their specific motives and methods for doing so shifted over time, with implications for whom within Latin American populations got counted, as what kind or category of person, and toward what ends. Of course, the particulars of this history varied considerably across individual countries. As analysis of classification practices in censuses of nineteen states across nearly two centuries revealed, Latin American states differed historically in their propensity to ethnoracially classify citizens on the census; they also differed in the specific questions and categories they used to do so. This variation follows from the preeminently political nature of the census, and the fact that census politics are enacted in specific historical and geographical contexts. Yet as the broad comparative and historical perspective adopted in this book revealed, the domestic politics of national censuses were embedded within international political and scientific fields. The histories of official ethnoracial classification in the censuses of Latin American states were shaped in relation to shifting international norms for how to be a modern nation and shifting international prescriptions for how to pursue national progress.

All of the Latin American states analyzed in this book shared a colonial history in which official ethnoracial classification was pervasive. In colonial Latin America, mercantilist Spanish and Portuguese imperial states counted and classified their subjects to advance fundamentally extractive aims. As seen in chapter 2, official ethnoracial classification served to construct a legally institutionalized social hierarchy that appeared to be rooted in a natural order. The identification of individual colonial subjects as "Indian," "black," or of some other caste, served as the administrative foundation for the construction of an elaborate bureaucratic architecture designed to both execute and rationalize regimes of systematic extraction, dispossession, and social control. Because colonial states typically counted and classified their subjects for particular, instrumental ends, certain categories of colonial subjects—whether taxable "castas" or tributary "indios"—were more likely to be counted, and subjected to the institutional repercussions of their official classification.

After the independence wars in early nineteenth-century Spanish Latin America, nationalists proclaimed the advent of new political communities. These new polities were defined in direct opposition to the naturalized ethnoracial hierarchies that had enabled and justified colonial rule. Yet, when it came time to produce statistical portraits of their newly national populations, the majority of Latin American states nevertheless engaged in official racial classification of their citizens.

Racial classification of citizens by the state flew in the face of independence-era promises, inscribed in newly penned constitutions, to construct color-blind liberal republics in the place of the colonial society of castes. By omitting race or color questions from national censuses, Latin American state builders could have upheld liberal promises to do away with official ethnoracial distinctions, while downplaying the historical legacies of colonial ethnoracial domination. Leaving questions about race or color out of the census would have also brought Latin American censuses into closer alignment with the international scientific norms for census content at the time—a goal to which the region's census officials aspired, as documented in chapter 3. Why, then, did postcolonial Latin American states engage in racial classification of their citizens?

Latin America's early national census agencies produced ethnoracial statistics with a twofold purpose. First, they sought to ground their claims to be distinctive, *sui generis*, nations. Like all other aspiring nations-in-formation, they needed proof that they were a distinctive people. While the act of taking a national census testified to their modern stateness, the content of census reports testified to their national distinctiveness. Latin American states used early national censuses to craft statistical portraits of modernizing nations, which they defined in racialist terms. Instead of defining their new nations in terms of shared values and beliefs, as communities of assent, political elites explicitly embraced racialist definitions of nationhood, claiming distinctive peoplehood rooted in shared descent. To be sure, they did not emulate the type of "ethnic" nationalism that was being cultivated in Germany around the same time. Latin American nationalisms championed racial mixture, not purity; race figured in official rhetoric as a principle of inclusion, not exclusion. Nor did Latin American idioms of nationhood mirror the "civic" nationalisms cultivated in France or (with evident hypocrisy) in the United States. Instead, in multiple variants of a common trope, Latin American nationalists made the idea of originating racial mixture a central and defining anchor of their claims to modern nationhood.

The production of ethnoracial statistics in the context of national censuses provided (supposedly) empirical, scientific grounding for nationalists' narratives. As shown in chapter 4, officials used censuses to describe the different racial types to be found in the national territory and to document how particular combinations of racial types had given rise to new national types. Leveraging the international prestige and scientific legitimacy of statistics, all but a few Latin American states conducted a national census in the nineteenth or early twentieth century in which their "national colors" were on full display.

At the same time, census officials produced racial statistics to deflect international scientific claims that the very thing that they claimed as their font of national distinctiveness—to wit, their unique combinations of ethnoracial mixture—undermined any hope of national progress. Latin America's early modernizers fastened on racial constructions of nationhood as they reconciled their aspirations for national progress with prevailing scientific theories of racial determinism. The onset of intensive and deliberate nation-state building in much of Latin America coincided with the rise to international prominence of "race science." Just as Latin American modernizers were drawing up (or importing) their roadmaps to a prosperous, civilized future, European and North American scientists were claiming they might as well not even bother.

In major works of late nineteenth-century racial determinist science, Latin American countries were invoked as evidence, writ large, of the deleterious effects of racial mixture on human populations. Latin Americans, however, refused to accept that "modern progress was meant only for white men in temperate zones."[2] Using the discursive, scientific, and organizational tools at their disposal—principal among them, newly created offices of national statistics—Latin American modernizers refuted predictions that racial miscegenation doomed their nations to degeneracy. In the pages of leather-bound volumes of national census results, and in the universal scientific language of statistics (at times with a creative flare, as seen in chapter 5), Latin American officials described how the very race mixture that distinguished them as unique peoples among others also set their populations on trajectories of demographic *re*generation. In the late nineteenth-century and into the first decades of the twentieth, official racial statistics were used to describe the distinctive racially mixed origins of Latin American nations while projecting an ever whiter and more homogenous future.

From the 1930s, scientific theories that called into question the validity of race as a scientific concept gained intellectual ground. In the wake of World War II, the political and moral legitimacy of the race concept became suspect as well. In this new international normative and scientific context, the explicit equation of national progress with racial progress had to be revisited. Latin American census officials sought ways to reconcile their commitments to the continued pursuit of national progress with the global delegitimization of "race" as a scientific concept and of "racial improvement" as a political project. As described in chapter 6, this reconciliation generally took the form of omission of direct race questions

---

[2] The quotation comes from historian Thomas Skidmore's classic work, *Black into White*, xxiii, with reference to the views of prominent nineteenth-century Brazilian intellectuals. Brazilians' skepticism of key claims of racial determinist science was shared by their contemporaries in many other Latin American countries, as this book has shown.

from the census, together with a proliferation of questions about cultural traits. While the terminology was recast, however, the underlying view that equated national progress with the homogenization and westernization of the population endured. In many countries, censuses continued to track "difference" within populations with an eye to both documenting and facilitating its ultimate disappearance into the national mass.

Toward the end of the twentieth century, the international mark of a modern nation changed yet again. Under pressure from domestic and transnational social movements, international governmental and nongovernmental organizations called on states to halt national development projects that ignored or aimed to assimilate minority populations. Instead, national governments were pressed to officially recognize and support enduring diversity within national populations. As described in chapter 7, by the early 2000s, a choir of domestic, regional, and international voices had come together on the same note: Latin American states should collect ethnoracial data in their censuses. The relative influence of domestic and international actors on the process of census reforms varied across countries, but in all cases some form of international pressure played a role. In the last decades of the twentieth century and the first decade of the twenty-first, nearly all Latin American states reintroduced census questions that asked citizens to identify their ethnoracial origins or identities.

Thus, across historical periods, census officials' decisions about how to describe populations and prescribe their path to development were shaped in relation to prevailing international norms of what a legitimate modern state is and prevailing international definitions of what it means to pursue national "progress" or "development." When nineteenth- and early twentieth-century nation-state builders in Latin America were confronted, on the one hand, with norms of nationhood that demanded some font of national distinctiveness, and on the other with scientific theories that pinned prospects for progress on having the right racial stuff, they used racial statistics to document how demographic processes at work in their populations produced racially one-of-a-kind and *re*generative nations. When international scientific and political norms later rejected the race concept, and with it, racial-determinist understandings of development, Latin America's modernizers reformulated the racialist rhetoric of nationalist claims to emphasize how mestizaje—either in the past or ongoing—guaranteed the *cultural* integration of their populations, in a "progressive" direction. And when, toward the end of the twentieth century, the mark of a modern nation became official recognition of enduring diversity rather than its eventual demise, Latin America's modernizers officially "unmixed" their mestizo nations, reinventing themselves as multicultural, multiethnic, or plurinational political communities.

In taking stock of how nineteen different states approached counting and classifying "diversity" within their populations over the course of two centuries, my historical analysis revealed common overarching tendencies across countries within historical periods, as well as change in the dominant tendency over time. Of course, the specific periodization fit the historical trajectories of census taking and nation making in some countries better than others, and in each period there were anomalous cases. Additionally, as the specific examples drawn from individual census reports to illustrate variants of broad regional trends revealed, each country's censuses had their own idiosyncrasies. The explanation for these idiosyncrasies lies in contingencies of domestic politics, especially the contests among actors within scientific and bureaucratic politics fields. Yet when any given census is placed in the context of the entire history of census taking by nineteen states in the region, it becomes apparent that the contingencies of domestic politics do not alone suffice to explain when or why Latin American states engage in official ethnoracial classification of their populations.

At least since the mid-nineteenth century, the ways that Latin American states counted and classified their citizens reflected the reconciliation of domestic political projects with evolving international norms of modern nationhood and international prescriptions for the pursuit of national progress. As internationally accepted definitions of national progress changed, so too did the ways Latin American states described their populations in censuses and prescribed their paths to progress or development.

From the first national censuses in the region to the present day, the questions and categories included on censuses have been influenced by politics. But the political field that shaped how Latin American states classified their populations on censuses was not constrained by national borders. The micropolitics of determining which questions and categories to use in counting and classifying populations were shaped historically by the macropolitics of efforts to build modern states and construct recognizably modern nations. This was true in the nineteenth century and it remains true at the beginning of the twenty-first. Thus, over the course of nearly two centuries, the relationship between domestic political actors and international norms and organizations played a decisive role in the rise, the fall, and the resurgence of official ethnoracial classification in Latin American censuses.

The New Politics of Official Ethnoracial Classification

In the early twenty-first century, as in prior historical periods, domestic politics and practices of official ethnoracial classification in Latin America are shaped in relation to international definitions of what constitutes a legitimate modern nation and what it means to pursue national "development." Yet in critical respects, the current politics of official ethnoracial classification in Latin America break from historical precedent. In contrast to the colonial uses of official ethnoracial classification to proscribe freedoms and entrench hierarchy, early twenty-first century states engage in official ethnoracial classification with the declared aim of enhancing "cultural liberty" and removing obstacles to individual mobility. And in contrast to nationalizing states' use of official ethnoracial classification to chart—and champion—the disappearance of internal distinctions within populations, early twenty-first-century states rely on official ethnoracial classification to document and display the enduring, multifaceted diversity of their nations.

As I have shown, Latin American national mythologies long championed the idea that distinctive nations were formed through the mixture and thus dissolution of categorical differences. Against this history, the recent embrace of questions about ethnoracial origins and identities on national censuses appears as a sort of tectonic ideological shift. Instead of insisting on the blending and disappearance of ethnoracial distinctions in their populations, Latin American states are now officially recognizing and institutionalizing clear, categorical divides.[3]

New methods and aims of official ethnoracial classification in Latin American censuses are symptomatic of the hard-fought politics of renegotiating relationships between citizens and states in the region. New facets of ethnoracial data collection in the region are also constitutive of new forms of politics. In the final pages, I point to three significant ways in which the contemporary politics and practices of official ethnoracial classification in Latin America break from historical precedent, and in so doing, open up new sites and modes of contestation in broader political struggles over recognition, rights, and redress for historically marginalized populations.

---

[3] As an aside, there is a certain historical irony in the fact that the official rejection of mestizo nationalisms in Latin America comes at the same moment when the United States is finally allowing its citizens to embrace multiracial origins by marking more than one race box on the census.

Democratizing Data Production

One striking feature of official ethnoracial classification in twenty-first century Latin American censuses that differs markedly from the past is that the enumerated are increasingly invited to participate in the design and analysis of the surveys used for their enumeration. Beginning in the early 2000s, as seen in chapter 7, international and regional organizations pressed Latin American states to add new questions to national censuses. In addition, they often encouraged government statistics offices to facilitate and enable the participation of representatives from indigenous and Afrodescendant organizations in the process of data production. The UN, the World Bank, CELADE, and other agencies supported the creation of training programs to provide indigenous and Afrodescendant individuals with access to the methods and tools used by statisticians, policy analysts, and government officials to collect and analyze census data. For example, a technical cooperation agreement between the Ministry of Health of Chile (MINSAL) and ECLAC to produce a socio-demographic report on the metropolitan indigenous population using census data included "training workshops for indigenous technical personnel on the REDATAM software and the use of censuses."[4] Financial and logistical support for such workshops demonstrated that calls by development agencies for greater inclusivity in the process of data production were not merely rhetorical.

Some agencies called for projects to go beyond the provision of technical training to incorporate input from members of ethnic minority populations on the design of survey questionnaires. The UN's Permanent Forum on Indigenous Issues, for example, flagged the need for more information on whether survey questions adequately addressed the needs of indigenous communities: "indigenous peoples' understanding of poverty, or land rights, often differs considerably from that of dominant or mainstream populations. This is rarely taken into account in the collection of relevant data."[5] In the leadup to the 2010 census round, the UN sponsored

---

[4] ECLAC, "Biennial Programme... 2007–2009." REDATAM (Retrieval of Data for small Areas by Microcomputer) is hierarchical database management software that can handle millions of records from varied sources at different scales, permitting rapid statistical analysis of demographic and other types of data and geographic mapping of results. The development of REDATAM software is supported by the regular budget of the United Nations and is used for large-scale hierarchical database management by many government agencies around the world.

[5] UN Department of Economic and Social Affairs, Division for Social Policy and Development, Secretariat of the Permanent Forum on Indigenous Issues, Report on "The Perspective of Information Received and Collected Within the Context of ILO Conventions Nos. 107 ad 169," 9.

conferences and seminars to ensure participation by representatives of indigenous and Afrodescendant groups. This was a primary objective of the 2008 CELADE/ECLAC conference held in Santiago, Chile, with funding from UNICEF, UNFPA, UNIFEM, and the WHO.[6] The workshop brought together "more than 100 experts from more than 20 countries, including from governmental and nongovernmental organizations, representatives of indigenous and Afrodescendant organizations, academics and technical experts from international agencies."[7]

Significantly, the meeting emphasized the importance of generating statistics that would be recognized as valid not only by governments and development agencies, but also by indigenous and Afrodescendant communities. Toward that end, a conference report recommended, "we should aim to obtain this information with the participation of the peoples (pueblos) and communities, which is what will make it appear legitimate in the eyes of the entire population."[8] The conference participants underscored that participation should be construed in the broadest possible terms. The final recommendation of the conference report was that "participation of [indigenous and Afrodescendant] peoples (pueblos) in the design of questions and the collection and analysis of data that refer to them should be institutionalized."[9] The CELADE conference report denotes a critical shift in how international development agencies and government agency personnel think about the relationship between the producers of demographic data, the individuals from whom data are collected, and the uses to which the data are put.

Efforts to ensure that voices of those who will be enumerated actually get taken into account in designing instruments for enumeration are still the exception rather than the rule, but current momentum favors those pressing national statistics offices to provide more opportunities for popular participation. It is conceivable that the continued legitimacy of the national census in the eyes of citizens will come to depend, in some contexts, on the existence of formal venues for public input into census operations. In theory, such forums could become arenas of substantive democratization in action—where the historical objects of statistical inquiry become subjects empowered with the authority, expertise, and resources to investigate themselves. A much more likely scenario, however, is that national statistics officials, in

---

[6]United Nations, "Censos 2010 y la inclusión del enfoque étnico."
[7]United Nations, "Censos 2010 y la inclusión del enfoque étnico," 5.
[8]United Nations, "Censos 2010 y la inclusión del enfoque étnico," 75.
[9]United Nations, "Censos 2010 y la inclusión del enfoque étnico," 79.

collaboration with experts working for international development agencies, maintain de facto control over design and execution of national surveys, while encouraging popular participation on carefully delimited issues with a range of acceptable outcomes more or less predetermined.

For those who generally support popular participation in governance, these changes seem like a positive development. But with democratization has come politicization. These innovations have opened up complicated new fields of politics, where there are struggles over recognition (which lines of ethnoracial distinction will get official sanction and which will remain statistically invisible?) and also over representation (who gets to speak on behalf of whom?). Of course politicization is not necessarily a bad thing, and in any case, the production of ethnoracial statistics has always been political. Historically, however, this fact was obscured through control of the means of enumeration and classification in the hands of an elite few. Indeed, historically, the symbolic authority of the census as a source of objective demographic knowledge hinged partly on the successful obfuscation of the politics of production of that knowledge. Recent developments in the region have brought the politics of data production into open view.

To the extent that the inherently political nature of producing official ethnoracial statistics becomes widely recognized, the authority of the census as a source of objective information could be eroded. This could undermine what remains of the state's capacity to pass off official census categories as mere description of demographic realities.[10] As the authority that had been rooted in the (ruse of) scientific objectivity of official statistics is diminished, the value of the census as a stake in ongoing political struggles could be diminished as well.

Yet as long as official census results continue to be a primary source of demographic information for the region, they will be leveraged to provide basic descriptions of Latin American populations and to inform policy prescriptions at multiple levels, the politics of their production notwithstanding. The democratization and politicization of the process of data production may invite critique, but in the absence of alternative sources of national data, the categories used in national censuses will continue to inform the categories through which Latin American societies are analyzed and understood.

---

[10] Put another way, the democratization of the process of demographic data production could undermine and erode the state's symbolic power in this domain. See Loveman, M. "The Modern State and the Primitive Accumulation of Symbolic Power."

Creating Constituencies for Categories

Another facet of contemporary census politics in Latin America that differs from the past is the rise of organized campaigns to persuade those who will be enumerated to embrace new classifications. Testifying to the earlier successes of states' ideological and political assimilationist projects, many Latin Americans who, by the varied criteria used by activists, social scientists, and others, "qualify" as indigenous or Afrodescendant, nonetheless do not choose to identify as such when given a choice. For example, although many observers suggest that approximately one quarter of Colombian's population is of African descent, in the 2005 census, "only 11 percent of the population self-identified as Afro-Colombian."[11] Undeterred, activists have collaborated with census agency staff and international agencies and foundations to wage informational campaigns that aim to persuade would-be Indians and blacks to identify as such on national censuses.

Activists in several countries have been working to strengthen domestic demand for government action on behalf of ethnoracially defined populations, in part by increasing the number of their fellow citizens who identify as indigenous or Afrodescendant. In one of the first efforts of this kind, in the runup to the 1990 census in Brazil, the Brazilian Black Movement, with support from the Ford Foundation, launched a publicity campaign to persuade Brazilians with any African ancestry to mark "black" instead of brown or white on the census. The campaign slogan admonished: "Don't let your color pass into white."[12] To take another example, prior to the 2005 census in Colombia, Afro-Colombian organizations waged a campaign to encourage Colombians to recognize the "beautiful faces of my black people" ("Las caras lindas de mi gente negra"). The organizations produced a television commercial featuring individuals with a range of Afrodescendant physical traits proclaiming themselves "morena," "negra," "mulata," "zamba," or "raizal," and concluding with the slogan: "In this census, make yourself counted. Proudly Afrodescendant." The advertisement was aired through an agreement with DANE and via social media such as YouTube.[13] In Panama prior to the 2010 census, a campaign with

---

[11] Seelke, "Afro-Latinos in Latin America and Considerations for US Policy," 5; Paschel, "The Beautiful Faces of My Black People."

[12] Nobles, "Responding with Good Sense."

[13] Estupiñán, "Afrocolombianos y el Censo 2005," fn8. The advertisement can be seen on YouTube ("Censo Afrocolombiano 2005"): http://www.youtube.com/watch?v=PY4uf49dMqg&feature=endscreen. For an analysis of this campaign, see Paschel, "'The Beautiful Faces of My Black People.'"

the same slogan did double duty as a commemoration of Afrodescendant women on the International Day of Women. The 30-second spot featured Afrodescendant men engaged in traditionally women's work (ironing, cooking, hanging laundry) and appealing to viewers to commemorate International Women's Day and to show gratitude to Afrodescendant Panamanian women in particular by proudly reporting their African descent on the census.[14]

While the net effect of these public information campaigns on census results is difficult to determine, Brazil and Colombia have seen slow but steady growth in the relative size of self-identified Afrodescendant populations over the past two decades.[15] Some observers attribute this growth to broad cultural shifts in the valuation of blackness, especially among younger cohorts; others note the importance of census agency publicity campaigns and the emergence of "incentives for people to identify as such."[16]

Campaigns to educate Latin American populations about the importance of responding to questions about ethnic or racial heritage escalated significantly in preparation for the 2010 census round. Domestic activists, census officials, national media outlets, and regional and international organizations worked together to launch major publicity campaigns to inform Latin Americans of African descent about the new census queries and to encourage them to acknowledge their African heritage in selecting a response. For example, a regional Census 2010 working group composed of Afrodescendant leaders partnered with the UN Development Fund for Women as well as a Brazilian communications firm to produce a four-part television series called *The Americas Have Color: Afrodescendants in 21st-century Censuses.*[17] According to a press release, the series was "created to inform the population of the Americas about the 2010–12 census round" and covered "the conditions of life of black men and women, black resistance throughout history and a panorama of public

---

[14] The advertisement, titled "Orgullosamente Afrodescendiente" can be seen on YouTube (by "censoafropanama2010"): http://www.youtube.com/watch?v=vidKl1YbGzk&feature=endscreen

[15] Telles and Paschel, "Beyond Fixed or Fluid."

[16] "Although self identification as black or Afrodescendant has been increasing throughout the region, it continues to be limited but census staff found that it can be increased by levels of information, awareness raising, recognition and incentives for people to identify as such" (Stubbs, 2006, cited in Telles, "Race and Ethnicity and Latin America's United Nations Millennium Development Goals").

[17] http://afrocensos2010.wordpress.com/author/afrocensos2010/. In Brazil, the series was called *As Américas têm cor*; In Spanish-speaking countries, it appeared as *Las Americas tienen color*. For video clips, see links from the blog "Série 'As Américas têm cor: Afrodescendente nos Censos do Século XXI'" (http://afrocensos2010.wordpress.com/videos/).

policies to confront racism."[18] The series described the living conditions of Afrodescendant populations in Brazil, Ecuador, Panama, and Uruguay and underscored the importance of self-identification as Afrodescendant in the census.

Publicity for new ethnoracial census questions often made explicit mention of racial prejudice, discrimination, and inequality as social ills that the new statistics would help to combat. In Brasil, for example, the *Americas Have Color* documentary series opened with a special episode of a weekly news program, *Cenas do Brasil* (Scenes of Brazil), in which journalist Lúcia Abreu discussed "the importance of declaring one's color on the 2010 Census, the evolution of demographic data that refer to color or race, and their contribution to the design of public policies."[19] In Panama, social movement organizations turned to the Internet, using websites and blogs to call on individuals to fight racism by embracing their racial identity on the census:

> Some individuals of all age groups *would not* like to be identified by their race at all, but to these individuals we clarify [that] we live in a racially partial world full of misconceptions and mis-perceptions and just plain *racial hatred*. However much you would like to forget your racial identity there are those people…that will forever keep reminding you of your race…[T]heir prejudices and erroneous notions can and do affect your economics, where you can live, and if and how you may travel, not to mention what you may study and to what vocations or professions you may aspire. We encourage you all to cooperate with this historic Census of 2010 and take the opportunity to thoroughly think out the question of your own racial identity, particularly those of you who are of African descent.[20]

Meanwhile, in Mexico, activists encouraged Mexicans of African descent to embrace their distinctive culture and contributions to Mexican history. Posters circulated as part of the "We All Count" campaign sought to cultivate

---

[18] Instituto Observatório Social, "Série censo e afrodescendientes é exibida em canais abertos de TV brasileiros."

[19] Instituto Observatório Social, "Série censo e afrodescendientes é exibida em canais abertos de TV brasileiros."

[20] Emphasis in original. The quotation comes from a blog on the website of The Silver People Heritage Foundation: Reid, "Panama's 2010 Census Promises to Be Interesting for Persons of African and Indigenous Descent." The blog also encouraged ethnic differentiation among those of African descent: "We further encourage you, the descendants of the Afro-Antilleans whose forefathers can be traced to the 'Silver People' to answer question 9 by stating that you identify yourself as: Other: Silver People."

feelings of communal pride among Mexicans of African descent. The photograph reproduced in figure 8.1 shows a flier plastered to a mural that reads "We All Count...and in this 2010 census, we also want to be counted as what we are: BLACKS. Because we are *proud* of our culture and of what we have given to this great nation." While Mexico's census agency did not include a question to enumerate Afro-Mexicans in the 2010 census, it announced plans to conduct another census in 2015 that would make Mexicans of African descent statistically visible as such.

Public campaigns encouraging Latin Americans to acknowledge and embrace the African part of their heritage, coupled with increasing mainstream media coverage of racial discrimination and prejudice, represented a significant break from decades of public silence around this issue. Campaigns to mobilize support for ethnoracial data collection on censuses and to persuade would-be indigenous and Afrodescendant individuals to identify as such have also contributed to the revival—in some cases the genesis—of ethnic distinctions *within* indigenous, Afrodescendant, and even mestizo populations.

While the censuses of some countries have traditionally recognized different indigenous groups (as in Mexico's detailed language queries), others have begun to officially recognize an array of distinct tribal identities on the census for the first time. Argentina's 2001 census, for example, listed seventeen distinct indigenous communities to which respondents

FIGURE 8.1 Publicity for the Todos Contamos Campaign in Mexico.
SOURCE: *Emeequis*, June, 30, 2013. http://www.m-x.com.mx/2013-06-30/el-inegi-realizara-un-inedito-censo-de-la-poblacion-afromexicana-en-agosto/

could claim to belong, in addition to an open-ended "other indigenous *pueblo*" option. Bolivia's 2012 census, its first as an official "plurinational state," would register more than thirty-seven distinct indigenous identities. Some states also disaggregated the "black" or "Afrodescendant" category. In Panama, for example, the 2010 census distinguished "colonial black," "Antillean black" and "black." Notably, such efforts to draw distinctions within the Afrodescendant population are directly at odds with social movement efforts in countries like Brazil to unite all those of African descent within a single identity category on the census. In Ecuador, meanwhile, activists called for subdivision of the "mestizo" category to distinguish those they consider to be bioculturally mixed Ecuadorians ("montubios") from the ideological construct of the state ("mestizo"), with all its now-discredited historical baggage.[21]

Major media campaigns tied to recent censuses have contributed to a broadened public awareness of the political stakes of the national census, with some unintended consequences. Informational campaigns have sought to underscore the distinctiveness of indigenous or Afrodescendant populations, while simultaneously drawing attention to shared cultural traditions or shared experiences of historical dispossession and contemporary discrimination. While these messages may resonate with some, they have produced backlash among others. In Brazil, for example, some critics have publicly denounced the practice of official racial classification by the state and argued against the dissemination of race-targeted social policies.[22] Brazil also witnessed the emergence of countercampaigns calling for Brazilians to embrace their "mixed" heritage. For example, an NGO based in Amazonia with the name "Nação Mestiça" (Mestizo Nation) sought to advance "the valorization of the process of miscegenation (mixture) between the diverse ethnic groups that created the Brazilian nationality, the promotion and defense of *pardo-mestiça* identity and the recognition of *pardo-mestiços* as cultural and territorial inheritors of the people from which they are descended." Arguing against campaigns to "unmix" Brazilians and echoing nationalists from the past, the group's slogan announced: "*A miscigenação une a nação*" (Miscegenation unites the nation).[23]

---

[21] Roitman, "Hybridity, Mestizaje, and Montubios in Ecuador."

[22] For an analysis of the public battle between proponents and critics of affirmative action in Brazilian universities, see Bailey and Peria, "Racial Quotas and the Culture War in Brazilian Academia."

[23] http://www.nacaomestica.org/ Blog posts on the "Mestizo Nation" website appear in both Portuguese and English, with coverage of various issues related to perceived discrimination against "mixed" Brazilians.

The reaction against census reforms has emerged especially forcefully in Bolivia, where critics charge that the census has been deliberately designed to artificially inflate the size of the indigenous population and "invisibilize" mestizos.[24] Controversy over Bolivia's census categories escalated in anticipation of the 2012 census. At a public workshop on the 2012 census plans, a presenter argued for the inclusion of the "mestizo" category on the census:

> To deny the 'ethnic reality' of bio-racial (or bio-ethnic) miscegenation is to deny the right of an enormous share of the Bolivian population to have the ability or liberty to self-perceive and self-identify as a human group that is distinct from the Spanish or indigenous-originaries; yet neither better nor worse than any of the other ethnic groups. But that's not all. It is to deny "Mestizos" recognition as such and, thereby, to deny them direct access to social, economic and cultural opportunities on conditions equal to those now enjoyed by Indians and criollos (whites).[25]

The emergence of opposition to recent census reforms is hardly surprising. Indeed, the very democratization and politicization of the census that enabled the introduction of new questions on recent censuses opened the door to a backlash. Groups that have emerged to defend official recognition of mestizos use many of the same arguments invoked by Afrodescendant and indigenous groups to demand visibility on censuses. For these critics, official ethnoracial classification is not inherently problematic; it is the depreciation or negation of "mixed" categories in favor of "absolute" or "pure" categories that is cause for concern.

The initial wave of reactions to the twenty-first-century resurgence of official ethnoracial classification in Latin America serves to remind that whatever the impetus to their production, once created, official ethnoracial statistics may be put to varied ends.[26] The coming flood of ethnoracial statistics may be produced with the best of intentions, but there is nothing to stop their use toward projects that are directly at odds with the aims of those who produce them. The possibility for "misuse" of official ethnoracial statistics is not an argument against their production. But given the very mixed history of the use of racial statistics by states, scientists, and political leaders in the history of Latin America as well as in other

---

[24] For more on this debate, see Zuazo, "Q'ueste los mestizos."
[25] Pinto Mosqueira, "Las categorías identitarias en la boleta censal."
[26] Zuberi, Thicker Than Blood.

contexts, it is a development to be watched closely in the decades ahead. The routinized production of official ethnoracial statistics in twenty-first-century Latin America is sure to have unintended consequences; new official categories will help cultivate new collective identities and political constituencies, not all of whom will see eye to eye.

Developing with Identities

The contemporary politics of official ethnoracial classification in Latin America also diverge from historical precedent in a third critical respect. From the nineteenth century through to the latter part of the twentieth the descriptive and prescriptive objectives of national censuses were tightly coupled. Latin American censuses documented increasingly integrated, assimilated, and homogenous nations, and they charted the path forward for a nation construed as an increasingly unitary whole. In the latter part of the twentieth century and beginning of the twenty-first, the alignment between the descriptive and prescriptive objectives of censuses was disrupted. Contemporary census politics are fraught with a fundamental tension between the project of describing the nation in numbers and the project of prescribing its path to development.

In the early twenty-first century, national censuses described Latin American nations as they were reconceived in multicultural and pluriethnic terms. With nationhood thus redefined, the very notion of national development as a process construed to improve the condition of the population taken as a unitary whole appeared untenable. Echoing an earlier generation of feminist critiques of one-size-fits-all approaches to development, activists on behalf of ethnoracially defined collectivities demanded to know what groups of individuals reaped the benefits, and which inherited the costs, of any given development project. When, in the early 2000s, the cultivation of diversity itself became an internationally prescribed *objective* of "development," as described in chapter 7, the implication was that development should be pursued through targeted efforts to improve the lot of a population's constituent ethnoracial parts. In practice, such prescriptions often ran counter to longstanding approaches to social policy and development projects throughout the region. The unsurprising result: escalating tensions among actors in pursuit of alternative versions of progressive social policy, and competing visions of development.

One manifestation of this tension is the growth and tenor of demands to put newly available official ethnoracial data "to use." By the latter part of the 2000s, the multiplicity of calls to produce more and better data about ethnoracial differences within Latin American populations gave way to increasing demands to *do* things with the new data. Initially, this mostly translated into the production of official and scholarly reports focused on statistical inequality between ethnoracial categories on various indicators of material well-being. As the authors of an IDB-sponsored report pointed out, "The inclusion of the ethnic variable in censuses and surveys is pointless if it isn't used in analyses."[27] International and regional development agencies began to generate comprehensive reports on the condition of Afrodescendant or indigenous communities in particular Latin American countries and in comparative perspective. For example, ECLAC committed resources to the production of statistical reports on the status of indigenous and Afrodescendant youth in Latin America based on results from the 2000 censuses. The World Bank and agencies of the United Nations also sponsored the production of reports on various aspects of health, education, and living conditions of minority populations in several parts of Latin America.

The publication of official statistics that documented the existence and plight of myriad ethnoracial subpopulations across Latin America directly confronted official mythologies of homogenous—or gradually homogenizing—nations. The authors of this new wave of statistical reports often complemented the dry reporting of numerical facts with passionate recriminations of historical omissions. This practice is exemplified in the conclusion to a UN-sponsored statistical atlas of indigenous diversity in Latin America. The final words of the more than 1000-page tome decried the historic and continued ethnocide against indigenous pueblos: "After reviewing this atlas, no one in their right mind can continue with the refrain of calling Latin America the most culturally homogenous region on the planet." The atlas used recent census and other survey data to document the tremendous human diversity of Latin America, and to argue that much more diversity would have survived had it not been for the imposition of "an ethnocidal regime in Latin America, which, under pretext of equality before the law, forgot not only about difference but also about dignity." Among the techniques used by Latin American states to commit ethnocide, the author highlighted "statistical ethnocide, when the supposed objectivity of numbers invisibilizes individuals, families and even entire societies and peoples."[28] The author called out the symbolic violence of classificatory omission in the history of census taking in Latin America.

---

[27] Renshaw and Wray, "Indicadores de bienestar y pobreza indígena."
[28] The quotations in the paragraph come from López, L. "Epílogos," 1077.

Going forward, Latin American states' efforts to pursue "development" would only be recognized as legitimate to the extent that the diversity of their populations was explicitly taken into account.

The tension between new imperatives to attend to ethnoracial distinctions and disparities within the population and traditional approaches to development is also manifest in escalating battles over the implementation of affirmative action programs in several countries in the region. Armed with a growing number of official reports and social scientific analyses of ethnoracial disparities in various outcomes, activists and their allies within state governments began to push for targeted social policies to ameliorate ethnoracial inequalities. The increased availability of ethnoracial statistics bolstered efforts to expand the meaning and benefits of social citizenship to include targeted redress for inequality along ethnoracial lines. Statistical documentation of ethnoracial inequality supported calls for states to supplement legal promises of protection from discrimination with proactive, corrective, and reparative measures to reduce existing disparities of condition and opportunity. In contexts where social movement actors or their allies occupy positions within the state, policies that directly address ethnoracial inequality became a visible priority.

Ethnoracially targeted affirmative action policies are already in place in parts of Latin America and there is pressure from both domestic activists and international organizations to introduce such initiatives across the region. As of 2013, Brazil had gone farthest down this path, with a broad range of affirmative action initiatives in government agencies, university admissions, and industries such as fashion and television. Ethnoracially targeted affirmative action programs of various sorts were also in place or on political agendas in almost every other country in the region. These initiatives ranged from policies focused on health services, nutrition, housing, poverty alleviation, and land titling, to educational benefits and guaranteed political representation. International organizations such as the IAC champion such initiatives, and advocate for the dissemination of affirmative action policies to the entire region.

Affirmative action policies generally rely upon official ethnoracial statistics both to justify their introduction and to monitor the results of their implementation. The implementation of affirmative action programs thus draws attention to the politics of official ethnoracial classification, and inevitably raises thorny questions about who qualifies for such programs. In many parts of Latin America, ethnoracial boundaries and identities remain malleable, at least on the margins; individual classifications may shift based on the proximate geographic, interactional, or social context.

This is not to say that ethnoracial classification is infinitely fluid. Generally speaking, the ways that individuals classify themselves and others are not unmoored from physical appearances, cultural traits, or social conditions. But in daily life, ethnoracial distinctions are often drawn in continuous or relative terms. This state of affairs is a legacy of twentieth-century nationalist projects that avoided the institutionalization of individual racial categorization, while emphasizing the insignificance or transience of socially evident ethnoracial divides. Against this backdrop, policies that require individuals to be sorted into one discrete category or another generate controversy: How does one draw the line separating "Indian" from "mestizo"? Who is "brown" enough to qualify for programs targeting "blacks"?

Programs that tie resources or opportunities to categorical ethnoracial identification force a determination of who counts as what. In democratic contexts, this question almost inevitably opens the door to debates over *who decides* who counts as what. Participants in such debates may also question who decides which categorical distinctions count at all. The distributional aims of affirmative action programs tend to bring the selective and subjective nature of official classification schemes into clear focus. Reflecting the politics of their production, affirmative action programs—just like initiatives to collect ethnic and racial statistics—make some categorical divides self-evidently relevant, while obscuring others from view.

As ethnoracially targeted social programs spread, controversies over why and how states classify citizens by race or ethnicity will likely escalate. Critics of these programs will point to opportunistic self-identification by individuals who do not merit targeted benefits; they will note how official categories will create or grow constituencies along those categorical lines; and they will warn of unintended consequences of well-meaning policies, including the consolidation of rigid group boundaries and attendant polarization or fragmentation of national societies.[29]

Those who support the aims of targeted social policies are likely to voice concerns about official ethnoracial classification as well. Policymakers and activists will debate whether the categories used for implementation effectively funnel resources or opportunities to the intended beneficiaries. In Bolivia, for example, the "indigenous" category has become so expansive

---

[29] For discussion of arguments for and against affirmative action in Brazil, see Guimarães, *Racismo e Anti-racismo no Brasil*; Telles, *Race in Another America*; Bailey and Peria, "Racial Quotas and the Culture War in Brazilian Academia"; Bailey, *Legacies of Race*.

that some believe targeted policies may miss their mark. As anthropologist Andrew Canessa observed:

> In recent years... when being indigenous can qualify you for particular aid or presenting concerns through the language of indigeneity has greater impact, the identification of indigenous people has become problematic and contentious. In lowland areas of Bolivia, for example, in certain cases the number of people identifying as belonging to an indigenous group has more than doubled in two years; in others people continue to be unwilling to identify themselves as such because of the profound racism in those areas. In highland areas the people who are most likely to identify themselves as indigenous are educated urban intellectuals or political activists, not the Aymara-speaking rural peasants who follow 'traditional' lifestyles.[30]

The ethnic or racial categories used to implement targeted social policies will never correspond perfectly to all of the relationally determined categorical distinctions that are operative in the lives of individuals and communities. In some contexts, official ethnoracial categories may inadvertently exclude individuals who merit inclusion based on policy makers' intent. In others, official categories will be too broad, diffusing the impact of initiatives to address explicitly ethnoracial facets of poverty and inequality. In either case, the political character of official ethnoracial classification will be exposed, fueling tensions amid broader struggles over the meaning of social citizenship and distribution of its promised benefits.

Perhaps the most blatant manifestation of the tension between the new norms of multicultural and pluriethnic nationhood and traditional goals of national development can be seen in ongoing struggles over large-scale development projects in many parts of Latin America. To take just one prominent example, the massive Belo Monte dam project in Brazil has provoked resistance by small groups of indigenous people whose homes and livelihoods will be destroyed by completion of the project. Repeated occupations of a road leading to the construction site, and the extensive

---

[30] Canessa, "Who Is Indigenous?," 209. Canessa notes that 20.4 percent of those identified as indigenous in the 2001 census do not speak an indigenous language or belong to a recognized indigenous community. "Anecdotal evidence suggests that some members of this group identified as indigenous in order to express a political alignment with the broader political goals of the new indigeneity; concern for natural resources, globalization, and U.S. hegemony. Scale is important here: on a global level many mestizo-creole Bolivians may see themselves as indigenous in terms of world power relations and because an indigenous identification makes them specifically Bolivian; on a more local level the same individuals may not identify with specific indigenous groups or peoples." Canessa, "Who Is Indigenous?," 208–9; cf. Nagel, "American Indian Ethnic Renewal."

FIGURE 8.2 Protesting the Belo Monte Dam Project in Brazil, 2012.

SOURCE: Elizondo, Gabriel and Maria Elena Romero. "Brazil Tribes Occupy Contentious Dam Site." *Al Jazeera*, last modified June 30, 2012. http://www.aljazeera.com/indepth/features/2012/06/201263012941975547.html

international media coverage of the ongoing conflict, left the path to "development" unclear. The state could not both protect the "cultural liberty" of indigenous peoples and complete construction of the hydroelectric dam; one version of the meaning of "development" and one vision of Brazil's national future had to win out over the other. This point came across clearly in photographs of the occupations broadcast to news outlets around the world (for example, see figure 8.2).[31] Poignant images of feather-adorned indigenous people standing up to bulldozers capture real conflicts of interest that promises of "development with identity" cannot wish away.

The politics of official ethnoracial classification are deeply implicated in these emerging conflicts over the meaning and goals of development in twenty-first-century Latin America. New census questions and categories generate official ethnoracial statistics that can be used both as information and as ammunition by those on different sides of these disputes. In previous decades, the disaggregation of poverty and health statistics by sex revealed the gendered nature of inequality in Latin America. Such statistics helped

---

[31] Elizondo and Romero, "Brazil Tribes Occupy Contentious Dam Site."

support a shift toward development strategies focused on women's roles in the distribution of scarce resources within families and communities. The coming flood of racial and ethnic statistics will likewise further expose severe ethnic and racial inequalities in some regions, and provide support for development project proposals that aim to reduce them. In some contexts, these projects may respond to real and pressing needs of historically neglected populations. In others, they may amount to what anthropologist Charles Hale terms "multicultural neoliberalism," serving primarily to *appear* to address inequalities while effectively dissipating bottom-up pressure for development strategies that would entail more substantive structural change.[32]

Meanwhile, international financial institutions and development organizations have announced their commitment to support projects that advance "development with identity." In practice, this will likely mean an increasing share of available resources are steered toward projects that promise to directly address the needs of indigenous or Afrodescendant communities (possibly sparking debates about their classification as such, as per the discussion above). Already, it means greater attention to the disparate impacts of development projects that are going to be undertaken anyway. As noted in chapter 7, the IDB and the World Bank now require an assessment of how funded projects will affect indigenous or Afrodescendant communities as a condition for loans. And with "cultural liberty" and reductions of ethnoracial inequality as explicit goals of development, ethnic and racial statistics become essential to assessment of project outcomes.

The institutionalized requirement to evaluate the effects of development projects on indigenous or Afrodescendant communities may resonate with some governments in the region. It may even be explicitly endorsed by those most open to the discursive embrace of the new international norms of multiethnic nationhood. But beyond the surface, such requirements will translate into unforeseen obstacles for the development plans of national governments. Many if not most large-scale infrastructural development projects in planning or in progress in the region already do or will impose disparate burdens on officially recognized indigenous or Afrodescendant communities. These are not all positive-sum games; there will be winners and losers as these projects are realized. The tensions and, in some cases, irreconcilable conflicts between commitments to "cultural liberty" and the broader and more traditional goals of "development" are likely to become a regular source of political conflict in Latin America as the twenty-first century unfolds.

---

[32] Hale, "Does Multiculturalism Menace?"; see also Anderson, M., "Garifuna Activism and the Corporatist Honduran State since the 2009 Coup."

Thus, the most recent chapter in the long history of official ethnoracial classification in Latin America has opened up an array of contentious sociological, political, and ethical issues. If history is any guide, the continued evolution and influence of international norms of modern nationhood, and of international standards for the proper measures and goals of development, will shape the dynamics and outcomes of these political struggles going forward. Just how these struggles will play out in different circumstances is impossible to predict. But one thing seems clear: the politics of official ethnoracial classification will be central to these unfolding disputes.

APPENDIX | The Database on Diversity in Latin American Censuses

SEVERAL OF THE TABLES that appear in this book were constructed from information that I compiled in a database on Diversity in Latin American Censuses (the D-LAC database). The database contains records for national censuses conducted or attempted in Latin America from the early nineteenth century through 2013. The records are organized by country and census year, with information about each census gleaned from a combination of sources including primary sources (copies of original census schedules and enumerator instructions), published census reports (including official descriptions of methods of data collection), published statistics (from which the content of the census questionnaire can sometimes be deduced), and secondary sources (including bibliographic surveys of Latin American censuses and historical monographs that discuss specific censuses in individual countries).

The information contained in the various sources used to construct the database is mostly consistent, but in some cases there are inconsistencies across types of sources. For example, a secondary source may report that a given census did not collect information about indigenous peoples, while a copy of the original enumerator instructions for the census indicates otherwise. Primary sources held precedence in my coding of censuses for all cases in which original or verifiable copies of original documents could be located. For many of the nineteenth- and early twentieth century censuses, primary materials are unavailable or incomplete. In these cases, I relied on information from published census reports, other official contemporary documents, and secondary sources (in that order), to determine what questions were asked and what categories used to enumerate a population in a given census.

For the purpose of presenting information in the tables found in this book, as well as for the historical analyses more generally, I had to make a number of decisions about which censuses to include and how to code the types of questions they used. For example, I had to decide whether to consider censuses that aspired to national coverage but fell far short in practice as "national censuses" for the purpose of my analysis (short answer: yes). I describe my general procedure for constructing each table found in this book in the chapters where the tables appear. Records describing the basis for coding decisions for each individual cell in each table and the sources upon which the decisions were based are contained in the D-LAC database. Below, I note some general clarifications about the content and coding of information reported in the tables.

One important clarification relates to the selection of censuses for inclusion in the tables. Many of the early efforts by Latin American states to take national censuses were basically failures, in terms of the amount or quality of information actually collected about the population. For this reason, in later years, national statistics offices often did not recognize the first attempts to take national censuses in the nineteenth or early twentieth centuries as national censuses at all. In general, I coded early efforts to conduct national censuses as such, regardless of their level of success or, relatedly, whether they were subsequently disowned by a more modern incarnation of a given country's national statistics agency. This means that for some countries, I have shaded a cell to indicate that a national census was attempted in a decade that is prior to the first officially recognized national census. This is the case, for example, for Chile in the 1830s and 1840s. Chile's statistics agency (INE) considers the 1854 census to be the country's first national census. Based on the work of historian Andrés Jaramillo, however, I included Chile's aspiring national censuses in the 1830s and 1840s in my set of national censuses analyzed in this book. On the other hand, there are also some known nineteenth-century censuses that do not appear in the tables because they did not aim for national coverage. This includes, for example, the 1905 census of the Callao province of Peru, the 1920 census of Callao and Lima, and two partial censuses in Uruguay in the 1880s.

Given my decision rule for including censuses in the tables for this book, Cuba's nineteenth-century censuses posed a distinctive challenge. Several censuses of Cuba conducted prior to the 1900s aspired to comprehensive coverage of the population, but since Cuba did not become independent until 1898, they were colonial censuses, not national ones. In the tables, I decided to shade the cells for Cuba's nineteenth century censuses to avoid the appearance that no general census was taken during those decades, even though technically those cells should be marked to distinguish them as colonial, not national, censuses.

Another important clarification is that some countries, in some periods, conducted more than one national census within a decade. The coding of individual cells in the tables is based on: (1) whether a country took a national census in that decade, and (2) what was asked in the census and/or how the results were reported. In the following cases, a country took more than one census in a single decade: Bolivia (1831, 1835); Colombia (1912 and 1918); Cuba (1841 and 1846, both colonial censuses); Honduras (1881 and 1887; 1901 and 1905; 1910 and 1916; 1930 and 1935; 1940 and 1945); Uruguay (1841 and 1846; 1881 and 1887); Venezuela (1920 and 1926). For these cases, the cell for the decade in question in all tables is coded based on information in *either* census for a given decade. Thus, for example, in table 6.1, the cell for these countries/decades is coded as "R" if either census taken within a given decade included a race or color question. The same general rule applies for coding of these cells for other types of census questions in subsequent tables in the book.

A final set of clarifications pertains to coding decisions related to the types of questions and categories about ethnoracial diversity that appeared on individual censuses. In some of the nineteenth and early twentieth-century censuses, there are official reports or secondary sources that state that "race" data were collected, but the original census forms or instructions to enumerators could not be located. In these cases, the respective cell in tables 3.3. and 6.1 is marked "R" while the cell in tables 6.2b has a question mark, because insufficient information is available to determine how the question was asked. In some cases, meanwhile, secondary reports indicate that enumerators collected information about indigenous peoples in certain provinces, even though the official enumerator instructions and the published national census results do not distinguish indigenous peoples from others in the population. According to Goyer and Domschke (*The Handbook of National Population Censuses*), this was the case, for example, in Chile's 1870 census. In the tables in chapter 6, a cell only indicates statistical visibility if the national census questionnaire and/or published results differentiate indigenous or Afrodescendant peoples within the population. When a statistics agency conducted a separate survey of indigenous or Afrodescendant populations in conjunction with a national census, this is indicated with an "S" code in tables 6.1a and 6.1b. Types of questions used within these separate censuses were not coded. When other codes appear within the same cell as an "S" code, this indicates that those other questions were asked on the national census.

BIBLIOGRAPHY

Abercrombie, Thomas. "Mothers and Mistresses of the Urban Bolivian Public Sphere: Postcolonial Predicament and National Imaginary in Oruro's Carnival." In *After Spanish Rule: Postcolonial Predicaments in the Americas,* edited by Mark Thurner and Andrés Guerrero, 176–220. Durham, NC: Duke University Press, 2003.

Afrochilenos...hacia la inclusión y el reconocimiento. "Exclusión de los afrodescendientes en Chile en el próximo censo nacional...¿ignorancia o racismo?" Blog entry by unnamed writer on *Afrochilenos...hacia la inclusión y el reconocimiento* (blog), September 20, 2011. http://afrochileno.blogspot.com/.

Agassiz, Louis J. R. and Elizabeth C. Agassiz. *A Journey in Brazil.* Boston: Ticknor and Fields, 1868.

Agudelo, Carlos. "The Afro-Guatemalan Political Mobilization: Between Identity Construction Processes, Global Influences, and Institutionalization." In *Black Social Movements in Latin America: From Monocultural Mestizaje to Multiculturalism,* edited by Jean Muteba Rahier, 75–91. New York: Palgrave MacMillan, 2012.

Aguirre Beltrán, Gonzalo. *La Población Negra de México, 1519–1810: Estudio Ethnohistórico.* Mexico City: Ediciones Fuente Cultural, 1946.

Albo, Xavier C. and Barrios, Franz X. *Por una Bolivia Plurinacional e Intercultural con Autonomías.* La Paz, Bolivia: PNUD Bolivia, 2006.

Alden, Dauril. "The Population of Brazil in the Late Eighteenth Century: a Preliminary Study." *Hispanic American Historical Review* 43, 2 (1963): 173–205.

Alonso, William and Paul Starr. "Introduction." In *The Politics of Numbers,* edited by William Alonso and Paul Starr, 1–6. New York: Russell Sage Foundation, 1987.

———, eds. *The Politics of Numbers.* New York: Russell Sage Foundation, 1987.

Althouse, Aaron P. "Contested Mestizos, Alleged Mulattos: Racial Identity and Caste Hierarchy in Eighteenth Century Pátzcuaro, Mexico." *The Americas* 62, 2 (2005): 151–75.

Alves, Marilda D. *O Desenvolvimento do Sistema Estatístico Nacional.* Rio de Janeiro: Fundação Instituto Brasileiro de Geografia e Estatistica, 1988.

Anaya, S. James. *Indigenous Peoples in International Law.* 2nd ed. New York: Oxford University Press, 2004.

Anderson, Benedict. *Imagined Communities: Reflections on the Origin and Spread of Nationalism.* London: Verso, 1991.

Anderson, Margo J. *The American Census: A Social History*. New Haven, CT: Yale University Press, 1988.

———. "The History of Women and the History of Statistics." *Journal of Women's History* 4, 1 (1992): 14–36.

Anderson, Margo J. and Stephen E. Fienberg. *Who Counts? The Politics of Census-Taking in Contemporary America*. New York: Russell Sage Foundation, 2000.

Anderson, Mark D. "Garifuna Activism and the Corporatist Honduran State Since the 2009 Coup" in *Black Social Movements in Latin America: From Monocultural Mestizaje to Multiculturalism*, edited by Jean Muteba Rahier, 53–73. New York: Palgrave MacMillan, 2012.

Andrews, George R. *Afro-Latin America, 1800–2000*. New York: Oxford University Press, 2004.

———. *Blacks and Whites in São Paulo, Brazil 1888–1988*. Madison: University of Wisconsin Press, 1991.

———. *The Afro-Argentines of Buenos Aires, 1800–1900*. Madison: University of Wisconsin Press, 1980.

Aparicio Wilhelmi, Marco. *Los Pueblos Indígenas y el Estado: El Reconocimiento Constitucional de los Derechos Indígenas en América Latina*. Barcelona: Editorial Cedecs, 2001.

Appadurai, Arjun. "Number in the Colonial Imagination." In *Modernity at Large: Cultural Dimensions of Globalization*, 114–35. Minneapolis: University of Minnesota Press, 1996.

Appelbaum, Nancy. *Muddied Waters: Race, Region, and Local History in Colombia, 1846–1948*. Durham, NC: Duke University Press, 2003.

Appelbaum, Nancy, Anne S. Macpherson, and Karin Alejandra Rosemblatt. *Race and Nation in Modern Latin America*. Chapel Hill: University of North Carolina Press, 2003.

Arcaya Urrutia, Pedro M., ed. *Censo de Venezuela en 1807*. Caracas: Italgráfica S.A., 1996.

Argentina. Comisión Directiva del Censo. *Segundo Censo de la República Argentina, Mayo 10 de 1895*. Buenos Aires: Taller Tip. de la Penitenciaria Nacional, 1898.

———. *Tercer Censo Nacional de la República Argentina*. Buenos Aires: G. Pesce, 1914.

———. *Tercer Censo Nacional*, levantado el 1° de junio de 1914, ordenado por la Ley 9108 durante la presidencia del Dr. Roque Saenz Peña, ejecutado cuando era president el Dr. Victorino de la Plaza. Comisión nacional: Alberto B. Martínez (president), Francisco Latzina, Emilio Lahitte (vocals). Buenos Aires, Talleres Gráficos de L.J. Rosso y Cia, 1916–1919, vol. 1.

———. Dirección General de Territorios Nacionales. *Censo de Población de los Territorios Nacionales, República Argentina, 1912*. Ministerio del Interior. Buenos Aires: Imp. G. Kraft, 1914.

Argentina. Instituto Nacional de Estadísticas y Censos. "Afrodescendientes." *Censo 2010: Año del Bicentario*. No date. http://www.censo2010.indec.gov.ar/index_afro.asp.

Argentina. Superintendente del Censo. *Primer Censo de la República Argentina Verificado en los Dias 15, 16 y 17 de Septiembre de 1869 Bajo la Dirección de Diego G. De La Fuente, Superintendente Del Censo*. Buenos Aires: Impr. del Porvenir, 1872.

———. *Segundo Censo de la República Argentina, mayo 10 d 1895, decretado en la administración del Dr. Saenz Peña, verificado en la del Dr. Uriburu. Comisión directive: Diego de la Fuente (president); Gabriel Carrasco, Alberto B. Martínez (vocals)*. Buenos Aires: Taller Tipográfico de la Penitenciaría Nacional, 1898.

Arguedas, Alcides. *Pueblo Enfermo*, 3rd ed. Santiago: Editorial Ercilla, 1937.

Arretz, Carmen, Rolando Mellafe, and Jorge L. Somoza. *Demografía Histórica En America Latina: Fuentes y Métodos*. San José, Costa Rica: Centro Latinoamericano de Demografía, 1983.

Azevedo, Aloysio Villela de. *Os Recenseamentos no Brasil*. Rio de Janeiro: IBGE, 1990.

Azevedo, Fernando de, ed. *As Ciências No Brazil*. São Paulo: Edições Melhoramentos, 1955.

———. *Brazilian Culture: An Introduction to the Study of Culture in Brazil*. Translated by William Rex Crawford. New York: MacMillan, 1950.

Badie, Bertrand. *The Imported State: the Westernization of the Political Order*. Stanford, CA: Stanford University Press, 2000.

Bailey, Stanley R. *Legacies of Race: Identities, Attitudes, and Politics in Brazil*. Stanford, CA: Stanford University Press, 2009.

Bailey, Stanley R. and Michelle Peria. "Racial Quotas and the Culture War in Brazilian Academia." *Sociology Compass* 4, 8 (2010): 592–604.

Banton, Michael. "Analytical and Folk Concepts of Race and Ethnicity." *Ethnic and Racial Studies* 2, 2 (1979): 127–38.

———. "Finding, and Correcting, My Mistakes." *Sociology* 39, 3 (2005): 463–479.

———. "International Norms and Latin American States' Policies on Indigenous Peoples." *Nations and Nationalism* 2, 1 (1996): 89–103.

———. *International Politics of Race*. Cambridge, MA: Polity Press, 2004.

———. *Racial Theories*. Cambridge: Cambridge University Press, 1987.

Barickman, Bert J. "Reading the 1835 Censuses from Bahia: Citizenship, Kinship, Slavery, and Household in Early Nineteenth-Century Brazil." *The Americas* 59, 3 (2003): 287–323.

Barié, Cletus Gregor. *Pueblos Indígenas y Derechos Constitucionales en América Latina: un Panorama*, 2nd ed. La Paz, Bolivia: Génesis, 2003. http://www.acnur.org/paginas/?id_pag=7562.

Barkan, Elazar. *The Retreat of Scientific Racism: Changing Concepts of Race in Britain and the United States Between the World Wars*. Cambridge: Cambridge University Press, 1992.

Barman, Roderick J. *Brazil: The Forging of a Nation, 1798–1852*. Stanford, CA: Stanford University Press, 1988.

———. "The Brazilian Peasantry Reexamined: The Implications of the Quebra-Quilo Revolt, 1874–1875." *Hispanic American Historical Review* 57, 3 (1977): 401–24.

Barreiro, José. 1989. "Indians in Cuba." *Cultural Survival Quarterly* 13, 3 (1989). http://www.culturalsurvival.org/publications/cultural-survival-quarterly/cuba/indians-cuba.

Barrientos, Pilar. "Are There Still 'Indians' in Argentina? Indigenous Peoples and the 2001 and 2010 Population Censuses." In *Everlasting Countdowns: Race, Ethnicity and National Censuses in Latin American States*, edited by Luis Fernando Angosto Ferrández and Sabine Kradolfer, 41–68. Newcastle upon Tyne: Cambridge Scholars Publishing, 2012.

Basadre, Jorge. *Chile, Peru y Bolivia Independientes*. Barcelona: Salvat Editores, 1948.
Basarás, Joachin Antonio de. *Origen, costumbres, y estado presente de mexicanos y philipinos*. New York: Hispanic Society of America, 1763.
Bashford, Alison. "Internationalism, Cosmopolitanism, and Eugenics." In *The Oxford Handbook of the History of Eugenics*, edited by Alison Bashford and Philippa Levine, 154–69. New York: Oxford University Press, 2010.
Batley, Richard. "The Politics of Administrative Allocation." *Urban Political Economy and Social Theory: Critical Essays in Urban Studies*, edited by Ray Forrest, Jeffrey W. Henderson, and Peter Williams, 78–111. Aldershot, UK: Gower, 1981.
Bauman, Zygmunt. *Modernity and the Holocaust*. Ithaca, NY: Cornell University Press, 1989.
Beattie, Peter. *The Tribute of Blood: Army, Honor, Race, and Nation in Brazil 1864–1945*. Durham, NC: Duke University Press, 2001.
Bendix, Reinhard. *Kings or People: Power and the Mandate to Rule*. Berkeley: University of California Press, 1978.
Benton, Joshiah H., Jr. *Early Census Making in Massachusetts 1643–1765*. Boston: C.E. Goodspeed, 1905.
Benton, Lauren. *Law and Colonial Cultures: Legal Regimes in World History, 1400–1900*. Cambridge: Cambridge University Press, 2002.
Bermúdez, Eduardo and Maria. M. Suárez. "Venezuela." In *No Longer Invisible: Afro-Latin Americans Today*, edited by Minority Rights Group, 243–69. London: Minority Rights Publications, 1995.
Biernacki, Richard. *Reinventing Evidence in Social Inquiry: Decoding Facts and Variables*. New York: Palgrave Macmillan, 2012.
Blanco, Jacqueline. "Logros y Contradicciones de la Jurisdicción Especial Indigena en Colombia" *Revista Diálogo de Saberes* 24 (2006): 51–68.
Boas, Franz. "Modern Populations of America." In *Proceedings of the Second Pan American Scientific Congress*, vol. 1, December 28, 1915, edited by Glen Levin Swiggett. Washington, DC: Government Printing Office, 1917.
Bolivia. Oficina Nacional de Inmigración, Estadística y Propaganda Geográfica. *Censo general de la población de la República de Bolivia según el empadronamento de 1.0 de septiembre de 1900*. La Paz, Bolivia: Taller Tipo-Litográfico de J.M. Gamorra, 1902–04. [1973].
Bonfil Batalha, Guillermo. *Utopía y Revolución: el Pensamiento Político Contemporáneo de los Indios en América Latina*. Mexico, D.F.: Editorial Nueva Imagen, 1981.
Bonilla-Silva, Eduardo. "The Essential Social Fact of Race." *American Sociological Review* 64, 6 (1999): 899–906.
———. "We Are All Americans!: The Latin Americanization of Racial Stratification in the USA." *Race & Society* 5 (2002): 3–16.
Borges, Dain. "'Puffy, Ugly, Slothful and Inert': Degeneration in Brazilian Social Thought, 1880–1940." *Journal of Latin American Studies* 25 (1993): 235–56.
Botelho, Tarcisio Rodrigues. "População e Nação no Brasil do Século XIX." PhD diss., Universidade de São Paulo, 1998.
Bourdieu, Pierre. "Identity and Representation." In *Language and Symbolic Power*, edited by John B. Thompson, 220–88. Translated by Gino Raymond and Matthew Adamson. Cambridge, MA: Harvard University Press, 1991.

———. *Pascalian Meditations*. Stanford, CA: Stanford University Press, 2000.

———. "Rethinking the State: Genesis and Structure of the Bureaucratic Field." In *State/Culture: State-Formation after the Cultural Turn*, edited by George Steinmetz, 53–75. Ithaca, NY: Cornell University Press, 1999.

———. "Social Space and Symbolic Power." In *In Other Words: Essays Towards a Reflexive Sociology*, 123–39. Translated by Matthew Adamson. Stanford, CA: Stanford University Press, 1990.

———. "The Social Space and the Genesis of Groups." *Theory and Society* 14, 6 (1985): 723–44.

Bourdieu, Pierre and Loïc Wacquant. *An Invitation to Reflexive Sociology*. Chicago: University of Chicago Press, 1992.

———. "On the Cunning of Imperialist Reason." *Theory, Culture & Society* 16, 1 (1999): 41–58.

Bourguet, M.-N. *Déchiffrer La France: La Statistique Départementale à L'Époque Napoléonienne*. Paris: Editions des Archives Contemporaines, 1988.

Boxer, Charles R. *Race Relations in the Portuguese Colonial Empire, 1415–1825*. Oxford: Clarendon Press, 1963.

———. "The Colour Question in the Portuguese Empire, 1415–1825." *Proceedings of the British Academy* 47 (1961): 113–38.

Brading, David A. "Nationalism and State-Building in Latin American History." *Ibero-Amerikanisches Archiv* 20, 1–2 (1994): 83–108.

Brazil. Conselho Nacional de Estatística. Serviço Nacional de Recenseamento. "Métodos dos Censos de População das Nações Americanas." In *Documentos Censitários*, Série D, n.1. Rio de Janeiro: Conselho Nacional de Estatística, 1952.

Brazil. Directoria Geral de Estatística. *Boletim Commemorativo da Exposição Nacional de 1908*. Rio de Janeiro: Typographia da Estatística, 1908.

———. *Recenseamento da população do Império do Brazil a que se procedeu no dia 10 de agosto de 1872*. Rio de Janeiro: Leuzinger e Filhos, 1873–1876.

———. *Recenseamento do Brazil realizado em 1 de setembro de 1920*. Rio de Janeiro: Typografia da Estatística, 1922.

———. *Relatorio apresentado à Assembléa Geral Legislativa na primeira sessão da nona legislatura pelo Ministro e Secretário de Estado dos Negócios do Império, Francisco Goncalves Martins*. Rio de Janeiro: Typographia Nacional, 1853.

———. *Relatorio. Trabalhos Estatísticos. Apresentado ao Illm e Exm. Sr. Conselheiro Dr. João Alfredo Corrêa de Oliveira, Ministro e Secretario D'Estado dos Negocios do Império Pelo Director Geral Interino Dr. José Maria do Coutto*. Rio de Janeiro: Typographia do Hypolito José Pinto, 1873.

———. *Relatorio. Trabalhos Estatísticos. Apresentado ao Illm e Exm. Sr. Conselheiro Dr. João Alfredo Corrêa de Oliveira, Ministro e Secretario D'Estado dos Negocios do Império Pelo Director Geral Conselheiro Manoel Francisco Correia*. Rio de Janeiro: Typographia Franco-Americana, 1874.

Brazil. Ministerio do Interior. *Relatorio apresentado ao Presidente da República dos Estados Unidos do Brasil pelo Dr. João Barbalho Uchôa Cavalcanti, Ministro do Estado dos Negocios do Interior em maio de 1891*. Rio de Janeiro: Imprensa Nacional, 1891.

Brewer-Carías, Allan R. *Las Constituciones de Venezuela: Estudio Preliminar*. Madrid: Centro de Estudios Constitucionales, 1985.

Bromley, Rosemary D. F. "Parish Registers as a Source in Latin American Demographic and Historical Research." *Bulletin of the Society for Latin American Studies* 19 (1974): 14–21.

Bronfman, Alejandra. *Measures of Equality: Social Science, Citizenship, and Race in Cuba, 1902–1940*. Chapel Hill: University of North Carolina Press, 2004.

Brubaker, Rogers. "Ethnicity without Groups." *Archives Européennes de Sociologie* XLIII, 2 (2002): 163–189.

———. "The Manichean Myth: Rethinking the Distinction between 'Civic' and 'Ethnic' Nationalism." In *Nation and National Identity: The European Experience in Perspective*, edited by Hanspeter Kriesi, Klaus Armingeon, Hannes Siegrist, and Andreas Wimmer, 55–71. Zurich: Rüegger, 1999.

———. *Nationalism Reframed*. Cambridge: Cambridge University Press, 1996.

———. *Citizenship and Nationhood in France and Germany*. Cambridge, MA: Harvard University Press, 1992.

Brubaker, Rogers, Mara Loveman, and Peter Stamatov. "Ethnicity as Cognition." *Theory and Society* 33 (2004): 31–64.

Brubaker, Rogers, Margit Feischmidt, Jon Fox, and Liana Grancea. *Nationalist Politics and Everyday Ethnicity in a Transylvanian Town*. Princeton, NJ: Princeton University Press, 2006.

Brysk, Alison. *From Tribal Village to Global Village: Indian Rights and International Relations in Latin America*. Stanford, CA: Stanford University Press, 2000.

Brysk, Alison and Carol Wise, "Liberalization and Ethnic Conflict in Latin America," *Studies in Comparative International Development* 32, 2 (1997): 76–105.

Bulmer-Thomas, Victor. *The Economic History of Latin America since Independence*. Cambridge: Cambridge University Press, 2003.

Bunge, Carlos Octavio. *Nuestra América*. Barcelona: Henrich y ca, 1903.

Burkholder, Mark A. and Lyman L. Johnson. *Colonial Latin America*, 3rd ed. New York: Oxford University Press, 1998.

Burleigh, Michael and Wolfgang Wippermann. *The Racial State: Germany, 1933–1945*. Cambridge: Cambridge University Press, 1991.

Buvinić, Mayra, and Jacqueline Mazza, eds. *Social Inclusion and Economic Development in Latin America*. Washington, DC: Inter-American Development Bank, 2004.

Cahill, David. "Colour by Numbers: Racial and Ethnic Categories in the Viceroyalty of Peru, 1532–1824." *Journal of Latin American Studies* 26 (1994): 325–46.

Calhoun, Craig. "'Belonging' in the Cosmopolitan Imaginary." *Ethnicities* 3, 4 (2003): 531–68.

———. *Nationalism*. Minneapolis: University of Minnesota Press, 1997.

Camargo, Alexandre de Paiva Rio. "Classificações Raciais e Formação do Campo Estatístico no Brasil (1872–1940)." In *Estatísticas nas Américas: por uma Agenda de Estudos Históricos Comparados*, edited by Nelson de Castro Senra and Alexandre de Paiva Rio Camargo, 229–64. Rio de Janeiro: Instituto Brasileiro de Geografia e Estatística, 2010.

Canadian Foundation for the Americas. "Report from the March 2nd 2006 Ottawa Roundtable 'Supporting Afro-Latino Communities, Is There A Role for Canada?'" FOCAL, Canadian Foundation for the Americas. 2006. http://www.focal.ca/pdf/focal_roundtable_jul06.pdf.

Canessa, Andrew. "Who Is Indigenous? Self-Identification, Indigeneity, and Claims to Justice in Contemporary Bolivia." *Urban Anthropology* 36, 3 (2007): 195–237.

Caplan, Jane and John Torpey. "Introduction." In *Documenting Individual Identity: The Development of State Practices in the Modern World*, edited by Jane Caplan and John Torpey, 1–12. Princeton, NJ: Princeton University Press, 2001.

Cardoso, Fernando Henrique and Enzo Faletto. *Dependency and Development in Latin America*. Berkeley: University of California Press, 1979.

Carnegie Endowment for International Peace. *The International Conferences of American States, 1889–1928: A Collection of the Conventions, Recommendations, Resolutions, Reports, and Motions Adopted by the First Six International Conferences of the American States, and Documents Relating to the Organization of the Conferences.* New York: Oxford University Press, 1931.

Carvalho, José Murilo de. *Os Bestializados. O Rio de Janeiro e a República Que Não Foi.* São Paulo: Companhia das Letras, 1987.

Castelló Yturbide, Teresa. "La indumentaria de las castas del mestizaje." *Artes de México: La pintura de castas* 8 (1990): 73–80.

Castillo Olivares, Mauricio. "INE realizará estudio sobre los afrodescendientes," *El Morro cotudo*, October 28, 2011, http://www.elmorrocotudo.cl/noticia/sociedad/ine-realizara-estudio-sobre-los-afrodescendientes.

Castleman, Bruce A. "Social Climbers in a Colonial Mexican City: Individual Mobility within the Sistema de Castas in Orizaba, 1777–1791." *Colonial Latin American Review* 10, 2 (2001): 229–49.

———. *Building the King's Highway: Labor, Society, and Family on Mexico's Caminos Reales, 1757–1804*. Tucson, AZ: University of Arizona Press, 2005.

———. "Workers, Work, and Community in Bourbon Mexico: Road Laborers on the Camino Real, 1757–1804." PhD diss., University of California, Riverside, 1998.

Centeno, Miguel A. "Blood and Debt: War and Taxation in Nineteenth-Century Latin America." *American Journal of Sociology* 102, 6 (1997): 1565–605.

———. *Blood and Debt: War and the Nation State in Latin America*. University Park, PA: Pennsylvania State University Press, 2002.

Centeno, Miguel A. and Fernando López-Alves, eds. *The Other Mirror: Grand Theory through the Lens of Latin America*. Princeton, NJ: Princeton University Press, 2001.

Chace, Russell E. "Protest in Post-Emancipation Dominica: The 'Guerre Negre' of 1844." *Journal of Caribbean History* 23, 2 (1989): 118–41.

Chackiel, Juan. "Censuses in Latin America: New Approaches." Paper presented at the Symposium on Global Review of 2000 Round of Population and Housing Censuses: Mid-Decade Assessment and Future Prospects, New York, August 7–10, 2001. http://unstats.un.org/unsd/demographic/meetings/egm/symposium2001/docs/symposium_14.htm.

Chalhoub, Sidney. *Visões da liberdade: Uma Historia das Últimas Décadas da Escravidão na Corte*. São Paulo: Companhia das Letras, 1998.

———. *Race and Closs in Colonial Oaxaca*. Stanford, CA: Stanford University Press, 1978.

Chance, John K. and William B. Taylor. "Estate and Class in a Colonial City: Oaxaca in 1792." *Comparative Studies in Society and History* 19 (1977): 454–87.

Charier, Alain. *Le Mouvement Noir au Vénézuela: Revendication Identitaire et Modernité Venezuela*. Paris: Harmattan, 2000.

Charney, Paul. *Indian Society in the Valley of Lima, Peru, 1524–1824*, Lanham, MD: University Press of America, 2001.

Chatterjee, Partha. *Nationalist Thought and the Colonial World: A Derivative Discourse?* Princeton, NJ: Princeton University Press, 1986.

Chesire, Edward. *The Results of the Census of Great Britain in 1851. With a Description of the Machinery and the Processes Employed to Obtain the Returns*. London: John William Parker and Son, 1854.

Chevalier, François. "Official *Indigenismo* in Peru in 1920: Origins, Significance, and Socioeconomic Scope." In *Race and Class in Latin America*, edited by Magnus Mörner, 184–96. New York: Institute of Latin American Studies, Columbia University, 1970.

Chile. Comisión Central del Censo. *Censo de la República de Chile levantado el 28 de noviembre de 1907*. Santiago, Chile: Sociedad "Impr. Universo," 1908.

Chile. Dirección General de Estadística. *Censo de población de la República de Chile levantado el 15 de diciembre de 1920*. Santiago, Chile: Soc. imp. Y litografía Universo, 1925.

Chile. Instituto Nacional de Estadísticas. *Retratos de nuestra identidad: los censos de población en Chile y su evolución histórica hacia el Bicentenario*. Santiago, Chile: FEYSER Ltda, 2009.

Chile. Ministerio de Planificación y Cooperación. *Ley Indígena*. Ley N° 19.253, Published 05.10.1993. Effective 28.09.1993. Last modified 13.11.1998, Ley 19.587.

Chile. Oficina Central de Estadística. *Censo general de la República de Chile levantado el 19 de abril de 1865*. Santiago, Chile: Imprenta Nacional, 1866.

Clark, A. Kim. "Race, 'Culture,' and Mestizaje: The Statistical Construction of the Ecuadorian Nation, 1930–1950" *Journal of Historical Sociology*, 11, 2 (2002): 185–211.

Coatsworth, John H. and Alan M. Taylor, eds. *Latin America and the World Economy since 1800*. Cambridge, MA: Harvard University Press, 1998.

Cole, Jeffrey A. *The Potosí Mita, 1573–1700: Compulsory Indian Labor in the Andes*, Stanford, CA: Stanford University Press, 1985.

Cole, Joshua H. *The Power of Large Numbers: Population, Politics, and Gender in Nineteenth-Century France*. Ithaca, NY: Cornell University Press, 2000.

Colombia. Ministerio de Gobierno. Pedro Maria Carreño. *Censo general de la República de Colombia, levantado el 5 de marzo de 1912*. Bogotá, Colombia: Imprenta Nacional, 1912.

Consejo Latinoamericano de Ciencias Sociales. *Fuentes para la demografía histórica de América Latina*. Mexico City: Celade, 1975.

Contreras, Carlos Alberto and Peter L. Reich. "Numbers and the State: An Overview of Government Statistical Compilation in Mexico Since the Colonial Period." In *Statistical Abstract of Latin America*, vol. 31, edited by James W. Wilkie, Carlos Alberto Contreras, and Catherine Komisaruk, 1251–62. Los Angeles: UCLA Latin American Center Publications, University of California, 1995.

Cook, Sherbourne F. and Woodrow W. Borah. *Essays in Population History: Mexico and the Caribbean*, vol. 1. Berkeley: University of California Press, 1971.

———. *Essays in Population History: Mexico and the Caribbean*, vol. 2. Berkeley: University of California Press, 1974.

———. "The Historical Demography of Aboriginal and Colonial America: An Attempt at Perspective." In *The Native Population of the Americas in 1492*, edited by William M. Denevan, 13–34. Madison: University of Wisconsin Press, 1976.

Cook-Martín, David and David Fitzgerald. "Liberalism and the Limits of Inclusion: Race and Immigration Law in the Americas, 1850–2000." *Journal of Interdisciplinary History* 41, 1 (2010): 7–25.

Cooper, Frederick. "Race, Ideology and the Perils of Comparative History." *American Historical Review* 101, 4 (1996): 1122–38.

Cooper, Frederick and Ann L. Stoler. "Introduction. Tensions of Empire: Colonial Control and Visions of Rule." *American Ethnologist* 16, 4 (1989): 609–21.

Cornell, Stephen and Douglas Hartmann. *Ethnicity and Race: Making Identities in a Changing World*. Thousand Oaks, CA: Pine Forge Press, 1998.

Corradi, Juan E., Patricia Weiss Fagen, and Manuel Antonio Garretón. *Fear at the Edge: State Terror and Resistance in Latin America*. Berkeley: University of California Press, 1992.

Costa, Emilia Viotti da. "The Myth of Racial Democracy: A Legacy of the Empire." In *The Brazilian Empire: Myths and Histories*, 2nd ed., edited by Emilia Viotti da Costa, 234–46. Chapel Hill: University of North Carolina Press, 2000.

Costa Rica. Dirección General de Estadística y Censos. *Censo de población de Costa Rica, 22 de mayo de 1950*. San José, Costa Rica: [s.n.], 1953.

———. *Censo general de la república de Costa Rica (27 de noviembre de 1864)*. San José, Costa Rica: Imprenta Nacional, 1868.

Cottrol, Robert. "Coming into Their Own? The Afro-Latin Struggle for Equality and Recognition." InterAmerican Foundation, 2012. http://www.iaf.gov/index.aspx?page=382.

Crawford, Elisabeth. *Nationalism and Internationalism in Science, 1880–1939: Four Studies of the Nobel Population*. Cambridge: Cambridge University Press, 1992.

Cuba. Oficina Nacional de los Censos Demográfico y Electoral. *Censos de población, viviendas, y electoral, enero 28 de 1953: Informe general*. Havana: P. Fernández, 1955.

Cunin, Elisabeth, coord. *Mestizaje, diferencia y nación: Lo "negro" en América Central y el Caribe*. Mexico City: Instituto Nacional de Antropología e Historia, 2010.

Cutter, Charles R. *The Legal Culture of Northern New Spain, 1700–1810*. Albuquerque: University of New Mexico Press, 1995.

Davis, F. James. *Who Is Black? One Nation's Definition*. University Park: Pennsylvania State University Press, 1991.

Daynes, Sarah and Orville Lee. *Desire for Race*. New York: Cambridge University Press, 2008.

de Gobineau, Joseph Arthur Comte. *Essai Sur L'Inégalité des Races Humaines (The Inequality of Human Races)*. Translated by Adrian Collins. London: William Heinemann, 1915.

de la Fuente, Alejandro. *A Nation for All: Race, Inequality, and Politics in Twentieth-Century Cuba*. Chapel Hill: University of North Carolina Press, 2001.

———. "Race, National Discourse, and Politics in Cuba." *Latin American Perspectives* 25, 3 (1998): 43–69.

de la Peña, Guillermo. "Orden Social y Educación Indígena en México: la Pervivencia de un Legado Colonial." In *La Heterodoxia Recuperada: en Torno a Angel Palerm*, edited by Susana Glantz, 286–99. Mexico City: Fondo de Cultura Economica, 1987.

de la Torre, Carlos and Jhon Antón Sanchez, "The Afroecuadorian Social Movement" In *Black Social Movements in Latin America: From Monocultural Mestizaje to Multiculturalism*, edited by Jean Muteba Rahier, 135–50. New York: Palgrave MacMillan, 2012.

de Lapouge, Georges Vacher. *L'Aryen: Son Rôle Social*. Paris: A. Fontemoing, 1899.

de Lapouge, Georges Vacher. *Les Sélections Sociales*. Paris: A. Fontemoing, 1896.

Deans-Smith, Susan. "Creating the Colonial Subject: Casta Paintings, Collectors, and Critics in Eighteenth-Century Mexico and Spain." *Colonial Latin American Review* 14, 2 (2005): 169–204.

Degler, Carl. *Neither Black nor White: Slavery and Race Relations in Brazil and the United States*. Madison: University of Wisconsin Press, 1970.

del Popolo, Fabiana. "Censos 2010 y la inclusión del enfoque étnico: Hacia una Construcción Participativa con Pueblos Indígenas y Afrodescendientes de América Latina." United Nations Economic Commission for Latin America and the Caribbean. Serie seminarios y conferencias, no. 57. Santiago, Chile: CEPAL, September 2009.

Delance, José M. *Bosquejo Estadístico de Bolivia*. La Paz, Bolivia: Universidad Boliviana, 1975.

Desrosières, Alain. *The Politics of Large Numbers: A History of Statistical Reasoning*. Cambridge, MA: Harvard University Press, 1998.

DiMaggio, Paul J. and Walter Powell. "The Iron Cage Revisited: Institutional Isomorphism and the Collective Rationality in Organizational Fields." *American Sociological Review* 48 (1983): 147–60.

Dirks, Nicholas B. "Castes of Mind." *Representations* 37 (1992): 56–78.

Dominican Republic. Oficina Regional de Estadística. "Cooperación Internacional." http://www.one.gob.do/index.php?module=articles&func=view&catid=212.

Domínguez, Virginia R. *White by Definition: Social Classification in Creole Louisiana*. New Brunswick, NJ: Rutgers University Press, 1994.

———. "Exporting U.S. Concepts of Race: Are There Limits to the Model?" *Social Research* 65, 2 (1998): 370–99.

Downing, Brian M. *The Military Revolution and Political Change: Origins of Democracy and Autocracy in Early Modern Europe*. Princeton, NJ: Princeton University Press, 1992.

Eckstein, Susan and Manuel Antonio Garretón Merino, eds. *Power and Popular Protest: Latin American Social Movements*. Berkeley: University of California Press, 2001.

Economic Commission for Latin America and the Caribbean. "Biennial Programme of Regional and International Cooperation Activities of the Statistical Conference of the Americas of ECLAC, 2007–2009." Santiago, Chile: ECLAC, 2008. http://www.eclac.org/publicaciones/xml/9/30209/LCL2814rev1i.pdf.

Economic Commission for Latin America and the Caribbean, Population Division (CELADE). International Seminar, "Pueblos indígenas y afrodescendientes de América Latina y el Caribe: relevancia y pertinencia de la información sociodemográfica para políticas y programas," Santiago de Chile, 27 de abril al 29 de abril de 2005. http://www.eclac.org/cgi-bin/getProd.asp?xml=/celade/noticias/paginas/7/21237/P21237.xml&xsl=/celade/tpl/p18f.xsl&base=/celade/tpl/top-bottom.xslt.

El Salvador. Dirección General del Censo. *Censo de Población del Municipio de San Salvador Levantado el 15 de Octubre de 1929*. San Salvador: Tipografia "La Unión," 1930.

Elizondo, Gabriel and Maria Elena Romero. "Brazil Tribes Occupy Contentious Dam Site." *Al Jazeera*, last modified June 30, 2012. http://www.aljazeera.com/indepth/features/2012/06/201263012941975547.html.

Elliott, John H. *Imperial Spain, 1469–1716.* New York: St. Martin's Press, 1964.

Emigh, Rebecca Jean, Dylan Riley, and Patricia Ahmed. *How Societies and States Count: A Comparative Genealogy of Censuses.* Unpublished manuscript.

Emirbayer, Mustafa and Matthew Desmond. *The Racial Order.* Chicago: University of Chicago Press, 2014.

Ertman, Thomas. *Birth of the Leviathan: Building States and Regimes in Medieval and Early Modern Europe.* Cambridge: Cambridge University Press, 1997.

Escobar, Arturo and Sonia E. Alvarez, eds. *The Making of Social Movements in Latin America: Identity, Strategy, and Democracy.* Boulder, CO: Westview Press, 1992.

Espeland, Wendy N. and Mitchell L. Stevens. "Commensuration as a Social Process." *Annual Review of Sociology* 24 (1998): 313–43.

Estefane, Andrés. "Imperial Uncertainties and Republican Conflicts: Archives, Diplomacy and Historiography in Nineteenth-Century Chile." *Early American Studies* 11, 1 (2013): 192–207.

Estrada, Daniela. "Afro-Chileans Seek Recognition in Census," *Final Call*, August 17, 2010, http://www.finalcall.com/artman/publish/World_News_3/article_7203.shtml.

Estupiñán, Juan Pablo. "Afrocolombianos y el Censo 2005: Elementos preliminares para el análisis del proceso censal con la población afrocolombiana." *Revista de Información Básica* 1, 1 (2006): under "artículo 7." http://www.dane.gov.co/revista_ib/html_r1/articulo7_r1.htm.

Evans, Ivan. *Bureaucracy and Race: Native Administration in South Africa.* Berkeley: University of California Press, 1997.

Finer, Samuel E. "State- and Nation-Building in Europe: The Role of the Military." In *The Formation of National States in Western Europe*, edited by Charles Tilly, 84–163. Princeton, NJ: Princeton University Press, 1975.

Fisher, Andrew B. and Matthew D. O'Hara. *Imperial Subjects: Race and Identity in Colonial Latin America.* Durham, NC: Duke University Press, 2009.

Fitzgerald, David and David Cook-Martín. *Culling the Masses: The Democratic Origins of Racist Immigration Policy in the Americas.* Cambridge, MA: Harvard University Press, 2014.

Fitzgerald, Keith. *The Face of the Nation: Immigration, the State and the National Identity.* Stanford, CA: Stanford University Press, 1996.

Fortoul, José Gil. *El Hombre y la Historia: Ensayo de la Sociología Venezolana.* Paris: Librería de Garnier Hermanos, 1896.

Foucault, Michel. "Governmentality." In *The Foucault Effect: Studies in Governmentality*, edited by Graham Burchell, Colin Gordon, and Peter Miller, 87–104. Chicago: University of Chicago Press, 1991.

———. *The History of Sexuality.* vol. 1, *An Introduction.* Translated by Robert Hurley. New York: Random House, 1978.

Francisco, Diego. "Chile: afrodescendientes quieren hacer parte de las estadísticas," *Globedia,* March 17, 2011, http://globedia.com/chile-afrodescendientes-hacer-parte-estadisticas.

Fredrickson, George M. *White Supremacy: A Comparative Study in American & South African History.* Oxford: Oxford University Press, 1981.

French, Jan Hoffman. *Legalizing Identities: Becoming Black or Indian in Brazil's Northeast.* Chapel Hill: University of North Carolina Press, 2009.

French, John D. "The Missteps of Anti-Imperialist Reason: Bourdieu, Wacquant and Hanchard's *Orpheus and Power*." *Theory, Culture & Society* 17, 1 (2000): 107–28.

Freyre, Gilberto. *The Masters and the Slaves: a Study in the Development of Brazilian Civilization.* 1st American ed. New York: Knopf, 1946.

Gamio, Manual. "Las Características Culturales y los Censos Indígenas." *América Indígena*, 2, 3 (1942): 15–19.

Garavito, César Rodríguez, Tatiana Alfonso Sierra, and Isabel Cavelier Adarve. *Raza y Derechos Humanos en Colombia: Informe sobre discriminación racial y derechos de la población afrocolombiana.* Bogotá: Ediciones Uniandes, 2009.

García Linera, Álvaro. "Estado plurinacional: Una Propuesta democrática y pluralista para la extinción de la exclusión de las naciones indígenas." In *La Transformación Pluralista del Estado,* edited by Álvaro García Linera, Luis Tapia Mealla y Raúl Prada Alcoreza, 19–92. La Paz, Bolivia: Muela del Diablo, 2007.

Geary, R. C. "Specific comments, La Trentième Session de L'Institut International de Statistique." *Revue IIS* 25, 1/3 (1957): 1–6.

Gellner, Ernest. *Nations and Nationalism.* Ithaca, NY: Cornell University Press, 1983.

Georgetown University, Edmund A Walsh School of Foreign Service and Center for Latin American Studies. *Political Database of the Americas.* http://pdba.georgetown.edu/IndigenousPeoples/introduction.html.

Gerstle, Gary. *American Crucible: Race and Nation in the Twentieth Century.* Princeton, NJ: Princeton University Press, 2002.

Giddens, Anthony. *The Nation-State and Violence.* Berkeley: University of California Press, 1987.

Glass, David V. *Numbering the People: The Eighteenth-Century Population Controversy and the Development of Census and Vital Statistics in Britain.* Farnborough, UK: D.C. Heath, 1973.

Goffman, Erving. *Stigma: Notes on the Management of Spoiled Identity.* Englewood Cliffs, NJ: Prentice-Hall, 1963.

Goldberg, David Theo. *Racist Culture: Philosophy and the Politics of Meaning.* Oxford: Blackwell, 1993.

———. *Racial Subjects: Writing on Race in America.* New York: Routledge, 1997.

Goldstein, Joshua R. "What's in an Order?: Reading Statistical Tables As Mental Artifacts." Paper presented at the Annual Meeting of the American Sociological Association, Washington DC, August 12–16, 2000.

González, Gustavo. "Indígenas-América Latina: El tabú del estado multiétnico," *Inter Press Service,* May 31, 2005. http://www.ipsnoticias.net/2005/05/indigenas-america-latina-el-tabu-del-estado-multietnico/.

Gorski, Philip. *The Disciplinary Revolution: Calvinism and the Rise of the State in Early Modern Europe.* Chicago: University of Chicago Press, 2003.

Goyer, Doreen S. and Elaine Domschke. *The Handbook of National Population Censuses: Latin America and the Caribbean, North America and Oceania.* Westport, CT: Greenwood Press, 1983.

Graham, Richard, ed. *The Idea of Race in Latin America, 1870–1940.* Austin: University of Texas Press, 1990.

Grandin, Greg. *The Blood of Guatemala: A History of Race and Nation.* Durham, NC: Duke University Press, 2000.

Grillo, Ralph. *Pluralism and the Politics of Difference: State, Culture, and Ethnicity in Comparative Perspective*. New York: Oxford University Press, 1998.

Gross, Ariela J. *What Blood Won't Tell: A History of Race on Trial in America*. Cambridge, MA: Harvard University Press, 2008.

Guatemala. Dirección General de Estadística. *Sexto censo de población, abril 18 de 1950*. Guatemala City: [Guatemala] Dirección General de Estatística, Officina Permanente del Censo, 1953.

Guatemala. Dirección General de Estadística. *VIII Censo de población, 26 de marzo de 1973*. Guatemala City: Dirección General de Estadística, 1975.

Guatemala. Dirección General de Estadística and Justo Rufino Barrios. *Censo general de la república de Guatemala, levantado el año de 1880*. Guatemala City: Estab. tip. de "El Progresso," 1881.

Guatemala. Dirección General de Estadística and Victor Sanchez Ocaña. *Censo general de la república de Guatemala levantado en 26 de febrero de 1893 por la Dirección General de Estadística y con los auspicios del Presidente Constitucional, General Don José María Reina Barrios*. Guatemala City: Tip. y encuad. "Nacional," 1894.

Guatemala. Ministerio de Fomento. Dirección General de Estadística. *Censo de la población de la república levantado el 28 de agosto de 1921*. Guatemala City: Talleres Gutenberg, 1924.

Guerrero, Andrés. "The Administration of Dominated Populations under a Regime of Customary Citizenship: The Case for Post-Colonial Ecuador." In *After Spanish Rule: Post-Colonial Predicaments of the Americas*, edited by Mark Thurner and Andrés Guerrero, 272–309. Durham, NC: Duke University Press, 2003.

Guglielmo, Thomas. A. *White on Arrival: Italians, Race, Color, and Power in Chicago, 1890–1945*. New York: Oxford University Press, 2003.

Guiilebeau, Christopher. "Affirmative Action in a Global Perspective: the Cases of South Africa and Brazil." *Sociological Spectrum* 19, 4 (1999): 443–65.

Guillaumin, Colette. "The Idea of Race and Its Elevation to Autonomous Scientific and Legal Status." In *Sociological Theories: Race and Colonialism*, 37–67. Paris: UNESCO, 1980.

Guimarães, Antonio Sérgio Alfredo. *Racismo e Anti-racismo no Brasil*. São Paulo: Editora 34 Ltda, 1999.

Haas, Peter. "Introduction: Epistemic Communities and International Policy Coordination." *International Organization* 46, 1 (1992): 1–35.

Hacking, Ian. "Biopower and the Avalanche of Printed Numbers." *Humanities in Society* 5 (1982): 279–95.

———. "Making Up People." In *Reconstructing Individualism: Autonomy, Individuality, and the Self in Western Thought*, edited by Thomas Heller, Morton Sosna, and David Wellbery, 222–36. Stanford, CA: Stanford University Press, 1986.

———. "Taking Bad Arguments Seriously (Ian Hacking on Psychopathology and Social Construction)." *London Review of Books*, vol 18, no. 16 (1997): 14–16.

———. "The Looping Effect of Human Kinds." In *Causal Cognition: A Multidisciplinary Debate*, edited by Dan Sperber, David Premack, and Ann James Premack, 351–394. Oxford: Clarendon Press, 1995.

———. *The Taming of Chance*. Cambridge: Cambridge University Press, 1990.

Hale, Charles. "Does Multiculturalism Menace? Governance, Cultural Rights, and the Politics of Identity in Guatemala." *Journal of Latin American Studies*, 34 (2002): 485–524.
———. "Political and Social Ideas in Latin America, 1870–1930." In *The Cambridge History of Latin America*: vol. 4, *c.1870 to 1930*, edited by Leslie Bethell, 367–414. Cambridge: Cambridge University Press, 1988.
Hammack, James T. "Report to the Statistical Society on the Proceedings of the Fourth Session of the International Statistical Congress, held in London, July 1860." *Journal of the Statistical Society of London* 24, 1 (1861): 1–21.
Hanchard, Michael. "Acts of Misrecognition: Transnational Black Politics, Anti-imperialism and the Ethnocentrisms of Pierre Bourdieu and Loïc Wacquant." *Theory, Culture & Society* 20, 4 (2004): 5–29.
———. *Orpheus and Power: The Movimento Negro of Rio de Janeiro and São Paulo, Brazil*. Princeton, NJ: Princeton University Press, 1994.
Haney-López, Ian. *White by Law: The Legal Construction of Race*. New York: New York University Press, 1996.
Harding, Philip and Richard Jenkins. *The Myth of the Hidden Economy: Towards a New Understanding of Informal Economic Activity*. Milton Keyes, UK: Open University Press, 1989.
Hatton, Timothy J. and Williamson, Jeffrey G. *The Age of Mass Migration. Causes and Economic Impact*. New York: Oxford University Press, 1998.
Helg, Aline. "Race and Black Mobilization in Colonial and Early Independent Cuba: A Comparative Perspective." *Ethnohistory* 44, 1 (1997): 53–74.
———. "Race in Argentina and Cuba, 1880–1930." In *The Idea of Race in Latin America, 1970–1940*, edited by Richard Graham, 37–69. Austin: University of Texas Press, 1990.
Hidalgo Pérez, Eloísa. "El Contenido de las *Relaciones Geográficas* Mexicanas y Venezolanas: Cambios e Influjos Ilustrados." In *Estudios Sobre América, Siglos XVI–XX: La Asociación Española de Americanistas en su Vigésimo Aniversario*, coordinated by Antonio Gutíerrez Escudero and María Luisa Lavíana Cuerto, 215–34. Seville: Asociación Española de Americanistas, 2005.
Hirschfeld, Lawrence A. *Race in the Making: Cognition, Culture, and the Child's Construction of Human Kinds*. Cambridge, MA: MIT Press, 1996.
Hirschman, Charles. "The Making of Race in Colonial Malaya: Political Economy and Racial Ideology." *Sociological Forum* 1, 2 (1986): 330–61.
———. "The Meaning and Measurement of Ethnicity in Malaysia: An Analysis of Census Classifications." *The Journal of Asian Studies* 46, 3 (1987): 555–82.
Hobsbawm, Eric. *Nations and Nationalism Since 1780*. Cambridge: Cambridge University Press, 1990.
Hobsbawm, Eric and Terence Ranger, eds. *The Invention of Tradition*. Cambridge: Cambridge University Press, 1983.
Hollinger, David. "Amalgamation and Hypodescent: The Question of Ethnoracial Mixture in the History of the United States." *The American Historical Review* 108, 5 (2003): 1363–1390.
Holloway, Thomas. *Immigrants on the Land: Coffee and Society in São Paulo, 1886–1934*. Chapel Hill: University of North Carolina Press, 1980.

Honduras. Dirección General de Estadística. *Breve noticia del empadronamiento general de casas y habitantes de la República de Honduras practicado el 18 de diciembre de 1910*. Tegucigalpa, Honduras: Tipografia Nacional, 1911.

———. *Resumen del censo general de población levantado el 29 de junio de 1930*. Tegucigalpa, Honduras: Tipografia Nacional, 1932.

Hooker, Juliet. "Indigenous Inclusion/Black Exclusion: Race, Ethnicity and Multicultural Citizenship in Latin America." *Journal of Latin American Studies* 37 (2005): 285–310.

Howard, David. *Coloring the Nation: Race and Ethnicity in the Dominican Republic*. Boulder, CO: L. Rienner Publishers, 2001.

Htun, Mala. "From 'Racial Democracy' to Affirmative Action: Changing State Policy on Race in Brazil." *Latin American Research Review* 39, 1 (2004): 60–89.

Hull, Cordell. *Report of the Delegates of the United States of America to the Seventh International Conference of American States: Montevideo, Uruguay, December 3–26, 1933*. Washington, DC: Government Printing Office, 1934.

Hutchinson, Elizabeth Quay. "La Historia Detrás de las Cifras: La Evolución del Censo Chileno y la Representación del Trabajo Femenino, 1895–1930." *Historia* 33 (2000): 417–434.

Ignatiev, Noel. *How the Irish Became White*. New York: Routledge, 1995.

Igo, Sarah E. *The Averaged American: Surveys, Citizens, and the Making of a Mass Public*. Cambridge, MA: Harvard University Press, 2007.

Iniciativas Ciudadanas por la Democracia Local (INCIDE). "Ley Antidiscriminación: Caso Lumbanga." video, 1:48. March 30, 2012. http://www.incide.cl/30/03/2012/ley-antidiscriminacion-caso-lumbanga.

Instituto Observatório Social. "Série censo e afrodescendientes é exibida em canais abertos de TV brasileiros," news release, UNIFEM, May 5, 2010. http://www.observatoriosocial.org.br/portal/en/node/568.

Inter-American Development Bank. "BID, Banco Mundial y Colombia Auspician Seminario Internacional Sobre Factores Raciales y Étnicos en Censos de América Latina," news release, November 7, 2000, http://www.iadb.org/es/noticias/comunicados-de-prensa/2000-11-07/bid-banco-mundial-y-colombia-auspician-seminario-internacional-sobre-factores-raciales-y-etnicos-en-censos-de-america-latina,799.html.

———. *Banco de Datos de Legislación Indígena*. Banco Interamericano de Desarrollo. Norway: NORLAT, 2003. http://www.iadb.org/Research/legislacionindigena/leyn/index.cfm?lang=es.

———. "IDB Approves $6,550,000 Loan to Nicaragua for Census and Statistics System," news release, February 27, 2004, http://www.iadb.org/en/news/news-releases/2004-02-27/idb-approves-6550000-loan-to-nicaragua-for-census-and-statistics-system,1390.html.

———. "Legislación Nacional por Pais." *Banco de Datos de Legislación Indígena*, 2013. http://www.iadb.org/Research/legislacionindigena/leyn/index2a.cfm?Language=Spanish.

Inter-American Dialogue. "Afro-Descendants in Latin America: How Many?," *Race Report*, Washington, DC: Inter-American Dialogue, January 1, 2003. http://www.thedialogue.org/PublicationFiles/Race%20Report%202003%20-%20Afro-Descendents%20in%20Latin%20America,%20How%20Many_.pdf.

———. "Constitutional Provisions and Legal Actions Related to Discrimination and Afro-Descendant Populations in Latin America," *Race Report*. Washington, DC: Inter-American Dialogue, August 1, 2004. http://www.thedialogue.org/PublicationFiles/RaceReport2004.pdf.

Inter-American Dialogue. "Gender and Diversity—IDB and Diversity," 2013. http://www.iadb.org/en/topics/gender-and-diversity/gender-and-diversity,1212.html.

Inter-American Statistical Institute. "Remarks of Stuart A. Rice." In *Second Inter-American Statistical Congress and Related Meetings, Bogotá, January 1950*, 22–3. Bogotá: Imprenta del Banco de la República, 1952.

International Labour Organization. *Convention No. 169—Indigenous and Tribal Peoples Convention, 1989 (No. 169)*. Geneva, adopted June 27, 1989. http://www.ilo.org/dyn/normlex/en/f?p=NORMLEXPUB:12100:0::NO::P12100_ILO_CODE:C169.

International Union of American Republics. "First Pan-American Scientific Congress." *Bulletin of the International Bureau of the American Republics*, XXVIII, 4–6 (1909): 580–98.

Ipsen, Carl. *Dictating Demography: The Problem of Population in Fascist Italy*. Cambridge: Cambridge University Press, 1996.

Jackson, Robert H. *Race, Caste, and Status: Indians in Colonial Spanish America*. Albuquerque: University of New Mexico Press, 1999.

———. "Race/Caste and the Creation and Meaning of Identity in Colonial Spanish America." *Revista De Indias* 55 (1995): 149–73.

Jackson, Robert H. and Gregory Maddox. "The Creation of Identity: Colonial Society in Bolivia and Tanzania." *Comparative Studies in Society and History* 35, 2 (1993): 263–84.

Jaramillo, Andrés Estefane. "'Un Alto en el Camino para Saber Cuántos Somos': los Censos de Población y la Construcción de Lealtades Nacionales, Chile, Siglo XIX." *História* 37, 1 (2004): 33–59.

Jenkins, Richard. *Rethinking Ethnicity: Arguments and Explorations*. London: SAGE Publications, 1997.

———. "Rethinking Ethnicity: Identity, Categorization and Power." *Ethnic and Racial Studies* 17, 2 (1994): 198–223.

Joppke, Christian. *Immigration and the Nation-State: The United States, Germany and Great Britain*. Oxford: Oxford University Press, 1999.

Katzew, Ilona. "Casta Painting: Identity and Social Stratification in Colonial Mexico." In *New World Orders: Casta Painting and Colonial Latin America*, edited by Ilona Katzew, 8–29. New York: Americas Society Art Gallery, 1996.

———. *Casta Painting: Images of Race in Eighteenth-Century Mexico*. New Haven, CT: Yale University Press, 2004.

Keith, Robert. *Conquest and Agrarian Change: the Emergence of the Hacienda System on the Peruvian Coast*. Cambridge, MA: Harvard University Press, 1976.

Kertzer, David and Dominique Arel, eds. *Census and Identity: The Politics of Race, Identity and Language in National Censuses*. Cambridge: Cambridge University Press, 2002.

———. "Censuses, Identity Formation, and the Struggle for Political Power." In *Census and Identity: The Politics of Race, Identity and Language in National Censuses*, edited by Kertzer, David and Dominique Arel, 1–42. Cambridge: Cambridge University Press, 2002.

Klein, Herbert S. *A Concise History of Bolivia*. Cambridge: Cambridge University Press, 2003.

Klein, Herbert S. and Ben Vinson III. *African Slavery in Latin America and the Caribbean*, 2nd rev. ed. Oxford: Oxford University Press, 2007.

Knibbs, Sir G. H. "The Evolution and Significance of the Census." *Professional Papers: Commonwealth Bureau of Census and Statistics*. Melbourne: Imperial Federation League of Australia, 1910.

Knight, Alan. "Racism, Revolution, and Indigenismo: Mexico, 1910–1940." In *The Idea of Race in Latin America, 1870–1940*, edited by Richard Graham, 71–113. Austin: University of Texas Press, 1990.

———. "Revolutionary Project, Recalcitrant People: Mexico, 1910–1940." In *The Revolutionary Process in Mexico: Essays on Political and Social Change*, edited by Jaime E. Rodríguez, 256–58. Los Angeles: UCLA Latin American Center Publications, University of California, Los Angeles, 1990.

Kohl, Philip L. "Nationalism and Archaeology: On the Constructions of Nations and the Reconstructions of the Remote Past." *Annual Review of Anthropology* 27 (1998): 223–46.

Kolchin, Peter. "Whiteness Studies: The New History of Race in America." *Journal of American History* 89 (2002): 154–73.

Kraay, Hendrick. "Transatlantic Ties: Recent Work on the Slave Trade, Slavery and Abolition." *Latin American Research Review* 39, 2 (2004): 178–95.

Kramer, Wendy. *Encomienda Politics in Early Colonial Guatemala, 1524–1544: Dividing the Spoils*. Boulder, CO: Westview Press, 1994.

Krüger, Lorenz, Lorraine J. Daston and Michael Heidelberger, eds. *The Probabalistic Revolution*, vol.1, Cambridge, Mass: MIT Press, 1987.

Lacerda, João Baptiste de. "The Métis, or Half-Breeds, of Brazil." 1911. In *Papers on Inter-Racial Problems Communicated to the First Universal Races Congress Held at the University of London, July 26–29, 1911*, edited by Gustav Spiller, 377–83. London: P. S. King & Son.

Lamont, Michèle and Virág Molnár. "The Study of Boundaries in the Social Sciences," *Annual Review of Sociology* 28 (2002): 167–95.

Larson, Brooke. *Trials of Nation Making: Liberalism, Race, and Ethnicity in the Andes, 1810–1910*. Cambridge: Cambridge University Press, 2004.

Lasso, Marixa. *Myths of Harmony: Race and Republicanism during the Age of Revolution, Colombia, 1795–1831*. Pittsburgh, PA: University of Pittsburgh Press, 2007.

Lee, Sharon M. "Racial Classifications in the US Census: 1890–1990." *Ethnic and Racial Studies* 16, 1 (1993): 75–94.

León, Nicolás. *Las Castas del México Colonial o Nueva España*. Mexico City: Talleres Gráficos del Museo Nacional de Arqueología, Historia y Etnografía, 1924.

Lesser, Jeffrey. *Negotiating National Identity: Immigrants, Minorities, and the Struggle for Ethnicity in Brazil*. Durham, NC: Duke University Press, 1999.

———. *Welcoming the Undesirables: Brazil and the Jewish Question*. Berkeley: University of California Press, 1995.

Levene, Ricardo. *Manual de historia del derecho argentino*, 5th ed. Buenos Aires: Depalma, 1985.

Lewin, Linda. *Surprise Heirs I: Illegitimacy, Patrimonial Rights, and Legal Nationalism in Luso-Brazilian Inheritance, 1750–1821*, vol. 1. Stanford, CA: Stanford University Press, 2003.

Library of Congress. Census Library Project. *General Censuses and Vital Statistics in the Americas: An Annotated Bibliography*. Washington, DC: Government Printing Office, 1943.

Lombardi, John. *People and Places in Colonial Venezuela*. Bloomington: Indiana University Press, 1976.

———. "Population Reporting Systems: An Eighteenth-Century Paradigm of Spanish Imperial Organization." In *Studies in Spanish American Population History*, edited by David J. Robinson, 11–44. Boulder, CO: Westview Press, 1981.

Lomnitz-Adler, Claudio. *Exits from the Labyrinth: Culture and Ideology in the Mexican National Space*. Berkeley: University of California Press, 1992.

López, Luis Enrique. "Epílogos." *Atlas Sociolingüístico de Pueblos Indígenas en América Latina*, vol. 2, edited by Inge Sichra 1077–79. UNICEF y FUNPROEIB Andes, Cochabamba: Imprenta Mariscal, 2009. http://www.proeibandes.org/atlas/tomo_2.pdf.

López, Raúl Necochea. "Demographic Knowledge and Nation-Building: The Peruvian Census of 1940" *Berichte Zur Wissenschaftsgeschichte* 33, 3 (2010): 280-96.

Loveman, Brian. *Chile: The Legacy of Hispanic Capitalism*, 3rd ed. New York: Oxford University Press, 2001.

———. *For la Patria: Politics and the Armed Forces in Latin America*. Wilmington, DE: Scholarly Resources Books, 1999.

———. *No Higher Law: American Foreign Policy and the Western Hemisphere since 1776*. Chapel Hill: University of North Carolina Press, 2010.

Loveman, Brian and Elizabeth Lira. *Las Suaves Cenizas del Olvido: Vía Chilena de Reconciliación Política, 1814–1932*. Santiago, Chile: LOM/DIBAM, 1999.

Loveman, Mara. "Blinded Like a State: The Revolt Against Civil Registration in 19th Century Brazil." *Comparative Studies in Society and History* 49, 1 (2007): 5–39.

———. "Census Taking and Nation Making in Nineteenth-Century Latin America." In *State and Nation Making in Latin America and Spain: Republics of the Possible*, edited by Miguel A. Centeno and Agustín E. Ferraro, 329–55. Cambridge: Cambridge University Press, 2013.

———. "Is 'Race' Essential? A Comment on Bonilla-Silva." *American Sociological Review* 64, 6 (1999): 891–99.

———. "Making 'Race' and Nation in the United States, South Africa and Brazil: Taking Making Seriously." *Theory and Society* 28, 6 (1999): 903–27.

———. "The Modern State and the Primitive Accumulation of Symbolic Power." *American Journal of Sociology* 110, 6 (2005): 1651–83.

———. "The Race to Progress: Census-Taking and Nation-Making in Brazil 1870–1920." *Hispanic American Historical Review* 89, 3 (2009): 435–70.

———. "The U.S. Census and the Contested Rules of Racial Classification in Early Twentieth-Century Puerto Rico." *Caribbean Studies* 35, 2 (2007): 3–36.

———. "Whiteness in Latin America: Measurement and Meaning in National Censuses (1850–1950)." *Journal de la Société des Américanistes* 95, 2 (2009): 207–34.

Loveman, Mara and Jeronimo O. Muniz. "How Puerto Rico Became White: Boundary Dynamics and Inter-Census Racial Reclassification." *American Sociological Review*, 72 (2007): 915–939.

Loveman, Mara, Jeronimo O. Muniz, and Stanley R. Bailey. "Brazil in Black and White?: Race Categories, the Census, and the Study of Inequality." *Ethnic and Racial Studies* 35, 8 (2012): 1466–83.

Lynch, John. *Spanish Colonial Administration, 1782–1810*. London: Athlone Press, 1958.

———. *The Spanish American Revolutions, 1808–1826*, 2nd ed. New York: W.W. Norton and Company, 1986.
Maclachlan, Colin M. "The Indian Labor Structure in the Portuguese Amazon, 1700–1800." In *The Colonial Roots of Modern Brazil*, edited by Dauril Alden, 199–230. Berkeley: University of California Press, 1973.
Maio, Marcos Chor. "UNESCO and the Study of Race Relations in Brazil: Regional or National Issue?" *Latin American Research Review* 36, 2 (2001): 1–34.
Maio, Marcos Chor and Ricardo Ventura Santos, eds. *Raça, Ciência e Sociedade*. Rio de Janeiro: Editora Fiocruz, 1996.
Mallon, Florencia. *Peasant and Nation: Making of Postcolonial Mexico and Peru*. Berkeley: University of California Press, 1995.
Mann, Michael. *The Sources of Social Power.* vol. 1, *A History of Power from the Beginning to AD 1760*. Cambridge: Cambridge University Press, 1986.
———. *The Sources of Social Power,* vol. 2, *The Rise of Classes and Nation-States, 1760–1914*. Cambridge: Cambridge University Press, 1993.
Marcílio, Maria L. "Levantamientos Censitários da Fase Proto-Estatística do Brasil." *Anais de História* 9 (1977): 63–75.
———. "Population." In *The Cambridge History of Latin America*, vol. XI, *Bibliographical Essays*, edited by Leslie Bethell, 180–3. Cambridge: Cambridge University Press, 1995.
Márquez, Gustavo, Alberto Chong, Suzanne Duryea, Jacqueline Mazza, and Hugo Ñopo. "Outsiders? The Changing Patterns of Exclusion in Latin America and the Caribbean." *2008 Report*. Washington, DC: Inter-American Development Bank and David Rockefeller Center for Latin American Studies, 2007. http://www.iadb.org/en/publications/publication-detail,7101.html?id=67316.
Martínez, Elena. *Genealogical Fictions: Limpieza de Sangre, Religion, and Gender in Colonial Mexico*. Stanford, CA: Stanford University Press, 2008.
Martínez-Echazábal, Lourdes. "*Mestizaje* and the Discourse of National/Cultural Identity in Latin America, 1845–1959." *Latin American Perspectives* 25, 100 (1998): 21–42.
———. "O Culturalismo dos anos 30 no Brasil e na América Latina: Deslocamento Retórico ou Mudança Conceitual?" In *Raça, Ciência e Sociedade*, edited by Marcos Chor Maio and Ricardo Ventura Santos, 107–24. Rio de Janeiro: Editora FioCruz, Centro Cultural do Brasil, 1996.
Marx, Anthony. *Making Race and Nation: A Comparison of the United States, South Africa and Brazil*. Cambridge: Cambridge University Press, 1998.
Marx, Gary. "Historians Work to Set Record Straight on Cuba." *Chicago Tribune*, August 17, 2004. http://www.latinamericanstudies.org/taino/record.htm.
Mattos, Hebe Maria. "Identidade Camponesa, Racialização e Cidadania no Brasil Monárquico: o Caso da 'Guerra dos Marimbondos' em Pernambuco a Partir da Leitura de Guillermo Palacios." *Almanack Brasiliense* 3 (2006): 40–6.
Mauri, Mónica Martínez. "The Social and Political Construction of Race and Ethnic Categories in National Censuses of Panama, 1911–2010." In *Everlasting Countdowns: Race, Ethnicity and National Censuses in Latin American States,* edited by Luis Fernando Angosto Ferrández and Sabine Kradolfer, 155–84. Newcastle upon Tyne: Cambridge Scholars Publishing, 2012.
Mazza, Jacqueline. "Todos Contamos II: National Censuses and Social Inclusion—A Back to Office Report." Washington, DC: Inter-American Development Bank, 2002.

McCaa, Robert. "*Calidad, Clase,* and Marriage in Colonial Mexico: the Case of Parral." *Hispanic American Historical Review* 64, 3 (1984): 497–501.

McCaa, Robert. "Missing Millions: the human cost of the Mexican Revolution." University of Minnesota Population Center, 2001. http://www.hist.umn.edu/~rmccaa/missmill/mxrev.htm

McCaa, Robert, Stuart B. Schwartz, and Arturo Grubessich. "Race and Class in Colonial Latin America: A Critique." *Comparative Studies in Society and History* 21 (1979): 421–42.

McCann, Frank. "The Formative Period of Twentieth-Century Brazilian Army Thought, 1900–1922." *Hispanic American Historical Review* 64, 4 (1984): 737–65.

McIntosh, Mary. "The Homosexual Role." *Social Problems* 16, 2 (1968): 182–92.

Mckeown, Adam. "Global Migration, 1846–1940." *Journal of World History* 15 (2004): 155–89.

Melo, Mario. "Guerra dos Maribondos." *Revista do Instituto Arqueológico, Histórico e Geográfico Pernambucano* 22 (1920): 38–47.

Menjívar, Cecilia, and Néstor Rodríguez, eds. *When States Kill: Latin America, the U.S., and Technologies of Terror.* Austin: University of Texas Press, 2005.

Mesa, Gloria Patricia Lopera. "Who Counts Indigenous People, How Are They Counted and What For? Census Policies and the Construction of Indigeneity in Colombia." In *Everlasting Countdowns: Race, Ethnicity and National Censuses in Latin American States,* edited by Luis Fernando Angosto Ferrández and Sabine Kradolfer, 94–127. Newcastle upon Tyne: Cambridge Scholars Publishing, 2012.

Mexico. Departamento de la Estadística Nacional. *Censo de población, 15 de mayo de 1930.* Mexico City: Talleres Gráficos de la Nación, 1932.

———. *Resumen del censo general de habitantes, de 30 noviembre de 1921.* Mexico City: Talleres Gráficos de la Nación, 1928.

Meyer, John. "The Changing Cultural Content of the Nation-State: A World Society Perspective." In *State/Culture: State Formation after the Cultural Turn,* edited by George Steinmetz, 123–43. Ithaca, NY: Cornell University Press, 1999.

———. "The World Polity and the Authority of the Nation-State." In *Institutional Structure: Constituting State, Society, and the Individual,* edited by George Thomas, John Meyer, Francisco Ramirez, and John Boli, 41–70. Newbury Park, CA: SAGE Publications, 1987.

Mignolo, Walter D. "Misunderstanding and Colonization: The Reconfiguration of Memory and Space." In *Le Nouveau Monde/Mondes Nouveaux. L'Experience Américáine,* edited by Serge Gruzinski and Nathan Wachtel, 271–308. Paris: éditions de l'Ecole des Hautes Etudes en Sciences Sociales, 1996.

Milliet, Sergio. "Recenseamentos Antigos." *Revista Brasileira de Estatística* 6, 62 (1955): 144–50.

Minority Rights Group, ed. *No Longer Invisible: Afro-Latin Americans Today.* London: Minority Rights Publications, 1995.

Mirow, Matthew C. *Latin American Law: A History of Private Law and Institutions in Spanish America.* Austin: University of Texas Press, 2004.

Mitchell, Timothy. "Everyday Metaphors of Power." *Theory and Society* 19, 5 (1990): 545–77.

Modood, Tariq. *Multiculturalism: A Civic Idea.* Cambridge: Polity Press, 2007.

Monmonier, Mark. *How to Lie with Maps.* Chicago: University of Chicago Press, 1991.

Montagu, Ashley. *Man's Most Dangerous Myth: The Fallacy of Race.* New York: Columbia University Press, 1942.

Mora, G. Cristina. *Making Hispanics: How Activists, Bureaucrats, and Media Constructed a New American*. Chicago: University of Chicago Press, 2014.

Morillo-Alicea, Javier. "'Aquel Laberinto de Oficinas': Ways of Knowing Empire in Late Nineteenth-Century Spain." In *After Spanish Rule: Post-Colonial Predicaments of the Americas,* edited by Mark Thurner and Andrés Guerrero, 111–40. Durham, NC: Duke University Press, 2003.

Mörner, Magnus. *Race Mixture in the History of Latin America*. Boston: Little, Brown and Company, 1967.

———. "Slavery and Race in the Evolution of Latin American Societies." *Journal of Latin American Studies* 8, 1 (1976): 127–35.

Morning, Ann. "Ethnic Classification in Global Perspective: A Cross-National Survey of the 2000 Census Round." *Population Research and Policy Review* 27, 2 (2008): 239–72.

Müller-Hill, Benno. *Murderous Science: Elimination by Scientific Selection of Jews, Gypsies and Others, Germany 1933–1945*. New York: Oxford University Press, 1988.

Mutume, Gumisai. "Development: World Bank Lambasted for Ignoring Racial Dimension of Poverty." *TerraViva,* World Social Forum, Porto Alegre, Brazil, January 25–30, 2001. http://www.ips.org/socialforum/0122/worldbank.htm.

Nagel, Joanne. "American Indian Ethnic Renewal: Politics and the Resurgence of Identity." *American Sociological Review* 60, 6 (1995): 947–65.

Nazzari, Muriel. "Vanishing Indians: The Social Construction of Race in Colonial São Paulo." *The Americas* 57, 4 (2001): 497–524.

Needell, Jeffrey D. *A Tropical Belle Epoque: Elite Culture and Society in Turn-of-the-Century Rio de Janeiro*. Cambridge: Cambridge University Press, 1987.

———. "History, Race, and the State in the Thought of Oliveira Vianna." *Hispanic American Historical Review* 75, 1 (1995): 1–30.

Nettl, J. P. "The State as a Conceptual Variable." *World Politics* 20, 4 (1968): 559–92.

Nicaragua. Constitución Politica de la República de Nicaragua. XXIII Legislatura, 2007. http://www.ineter.gob.ni/Constitucion%20Politica%20de%20Nicargua.pdf.

Niezen, Ronald. *The Origins of Indigenism: Human Rights and the Politics of Identity*. Berkeley: University of California Press, 2003.

Nixon, James William. *A History of the International Statistical Institute, 1885–1960*. The Hague: International Statistical Institute, 1960.

Nobles, Melissa. "'Responding with Good Sense:' The Politics of Race and Censuses in Contemporary Brazil." PhD diss., Yale University, 1995.

———. *Shades of Citizenship: Race and the Census in Modern Politics*. Stanford, CA: Stanford University Press, 2000.

Noiriel, Gérard. "The Identification of the Citizen: The Birth of Republican Civil Status in France." In *Documenting Individual Identity: The Development of State Practices in the Modern World*, edited by Jane Caplan and John Torpey, 34–68. Princeton, NJ: Princeton University Press, 2001.

North, S.N.D. "The Standardization of Census and Commercial Statistics in the American Republics." In *Proceedings of the Second Pan American Scientific Congress*, edited by Glen Levin Swiggett, 617–25. Washington, DC: Government Printing Office, 1917.

Nunn, Fredrick. *Yesterday's Soldiers: European Military Professionalism in South America, 1890–1940*. Lincoln: University of Nebraska Press, 1983.
O'Crouley, Pedro A. *A Description of the Kingdom of New Spain*. Translated and edited by Sean Galvin. New York: J. Howell, 1972.
Oliveira, Maria Luiza Ferreira de. "Sobreviver à Pressão Escapando ao Controle: Embates em Torno da 'Lei do Cativeiro' (a Guerra dos Marimbondos em Pernambuco, 1851–1852)." *Almanack Braziliense* 3 (2006): 47–55.
Olzak, Susan. *The Global Dynamics of Ethnic and Racial Mobilization*. Stanford, CA: Stanford University Press, 2006.
Omi, Michael and Howard Winant. *Racial Formation in the United States: From the 1960s to the 1990s*. New York: Routledge, 1994.
Organización de Estados Iberoamericanos. "Declaratoria de Cartegena—Agenda Afrodescendiente en las Américas." Dec.30, 2010. http://www.oei.es/afro03.php.
Otero, Hernán. *Estadística y Nación: Una Historia Conceptual del Pensamiento Censal de la Argentina Moderna 1896–1914*. Buenos Aires: Promoteo Libros, 2006.
Ozlak, Oscar. "The Historical Formation of the State in Latin America: Some Theoretical and Methodological Guidelines for Its Study." *Latin American Research Review* 16, 2 (1981): 3–32.
Palacios, Guillermo. "A 'Guerra dos Maribondos': Uma Revolta Camponesa no Brasil Escravista (Pernambuco, 1851–1852)—Primeira Leitura." *História: Questões e Debates* 10, 18–19 (1989): 7–75.
Panama. Contraloría General. Dirección General de Estadística. *Boletín del censo de la República de Panamá*. Panama City: Imprenta Nacional, 1911.
Panama. Dirección General del Censo. *Boletin Nº. 1. Censo demográfico de la Provincia de Panamá, 1920*. Panama City: Imprenta Nacional, 1922.
———. *1930 Censo Demográfico*. Panama City: Imprenta Nacional, 1931–1932, 2 vol.
Panama. Oficina del Censo. *Censo de población, 1940*. Panama City: Imprenta Nacional, 1943–1945.
Paschel, Tianna S. "'The Beautiful Faces of My Black People': Race, Ethnicity and the Politics of Colombia's 2005 Census." *Ethnic and Racial Studies* 36 (2013): 1–20.
———. "The Right to Difference: Explaining Colombia's Shift from Color-Blindness to the Law of Black Communities." *American Journal of Sociology* 116, 3 (2010): 729–69.
Paschel, Tianna S. and Mark Q. Sawyer. "Contesting Politics as Usual: Black Social Movements, Globalization, and Race Policy in Latin America." *Souls: A Critical Journal of Black Politics, Culture, and Society* 10, 3 (2008): 197–214.
Pascoe, Peggy. *What Comes Naturally: Miscegenation Law and the Making of Race in America*. New York: Oxford University Press, 2009.
Patriarca, Silvana. *Numbers and Nationhood: Writing Statistics in Nineteenth-Century Italy*. Cambridge: Cambridge University Press, 1996.
———. "Statistical Nation Building and the Consolidation of Regions in Italy." *Social Science History* 18, 3 (1994): 359–76.
Peachy, Keith. "The Revillagigedo Census of Mexico, 1790–1794: A Background Study." *Bulletin of the Society for Latin American Studies* 25 (1976): 63–80.
Pearce, Adrian J. "The Peruvian Population Census of 1725–1740." *Latin American Research Review* 36, 3 (2001): 69–104.

Peru. Dirección de Estadística. "Resumen del Censo General de habitantes del Perú: hecho en 1876." Lima: Imprenta del estado, 1878.

———. *Censo nacional de población y ocupación, 1940*. Lima: publisher unknown, 1944.

Peru. Dirección Nacional de Estadística y Censos. *Resultados del VI Censo Nacional de Población*. vol. I: 5. Lima: Talleres Gráficos de la Dirección Nacional de Estadística y Censos, 1966.

Peru. Instituto Nacional de Estadística e Informática. "Analizaron recolección de información sobre poblaciones indigenas y afrodescendientes," news release, October 2002, http://www.inei.gob.pe/web/NotaPrensa/Attach/4668.pdf.

Petersen, William. "Politics and the Measurement of Ethnicity." In *The Politics of Numbers*, edited by William Alonso and Paul Starr, 187–233. New York: Russell Sage Foundation, 1987.

Peyser, Alexia and Juan Chackiel. "La Identificación de Poblaciones Indígenas en los Censos de América Latina." Pp. 353–369 in Economic Commission for Latin America and the Caribbean, *América Latina: Aspectos Conceptuales de los Censos del 2000*. Serie Manuales. Santiago, Chile: CELADE, 1999.

Phelps, Elizabeth, ed. *Proceedings of the International Statistical Conferences*. First session of the Inter American Statistical Institute, Sept. 6-18 (Washington, DC: vol. 4), 1947.

Pinto Mosqueira, "Las categorías identitarias en la boleta censal: Alcances y efectos. La Categoría 'Mestizo'." Presented at *Taller para el debate public o del Censo 2012*, Santa Cruz de la Sierra, Bolivia, February 3, 2012. http://www.radioiyambae.com/sitio/recursos/Mestizaje%20en%20el%20censo%202012.pdf.

Piza, Edith and Fulvia Rosemberg. "Color in the Brazilian Census." In *Race in Contemporary Brazil*, edited by Rebecca Reichmann, 37–52. University Park: Pennsylvania State University Press, 1999.

Platt, Lyman D. *Latin American Census Records*, 2nd ed. Salt Lake City, UT: Instituto Genealógico e Histórico Latinoamericano, 1989.

Poggi, Gianfranco. *The State: Its Nature, Development, and Prospects*. Stanford, CA: Stanford University Press, 1990.

Pollak-Eltz, Angelina. "Migration from Barlovento to Caracas." In *The Venezuelan Peasant in Country and City*, edited by Luise Margolies, 29–54. Caracas: Ediciones Venezolanas de Antropología, 1979.

Porter, Bruce D. *War and the Rise of the State: The Military Foundations of Modern Politics*. New York: Free Press, 1994.

Porter, Theodore M. *The Rise of Statistical Thinking, 1820–1900*. Princeton, NJ: Princeton University Press, 1986.

Powell, T. G. "Mexican Intellectuals and the Indian Question, 1876–1911." *Hispanic American Historical Review* 48, 1 (1968): 19–36.

Powers, Karen. *Andean Journeys: Migration, Ethnogenesis, and the State in Colonial Quito*. Albuquerque: University of New Mexico Press, 1995.

Price, Richard. *Maroon Societies: Rebel Slave Communities in the Americas*, 3rd ed. Baltimore: Johns Hopkins University Press, 1996.

Prieto, René. "The Literature of Indigenismo." In *The Cambridge History of Latin American Literature,* Vol. 2. Twentieth Century, edited by Roberto González Echevarría and Enrique Pupo-Walker, 138–63. Cambridge: Cambridge University Press, 1996.

Quijano, Aníbal. "Colonialidad del Poder, Eurocentrismo y América Latina." In *La Colonialidad del Saber: Eurocentrismo y Ciencias Sociales,* compiled by Edgardo Lander. Buenos Aires: CLACSO, 2000.

Radcliffe, Sarah and Sallie Westwood. *Remaking the Nation: Place, Identity and Politics in Latin America.* London: Routledge, 1996.

Rahier, Jean Muteba, ed. *Black Social Movements in Latin America: From Monocultural Mestizaje to Multiculturalism.* New York: Palgrave MacMillan, 2012.

———. "The Study of Latin American 'Racial Formations': Different Approaches and Different Contexts." *Latin American Research Review* 39, 3 (2004): 282–93.

Randeraad, Nico. *States and Statistics in the Nineteenth Century.* Manchester, UK: Manchester University Press, 2010.

———. "The International Statistical Congress (1853–1876): Knowledge Transfers and their Limits." *European History Quarterly* 41, 1 (2011): 50–65.

Rappaport, Joanne. "'Asi lo Paresçe por su Aspeto': Physiognomy and the Construction of Difference in Colonial Bogotá." *Hispanic American Historical Review* 91, 4 (2011): 601–31.

Regalsky, "Bolivia: Indigenous Identities and Collective Subjects in the Andes." In *Everlasting Countdowns: Race, Ethnicity and National Censuses in Latin American States,* edited by Luis Fernando Angosto Ferrández and Sabine Kradolfer, 69–93. Newcastle upon Tyne: Cambridge Scholars Publishing, 2012.

Reid, Lydia M. "Panama's 2010 Census Promises to Be Interesting for Persons of African and Indigenous Descent." *The Silver People Heritage Foundation* (blog), May 5, 2010. http://thesilverpeopleheritage.wordpress.com/2010/05/05/panamas-2010-census-promises-to-be-interesting-for-persons-of-african-and-indigenous-descent/.

Reiter, Bernd and Kimberly Eison Simmons, eds. *Afro-Descendants, Identity, and the Struggle for Development in the Americas.* East Lansing: Michigan State University, 2012.

Renan, Ernest. *Qu'est-ce qu'une nation?* Translated by Ida Mae Snyder. Paris: Calmann-Levy, 1882.

Renshaw, Jonathan and Natalia Wray. "Indicadores de bienestar y pobreza indígena," prepared for Inter-American Development Bank, 2004. http://www.comunidadandina.org/sociedad/indicadores_indigenas.pdf.

Richards, Patricia. *Pobladoras, Indígenas, and the State: Conflicts over Women's Rights in Chile.* New Brunswick, NJ: Rutgers University Press, 2004.

Robinson, David J. "Indian Migration in Eighteenth-Century Yucatán: The Open Nature of the Closed Corporate Community." In *Studies in Spanish American Population History,* edited by David J. Robinson, 149–69. Boulder, CO: Westview Press, 1981.

———, ed. *Studies in Spanish American Population History.* Boulder, CO: Westview Press, 1981.

Rodrigues, Raimundo Nina. *Os Africanos no Brasil,* 3rd ed. São Paulo: Companhia editora nacional, 1945.

Rodríguez, Clara E. *Changing Race: Latinos, the Census, and the History of Ethnicity in the United States.* New York: New York University Press, 2000.

Rodríguez, Julia. *Civilizing Argentina: Science, Medicine and the Modern State.* Chapel Hill: University of North Carolina Press, 2006.

Rodríguez-Piñero, Luis. *Indigenous Peoples, Postcolonialism and International Law: The ILO Regime (1919–1989)*. Oxford: Oxford University Press, 2005.

Roediger, David R. *The Wages of Whiteness: Race and the Making of the American Working Class*. London: Verso, 2007.

Roitman, Karem. "Hybridity, Mestizaje, and Montubios in Ecuador." QEH Working Paper Series Working Paper 165, Oxford Department of International Development, University of Oxford, 2008. http://www3.qeh.ox.ac.uk/pdf/qehwp/qehwps165.pdf.

Roth, Wendy. *Race Migrations: Latinos and the Cultural Transformation of Race*. Stanford, CA: Stanford University Press, 2012.

Sánchez, Enrique, ed. *Derechos de los Pueblos Indígenas en las Constituciones de América Latina*. Bogotá: Disloque Editores, 1996.

Sánchez, Enrique and Paola García. "Los Afrocolombianos." In *Más Allá de los Promedios: Afrodescendientes en América Latina*, edited by Josefina Stubbs and Hiska N. Reyes. Washington, DC: The World Bank, 2006. http://documents.worldbank.org/curated/en/2006/02/6838413/los-afrocolombianos.

Sánchez-Albornoz, Nicolás. "Population." In *The Cambridge History of Latin America*, vol. 9, edited by Leslie Bethell, 59–66. Cambridge: Cambridge University Press, 1995.

———. *The Population of Latin America*. Berkeley: University of California Press, 1974.

Sánchez-Alonso, Blanca. "Algunas Reflexiones Sobre las Políticas de Inmigración en América Latina en la Época de las Migraciones de Masas." *Estudios Migratorios Latinoamericanos* 53 (2004): 155–177.

———. "El Nuevo Orden Parroquial de la Ciudad de México: Población, Etnia y Territorio (1768–1777)." *Estudios de Historia Novohispana* 30 (2004): 63–92.

Santos, Boaventura de Sousa. *La Reinvención del Estado y el Estado Plurinacional*. Cochabamba, Bolivia: CEJIS, CENDA, CEDIB, 2007.

Santos, Ricardo Ventura. "Da Morfologia ás Moléculas, de Raça a População: Trajetórias Conceituais em Antropologia Física no Século XX." In *Raça, Ciência e Sociedade*, edited by Marcos Chor Maio and Ricardo Ventura Santos, 125–39. Rio de Janeiro: Editora FioCruz, 1996.

Scarano, Francisco. "Censuses in the Transition to Modern Colonialism: Spain and the United States in Puerto Rico." In *Colonial Crucible: Empire in the Making of the Modern American State*, edited by Alfred W. McCoy and Francisco A. Scarano, 210–19. Madison: University of Wisconsin Press, 2009.

Schor, Paul. *Compter et Classer: Histoire des Recensements Américains*. Paris: Éditions EHESS, 2008.

Schwaller, Robert C. " 'For Honor and Defence': Race and the Right to Bear Arms in Early Colonial Mexico." *Colonial Latin American Review* 21, 2 (2012): 239–66.

Schwarcz, Lilia M. *O Espetáculo das raças: Cientistas, instituições, e questão racial no Brasil 1870–1930*. São Paulo: Companhia das Letras, 1993.

Schwartz, Stuart B. "Colonial Brazil, c.1580–c.1750: Plantations and Peripheries." In *The Cambridge History of Latin America*. vol. 2, *Colonial Latin America*, edited by Leslie Bethell, 421–500. Cambridge: Cambridge University Press, 1984.

———. *Sugar Plantations in the Formation of Brazilian Society: Bahia, 1550–1835*, New York: Cambridge University Press, 1985.

Schwarz, Barry. *Vertical Classification*. Chicago: University of Chicago Press, 1981.

Schweber, Libby. *Disciplining Statistics: Demography and Vital Statistics in France and England, 1830–1885*. Durham, NC: Duke University Press, 2007.

Scott, James. *Seeing Like a State: How Certain Schemes to Improve the Human Condition Have Failed*. New Haven, CT: Yale University Press, 1999.

Second Inter-American Statistical Congress. "Summary, Participants, Program and Resolutions" Bogotá, Colombia, January 1950. Washington, DC: Pan-American Union, Division of Conferences and Organizations, 1951.

Seelke, Claire Robando. "Afro-Latinos in Latin America and Considerations for US Policy." *Congressional Research Service Report for Congress*, updated November 21, 2008. http://www.fas.org/sgp/crs/row/RL32713.pdf.

Seltzer, William. "On the Use of Population Data Systems to Target Vulnerable Populations." *Conyuntura Social* 32 (2005): 31–44.

Seltzer, William and Margo J. Anderson, "Census Confidentiality under the Second War Powers Act (1942–1947)." Paper presented at the 2007 Meeting of the Population Association of America, New York, March 29–31.

Sen, Amartya. *Development as Freedom*. New York: Random House, 1999.

Senra, Nelson de Castro. *História das Estatísticas Brasileiras*. Rio de Janeiro: Instituto Brasileiro de Geografia e Estatística –IBGE, Centro de Documentação e Disseminação de Informações, 2006.

Senra, Nelson de Castro and Alexandre de Paiva Rio Camargo, eds. *Estatísticas nas Américas: Por Uma Agenda de Estudos Históricos Comparados*. Rio de Janeiro: Instituto Brasileiro de Geografia e Estatística -IBGE, Centro de Documentação de Informações, 2010.

Sheriff, Robin. *Dreaming Equality: Color, Race, and Racism in Urban Brazil*. New Brunswick, NJ: Rutgers University Press, 2001.

Sherman, William L. *Forced Native Labor in Sixteenth-Century Central America*. Lincoln: University of Nebraska Press, 1979.

Sieder, Rachel, ed. *Multiculturalism in Latin America: Indigenous Rights, Diversity and Democracy*. London: Institute of Latin American Studies, 2002.

Sikkink, Katherine and Margaret Keck. *Activists Beyond Borders: Advocacy Networks in International Politics*. Ithaca, NY: Cornell University, 1998.

Simon, Patrick. "Collecting Ethnic Statistics in Europe: A Review." *Ethnic and Racial Studies* 35, 8 (2012): 1366–91.

Simpson, Lesley Byrd. *The Encomienda in New Spain*. Berkeley: University of California Press, 1966 [c. 1950].

Skerry, Peter. *Counting on the Census? Race, Group Identity, and the Evasion of Politics*. Washington DC: Brookings Institution Press, 2000.

Skidmore, Thomas. *Black into White: Race and Nationality in Brazilian Thought*. Oxford: Oxford University Press, 1993.

———. "Racial Ideas and Social Policy in Brazil, 1870–1940." In *The Idea of Race in Latin America, 1870–1940*, edited by Richard Graham, 7–36. Austin: University of Texas Press, 1990.

Skrentny, John D. *The Ironies of Affirmative Action: Politics, Culture and Justice in America*. Chicago: University of Chicago Press, 1996.

Smith, Anthony. *The Ethnic Origins of Nations*. Oxford: Blackwell, 1986.

Smith, Rogers. *Stories of Peoplehood: The Politics and Morals of Political Membership.* Cambridge: Cambridge University Press, 2003.

Snipp, Matthew. "Racial Measurement in the American Census: Past Practices and Implications for the Future." *Annual Review of Sociology* 29 (2003): 563–88.

Sobrequés i Vidal, Santiago. "Censo y Profesión de los Habitantes de Gerona en 1462." *Anales del Instituto de Estudios Gerundenses* VI (1951), 193–246.

Soifer, Hillel. "Elite Preferences, Administrative Institutions, and Educational Development During Peru's Aristocratic Republic, 1895–1919" Ch.12 in Miguel Centeno and Agustín Ferraro, eds. *State and Nation Making in Latin America and Spain: Republics of the Possible.* Cambridge: Cambridge University Press, 2013.

Sommer, Doris. *Foundational Fictions: The National Romances of Latin America.* Berkeley: University of California Press, 1991.

———. "Irresistible Romance: the Foundational Fictions of Latin America." In *Nation and Narration*, edited by Homik Bhabha, 71–98. London: Routledge, 1990.

Souto Mantecón, Matilde. "Composición Familiar y Estructura Ocupacional de la Población de Origen Español en Jalapa de la Feria (1791)." *Estudios de Historia Novohispana* 27 (2002): 91–122.

Souza e Silva, Joaquim Norberto de. *Investigações Sobre os Recenseamentos da População Geral do Império e de Cada Província de per si Tentados Desde os Tempos Coloniais Até Hoje.* São Paulo: Instituto de Pesquisas Economicas, 1986 [1870].

Stabb, Martin S. "Indigenism and Racism in Mexican Thought, 1857–1911." *Journal of Inter-American Studies* 1 (1959): 405–43.

Starr, Paul. "Social Categories and Claims in the Liberal State." In *How Classification Works*, edited by Mary Douglas and David Hull, 154–79. Edinburgh: Edinburgh University Press, 1992.

———. "The Sociology of Official Statistics." In *The Politics of Numbers*, edited by William Alonso and Paul Starr, 7–57. New York: Russell Sage Foundation, 1987.

Stavenhagen, Rodolfo. "Indigenous Peoples and the State in Latin America: An Ongoing Debate." In *Multiculturalism in Latin America: Indigenous Rights, Diversity, and Democracy,* edited by Sieder, Rachel, 24–44. New York: Palgrave MacMillan, 2002.

Steinmetz, George, ed. *State/Culture: State Formation after the Cultural Turn.* Ithaca, NY: Cornell University Press, 1999.

———. *The Devil's Handwriting: Precoloniality and the German Colonial State in Qingdao, Samoa, and Southwest Africa.* Chicago: University of Chicago, 2007.

Stepan, Nancy L. *The Hour of Eugenics: Race, Gender, and Nation in Latin America.* Ithaca, NY: Cornell University Press, 1991.

Stern, Peter. 1994. "Gente de Color Quebrado: Africans and Afromestizos in Colonial Mexico." *Colonial Latin American Historical Review* 3, 2 (1994): 185–205.

Stern, Steve J. *Peru's Indian Peoples and the Challenge of the Spanish Conquest: Huamanga to 1640*, 2nd ed. Madison: University of Wisconsin Press, 1993.

Stolcke, Verena. "Sexo es para Gênero Como Raça para Etnicidade?" *Estudos Afro-Asiáticos* 20 (1991): 101–19.

Stoler, Ann L. "Rethinking Colonial Categories: European Communities and the Boundaries of Rule." *Comparative Studies in Society and History* 31, 1 (1989): 134–61.

Stuchlik, Milan. "Chilean Native Policies and the Image of the Mapuche Indians." In *The Conceptualisation and Explanation of Processes of Social Change*, vol. 3, edited by David Riches, 33–54. Belfast: Queen's University Papers in Social Anthropology, 1979.

Sue, Christina. "An Assessment of the Latin Americanization Thesis." *Ethnic and Racial Studies* 32, 6 (2009): 1058–70.

Sulmont, David, and Néstor Valdivia. "From Pre-Modern 'Indians' to Contemporary 'Indigenous People': Race and Ethnicity in Peruvian Censuses 1827–2007" In *Everlasting Countdowns: Race, Ethnicity and National Censuses in Latin American States*, edited by Luis Fernando Angosto Ferrández and Sabine Kradolfer, 185–220. Newcastle upon Tyne: Cambridge Scholars Publishing, 2012.

Tarrow, Sidney. *Power in Movement: Social Movements and Contentious Politics*. Cambridge: Cambridge University Press, 1994.

Telles, Edward E. "US Foundations and Racial Reasoning in Brazil." *Theory, Culture & Society* 20, 4 (2003): 31–47.

———. "Race and Ethnicity and Latin America's United Nations Millennium Development Goals." *Latin American and Caribbean Ethnic Studies* 2, 2 (2007): 185–200.

———. *Race in Another America: The Significance of Skin Color in Brazil*. Princeton, NJ: Princeton University Press, 2004.

Telles, Edward E. and Tianna Paschel. "Beyond Fixed or Fluid: Degrees of Fluidity in Racial Identification in Latin America." Paper presented at the Latin American Studies Association Meeting, San Francisco, May 25, 2012. http://perla.princeton.edu/files/2012/05/BeyondFixedorFluid.pdf.

Tena Ramírez, Felipe. *Leyes Fundamentales de México 1808–1998*, 21st ed. Mexico City: Porrúa, 1998.

Terán, Oscar. *Vida intelectual en el Buenos Aires fin-de-siglo (1880–1910): derivas de la "cultura científica."* Buenos Aires: Fondo de Cultura Económica, 2000.

Thistlethwaite, Frank. "Migration from Europe Overseas in the Nineteenth and Twentieth Centuries." Reprinted in *A Century of European Migrations, 1830–1930*, edited by Rudolph J. Vecoli and Suzanne M. Sinke, 17–57. Chicago: University of Illinois Press, 1991.

Thompson, Alvin O. *Flight to Freedom: African Runaways and Maroons in the Americas*. Mona, Jamaica: University of the West Indies Press, 2006.

Thurner, Mark and Andrés Guerrero, eds. *After Spanish Rule: Post-Colonial Predicaments of the Americas*. Durham, NC: Duke University Press, 2003.

Tilly, Charles. *Durable Inequality*. Berkeley: University of California Press, 1998.

———. *Coercion, Capital, and European States, AD 990–1992*. Cambridge: Blackwell, 1990.

———. "Epilogue: Now Where?" In *State/Culture: State Formation after the Cultural Turn*, edited by George Steinmetz, 407–19. Ithaca, NY: Cornell University Press, 1999.

———, ed. *The Formation of National States in Western Europe*. Princeton, NJ: Princeton University Press, 1975.

Torpey, John. *The Invention of the Passport: Surveillance, Citizenship and the State*. Cambridge: Cambridge University Press, 2000.

Tovar Pinzón, Hermes, Jorge Andrés Tovar Mora, and Camilo Ernesto Tovar Mora. *Convocatoria al poder del número: censos y estadísticas de la Nueva Granada, 1750–1830*. Santa Fé de Bogotá, Colombia: Archivo General de la Nación, 1994.

Travis, Carole, ed. *A Guide to Latin American and Caribbean Census Material: a Bibliography and Union List*. Boston: G.K. Hall, 1990.

Tsing, Anna. "Indigenous Voice." In *Indigenous Experience Today*, edited by Marisol de la Cadena and Orin Starn, 33–68. Oxford: Berg, 2007.

Twinam, Ann. *Public Lives, Private Secrets: Gender, Honor, Sexuality, and Illegitimacy in Colonial Spanish America*. Stanford, CA: Stanford University Press, 1999.

———. "Purchasing Whiteness: Conversation on the Essence of Pardo-ness and Mulatto-ness at the End of Empire." In *Imperial Subjects: Race and Identity in Colonial Spanish America*, edited by Andrew B. Fisher and Matthew D. O'Hara, 141–66. Durham, NC: Duke University Press, 2009.

United Nations. "World Conference against Racism, Racial Discrimination, Xenophobia and Related Intolerance: Declaration." New York: United Nations, 2002. http://www.un.org/en/ga/durbanmeeting2011/pdf/DDPA_full_text.pdf.

United Nations Department of Economic and Social Affairs. Division for Social Policy and Development. Secretariat of the Permanent Forum on Indigenous Issues. "The Perspective of Information Received and Collected Within the Context of ILO Conventions Nos. 107 and 169, and Other Relevant ILO Conventions." Paper presented at Workshop on Data Collection and Disaggregation for Indigenous Peoples, New York, January 19–21, 2004. http://www.un.org/esa/socdev/unpfii/documents/workshop_data_ilo.doc.

———. "Workshop on Data Collection and Disaggregation for Indigenous Peoples." New York, January 19–21, 2004. http://social.un.org/index/IndigenousPeoples/CrossThematicIssues/DataandIndicators.aspx.

United Nations Department of Social Affairs and United Nations Statistical Office. *Population Census Methods*. New York: United Nations, 1949.

United Nations Development Programme. "Human Development Report 2004: Cultural Liberty in Today's Diverse World." New York: UNDP, 2004.

———. "Visibilidad estadística: Datos sobre población afrodescendiente en censos y encuestas de hogares de América Latina." Panama City, Panama: UNDP, 2012. http://www.slideshare.net/escuelaelectoral/visibilidad-estadistica-datos-de-poblacion-afrodescendiente-en-america-latina.

United Nations. Economic Commission for Africa. *African Recommendations for the 1970 Population Censuses*. Addis Ababa, Ethiopia: Economic Commission for Africa, 1968.

United Nations. Economic Commission for Asia and the Far East. *Asian Recommendations for the 1970 Population Censuses*. New York: United Nations, 1967.

United Nations Educational, Scientific and Cultural Organization. *The Race Question in Modern Science. The Race Concept: Results of an Inquiry*. Paris: UNESCO, 1952. http://unesdoc.unesco.org/images/0007/000733/073351eo.pdf.

United Nations. Statistical Office. *Principles and Recommendations for National Population Censuses*. New York: United Nations, 1958.

United States. Delegates to the International Statistical Congress. *Report of the Delegates to the International Statistical Congress Held at St. Petersburg in August, 1872*. Washington, DC: Government Printing Office, 1875.

United States War Department. Cuban Census Office. *Census of Cuba, 1899*. Washington, DC: Government Printing Office, 1900.

Uruguay. Dirección General del Censo. *Censo General (1895–1896)*. Montevideo, Uruguay: Imprenta Vapor de la Nación, 1897.

Valdez, Carlos. "Bolivia's Census Omits 'Mestizo' as Category," *The Big Story, Associated Press,* November 21, 2012. http://bigstory.ap.org/article/bolivias-census-omits-mestizo-category.

Van Cott, Donna Lee. "Andean Indigenous Movements and Constitutional Transformation: Venezuela in Comparative Perspective." *Latin American Perspectives* 30, 1 (2003): 49–69.

———. *Indigenous Peoples and Democracy in Latin America*. New York: St. Martin's Press, 1994.

———. *The Friendly Liquidation of the Past: The Politics of Diversity in Latin America*. Pittsburgh, PA: University of Pittsburgh Press, 2000.

Van Dijk, Teun. *Ideología, una Aproximación Multidisciplinaria*. Barcelona: Gedisa, 1998.

Vandellós, José A. "Ensayo de Demografía Venezolana," Dirección General de Estadística y Censos Nacionales. Caracas: Lit. y Tip. Casa de especialidades, 1938.

Vandiver, Marylee Mason. "Racial Classifications in Latin American Censuses." *Social Forces* 28 (1949): 138–146.

Varnhagen, Francisco Adolfo de. "Relatorio Acérca dos Trabalhos do Congresso Estatistica de St. Petersburg em Agosto de 1872, Apresentado Ao Governo Imperial Pelo Delegado Official do Brazil, Barão do Porto Seguro," 1872, appended to *Relatario do Ministério dos Negócios do Império apresentado em dezembro de 1872*. Rio de Janeiro: Typographia Nacional, 1872.

Vasconcelos, José. *The Cosmic Race/La Raza Cósmica*. Translated by Didier T. Jaén. Los Angeles: California State University, 1979.

Venezuela. Dirección General de Estadística y Censos Nacionales. *Quinto censo nacional de los Estados Unidos de Venezuela... levantado en los días 31 de enero y 1, 2 y 3 de febrero de 1926*. Caracas: Tip. Universal, 1926.

Venezuela. Ministerio de Fomento. Dirección de Estadística. Oficina Central del Censo Nacional. *Octavo censo general de población, 26 de Noviembre de 1950*. Caracas: Ministerio de Fomento, 1957.

———. Dirección de Estadística. *VII censo nacional de población levantado el 7 de diciembre de 1941*. Caracas: Dirección General de Estadística, 1944–1947.

———. *Resumen general del sexto censo de población, 26 de diciembre de 1936*. Caracas: Tip. Garrido, 1938.

Ventresca, Marc J. "When States Count: Institutional and Political Dynamics in Modern Census Establishment, 1800–1993." PhD diss., Stanford University, 1995.

———. "Global Policy Fields: Conflicts and Settlements in the Emergence of Organized International Attention to Official Statistics, 1853–1947." Institute for Policy Research Working Paper WP-02-45, Northwestern University, 2002. http://www.ipr.northwestern.edu/publications/papers/2002/ipr-wp-02-45.html.

Vianna, Francisco José de Oliveira. *Evolução do Povo Brasileiro*, 2nd ed. São Paulo: Companhia Editora Nacional, 1933.

———. "Raça e pesquisas estatísticas." *Correio Paulistano* 25 September, 1926, p. 3.

Villaramín, Juan and Judith Villaramín. "Colonial Censuses and Tributary Lists of the Sabana de Bogotá Chibcha: Sources and Issues." In *Studies in Spanish American*

Population History, edited by David J. Robinson, 45–92. Boulder, CO: Westview Press, 1981.

———. "Native Colombia: Contact, Conquest, and Colonial Populations." *Revista de Indias* LXIII 227 (2003): 105–34.

Vinson, Ben. *Bearing Arms for His Majesty: the Free-Colored Militia in Colonial Mexico.* Stanford, CA: Stanford University Press, 2001.

Voelz, Peter. *Slave and Soldier: The Military Impact of Blacks in the Colonial Americas.* New York: Garland Publishing, Inc., 1993.

vom Hau, Matthias, and Hillel Soifer. "Unpacking the 'Strength' of the State: The Utility of State Infrastructural Power." *Studies in Comparative International Development* 43 (2008): 219–30.

Wacquant, Loïc. "For an Analytic of Racial Domination." *Political Power and Social Theory* 11 (1997): 221–34.

Wade, Peter. *Blackness and Race Mixture: The Dynamics of Racial Identity in Colombia.* Baltimore: John Hopkins University Press, 1993.

———. *Race and Ethnicity in Latin America.* London: Pluto Press, 2010.

———. *Race, Nature and Culture: An Anthropological Approach.* London: Pluto Press, 2002.

Wagley, Charles. "On the Concept of Social Race in the Americas." In *Contemporary Cultures and Societies in Latin America*, edited by Dwight B. Heath and Richard N. Adams, 531–45. New York: Random House, 1965.

Warren, Sarah. "A Nation Divided: Building the Cross-Border Mapuche Nation in Chile and Argentina." *Journal of Latin American Studies* 45, 2 (2013): 235–64.

Weber, Eugen. *Peasants into Frenchmen: the Modernization of Rural France, 1870–1914.* Stanford, CA: Stanford University Press, 1976.

Weber, Max. *Economy and Society.* Berkeley: University of California Press, 1968.

Westergaard, Harald. *Contributions to the History of Statistics.* London: King, 1932.

Wightman, Ann. *Indigenous Migration and Social Change: the Forasteros of Cuzco, 1570–1720.* Durham, NC: Duke University Press, 1990.

Willcox, Walter F. "Census." In *Encyclopedia of the Social Sciences*, vol. 2, edited by R. A. Seligman, 295–300. New York: MacMillan Company, 1930.

Williams, John Hoyt. "Observations on the Paraguayan Census of 1846." *Hispanic American Historical Review* 56, 3 (1976): 424–437.

Wilmer, Franke. *The Indigenous Voice in World Politics: Since Time Immemorial.* Newbury Park, CA: Sage, 1993.

Wimmer, Andreas. *Nationalist Exclusion and Ethnic Conflict: Shadows of Modernity.* Cambridge: Cambridge University Press, 2002.

———. "The Making and Unmaking of Ethnic Boundaries. A Multilevel Process Theory." *American Journal of Sociology* 113, 4 (2008): 970–1022.

———. "Who Owns the State? Understanding Ethnic Conflict in Post-Colonial Societies." *Nations and Nationalism* 3, 4 (1997): 631–65.

Winant, Howard. *The World Is a Ghetto: Race and Democracy Since World War II.* New York: Basic Books, 2001.

Wolfe, A. B. "Population Censuses before 1790." *Journal of the American Statistical Association* XXVII, 180 (1932): 357–70.

Woolf, Stuart. "Statistics and the Modern State." *Comparative Studies of Society and History* 31 (1989): 588–604.

World Bank. "The 'Todos Contamos' Workshop." *La Ventana Newsletter* 1 (August 2001): 1–6. http://www-wds.worldbank.org/servlet/WDSContentServer/WDSP/IB/2002/09/07/000094946_02082104034383/Rendered/PDF/multiopage.pdf.

Wright, Carroll D. and William Hunt. *The History and Growth of the United States Census.* Washington, DC: Government Printing Office, 1900.

Wright, Winthrop R. *Café con Leche: Race, Class, and National Image in Venezuela.* Austin: University of Texas Press, 1993.

Yashar, Deborah J. *Contesting Citizenship in Latin America: The Rise of Indigenous Movements and the Postliberal Challenge.* Cambridge: Cambridge University Press, 2005.

———. "Democracy, Indigenous Movements, and the Postliberal Challenge in Latin America." *World Politics* 52, 1 (1999): 76–104.

Young, Crawford. "Ethnicity and the Colonial and Postcolonial State in Africa." In *Ethnic Groups and the State*, edited by Paul Brass, 57–93. London: Croom Helm, 1985.

Zahn, Friedrich. *50 Années de L'Institut International de Statistique.* Munich: Institut International de Statistique, 1934.

Zerubavel, Eviatar. "Lumping and Splitting: Notes on Social Classification." *Sociological Forum* 11, 3 (1996): 421–33.

———. *Social Mindscapes: an Invitation to Cognitive Sociology.* Cambridge, MA: Harvard University Press, 1997.

———. *The Fine Line: Making Distinctions in Everyday Life.* New York: Free Press, 1991.

Zolberg, Aristide. "International Migration Policies in a Changing World System." In *Human Migration: Patterns and Policies*, edited by William McNeill and Ruth Adams, 241–86. Bloomington: Indiana University Press, 1978.

———. "Matters of State: Theorizing Immigration Policy." In *The Handbook of International Migration: The American Experience*, edited by Charles Hirschman, Josh DeWind, and Philip Kasinitz, 71–93. New York: Russell Sage, 2000.

Zuazo, Moira. "Q'ueste los mestizos: Diálogo con tres estudios sobre mestizaje y condición indígena en Bolivia." *Tinkazos* 9, 21 (2006). http://www.eforobolivia.org/blog.php/?p=10827.

Zuberi, Tukufu. *Thicker Than Blood: How Racial Statistics Lie.* Minneapolis: University of Minnesota Press, 2001.

Zúñiga, Roberto Herrera. "Las metáforas del racismo: apuntes sobre el positivismo boliviano." *Revista de Filosofía Universidad Costa Rica* XLVII, 122 (2009): 39–47.

INDEX

Figures and tables are indicated by "f" and "t" following the page numbers.

Abercrombie, Thomas, 83
Abreu, Lúcia, 314
Activism for census reforms, 279–283, 285, 297, 312–318
Affirmative action initiatives, 4, 276–277, 316, 320–322
Afrodescendant populations
  census questions used for identification of, 254t, 256–263t
  demographic disappearance of, 241–248, 241t
  mobilization of, 274–278, 279–280
  statistical omission of, 28n79, 191–200
  visibility in censuses, 241–243, 241t, 252–256, 253t, 254t, 256–263t
Agassiz, Louis, 126, 129
Age
  classification by, 3, 26, 93, 94, 118
  legal rights based on, 61
  military eligibility and, 26, 50
  Portuguese population count in Brazil by age and sex, 56
  statistical tables organized by, 183, 184f
The Americas Have Color: Afrodescendants in 21st-century Censuses (documentary series), 313–314
Andrews, George Reid, 73
Apartheid, 4, 11, 16

Appadurai, Arjun, 55, 58
Argentina
  census questions regarding ethnoracial diversity in, 256t, 264, 279, 315–316
  ILO 169, ratification of, 273t
  immigration to, 145, 150–153, 152f, 184f
  indigenous populations in, 189–191, 190f, 270
  mestizaje in, 130, 155–156, 157
  national censuses in, 7n9, 102, 104, 106, 111, 112n94
  national statistics agency in, 102, 103t
  postindependence denouncement of racial classification, 79–80
  race science on degeneration in, 130
  racial composition of, 144–145, 193, 194f
  racial statistics, presentation of, 183, 184f, 194f
  reform of censuses in, 264n5, 300
  selective omission of racial statistics in, 28n79, 145, 192–193, 194f
  visibility of minority populations in censuses of, 233–236, 233–234t, 241–243, 241t, 252–256, 253–254t
  whitening of populations in, 131
Arguedas, Alcides, 129–130

Asian populations
    enumeration of, 172, 173, 182–183, 193, 195, 198–200
    exclusionary immigration policies for, 146–147
    statistical invisibility of, 295n96
Average man concept, 25, 31, 88
Aztec empire, 20n49, 68

Banton, Michael, xv, 250n2
Belo Monte dam project, 322–323, 323*f*
Birthplace. *See* Place of birth
Boas, Franz, 218
Bolivia
    census questions regarding ethnoracial diversity in, 253*t*, 254*t*, 257*t*, 317
    enumerator instructions in, 174–175
    ILO 169, ratification of, 273, 273*t*
    indigenous populations in, 133–135, 236, 264, 270, 321–322
    mestizaje in, 156, 160–161
    multicultural reforms in, 270
    national statistics agency in, 103*t*
    opposition to racial classification practices in, 317
    race science on degeneration in, 129–130
    racial composition of, 141, 144, 195, 196*f*
    racial improvement, portrayals of, 131–132, 133–135
    reform of censuses in, 299
    selective omission of racial statistics in, 195, 197*f*, 198
    uncounted populations in, 187
    visibility of minority populations in censuses of, 233–236, 233–234*t*, 241*t*, 252–256, 253–254*t*
Borah, Woodrow W., 67n80, 73n103
Bourdieu, Pierre, 17
Brazil
    affirmative action initiatives in, 277, 279, 320
    Afrodescendant movements in, 275
    antidiscrimination campaigns in, 277
    Belo Monte dam project, 322–323, 323*f*
    campaign to increase black classification in, 312, 313, 314
    census questions regarding ethnoracial diversity in, 255, 257*t*, 264
    colonial census taking in, 51–52, 53, 56
    DGE (General Directorate of Statistics), 104n79, 107, 176
    enumerator instructions in, 174, 176
    ILO 169, ratification of, 273*t*
    immigration to, 147, 148–150, 150*f*
    indigenous populations in, 137–138
    labor extraction practices in, 51–52
    mestizaje in, 155
    national censuses in, 101, 104
    national statistics agency in, 102, 103*t*, 107, 176
    opposition to racial classification practices in, 316
    politics influencing collection of racial statistics, 244–245
    race science on degeneration in, 125, 126, 129, 166
    racial composition of, 141–143, 141*f*
    racial improvement, portrayals of, 132, 137–138, 166
    racial statistics, presentation of, 141, 141*f*, 185, 202, 202*f*
    reform of censuses in, 279, 285, 299
    report on comparability of race data, 216–217
    selective omission of racial statistics in, 198
    slave classification in, 68
    visibility of minority populations in censuses of, 233–236, 233–234*t*, 241–245, 241*t*, 252–256, 253–254*t*, 255, 257*t*
    whitening of populations in, 229–230, 245
Brazilian Black Movement, 312
Brubaker, Rogers, xiv, 21
Bunge, Carlos Octavio, 130

Calidad (quality), 45–46, 73, 76, 90, 148
Canadian Foundation for the Americas (FOCAL), 286
Canessa, Andrew, 273n34, 322
Cardoso, Fernando Henrique, 36n106, 279
Cartagena Declaration, 289–290
Casta paintings, 63n75, 64, 64n76, 66, 66n77, 67*f*
Casta system, 44n4, 59, 61, 63–64, 64–65*f*, 68–70
Caste, classification by, 26, 45, 56
Castizos, xii, 63, 69, 70, 74, 76
Castleman, Bruce, 66n79, 74
Castro, Fidel, 246
Categorical classification, 3, 12,–14, 16, 18, 22, 28, 32, 37, 43–44, 59–62, 80, 137, 173, 183, 191, 308, 321.
  See also Ethnoracial classification
CELADE (Centro Latinoamericano y Caribeño de Demografía), 289, 309, 310
Census Bureau, U.S., 18n41, 176–177, 223, 226, 282, 284
Census reforms, 250–300
  actors involved in, 251, 266–269, 278
  democratization influencing, 265–267
  development goals of, 252, 291–293, 318–324
  direct logistical support and public advocacy for, 285–287
  diversity, recognition of, 250–256, 253–254*t*, 264–265, 306
  domestic activists and, 285, 306
  ethnoracial classification, modifications to queries of, 253–254*t*, 257–258, 256–263*t*, 264–265, 285–288
  future challenges of, 299–300
  holdouts to ethnoracial data collection, 294–298
  international influence on, 281–294, 306
  multiculturalism and, 267–278, 307
  opposition to, 300, 316–318
  public information campaigns and, 312–316
  regional organizational support for, 289–290
  as target of social activists, 278–281
Census taking. *See also* National censuses
  for conscription purposes, 24, 48, 49–50, 56
  for household and demographic information, 52–55
  for labor extraction practices, 50–52
  nation making and, 28–30, 82, 85–87, 121–122, 201, 205
  reforms, 250–300.
    See also Census reforms
  as social control method, 55, 58
  standardization of methods for, 91–92, 93–97, 115, 117–119, 223–225, 281
Centro Latinoamericano y Caribeño de Demografía (CELADE), 289, 309, 310
Certification of whiteness, 70–71
Chile
  census questions regarding ethnoracial diversity in, 258*t*, 295–298
  democratization of data production in, 309
  ILO 169, ratification of, 273, 273*t*
  indigenous population counts in, 188–189
  mestizaje in, 189
  national censuses in, 7n9, 100, 105–106, 112n94
  national statistics agency in, 102, 103*t*
  postindependence denouncement of racial classification, 79
  selective omission of racial statistics in, 191–192, 193–194
  visibility of minority populations in censuses of, 233–236, 233–234*t*, 241–243, 241*t*, 252–256, 253–254*t*
  whitening of populations in, 131
Church, population registers kept by, 53–55
Citizenship, classification by, 3
Civic constructions of nationhood, 20–23, 79, 122, 123, 304
Civil registration, 53n40

Index | 365

Civil status. *See* Marital status
Classificatory mobility, 70–71, 72–76
Colombia
- Afrodescendant movements in, 275
- antidiscrimination campaigns in, 277
- campaign to increase classification as black in, 312, 313
- census questions regarding ethnoracial diversity in, 258*t*, 264
- DANE (Departamento Administrativo Nacional de Estatística), 280, 286, 312
- ILO 169, ratification of, 273, 273*t*, 280
- multicultural reforms in, 268
- national censuses in, 121
- national statistics agency in, 101, 103*t*
- racial improvement, portrayals of, 132
- reform of censuses in, 279–280, 285, 289, 299
- selective omission of racial statistics in, 199
- visibility of minority populations in censuses of, 233–236, 233–234*t*, 241–243, 241*t*, 252–256, 253–254*t*

Colonial Latin America, 43–78. *See also* Latin America; Portuguese America; Spanish America; *specific countries*
- casta paintings, 63n75, 64, 64n76, 66, 66n77, 67*f*
- casta system in, 44n4, 59, 61, 63–64, 64–65*f*, 68–70
- census taking, motives and methods of, 47–59, 303
- Church, population registers kept by, 53–54
- classificatory mobility in, 70–71, 72–76
- discretionary power in classification practices in, 73–74
- diversity in, 44
- ethnoracial classification in, 39, 44–46, 59–62, 66–71
- historical analysis of, 46–47
- Indian classification in, 16n33, 43n3, 67–68
- labor extraction practices in, 50–52
- *limpieza de sangre* ideology in, 62–63, 68–70
- military strength, assessment of, 48, 49–50
- naturalization of social divides in, 39, 44, 47, 59, 76
- population as strategic resource in, 39, 43–44
- resistance to racial categories in, 71–76
- slave classification in, 68
- tributary systems in, 50–51

Color-blind states, official ethnoracial classification in, 82–85
Conferences of American States, 117n104, 118, 119
Conscription, census taking for purposes of, 24, 25, 48–50, 56, 70, 101
Cook, Sherbourne F., 67n80
Costa Rica
- census questions regarding ethnoracial diversity in, 253–254*t*, 258*t*
- enumeration of indigenous populations in, 187, 236
- ILO 169, ratification of, 273, 273*t*
- national censuses in, 106, 110
- national statistics agency in, 103*t*
- visibility of minority populations in censuses of, 233–236, 233–234*t*, 241–243, 241*t*, 252–256, 253–254*t*
- whitening of populations in, 229, 230n52, 248

Creoles, 69, 74, 80, 83, 128, 185n35, 261*t*, 264
Cuba
- census questions regarding ethnoracial diversity in, 253–254*t*, 259*t*, 295–296
- national censuses in, 8n11, 143, 143n50, 148, 185
- national statistics agency in, 103*t*
- politics influencing collection of racial statistics, 245–247

366 | Index

racial composition of, 143–144, 230,
    230–231*f*
racial improvement, portrayals
    of, 132, 230
visibility of minority populations in
    censuses of, 233–236, 233–234*t*,
    241–243, 241*t*, 252–256, 253–254*t*
whitening of populations in, 230,
    230–231*f*, 245–246
Cultural anthropology, 218
Cultural attributes as measures of racial
    differences, 226–232, 236–240, 238*f*,
    305–306
Cultural liberty, 291–292, 308, 317, 323, 324

De Gobineau, Arthur, 125, 126, 127
De la Fuente, Alejandro, 148
Delance, Jorge, 133–134, 156
De Lapouge, Vacher, 126, 137, 143, 145
Democratization
    census reforms, influence on, 265–267
    of data production, 309–311
Department of War, U.S.
    See War Department, U.S.
Desrosières, Alain, 25n72, 30n87
Disabilities, classification by, 3, 93, 94, 203
Discrimination
    antidiscrimination campaigns, 276–277
    ethnoracial classification to combat, 4
    limpieza de sangre and, 62–63, 68–70
Diversity. *See also* Racial and ethnic
    differences
    census reforms, recognition of, 250–252,
        253–256, 253–254*t*, 264–265, 306
    in colonial Latin America, 44
    nation making, challenges for, 19–20, 21
Domestic activists, 244–245, 249, 251, 267,
    273, 274–280, 285, 291, 295–297,
    312, 314, 316, 318, 320–322
Dominican Republic
    census questions regarding ethnoracial
        diversity in, 259*t*, 295, 296
    national censuses in, 8n12

national statistics agency in, 102, 103*t*
racial improvement, portrayals of, 132
selective omission of racial statistics in, 199
visibility of minority populations in
    censuses of, 233–236, 233–234*t*,
    241–243, 241*t*, 252–256, 253–254*t*
Domschke, Elaine, 188n39, 329
*Draft Declaration of Principles for the
    Defense of Indigenous Nations and
    Peoples of the Western Hemisphere*
    (UN), 272

Economic Commission on Latin America
    and the Caribbean (ECLAC), 282,
    287, 289, 297, 309, 310, 319
Ecuador
    Afrodescendant movements in, 277
    census questions regarding ethnoracial
        diversity in, 259*t*, 316
    ILO 169, ratification of, 273, 273*t*
    Indian classification in, 83–84
    multicultural reforms in, 268, 277
    national statistics agency in, 102, 103*t*
    reform of censuses in, 300
    visibility of minority populations in
        censuses of, 233–236, 233–234*t*,
        241–243, 241*t*, 252–256, 253–254*t*
Education
    classification by, 118
    constitutional provisions for, 269
    racial classification, implications for, 62
El Salvador
    census questions regarding ethnoracial
        diversity in, 259–260*t*
    national statistics agency in, 102, 103*t*
    racial improvement, portrayal of, 144
    visibility of minority populations in
        censuses of, 233–236, 233–234*t*,
        241–243, 241*t*, 252–256, 253–254*t*
Enumerator instructions for census taking,
    171–172, 173–177, 178–180
Essay on the Inequality of the Races
    (de Gobineau), 125

Index | 367

Ethnic constructions of nationhood, 20–23, 122, 304
Ethnic group, use of term, 14, 221–222, 223
Ethnocide, statistical, 191, 319
Ethnoracial classification, 3–42, 301–325.
   See also Racial and ethnic differences
   affirmative action initiatives and, 4, 277, 279, 320–322
   analytic approach to, 32–34
   in colonial Latin America, 39, 44–46, 59–62, 66–71
   comparative approach to, 10, 11, 34–37
   constituencies for categories, creation of, 312–318
   exclusionary vs. inclusionary results of, 4–5, 12
   historical analysis of, 7–8, 10, 11, 301–307
   in Latin America. See Latin America; specific countries
   international guidelines for census content and, 111–115, 112n94, 113t, 117, 119–120
   motivations for, 4–5, 8, 12–13, 22
   nation making and, 19–23.
      See also Nation making
   naturalization of social divides and, 13–19.
      See also Naturalization of social divides
   official vs. informal, 18–19
   people, defining and redefining through, 20, 23–24, 44
   political nature of, 301–302, 307, 308, 311, 318, 320–325
   racial statistics and, 121–206.
      See also Racial statistics
   terminology, 37–39
Eugenics, 23, 126, 127, 130, 144, 155, 217–220
European Union, 282
Exclusion
   ethnoracial classification resulting in, 4–5, 12
   in immigration policies, 22, 146–147, 224

Family lineage
   classification by, 74, 93, 94
   legal rights based on, 61, 66
   racial ascription influenced by, 46
Fertility rates, racial differences in, 140–141, 144, 145
FOCAL (Canadian Foundation for the Americas), 286
Ford Foundation, 285, 288, 292n92, 312
Fortoul, José Gil, 194–195, 242–243
France, defining source of nationhood in, xiv, 8, 98, 122, 324
Freyre, Gilberto, 218, 228
Funding for national censuses, 282, 282n56–57, 281–284, 293

Gamio, Manuel, 218, 236–237
Gender. See Sex
General Directorate of Statistics (DGE), 104n79, 107, 176
Gente de razón (people of reason), 67, 67n80
Germany, defining source of nationhood in, 122, 304
Goyer, Doreen S., 188n39, 329
Grillo, R. D., 20n49, 54n41
Guatemala
   Afrodescendant movements in, 277
   census questions regarding ethnoracial diversity in, 260t
   cultural attributes as measures of indigenous populations, 239–240
   enumerator instructions in, 173, 175
   ILO 169, ratification of, 273, 273t
   immigration to, 147–148
   indigenous populations in, 135
   language groups in, 137, 138f
   mestizaje in, 158–160, 159f
   multicultural reforms in, 268
   national statistics agency in, 102, 103t
   racial improvement, portrayals of, 131–132
   racial statistics, presentation of, 182, 183

selective omission of racial statistics in, 195–196
uncounted populations in, 187
visibility of minority populations in censuses of, 233–236, 233–234*t*, 241–243, 241*t*, 252–256, 253–254*t*
Guerrero, Andrés, 83–84

Hacking, Ian, 15, 15n27–28, 16, 88, 91n38
Hale, Charles, 324
Head-tax systems, 50
Honduras
  Afrodescendant movements in, 275
  census questions regarding ethnoracial diversity in, 260*t*
  ILO 169, ratification of, 273, 273*t*
  multicultural reforms in, 276
  national censuses in, 139
  national statistics agency in, 102, 103*t*
  uncounted populations in, 187
  visibility of minority populations in censuses of, 233–236, 233–234*t*, 241–243, 241*t*, 252–256, 253–254*t*
Hooker, Juliet, 276
Household censuses, 47n12, 48, 52–55
Huamanga communities, tributary systems in, 51
Human Development Report (UNDP), 291–293
Human rights legislation for indigenous populations, 271–274, 273*t*

IAC. *See* Inter-Agency Consultation on Race in Latin America
IASI (Inter-American Statistical Institute), 223–224
IBGE (Instituto Brasileiro de Geografía e Estatística), 279
ICERD (International Convention on the Elimination of all Forms of Racial Discrimination), 284
IDB. *See* Inter-American Development Bank

ILO 169. *See* International Labor Organization Convention 169
Immigration
  exclusionary policies on, 6n8, 22, 130, 146–147, 198, 219, 224, 266
  incentive programs for, 146
  as method for demographic improvement, 145–153
  racial statistics on, 145–153, 150*f*, 194*f*
Incan empire, 68, 102n75
Income, race as factor in distribution of, 288
Indian classification. *See also* Indigenous populations
  civilized vs. uncivilized, 186–191
  in colonial Latin America, 16n33, 43n3, 67–68
  invention of, 16, 43
Indigenous populations. *See also* Indian classification
  census questions used for identification of, 234*t*, 254*t*, 255–256, 256–263*t*, 264–265
  Draft Declaration of Principles for the Defense of Indigenous Nations and Peoples of the Western Hemisphere (UN), 272
  enumeration, approaches to, 234*t*, 235
  human rights legislation and, 271–274, 273*t*
  mobilization of, 269, 270–274, 277–278
  Permanent Forum on Indigenous Issues (UN), 274
  training workshops on use of censuses for, 309–310
  visibility in censuses, 233–240, 233–234*t*, 252–253, 253–254*t*, 256
  Working Group on Indigenous Populations (UN), 272
Infirmities. *See* Disabilities
Informal vs. official classifications, 18–19
Inheritance, implications of racial classification for, 45, 62, 71
Institutional isomorphism, 86

Institutionalization of racial categories, 5, 11–12, 14, 35
Inter-Agency Consultation on Race in Latin America (IAC), 288, 291, 292–293, 320
Inter-American Development Bank (IDB), 282, 284, 286, 287, 288, 291, 293, 319, 324
Inter-American Dialogue organization, 270, 288, 291
Inter-American Statistical Institute (IASI), 223–224
International Convention on the Elimination of all Forms of Racial Discrimination (ICERD), 284
International Expert Workshop on Data Collection and Disaggregation for Indigenous Peoples (UN), 288–289
International Labor Organization Convention 169 (ILO 169), 272–274, 273t, 280
International Statistical Congress (ISC)
  accomplishments of, 90–91
  adaptations to recommendations of, 109–111
  census taking, standardization of methods for, 91–92, 93–96, 281
  establishment of, 81, 88, 89–90
  Latin American participation in, 106–109, 108t, 110–111
  national statistics agencies and, 101–102, 103t
  racial statistics, inattention to, 114–115, 117–118
  statistical best practice recommendations, 82, 90, 93–95
  successor to, 96
International Statistical Institute (ISI), 96–97, 109, 114–115, 114n98, 115n100, 116t
ISC. *See* International Statistical Congress

Jackson, Robert, 33, 73n105
Jaramillo, Andrés, 328
Jenkins, Richard, 18n39, 19
Jesuit missionaries, 51–52
A Journey in Brazil (Agassiz & Agassiz), 126

Knight, Alan, 16, 16n33, 43n3

Labor extraction practices, 50–52
Lacerda, João Batista de, 128–129
Language
  classification by, 93, 94, 114, 135–137, 136f, 138f, 157, 192, 225–227, 233–237, 254t, 255, 256–263t, 315
Lapouge, Georges Vacher de, 126, 137, 143
Latin America. *See also specific countries*
  affirmative action initiatives in, 279, 281, 322, 323
  Afrodescendant movements in, 274–278, 279–280, 285, 312–318
  antidiscrimination campaigns in, 276–278
  colonial Latin America, 43–78.
    See also Colonial Latin America
  democratic reforms in, 265–267
  immigration to, 145–153, 150f, 152f
  inclusionary racial distinctions in, xv, 304
  indigenous movements in, 267, 270, 271–275, 279–280
  ISC participation by, 106–109, 108t, 110–111
  modernization projects and censuses in, 6–7, 87, 98–99, 103–104
  multicultural reforms in, 267–278, 306
  national censuses in, 79–120.
    See also National censuses
  national statistics agencies in, 101–102, 103t
  nationhood, defining source of, 122–123
  postindependence denouncement of racial classification, 79–81, 82
  race science view of, 125–128
  racial statistics, 121–206. *See also* Racial statistics
  slave classification in, 80

Law of normal distribution, 88
League of Nations, 97, 115, 117, 219, 222, 224
Le Bon, Gustav, 127, 143
Limpieza de sangre (cleanness of blood), 62–63, 68–70
Literacy
　as requirement for political participation, 83
　as requirement for census enumerators, 171
Lombardi, John, 43, 50, 54n44, 57, 60
Lomnitz-Adler, Claudio, 61
Looping effect, 16

Making Race and Nation (Marx), 35
Marital status (civil status)
　classification by, 3, 56, 61, 93, 94, 118, 178n26
　legal rights based on, 61
Martí, José, 245
Martínez, Alberto, 153, 156n83
Marx, Anthony, 35
Matrículas (Spanish household censuses), 52
McCaa, Robert, 45–46
MDGs (Millennium Development Goals), 291
Menezes, Luiz Cesar de, 55
Mestizaje (race mixture)
　census accounts of, 153–164
　colonial conceptions of, 62–69, 64*f*, 65*f*, 67*f*
　Indianness, shift away from, 157–160, 189, 232–240
　as national ideal, xii, 164, 231–233, 248–250
　racial progress through, 128–132, 153–154, 156–157, 228–229, 231–233, 247–249
　whitening effects of, 131, 140, 153–156, 158, 161–162, 164–166
Mestizo Nation organization, 316

Mestizos, 63, 69, 70, 160, 173–174, 231–232
Mexico
　Afrodescendant movement in, 314–315
　campaign to increase black classification in, 314–317
　census questions regarding ethnoracial diversity in, 260–261*t*
　colonial census taking in, 69–70
　cultural attributes as measures of indigenous populations, 226–228, 236–237
　discretionary power in classification practices in, 73
　ILO 169, ratification of, 273, 273*t*
　language groups in, 135–137, 135n37, 136*f*
　national statistics agency in, 102, 103*t*, 109
　postindependence denouncement of racial classification, 80
　racial improvement, portrayals of, 131–132
　racial statistics, presentation of, 181–182, 181*f*
　segregated militias in, 70
　visibility of minority populations in censuses of, 233–236, 233–234*t*, 241–243, 241*t*, 252–256, 253–254*t*
Millennium Development Goals (MDGs), 291
Modernization projects, 6–7, 87, 98–99, 103–104
Modern states categorical classification in, 3, 19
　diversity challenges in, 20, 21
　national censuses in, 24–27
　system of states, xiv, 28, 36
Montagu, Ashley, 221
Morales, Evo, 264n7, 270
Moral statistics, 15n28, 58, 91, 92
Morelos, José María, 80
Morelos, René, 130
Mortality rates, racial differences in, 140, 144, 145

Index | 371

Mulattos, 63, 68, 126, 148, 156, 176–177, 191, 213
Multicultural neoliberalism, 324
Multicultural reforms, 267–278, 308

National censuses, 79–120.
  See also Census taking
  adaptations to international model of, 109–111
  challenges of first national censuses, 100–101
  ethnoracial classification in, 111–115, 112n94, 113t, 117, 119–120
  funding for, 282, 282n56–57, 281–284, 293
  global model, origins and construction of, 87–97
  implementation of, 105–109
  international norms and actors influencing, 9, 10–11, 85, 99, 284–298, 306
  international visibility of, 82, 84
  legitimacy of, 30, 30n87
  mestizaje, accounts of, 153–157, 160–164
  modernization projects and, 6–7, 87, 97–99, 103–104
  in modern states, 24–27
  national statistics agencies, 101–102, 103t
  objectives and motivations of, 87, 99–100, 166, 304
  political nature of, 8–11, 33, 84–85, 245, 303
  racial queries, removal of, 207–210, 208t, 211–218
  racial statistics from, 121–206.
    See also Racial statistics
  reforms, 250–300.
    See also Census reforms
  science of human progress and, 9, 30–31
  symbolic function of, 28, 104–105
  as venues for documenting racial progress, 207–249. *See also* Racial progress
Nationality
  classification by, 14, 19, 118, 137, 224
  immigration statistics by, 150, 151
  statistical tables organized by, 182–183, 184t
National particularity, 122–123, 135, 166
National statistics agencies, 101–102, 103t
Nationhood
  bonds of, 20
  civic and ethnic constructions of, 20–23
  defining sources of, 122–123
Nation making
  census taking and, 28–30, 82, 83–91, 121–122, 201–206
  diversity as challenge for, 19–20, 21
  race science influencing, 21–22, 21n60, 23
  racial statistics as demonstration of, 122–124, 166
Nation-states as cultural model, 86–87, 97–99
Naturalization of social divides
  category and categorized, interactions between, 16–17, 19
  in colonial Latin America, 39, 44, 47, 59, 76
  defined, xv, 13
  factors affecting, 16–18
  implications of, 19
  racial statistics perpetuating, 170, 180–183, 186, 200
  self-concept influenced by, 14–16, 17
  states, role in, 13–15, 35–36
  terminologies used in, 14
Natural selection, racial statistics on, 140–145
Neoliberal reforms, 267, 269, 324
Nicaragua
  Afrodescendant movements in, 276
  census questions regarding ethnoracial diversity in, 256, 261t, 264
  funding for censuses, 293
  ILO 169, ratification of, 273, 273t

indigenous population counts in, 188
multicultural reforms in, 268–269
national statistics agency in, 102, 103*t*
visibility of minority populations in censuses of, 233–236, 233–234*t*, 241–243, 241*t*, 252–256, 253–254*t*
Nobles, Melissa, 33, 245, 247n52, 285n65
Nominal identities, 18n39
North, S. N. D., 117, 118

Occupation
classification by, 3, 29, 74, 93, 94, 119, 229
legal rights based on, 45, 61
Official vs. informal classifications, 18–19
O'Higgins, Bernardo, 79
"On the Races and their Relations" (Delance), 133–134, 156
Organization of IberoAmerican States (OEI), 289–290
Otero, Hernán, 145n55, 213

Panama
campaign to increase black classification in, 313–314, 316
census questions regarding ethnoracial diversity in, 258, 261*t*, 316
enumerator instructions in, 174
mestizaje in, 161–163
national statistics agency in, 102, 103*t*
racial composition of, 162, 162–163*f*
selective omission of racial statistics in, 199
visibility of minority populations in censuses of, 233–236, 233–234*t*, 241–243, 241*t*, 252–256, 253–254*t*
whitening of populations in, 229
Pan-American Scientific Congresses, 117–119, 219
Paraguay
census questions regarding ethnoracial diversity in, 262*t*
ILO 169, ratification of, 273, 273*t*

multicultural reforms in, 268–269
national statistics agency in, 102, 103*t*
visibility of minority populations in censuses of, 233–236, 233–234*t*, 241–243, 241*t*, 252–256, 253–254*t*
Passing, 69, 74–75
Patriarca, Silvana, 92
Patriotic statistics, 29
Patronato Real concessions, 53
People, as nation, defining and redefining, 20, 23–24, 44
Permanent Forum on Indigenous Issues (UN), 272, 275, 288, 309–310
Peru
census questions regarding ethnoracial diversity in, 256, 263*t*
cultural attributes as measures of indigenous populations, 237, 238*f*
enumerator instructions in, 173–174, 178
ILO 169, ratification of, 273, 273*t*
multicultural reforms in, 268
national statistics agency in, 102, 103*t*
postindependence denouncement of racial classification, 79
racial improvement, portrayals of, 131–132
racial statistics, presentation of, 183, 185*f*
reform of censuses in, 300
tributary systems in, 51
visibility of minority populations in censuses of, 233–236, 233–234*t*, 241–243, 241*t*, 252–256, 253–254*t*
Place of birth
classification by, 93, 94
legal rights based on, 61
Place of residence
classification by, 3, 93
racial ascription influenced by, 46, 74
Political arithmetic, 89
Political construction of racial differences, 5, 8, 11
"Population Census Methods" (UN), 224–225

Population registers, 53–55. *See also* Census taking; National censuses
Portuguese America. *See also* Colonial Latin America
  census taking in, 51–53, 55–57
  Church, population registers kept by, 53–54
  colonies established in contested regions of, 49
  labor extraction practices in, 50, 51–52
  official ethnoracial classification in, 62, 66
Positivism, 109, 125, 129, 130, 227, 236
Prejudice, 175, 176, 214, 216, 220n28, 232, 314
"Principles and Recommendations for National Population Censuses" (UN), 224–225
"Program for Improvement and Coordination of Statistics in the Western Hemisphere" (IASI), 223
"Program for Improvement of Household Surveys and Measurement of Living Conditions in Latin America" (ECLAC), 282
Property ownership
  classification by, 26
  constitutional provisions for, 269
  legal rights based on, 45
  racial classification, implications for, 62
Public information campaigns for new census categories, 312–317

Quetelet, Adolphe, 25, 25–26n72, 88, 89–90, 101, 105, 192

Race. *See also* Race science; Racial and ethnic differences
  classification by, 3–4, 26. *See also* Ethnoracial classification
  statistical tables organized by, 141*f*, 159*f*, 162–163*f*, 181*f*, 185*f*, 194*f*, 196*f*, 197*f*, 202*f*
  use of term, xii, 37–38, 220–221, 222

The Race Question (UNESCO), 220, 221
Race science
  Latin America as viewed by, 125–128
  nation making, influence on, 21–22, 21n60, 23, 121–168
  racial statistics as response to development predictions, 40, 128–132, 165, 166–167, 168, 304–306
  rejection of, 217–222
Racial and ethnic differences. *See also* Diversity; Ethnoracial classification
  cultural attributes as measures of, 226–232, 237–240, 238*f*, 306–307
  documentation using racial statistics, 132–138
  identification of, 73, 171, 258, 314–317
  in fertility and mortality rates, 140, 144, 145
  institutionalization of, 5, 11–12, 35
  political construction of, 5, 8, 11
  social construction of, 13
Racial determinist theories, 123–124, 125–128, 130, 217–222, 306
Racial drift, 74
Racial Impact Statement (RIS), 292–293
Racial particularity, 40, 122–123, 132–138
Racial progress, 121–168, 207–251
  Afrodescendant populations, purported demographic disappearance of, 241–248, 241*t*
  charting, 139–163
  Indians, purported demographic disappearance of, 232–240, 233–234*t*
  mestizaje as promoting, 153–156, 226–227, 228–232, 247–249
  racial determinism, displacement of, 217–222
  whitening populations as, 40, 165, 198, 229, 246, 247
Racial statistics
  audiences targeted for use of, 165–168
  collecting, 171–180, 201

displacement of indigenous groups in, 186–191
documenting racial difference using, 132–138
enumerator discretion in production of, 171–176, 178–180
identification practices and, 73, 171, 256, 312–317
inclusion in early censuses, 111–114, 112n94, 113*t*
as indicators of national progress, 139–140, 164–165, 170
international comparability of, 216–217
on mestizaje, 153–164
nation making demonstrated through, 122–124, 166
on natural and social selection, 140–145, 141*f*
hierarchy of races perpetuated through, 170, 180–183, 186, 200
politics influencing collection of, 244–247
presentation and organization of, 180–186, 201–203
reliability of, 174, 175, 176–178, 210, 213, 215, 217
as response to race science development predictions, 40, 128–132, 165, 166–167, 305–306
selective omission of, 191–200, 197*f*, 243, 244
statistic congresses inattention to, 114–115, 117–119
validity of, 210, 211, 213–215, 244, 247
Ramirez, Nelson, 217
Religion
classification by, 14n23, 93, 94, 114, 225
legal rights based on, 61, 66
omission of queries on, 191–192, 217
Residence. *See* Place of residence
Revillagigedo military census, 70
Rodrigues, Nina, 129

Rodríguez-Piñero, Luis, 271–272
Romero, Sílvio, 128

San Martín, José de, 7, 79
Scenes of Brazil (news program), 314
Science of human progress, national censuses and, 9, 30–31
Sex
classification by, 3, 26, 94, 118
legal rights based on, 61, 66
Portuguese population count in Brazil by age and sex, 56
poverty and health statistics by, 323
statistical tables organized by, 183, 184*f*, 189, 229, 238*f*, 283, 323
Sickness and infirmities. *See* Disabilities
Skidmore, Thomas, 128, 167n99, 305n2
Slave classification, 68, 80
Smith, Mayo, 212
Smithsonian Institute, 295
Social Darwinism, 125, 143, 228
Social prejudice, 175, 176, 214, 314
South Africa, apartheid in, 11, 16
Soviet Union, ethnoracial classification in, 16
Spanish America. *See* Colonial Latin America
Spencer, Herbert, 109, 127
Staatenkunde field of study, 89
Starr, Paul, 27, 57–58
State building, xiv, 10, 24, 31, 35–36, 85, 110, 205, 305
Statistical ethnocide, 191, 319
Statistics and Sociology (Smith), 212
Stern, Peter, 72
Stern, Steve, 51

Telles, Edward, 299
Todos Contamos campaign, 286–288, 294, 314–316, 315*f*
Tributary systems, 39, 50–51, 68, 71–73, 79, 80n8

"Uniformity and Cooperation in the Census Methods of the Republics of the American Continent" (North), 117
United Nations (UN)
    on data collection methods, 224–226, 281, 288–289
    on human development, 291–292
    on indigenous populations, 271–272, 288–289, 309–310
    Millennium Development Goals, 291
    on statistical ethnocide, 319
United Nations Development Programme (UNDP), 291–292, 297
United Nations Educational, Scientific, and Cultural Organization (UNESCO), 219–222, 220n27, 222n34, 297
United Nations Population Fund (UNFPA), 281, 289, 310
United Nations World Conference against Racial Discrimination, Racism, Xenophobia, and Related Intolerance (UNWCAR), 274, 282, 284, 286
United States.
    Census Bureau, 11n17, 18n41, 223, 226, 282
    Congressional Research Service, 286–287
    enumerator instructions in, 176–180
    ethnoracial classification in, xi, 176–178
    exclusionary racial distinctions in, xv
    immigration policies of, 223–224
    institutionalization of racial differences in, 5
    nationhood, defining source of, 122
    sociology of race in, 32, 36
Upward mobility, xii, 61, 70–71, 72–76, 308
Ureña, Francisco Cáceres, 296
Uruguay
    campaign for Afro-descendant classification in census, 314
    census questions regarding ethnoracial diversity in, 256, 263t
    early national censuses in, 103
    national statistics agency in, 102, 103t
    visibility of minority populations in censuses of, 233–236, 233–234t, 241–243, 241t, 252–256, 253–254t
Uti possidetis principle, 49, 49n17

Van Cott, Donna Lee, 267n13, 270
Varnhagen, Baron von, 107, 108t
Vasconcelos, José, 228
Venezuela
    census questions regarding ethnoracial diversity in, 256, 263t
    cultural attributes as measures of indigenous populations, 239–240
    ILO 169, ratification of, 273, 273t, 274
    indigenous populations in, 157–158, 187–188, 239–240, 272–274
    mestizaje in, 157–158
    national censuses in, 7n9, 106
    national statistics agency in, 102, 103t
    omission of racial queries on censuses in, 194–195, 213–214, 242–245
    postindependence denouncement of racial classification, 80
    racial improvement, portrayals of, 132
    slave classification in, 68
    visibility of minority populations in censuses of, 233–236, 233–234t, 241–243, 241t, 252–256, 253–254t
Vianna, Oliveira, 137–138, 141–142, 143, 148–149, 166

War Department, U.S., 143, 143n50, 144, 185, 245
We All Count campaign, 286–288, 314–315, 315f
Wealth
    influence on racial classification of, 45, 69
    legal rights based on, 61
    race as factor in distribution of, 288
Weber, Max, 3

Whiteness, certification of, 70–71
Whitening populations
   immigration as method of, 145–153
   mestizaje as method of, 153–164
   natural and social selection as method of, 140–145
   as racial progress, 40, 165, 198, 229, 246, 247

Working Group on Indigenous Populations (UN), 272
World Bank, 251, 281–284, 286–288, 291, 293–294, 309, 319, 324
World Conference against Racism, 274, 282, 284, 286

Yashar, Deborah, 269

i

Made in the USA
Lexington, KY
01 October 2014